Limited Classical Reprint Library

THE BACKGROUND OF THE GOSPELS

OR

JUDAISM IN THE PERIOD BETWEEN THE OLD AND NEW TESTAMENTS

The Twentieth Series of the Cunningham Lectures

BY

WILLIAM FAIRWEATHER, M.A., D.D.(Edin.)

MINISTER OF
DUNNIKIER UNITED FREE CHURCH
KIRKCALDY

1920
1977
Reprint

THIRD EDITION

Klock & Klock Christian Publishers
2527 GIRARD AVE. N.
MINNEAPOLIS, MINNESOTA 55411

Originally published by
T & T Clark
1920

Printed by Klock and Klock in the U.S.A
1977 reprint

FOREWORD

'In the fulness of time,' wrote the apostle Paul, 'God sent forth His Son.' The coming of Christ marked the period of release from the state of spiritual infancy and servitude, and of entrance into the blessings promised by the prophets.

But how had the world been prepared for 'the fulness of time'?

In a most delightful way, William Fairweather sums up the effect of legalism on the Jewish people, the rise of the Pharisees, the diffusion of Greek culture, the establishment of *Pax Romana*, the widespread Messianic expectation and general moral helplessness, and shows how the world was ready for change--for the coming of Christ.

In developing his theme, Dr. Fairweather begins with the Maccabean revolt and ends with the destruction of Jerusalem by Titus. His careful blending of history and theology makes *The Background of the Gospels* indispensable to the study and proper understanding of the life and ministry of Christ. Only once does he stumble, and that is in his treatment of the Jewish apocalyptic movement. In this section he assigns the Book of Daniel to the Maccabean period. It is a regrettable error, but does not detract from the overall value of his fine book.

Cyril J. Barber
Author,
The Minister's Library

PREFACE

———✦———

THIS volume has been prepared in fulfilment of the duty laid upon me in connexion with my appointment to the Cunningham Lectureship, and is now published in accordance with the terms of that appointment.

Chapters VI. and VIII. are additional to those which formed the subject of Lectures in Edinburgh in February and March 1907.

The notes in the Appendix consist partly of illustrative quotations, and partly of discussions on points which could not suitably be handled in the body of the book.

For the convenience of students, I also append a bibliography of the literature bearing on the period under review. While the acknowledgments made throughout the volume will shew my indebtedness to many of these writings, it is only right to say that I am under special obligation to two living scholars: I owe much to Schürer's great work on the history, and still more to Bousset's particularly illuminating treatment of the religion, of the later Judaism.

To the Rev. Principal Skinner, D.D., of Westminster College, Cambridge, for valued counsel with regard to the general plan of the book, as well as for various sugges-

tions with reference to particular points; to the Rev
George Steven, M.A., Edinburgh, who kindly read the
manuscript; and to my brother, the Rev. G. M.
Fairweather, M.A., Berwick-on-Tweed, who has revised
the proof-sheets, I beg to offer my grateful acknowledgments.

In dealing with the theme chosen, namely, " The
Background of the Gospels, or Judaism in the Period
between the Old and New Testaments," I have been very
conscious of the difficulty of doing it justice within the
limits of a few chapters. The period embraced is that
beginning with the Maccabæan revolt and ending with
the destruction of Jerusalem under Titus. These two important events, separated by an interval of two hundred
and thirty-five years, mark off a well-defined section of
the history of the nation. The external history has
been narrated only so far as necessary to make clear the
development of Judaism. Some readers may feel that
here and there, as in Chapter III., many of the historical
details might have been dispensed with, but in view of the
vital significance of the Maccabæan movement for the
later Judaism, I have deemed it best to give reasonable
prominence to the facts.

This period of Judaism is one so characterised by
opposing tendencies that at first sight it seems difficult
to discover a line of development running through the
varying phenomena of the national life. Closer investigation, however, makes it clear that the later Judaism
represents a religion in the stage of transition from a
narrower to a wider phase. We see here the national on
the way to become universal, and the ceremonial in process of being superseded by the spiritual. In this move-

ment, which was greatly stimulated by the Diaspora and the Jewish propaganda carried on among the heathen, Palestinian Judaism shared in virtue of the mere fact that it was the acknowledged centre of the religion which was fast becoming world-wide. But in Palestine the drift towards a universal religion was also strengthened by the simultaneous tendency towards the detachment of piety from the national life, and by the creation of new spiritual forms in which it could express itself, such as the synagogue service, the canon of the Holy Scriptures, and the cultivation of life under the Law. The mainspring of all this was the Maccabæan struggle, which made Judaism quite a different thing from what it had been before. No doubt the development began as far back as the Exile, but until it received an impulse from the Maccabæan crisis it had always lacked the power of expansion and of organisation. Ever since the Restoration there had been only a Jewish "congregation"; henceforth there was a Jewish "Church."

Yet in Judaism we have a striking instance of arrested development. From the religious standpoint the results of the Maccabæan movement were disappointing. It failed to secure the emancipation of piety from the fetters of the national particularism. It paved the way for Pharisaism. Under the influence of the scribes, Judaism became a religion of ceremonial observance based upon the Law, and retaining a national character, partly on account of the religious value attached to custom, and partly in virtue of its Messianic hope. Although distinctly national, the Jewish hope for the future certainly assumed at the same time a wider scope in the apocalyptic literature, which furnished Judaism with many new ideas. Whether these are to be regarded merely as a normal development of Old Testament religion, or as derived in part at least from foreign religions, such as the Persian, is a question much discussed among scholars at the present time.

The special type of religious life and thought represented in Hellenistic Judaism was really an offshoot from the main stem, and lends itself accordingly to separate treatment.

These preliminary observations may serve to indicate the general line which it has been my endeavour to follow. Chapter I. is devoted to a discussion of the fundamental characteristics of Judaism, and Chapter II. deals with Palestinian Judaism: Pre-Maccabæan. We are thus enabled to relate the particular epoch dealt with to the earlier aspects of Judaism. The history of the Maccabæan struggle, as the great dividing line of the period, next demands attention. This is naturally followed by a discussion of Palestinian Judaism: Post-Maccabæan. Chapter V. treats of the Herodian age, which saw the beginnings of rabbinism and the rise of the Zealots. Thereafter the apocalyptic movement and literature, as a phenomenon of cardinal importance for our period, calls for special notice. Finally, we turn to Alexandrian Judaism as a development of exceptional interest and significance in relation to Hellenistic culture. I could have wished also, by way of completing our survey, to advert to the development of doctrine during the inter-Testamental period, but must content myself with a reference to the article on this subject contributed by me to Hastings' *Dictionary of the Bible* (Extra Volume).

It would have been a satisfaction to myself could I have dealt more fully with the bearings of the whole subject upon the New Testament; but apart from the difficulty of doing this without unduly encroaching upon the domain of New Testament theology, considerations of space seemed to preclude the attempt. As it is, I trust that the more essential points have not been altogether overlooked, and that readers will at least find in these pages something to arouse or deepen their interest in the period between the Testaments. For long this period has suffered strange neglect. At the hands of Old Testament and New Testament expositors alike it has received only scant and passing notice. Of late, however, it has been justly attracting increased attention as the historical soil on which the Gospels grew up, and as therefore vital to an intelligent acquaintance with their contents. There is still much work to be done in connexion with this obscure but important period, and it is to be hoped that among the rising generation of theological students some will devote their energies to an independent study of its unsolved problems.

W. FAIRWEATHER.

KIRKCALDY, *October,* 1908.

PREFACE TO THE SECOND EDITION

THE issue of a Second Edition has enabled me to correct some misprints, and a few other errors which have been kindly pointed out in the helpful criticisms of various reviewers.

No very material alteration has been made either in the substance or in the form of the book, although here and there obscurities have been removed, expressions of opinion modified, and additional details supplied. One or two supplementary Notes have been written, and the Bibliography has been considerably enlarged and brought up to date.

Some reviewers have suggested that the quotations from French and German authorities, given in the Appendix, should be translated for the benefit of students to whom these languages are not familiar, but I have not thought it necessary to give effect to the suggestion. Besides following in this particular the precedent set by previous Lecturers, I have reason to believe that many of those likely to read the book will prefer to have the citations in the original.

W. F.

KIRKCALDY, *7th September* 1911.

CONTENTS

CHAPTER I.

THE FUNDAMENTAL CHARACTERISTICS OF JUDAISM.

CHAPTER II.

PALESTINIAN JUDAISM: PRE-MACCABÆAN.

CHAPTER III.

THE MACCABÆAN STRUGGLE.

Contents

CHAPTER IV.

PALESTINIAN JUDAISM: POST-MACCABÆAN.

CHAPTER V.

THE HERODIAN AGE.

b

CHAPTER VI.

THE APOCALYPTIC MOVEMENT AND LITERATURE.

PART I.

CHAPTER VII.

THE APOCALYPTIC MOVEMENT AND LITERATURE.

PART II.

CHAPTER VIII.

HELLENISTIC JUDAISM.

LIST OF NOTES.

(SEE APPENDIX I.)

LITERARY SOURCES.

CHAPTER V.

CHAPTER VI.

CHAPTER VII.

CHAPTER VIII.

THE BACKGROUND OF
THE GOSPELS

———◆———

LITERARY SOURCES.

1. Canonical Literature falling within this Period.—
" Between the Testaments" connotes in reality a much
shorter space of time than it has been usual to suppose.
There is a widespread popular error to the effect that
chronologically as well as actually the Old Testament
ends with Malachi, and that there is no subsequent
canonical literature. The general trend of recent
Biblical criticism favours the view that in seeking to
explore the inter-Testamental period we are not dealing with such unknown territory as it has long been
customary to assume. If its conclusions are correct,
then we can claim as historical sources for the Greek
period of Jewish history (B.C. 332–167) the work of
the Chronicler (including 1 and 2 Chronicles, and Ezra
–Nehemiah), the Book of Esther, Ecclesiastes, Zechariah
ix.–xiv., the Book of Daniel, Joel, and many Psalms.
Roughly, the interval of four centuries is thus reduced to
one of two, representing the seven or eight generations
that divide the Maccabæan revolt from the destruction

of Jerusalem by Titus.   Even within this limit we may,
with a high degree of probability, place some of the later
psalms.   In view of this, and of the fact that the
Gospels, though written fully two generations later, go
back to the birth of Christ, we may say that the
canonical hiatus extends to not more than a century
and a half.   This is in marked contrast to the "four
centuries of silence" which were formerly regarded as an
impenetrable veil hung between the Old and New
Dispensations.   Yet even so the gap is considerable.
Although the canonical books of the Old Testament
enable us for many centuries together to place ourselves
alongside of the life of the Jewish people, the last link
in the chain they supply stops materially short of the
point at which the New Testament again brings us into
touch with the national history.   The period thus
affected is obviously of great importance as that which
immediately preceded the Advent of Christ and
determined the whole future of Judaism.   It was an
age of fierce antagonisms, but of marked development,
during which, as Fritzsche has said, "Judaism shed its
finest blood and fulfilled its world-historic mission for
the salvation of all nations in order soon, and again in
despair, struggling and battling, to withdraw from the
political arena for ever."

2. *Apocrypha and Pseudepigrapha.*—We name next
as undisputed authorities here the Old Testament
Apocrypha and the writings known as Pseudepigrapha.
Apart from any question of canonicity, the former are
invaluable as reflecting the inner life of the Jewish
people during this obscure but interesting period.
Although the Wisdom of Sirach or Ecclesiasticus is the

only one of these books bearing an approximate date (the Euergetes mentioned in the prologue being presumably Ptolemy VII. Physcon [1]), nearly all of them admittedly belong to the two centuries immediately preceding the Christian era. That the Wisdom of Solomon and 2 (4) Esdras may date from the first century A.D. does not really remove them from this category, in view of the fact that the earliest of the New Testament books were written in the latter half of that century. Towards filling the gap between the Testaments quite as much help is afforded by the Pseudepigrapha, including the Jewish apocalyptic literature, of which, apart from the Book of Daniel, the most notable extant specimens are the Book of Enoch and the Sibylline Oracles. All of these are valuable sources for the religion of the age.

3. *Josephus.*—As the great Jewish historian of the period, Josephus is necessarily also a leading authority. The last nine books of his *Antiquities of the Jews*, which deal with the post-Biblical history, are, however, of very unequal merit, and the account given of the long interval between Nehemiah and Antiochus Epiphanes is unfortunately most inadequate, being mainly founded on picturesque legends about Alexander the Great and Ptolemy Philadelphus. The time between Alexander and the Maccabees is almost a blank. Josephus makes no reference to the rise of synagogues among the Jews, and presumably had no idea of the epoch-making importance of the period. Schürer suggests that his careless execution of this part of the history must have been due to "utter weariness," but it is probably nearer

[1] See Note 1, p. 363.

the truth to say that he had no information, except in the form of floating legends which he made the most of. For the forty years, B.C. 175–135, the main sources drawn upon by Josephus are the First Book of Maccabees and the Roman history of the Greek Polybius; for the century following, that is, for the time of the Hasmonæans, from John Hyrcanus to the defeat of Antigonus (B.C. 135–37), he has used the Greek historian and geographer Strabo and Nicolaus of Damascus. In spite of his weakness both as a man and as an author, it must in fairness be said that apart from his works the history of this latter period could scarcely have been written at all.

4. *Notices of Greek and Roman Writers.*—Direct references on the part of classical authors are very scanty. Among the Greek, in addition to those already named, may be mentioned Diodorus Siculus, whose works contain a fragment upon Antiochus Epiphanes;[1] Plutarch, some of whose "Lives" fall within the scope of our period; and Appian, the eleventh book of whose history is entitled Συριακή. The Roman include Cicero, whose letters and speeches furnish much material for the history of Syria from B.C. 57–43; Tacitus, whose history contains a brief sketch of Jewish annals down to the war with Titus; Suetonius (*Vitæ XII. Imperatorum*); and Justinus's epitome of the lost historical work of Trogus Pompeius—a valuable source for the history of the Seleucid era. Besides what can be gathered from those writers who deal specially with the history of Syria, some very informing allusions to contemporary Judaism occur in the satires of Horace and

[1] xxix. 32.

Juvenal. Such sidelights, although all too inconsiderable, provide us with a fairly vivid picture of the real background of Jewish history during the Greek dominion.

5. *Inscriptions on Monuments and Coins, and Evidence from Papyri.*—With regard to the witness of the coins, it is enough to refer to Madden's *Coins of the Jews* (1881), now the standard work on Jewish numismatics. Here also will be found enumerated the Jewish inscriptions referring to our period. These consist largely of Hebrew-Greek epitaphs from Palestine and the catacombs at Rome, but include some synagogue inscriptions from Palmyra. Among those in Hebrew, collected by Chwolson, is the epitaph of the *Benê Chesir* on the reputed tomb of St. James at Jerusalem, dating from the Herodian age. The non-Jewish inscriptions from which help can be got towards the elucidation of our subject have been collected in the *Corpus Inscriptionum Græcarum*, tome iii., and in the *Corpus Inscriptionum Latinarum*, tome iii. One marble monument is worthy of special note. On the walls of the temple at Ancyra in Galatia there was engraved in both Latin and Greek a record of the chief events in the reign of Augustus. This has been preserved virtually entire, and is a valuable authority for that emperor's reign (B.C. 28–A.D. 14). Some light has recently been got from Greek inscriptions and papyri.[1] At Pergamum, for instance, in 1885, was discovered an inscription on a marble stele recording the honours paid to Eumenes king of Pergamum and his brother Attalus by the council and people of Antioch for service rendered to the State in

[1] See Note 2, p. 365.

aiding Antiochus to secure his throne.   They were made
the recipients of golden crowns, and the decree was
ordered to be engraved on stone tablets at Antioch, in
Daphne, and in Pergamum.   This inscription is printed
in Driver's *Daniel*, p. 207 f.   Special interest attaches
to the Nabatæan inscriptions edited by De Vogüé
(1868) and Euting (1885).   Some Scottish gleaners
in this interesting field have earned the gratitude of
students—notably Prof. W. M. Ramsay, by his inde-
fatigable researches in Asia Minor, and Principal Sir
G. A. Smith and Dr. Ewing, by their collection of
Greek and other inscriptions in Gilead and the Hauran.
It must be acknowledged, however, that for the epoch
subsequent to Alexander the Great the results obtained
as yet from the investigation of the monuments are, so
far as the fortunes of Palestine are concerned, comparatively slight.   See, however, some interesting
particulars given in Deissmann's *Bible Studies*.

6. *Rabbinical Literature.*—Although the mass of
writings known as the Mishna and the Targums are
entirely of a date subsequent to the Christian era, they
certainly embody fragments of pre-Christian origin, and
really reflect to a considerable extent the religious thought
and life of the period under review.   At the same time,
in view of the fact that none of these writings were
completed before the third or fourth, and some of them
not before the fifth or sixth, century A.D., they must
obviously be used with caution as sources for determining the character of social and religious life, as
well as the evolution of doctrine, in the period that
elapsed between the cessation of prophecy and the
Advent of Christ.   We can accept them as authorities

for our period only in so far as they contain sayings which can be referred to rabbinic teachers who lived within it, such as Simon ben Shetach, Hillel, Shammai, or Gamaliel.

In what has been said we have viewed the sources according to their character. It may be useful if we view them also according to their date, and irrespective of their character. Without entering upon the discussion of debatable points, we shall simply tabulate the conclusions rendered most probable in the light of recent research.

I. PRE-MACCABÆAN.

1. *Palestinian*—Ecclesiasticus, Tobit.
2. *Hellenistic*—Translation of Pentateuch.

II. WORKS BELONGING TO THE MACCABÆAN AGE.

1. *Palestinian.*

The (probably) Maccabæan Psalms (*e.g.* xliv., lxxiv., lxxix., lxxxiii.); Esther; Zechariah ix.–xiv.; (?) Last recension of Ezra–Nehemiah–Chronicles; (?) Joel; Ecclesiastes; Daniel; 1 (Ethiopic) Enoch; Jubilees; Testaments of the XII. Patriarchs; Psalms of Solomon; (probably) Judith; 1 Maccabees.

2. *Hellenistic.*

Letter of Aristeas; Fragments of Aristobulus (Bousset, however, places both of these as late as the Herodian age); 1 (3) Esdras; Completion of Septuagint translation; the Jewish Sibyllines; Fragments of Greek writers transmitted by Alexander Polyhistor.

III. WRITINGS OF THE POST-MACCABÆAN OR HERODIAN AGE.

1. *In Palestinian Judaism.*

Assumption of Moses; 2 (Slavonic) Enoch; Life of Adam and Eve; Apocalypse of Abraham; Legend of Joseph and Aseneth; Martyrdom of Isaiah.

2. *In the Diaspora.*

The Jewish Sibyllines, III. 46–92; Pseudo - Hecatæus; Additions to the Septuagint—(*a*) Epistle of Jeremiah; (*b*) Additions to Daniel and Esther; The Book of Wisdom; 2 Maccabees; 3 Maccabees; 4 Maccabees; Philo.

IV. WORKS WRITTEN AFTER THE DESTRUCTION OF JERUSALEM (A.D. 70).

1. *Palestinian*—2 (4) Esdras; Apocalypse of Baruch.
2. *Hellenistic*—Book IV. of the Sibyllines; Josephus.

V. CONTEMPORARY LITERATURE.

Roman and Greek writers from Hecatæus and Manetho to Tacitus (collected by Th. Reinach); New Testament literature; Shepherd of Hermas; the Didache; Jewish writings in a Christian setting (Ascension of Isaiah; 3 Baruch; Sibyllines, Books I.–II., V., VIII.).

VI. THE LATER JEWISH LITERATURE.

Mishna; Gemara; Talmud (Babylonian and Palestinian); Halacha (purely legal); Haggada (exegesis, fables, etc.); Targums; Midrashim (commentaries).

Smaller (haggadic and apocalyptic) writings not belonging to official Judaism. In a slightly changed form these became Christian literature.

CHAPTER I

THE FUNDAMENTAL CHARACTERISTICS OF JUDAISM

CHAPTER I.

THE FUNDAMENTAL CHARACTERISTICS OF JUDAISM.

THE terms Jew, Jewish, and Judaism are often popularly used in such a way as practically to cover the whole field of Old Testament history and revelation. In reality, however, they do no such thing, being only of post-exilic application. The Jews are not to be identified with the Hebrew or Israelitish nation as a whole, but only with that section of it, chiefly composed of the tribe of Judah, which returned from Babylon about half a century after the destruction of Jerusalem, to take up the arduous task of restoration. This had to be prosecuted under new conditions, and its prosecution gave rise to peculiar developments. It is to the particular facts and ideas connected with these far-reaching changes that the term Judaism is properly applied. So used, it denotes at once a special form of religion, and a distinct nationality, which is the sole possessor, as it is the unique product, of that religion.

What, then, it may be asked, are the fundamental characteristics of Judaism?

1. *Legalism.*—We cannot even begin to study the history of this period without recognising that there is a spirit in Judaism as well as in Hellenism. If less subtle, it is equally pronounced. The fundamental idea

of Judaism is that the religious relationship between God and His people is legal and national. For the Jews religion meant a church based upon a law-code. It was the special possession of a particular people, and everything connected with it had the binding force of statute-law. Gradually the whole life of the community was brought under the sweep of the legal principle. Laws civil and social, as well as moral and ceremonial, were viewed as the commandments of God. A halo of sanctity was thus cast around Jewish national custom, for everything that differentiated the Jews from other men became part of their religion. The resultant very complex body of Jewish law was accounted the true religion in contrast to the false religions of the Gentiles. At the same time the God of all the earth was held to have delivered to Israel its Law with a view to the ultimate acceptance of that Law by the nations generally.

That Judaism was built upon the Law was fully recognised by the Jews themselves. For them law was the embodiment of the Divine wisdom.[1] As such it was not subject to change like other laws. According to Philo it was an image of the eternal order of the cosmos. Our Lord Himself expressly repudiated the idea that He came to destroy the Law, and spoke of it as destined to outlast the world itself.[2] The Law was also viewed as an inalienable possession. " Though we be deprived of our wealth, of our cities, or of the other advantages we have," says Josephus, " our Law continues immortal." [3] So, too, the author of the Syriac Apocalypse

[1] Sir. xxiv. 8 ff.   [2] Matt. v. 18; Luke xvi. 17.
[3] *c. Apion*, ii. 39.

of Baruch, writing after the final destruction of the Jewish
State, says, "We have nothing now except the Almighty
and His Law." [1] In the Law, however, they had the
very substance of life, and the guarantee of a portion
in the world to come.[2] This was expressed by Hillel
in the aphorism, "much law, much life." [3] Sirach's
identification of the Law with Divine wisdom seems to
have led to its being regarded as a pre-existent heavenly
hypostasis.[4]

For the germs of this whole conception we must go
back to an earlier period of the national history. The
ideal of the God whose chosen they were had been
shaping itself in the minds of the finer spirits in Israel
even from the days of the wilderness wanderings, and
had found expression in the Decalogue. Another stage
in the growth of the Jewish idea of religion is reached
with the conception of the covenant relation between
Jahweh and His people as formulated in the prophetic
period, particularly by the Deuteronomist and Jeremiah.[5]

A recent writer has classified the ties which bind a
man to his God as being those of interest, obligation,
and love.[6] The prophets represent the pure form of

[1] lxxxv. 3. Cf. Goldsmith's line: "Our God is all we boast below."
[2] Ps. xl. 8; 2 (4) Esd. vii. 129, ix. 31, xiv. 22, etc.
[3] *Pirke Aboth*, ii. 8.
[4] *Assumption of Moses*, i. 11, where Clemens (in Kautzsch) reads *legem*
instead of *plebem*: "He has created the world for the sake of His Law."
[5] Closely connected with this is the thought of God's authority as Judge,
so often appealed to in the Psalms. Not that Divine grace is here excluded;
on the contrary, this is frequently set forth as the basis of the covenant relation (Deut. vii. 7 f.; Isa. xliii.; Ps. c. 3), which is essentially a moral one,
involving mutual obligations. The creation of such a relation could not affect
the essential character of Jahweh as merciful and gracious, and human merit
could in no case be commensurate with the mercies vouchsafed by God
(Gen. xxxii. 1).
[6] Sabatier, *Religions of Authority and the Religion of the Spirit*, p. 282 f.

the second of these ties.   They uniformly inculcate a
spiritual obedience.[1]   Even among the prophets, however,
there is a certain difference of attitude with respect to
the legal conception of religion.   And this is true of
prophets chronologically and theologically so near of
kin as Jeremiah and Ezekiel.   Jeremiah is far from
being enamoured of external law as a means of setting
forth the claims of God upon the homage of man.   He
prefers to regard obedience not as compliance with a
command, but as the spontaneous fruit of an inward
life grounded upon the pardoning love of God and
sustained by personal communion with Him, and thinks
of the Law as graven not on stone, but on the heart.
Although Ezekiel also dwells upon the need of a new
heart in order to fit Israel for obedience to the Divine
will, his conception of obedience is still that of compliance with the written Law, and his final ideal is that
of a community in which the details of life will be
regulated by definite enactment.

The spirit of the later Judaism is different from that
of the prophets, for while equally with the latter it lays
stress upon the obligatory in man's relation to God, it
seeks to reduce this to set terms.   It was this standpoint of Ezekiel, and not Jeremiah's, which was generally
adopted after the Exile.   The opposition which the Jews
met with from the surrounding peoples helped to intensify
their legalistic spirit.   It was, moreover, upon that side
of the Law which related to custom and ceremony that
special stress was laid.   In this direction the development
of legalism was extraordinary, and just herein lay the
peculiarity of Judaism.   Even the heathen had morality

[1] 1 Sam. xv. 22; Isa. i. 19; Hos. vi. 6.

to some extent, but in virtue of the rules observed by him in daily life the Jew proudly differentiated himself from other men. The root factor in this separation between Jew and Gentile was the rite of circumcision. All other provisions of the Law which so effectually fenced off the Jewish people from those of other nationalities were based upon this. The relations of the circumcised to the uncircumcised were carefully defined. Distinctions were drawn between clean and unclean meats. Rules were laid down with regard to sabbath observance, festivals, ablutions, etc. Principles were applied in endless detail, and life girdled with a belt of legalism. The idea was to leave no contingency unprovided for in the legalistic code. It was of course impracticable, although the attempt to realise it had certainly its heroic as well as its ridiculous side. Ultimately in the hands of the Pharisees religion degenerated into mere ritual, and supreme importance was attached to the precise observance of every jot and tittle of the external law. Not that such an attitude was incompatible with a pure zeal for righteousness. The case of St. Paul is sufficient proof to the contrary; but it also shews that the most earnest efforts after righteousness, when pursued on such lines, are of no avail to secure inward peace.[1]

The materials are not to hand for tracing the process by which the Law was thus expanded in detail. It cannot have begun in Ben Sira's time, for with him law and morality (wisdom) are practically identical. But the conflicts resulting from the advance of Hellenism revived the pronounced Jewish sentiment of early post-

[1] Rom. vii. 7 ff.

exilic times. This is already apparent from the Book of Daniel.[1] Even in the Maccabæan period, however, the Law does not seem to have become the burdensome yoke which it had become in New Testament times. The age was not favourable to such a development of legal niceties; rather did it lead the pious to indulge in dreams and forecasts of the future. Their strength, moreover, was spent in fighting the Maccabæan dynasty. It was pre-eminently during the Herodian age that Judaism assumed its *legalistic* character. Quickened by the experiences of the Maccabæan period, the intense spirit of the Jewish people threw itself with almost fanatical energy into the task of perfecting the Law, and it is practically to the colossal diligence of that epoch that we owe the development of Judaism as we know it.

If not perhaps to the same extent, the influences that were at work in Palestine affected the Diaspora as well.[2] While in previous times Jewish soldiers had frequently served in the Egyptian army, about the middle of the first century B.C. Jews began to claim exemption from military service as incompatible with the requirements of their religion. In the Dispersion the lack of the Temple led only to a greater importance being attached to religious ceremony, the sabbath being even more strictly kept than in Palestine.[3] Jews were everywhere known for their practice in this respect, as well as for their exclusiveness, and their avoidance of certain kinds of food as unclean. The ceremonial Law was the specialty of Judaism, and its requirements were satisfied not because of any spiritual relationship to its separate

[1] i. 8 ff., vi. 10 ff.   [2] See Note 3, p. 365.
[3] Philo, *De Vita Mosis*, ii. 4; Euseb. *Præp. Ev.* viii. 7; Jos. *Ant.* xvi.

prescriptions on the part of those who kept it, but simply on the ground that they represented the will of God. Religion was a matter of obedience, and obedience meant outward conformity to rule.

The standpoint of later Judaism differed therefore from that of the prophets not only in regard to the place given to Law as such, but also in its estimate of what were " the weightier matters of the law." While the prophets protested against the popular view that it was by ceremonial acts of worship that men could best please God, and while they placed in the forefront the necessity of obedience to His moral commands, post-exilic Judaism was developed in the very opposite direction. It magnified the ceremonial at the expense of the ethical. The prophets preached the necessity of justice, mercy, and humility,[1] and set a higher value upon the knowledge of God than upon burnt-offerings.[2] After the Exile the position was completely reversed. The teachers of the people insisted upon the most punctilious discharge of every ceremonial ordinance, even where that might mean neglect of moral duties. Morality began to be smothered with ceremony. There was such a shifting of the centre of gravity that it was no longer sin that men were concerned to avoid, but Levitical defilement. Subsequent at least to the Maccabæan age, law and morality were no longer identical; morality was largely conditioned by its connexion with law, and that in several directions.

There was no proper appreciation of the distinction between great moral duties and little points of petty casuistry. Great duties and small were mixed together

---

[1] Mic. vi. 8.   [2] Hos. vi. 6.

in the most casual way.[1]   There was no sense of
spiritual proportion tending to frame life into a moral
unity.   This finds ample illustration in the ethical literature of the period, which often mechanically groups
together numerical lists of otherwise unconnected things.[2]
No doubt there were exceptions to the general
artificiality.   Recorded sayings of learned teachers like
Hillel, Gamaliel, and others, prove that their moral sense
was not crushed under the terrible incubus of the Law,
and that in spite of all their hair-splitting they were
not destitute of true spiritual perception or incapable of
a free and earnest outlook upon life.   It was a scribe
who said to Jesus, "Master, which is the great
commandment in the law?"   Yet these were but
occasional gleams of clearer spiritual apprehension, and
the verdict of Jesus that Pharisaism tithed mint and rue
and all manner of herbs, and passed over judgment and
the love of God,[3] must be accepted as an accurate
estimate of the essential spirit of later Jewish ethics.

Another limitation imposed upon Jewish morality by
its association with legalism is seen in its predominantly
negative character.   Even the Golden Rule—to take
a familiar example—was expressed by Hillel in negative
form : " Do not to others what ye would not that they
should do to you "—a very inferior version as compared
with the positive precept given in the Sermon on the
Mount : " Whatsoever ye would that men should do to
you, do ye even so to them." [4]   Only two commandments of the Decalogue are positive; all the rest take

---

[1] See Note 4, p. 367.
[2] Prov. xxx. 15, 18, 24 ; Sir. xxv. 1, 7, etc.
[3] Luke xi. 42.   [4] Matt. vii. 12.

the form, "Thou shalt not." And the latter is the
keynote of the Jewish legislation generally. Its main
burden is prohibition. The pious Jew must not slander,
must not be angry, must not give offence, and so on.
As might be expected from its prevailingly negative
standpoint, Jewish ethic favours the passive rather than
the active virtues; it takes more account of meekness
and patience than of strenuousness and courage.

A further feature of Jewish ethic as conditioned by
the Law is its narrow particularism. It lacks width of
horizon, and has no outlook into the universal. In character and scope it is essentially national. Morality is
viewed from a purely Jewish standpoint. An Israelite's
duties are regarded as limited to his own people,[1] and
even within this circumscribed area the tendency towards
particularism asserted itself more and more—witness the
sharp division between poor and rich, oppressed and
powerful, pious and godless, revealed in the Psalms. In
like manner Ben Sira says, "Give to the good man, and
help not the sinner."[2] The cleavage is still more pro-
minently reflected in the later apocalyptic literature.
That Jewish ethics assumed an ecclesiastical as well as
a national character is proved by what the Gospels
disclose as to the common estimate of "publicans and
sinners," and the relations between Jews and Samaritans.
Jesus had a new answer to the question, "Who is my
neighbour?" He also sums up the spirit of Jewish
morality in one keen, incisive word: "Thou shalt love
thy neighbour and hate thine enemy."[3] In practice,
however, this position was not always strictly adhered to.
The gentle Hillel, for example, had such faith in the

---

[1] Tob. iv. 13.   [2] xii. 7.   [3] Matt. v. 43.

educative power of the Law that, in contrast to the school of Shammai, who would have none but intelligent pupils of good family, he welcomed all who desired instruction. It is also the case that the missionary effort put forth in the interests of Judaism [1] helped to detach Jewish morality from its narrow basis. But its particularism was never wholly removed. It was only in so far as the Gentile was a potential Jew that he possessed any interest for a son of Israel. Pure well-wishing towards man as man was a sentiment foreign to Judaism. Although it is true that Philo and some other Jewish writers kept the specifically Jewish in the background, it must be remembered that in general they wrote from an apologetic standpoint, and that they do not represent the position of the average Jew of the Dispersion, whose ethical particularism was scarcely less pronounced than that of his brethren in Palestine.

It still remains to point out that while, like all ecclesiastical piety, Judaism was distinguished by the practice of benevolence, and even classed almsgiving along with prayer and fasting as of primary importance for the religious life, its legalistic trend directly fostered an atmosphere of unreality. Truth was valued not for its own sake, but only as a legal and social asset. To bear false witness against a neighbour was strongly forbidden, but for truth in the sense of sincerity there was small appreciation. Doubtless among the pious there were Israelites in whom there was no guile, but of the rank and file it was lamentably true that so long as outward appearances were kept up they were content. Jesus directed a constant polemic against the pretence

[1] See Note 5, p. 368.

and hypocrisy rampant in His time. That men had deviated so far from the path of reality was in some measure due to the twist given to their moral nature by a situation in which, while it was necessary to conform to the rules of piety, so many failed to share the ideals of the truly pious.

In Judaism, therefore, we have an unsuccessful attempt to establish religion on an ethical basis. Its morality is not a pure morality, but a morality conditioned on various sides by the Law.

2. *Religious Fellowship.*—To the Maccabæan revolt Judaism owed the powerful impulse which at once renewed its own life and enabled it to become a significant factor in the religious history of the world. From that time two great currents—the ecclesiastical and the national—once more began to act simultaneously upon the life of the Israelitish people. At first the national was the more vigorous, for the Maccabæan movement was above all a national revival; but the ecclesiastical tendency grew stronger and stronger till ultimately it became predominant, and the whole development resulted in the evolution of the Jewish " Church."

It was not long before the new nationalism ceased to command the unanimous support of the Jewish people. No sooner had religious freedom been conceded by the Syrians than the Ḥasīdîm, the flower of Israelitish piety, dissociated themselves from the Maccabæan leaders. Their aims being purely religious, they declined to fight for political independence. Although the treachery of Alcimus, the newly installed Aaronic high priest, coupled with the victory of Judas over Nicanor, again gave solidarity to the Jewish nation for some thirty years, an

acute cleavage between the pious and the priestly aristocracy shewed itself in the time of John Hyrcanus.   Under
Alexander Jannæus it assumed such alarming proportions as seriously to threaten the stability of the
Hasmonæan dynasty.   By the time of Pompey the
Maccabees were pilloried in the Psalter of Solomon as
usurpers, and their overthrow ascribed to the just
judgment of God.· To such a degree had piety cut
itself adrift from the political life of the nation.   The
more the pious succeeded in organising themselves into
a church, the more was religion detached from its
connexion with politics.

In the life of the Jewish people, then, the ecclesiastical
tendency was fast gaining the ascendancy when Herod
came to the throne, and it was in his day that it became
absolutely predominant.   How was it that the Pharisees,
who were at variance with the Maccabæan high priests,
came to terms with a ruler like Herod?   We know that
their leaders Sameas and Polion advised the people to
open the city gates to him when, jointly with the Roman
general Sosius, he besieged Jerusalem; that they readily
became his subjects; and that Herod on his part took
care to humour them.   The real reason for this surprising turn of affairs was that foreign supremacy was
essential to the successful development of Pharisaism.
Under Herod's régime all responsibility for the secular
side of the national life was removed from the shoulders
of the pious.   They took nothing to do with the conduct
of war, the arrangement of treaties, the raising of taxes,
the erection of public buildings, etc.   These were things
which had no connexion with religion.   A semi-heathen
like Herod might be as worldly as he chose in his

administration of such matters. In this way the
Pharisees got rid of the troublesome sense of responsibility which they had in connexion with the worldliness
of the high priestly rulers. At the same time the way
was cleared for their exclusive devotion to the perfecting of legalism in the sphere of religion. The Herodian
age accordingly came to be of prime significance for the
development of Jewish piety. During that period the
Pharisees concentrated their efforts upon the one task of
controlling the religious life of the people. And they
achieved wonderful results within their chosen sphere.
Relieved from all care about externals, and no longer
spending their strength in opposition to the ruling
house, they applied themselves with prodigious industry to the development of the Law, and moulded
Judaism into the form with which the New Testament
has made us familiar.

As compared with the Romans, Herod was fortunate
in being thoroughly acquainted with the spirit and the
prejudices of the Jews. He knew their peculiarities,
and respected their scruples, in a way not possible for
the imperial rulers. This explains how the yoke of the
latter proved more galling to the Jews than that of the
Idumæan, and how at length the national sentiment
recovered itself and rose to such a pitch of frenzy that
the Pharisaic ideals were abandoned for a fanatical and
hopeless war, which destroyed the Jewish nation, and
left only the Jewish " Church." Thereafter in the hands
of the Pharisees and the rabbis—henceforth its only
possible leaders—Judaism not only entrenched itself so
to speak within an impregnable fortress, but united in
an indissoluble fellowship the totality of Jews through-

out the world. It was really in virtue of the extraordinary spread of Judaism in the Dispersion subsequent
to the Maccabæan movement that it developed into a
Church; for, after all, the steps taken towards the
denationalisation of piety had practically only restored
the *status quo* prior to the conflicts provoked by the
introduction of Greek culture.

Down to the Maccabæan period the growth of
Judaism had been as nothing compared to the expansion
which it underwent in the days of the later Hasmonæans
and Herod, both in Palestine itself and beyond. There
was thus gradually formed a new fellowship unconnected
with the national life, world-wide, multilingual, yet
binding all its members into a close spiritual unity,
and surpassing in its intensity anything previously
witnessed on the field of religion. Josephus recognises
this special characteristic of Judaism when he points out
that constitutionally it is neither a monarchy, nor an
oligarchy, nor a democracy, but a *Theocracy*.[1]   The
designation is appropriate enough; it was a new word
coined to describe a new thing—the development of
the national religion into the Church.

All this meant much for Judaism. The formation
of the new religious fellowship turned it into a great
spiritual power, and gave it the consciousness of
superiority to the vaunted culture of the Greeks. From
the lofty pedestal of those in possession of a truer
theology and a higher morality the Jews regarded with a
scornful compassion the superstitions and vices of the
heathen world, and confidently asserted that the Jewish
wisdom far surpassed the Greek philosophy in antiquity

[1] *c. Apion*, ii. 17.

as well as in merit. Nor was it any merely national tie
that held together the Jewish Church—as even the
inhabitants of Jerusalem must have perceived when on
festal occasions the city was thronged with worshippers
from every country under heaven. In Judaism as
detached from the political life of the nation there had
arisen a great spiritual force which no geographical
barriers could affect.

By far the most important factor in enabling Judaism
thus to grip an entire race was the synagogue. Although
it is difficult to trace the origin of this great institution,
it was undoubtedly post-exilic, and perhaps later than is
usually supposed.[1] The primary object of the weekly
service was "to hear the Law and to learn it accurately."[2]
Every synagogue thus became a centre of national and
religious instruction. Comparatively few could attend a
Beth-ha-Midrash, or special centre where the ·scribes
supervised the studies of those who wished to become
experts in the Law, so that, apart from parental
instruction, the people generally were dependent upon
the synagogue for such rudimentary knowledge of it
as was necessary to every Jew. Nor did it prove an
inefficient instrument for securing the end in view. By
means of this powerful institution post-exilic Judaism
was kept in ever closer touch with the Law. Josephus
could make the proud boast that while no Roman
procurator could dispense with the services of skilled
lawyers, "if any one should question one of us concerning

---

[1] Bousset. The new spirit which prompted the culture of the Law led
also to the multiplication of synagogues in the Diaspora as well as in Palestine. By the first century of our era, according to the Rabbinic legend,
Jerusalem alone had between four and five hundred; but this is obviously
an exaggeration.   [2] *c. Apion*, ii. 18.

the laws, he would more easily repeat all than his own name." [1]   This was largely the result of the synagogue service.   The instruction thus communicated was both theoretical and practical, and was imparted largely by the scribes.   Not that they held any official position analogous to that of the priests in the Temple.   Any competent male worshipper was permitted to teach.   In New Testament times our Lord and His apostles often availed themselves of this liberty.   But naturally the leading part in the exposition of Holy Scripture was taken by those who had a professional knowledge of it. The synagogue also served the important purpose of being a house of prayer in which pious hearts could hold fellowship with God apart from any priestly ritual.[2]

[1] *c. Apion*, ii. 19.

[2] Without entering into details regarding the buildings in which the sabbath assemblies were held, or the officials who were responsible for the general management and particular discharge of the affairs of the congregation— on these points see Schürer, II. ii. p. 63 ff.—we may here advert to the leading features and recognised order of the service.   The principal diet of worship was held on the forenoon of the sabbath, and began with the recitation of the Shěma', a thankful confession of Jahweh as the God who delivered Israel from Egypt.   It consists of three extracts from the Pentateuch (Deut. vi. 4–9, xi. 13–21; Num. xv. 27–41, *Shěma*ʿ being the Hebrew word with which the first of these passages begins), with certain benedictions prefixed and appended. Then with the formula, "Bless ye Jahweh," the reader summoned the people to pray.   This they did standing, and with their faces turned towards the Holy of Holies, *i.e.* towards Jerusalem.   An authorised form of prayer was pronounced by an adult worshipper, who stood in front of the chest con- taining the rolls of the Law.   Only certain responses, including the Amen, were uttered by the congregation.   Next came the readings from the Law and the Prophets (Luke iv. 17; Acts xiii. 15), with translation into the Aramaic vernacular, the Septuagint translation being used, however, in the synagogues of the Dispersion.   The lessons were read by adult members, precedence being given to priests and Levites if any such were present. Then followed a homiletic discourse based upon the passages read, the preacher being frequently, but not necessarily, a scribe.   The service was concluded by the priestly benediction, to which the whole assembly gave the responsive Amen.   This item was plainly borrowed from the Temple ritual. If no priest were present, the blessing took the form of a prayer.

It is clear, therefore, that the synagogue was school and church in one; and in view of the two great functions which it discharged, its value for the religious life of Judaism can scarcely be overestimated. It enjoyed great popularity, and had great influence. More than any other agency, it helped to bind Judaism into a uniform and compact whole. By fostering freedom of speech it broke down the sharp distinction between priests and laity, and by its democratic basis saved religion from the domination of the learned. It created also a new conception of worship, in accordance with which prayer took the place of animal sacrifices, and spiritual edification was derived from the study of God's Word. The sabbath was freed from its ceremonial character, and transformed into a day of hallowed fellowship. For the devout Jew the Temple and its ritual were no longer a necessity. All this was the fruit of that most typical illustration of the genius of Judaism—the synagogue. And here let it be noted as a fact of cardinal importance, that the first Christian gatherings for worship on Sundays were, as regards their arrangements generally, modelled upon the synagogue. Whatever may be the case with respect to the Roman and Anglican Churches, our Presbyterian worship is moulded not after the Temple ritual, but upon the service of the synagogue.

The Jewish Church succeeded in enveloping the entire life of the people with a religious atmosphere. From earliest childhood every one began to breathe it, and it was scarcely possible for any to withdraw themselves from it. Although it is difficult to say how far systematic religious instruction was given in elementary schools during our period, the testimony of Philo and

Josephus is very significant. According to Philo, the Jews "are taught, so to speak, from their swaddling-clothes by their parents, teachers, and those who bring them up, even before instruction in the sacred laws and the unwritten customs, to believe in God the one Father and Creator of the world."[1] Equally emphatic is the statement of Josephus: "Our principal care of all is this, to educate our children well."[2] Now the Jewish Church never relaxed its hold upon its members; it controlled their lives throughout. And the forms of religious life which it established, and by means of which it retained its power over the community, have stood the test of time. What, then, were these? Prayer, fasting, and almsgiving were undoubtedly the three principal points of Judaistic piety,[3] and those which stamped upon it its distinctive character.

The duty of prayer in accordance with a set formula, and at stated times, seems to have been generally recognised by the middle of the first century A.D. While Josephus represents it as incumbent on every Jew to pray twice daily (morning and evening), later rabbinical writers[4] require prayer to be offered three times (morning, afternoon, and evening). The forms in use were probably the *Shěma'* and the *Shemoneh-Esreh*. At meal-times also the Divine goodness was expressly acknowledged.[5] Although such regulated devotion frequently degenerated into mere formalism, it nevertheless helped, by thrusting the idea of God into

---

[1] *Leg. ad Caium*, 31.   [2] *c. Apion*, i. 12.
[3] Tob. xii. 8 ; Matt. vi. 1–18.   [4] *Berachoth*, iv. 1.
[5] Matt. xiv. 19 ; Rom. xiv. 6, etc. In the *Sibyllines*, however, this is alluded to as a special mark of piety (Book IV. 26).

everyday life, to raise the general level of piety in the community. In the fact that a teacher was expected by his disciples to teach them to pray[1] we have a significant illustration of the degree to which the synagogue service influenced public life.

Another prominent element in the framework of Jewish piety was that of fasting. The great statutory fast-day was the Day of Atonement, although after the Exile several other annual fast-days were instituted. Fasting was chiefly, but not exclusively, an expression of penitence. Special fast-days were observed in view of public calamities, such as reverses in war, plague, or drought; as a means of averting threatened disaster; and by way of seeking the Divine favour in connexion with some undertaking. Private fasting, though not required by law, was not uncommon. In New Testament times Pharisees who valued a reputation for piety fasted twice in the week.[2] The disciples of John and the Essenes were also given to fasting, and it was a reproach levelled against Jesus and His disciples that they did not fast.[3] Along with prayer, fasting was resorted to as a cure for demoniac possession.[4] Although Jesus did not bind His disciples to a practice which was not in harmony with the essentially joyful character of the Messianic age,[5] fasting became customary in the Christian Church from an early date.[6]

Almsgiving likewise played an important part in the religious life of later Judaism, the machinery for the care of the poor being supplied by the synagogue. The

---

[1] Luke xi. 1 f.   [2] Luke xviii. 12.   [3] Mark ii. 18.
[4] Matt. xvii. 21.   [5] Mark ii. 19.
[6] Acts xiii. 3, xiv. 23; 1 Cor. vii. 5; 2 Cor. vi. 5.

Church's peculiar ability to handle the social problem increased its influence in the State, although at the same time in ecclesiastical hands the idea of charity became externalised. To some extent, indeed, this had already taken place with the very introduction of the word "alms," which, frequently as it is used in the Apocrypha, nowhere occurs in the Old Testament. But the process grew with the lapse of time. The whole scheme of moral teaching, as handed down by tradition through successive generations of scribes and summed up in almsgiving, prayer, and fasting, soon became very mechanical, and, as our Lord has shewn in the Sermon on the Mount, quite unfitted to advance true religious life. The practice of collecting alms on Sundays in apostolic times [1] was no doubt taken over from the synagogue.

Judaism, then, had become a great religious fellowship, limited to no single country. And yet it did not succeed in completely detaching itself from the national life. It fell down, so to speak, between two stools—the State and the Church. In the end the spirit of exclusiveness triumphed over the tendency towards expansion. Although no longer merely a national, Judaism had nevertheless not become a universal, religion. It was virtually confined to Jews, even proselytes becoming Jews after a fashion. Under the guidance of the rabbis of Palestine it became a religion of persistent ceremonialism, and ultimately Christianity served itself heir to its missionary zeal.

3. *Individualism.*—The standpoint of the later Judaism differs from that of the prophets. In one

---

[1] 1 Cor. xvi. 2.

sense it was a development of prophetic teaching, or perhaps it might be nearer the truth to say that it was a practical application of it. Its significance lies in the fact that it was an attempt to embody the Mosaic ideas in actual practice, and to translate the theocratic conceptions of the prophets into terms of individual religion. The individual had already been "discovered" by Jeremiah and Ezekiel. To Jeremiah it was given to perceive that religion essentially consists in personal communion with God, and that as a purely spiritual thing it could not be injuriously affected by the dissolution of the national life. Rather would this help on its perfect realisation in the future Messianic age. Ezekiel, on the other hand, was called to apply the new truth to the immediate circumstances of the time, and on this basis to organise the religious community of the future. Hence the emphasis laid by him on individual responsibility. His message is that God will no longer deal with men in the aggregate, but as units. Ezekiel knows nothing of that philosophy according to which "the individual withers, and the world is more and more." For him each individual stands in a direct personal relation to God, and is accountable for his own free actions, and for no other. The Divine righteousness is discriminating, and every man's destiny will be in keeping with his own character.

Although the tendency towards individualism had begun thus early, it was only in the period subsequent to the Maccabæan revolt that it created for itself definite and fixed forms. It was not exclusively Jewish. The drift of Judaism in this direction was in reality part of a larger movement already traceable in the Persian kingdom, and still more in evidence during the age of the Ptolemies and the Seleucidæ. What lay at the root of this movement was the loss by so many States of their political independence. In consequence of this, importance was no longer attached to the national and political aspect of Deity. The bond between a god and his worshippers came to be viewed as a purely personal one. From being a national concern religion was transformed into a matter of individual moment. It was cultivated by select guilds, such as those of the priests of Egypt, the astrologers of Chaldæa, and the different schools of philosophers in Greece. Not only so ; each man for himself looked to the heavenly powers, chiefly perhaps as a protection from sickness and other misfortunes. Hence, for example, the extraordinary spread of the cult of Æsculapius, the god of medicine. There was no longer any endeavour to realise a great living fellowship ; all religions were tending towards universalism and individualism.[1] And in this world-wide stream of development Judaism shared. With its growing detachment from the national life, and its adoption of ecclesiastical forms, piety became a matter of individual choice and of personal responsibility for the fulfilment of the Law. To have been born a Jew was no longer equivalent to membership in the congregation of the saints. So sharply was the line drawn between the pious and the godless, that these two classes were almost as far apart as Jew and heathen. Piety was thus simply and solely the devotion of the individual heart. Its adequate exercise depended upon no priestly functionary, and it was open to any one by

[1] Ed. Meyer, *Geschichte des Alterthums*, iii. p. 169 f.   See Note 6, p. 369.

personal acquirements and zeal to reach the front rank in the new spiritual aristocracy of holiness.

Important as was the public service of the Temple in welding the theocracy into a unity, and in promoting its organisation, Judaism depended still more upon strict obedience to its precepts on the part of the individual. Not that this private worship was in any way opposed to the public ritual; they were related through the Day of Atonement, and through the sin and trespass offerings. But the title to be a Jew had to be laboriously earned. It was not gained simply by periodical visits to the Temple, or by payment of the sacred dues. Judaism flourished not only in Jerusalem, but in the Diaspora as well. Wherever Jews were found they worked hard to build up, and to constitute themselves units in, a nation whose distinguishing feature was holiness, and whose territory was wide as the globe itself. The holiness they sought to attain was that of perfect compliance with the requirements of the Law, which contained in concrete form the principles propounded by the prophets. This they pursued with unconquerable ardour, even under the most disadvantageous conditions. The code of regulations as to ceremonial observances came to be encyclopædic, and the self-discipline involved in carrying them out, tremendous. Life was so girdled with legalism as to leave but small opportunity for going astray. Positive enactments were viewed as safeguards against sin, and therefore as conducive to holiness. For the idea essentially bound up with holiness was not that of doing good, but that of shunning evil.

But while there was thus ample scope and real

necessity for individualism, there were also in Judaism controlling and co-ordinating forces which tended to shape it into one harmonious whole. The very act of circumcision, as the indelible mark of the covenant, already told powerfully in this direction. All the subsequent training of a Jewish boy was also carefully calculated to counteract the centrifugal tendencies of individualism, and to create an *esprit de corps* among the sons of Israel. What was aimed at was universal instruction in the Law with a view to the realisation of the prophetic ideal : " All thy children shall be taught of Jahweh, and great shall be the peace of thy children." [1] These words may remind us that, intolerable as they might appear to us, and intolerable as they ultimately became even to the Jews themselves,[2] the requirements of the Law were not generally felt to be so irksome as might be supposed. It is wonderful what men can become inured to ; and the Law's demands being of an external kind, could at least be met and paid to the uttermost farthing. If, moreover, on the one hand the system was fitted to create an artificial conscience by demanding obedience to prescriptions which had no obvious relation to the moral sense, it tended on the other hand to give rise to a feeling of contentment with obedience to the letter of the Law. One who rendered such obedience felt that he had done what was required of him, and he only needed to keep pace with the hourly demands made upon him in order to rid himself of all troublesome questions regarding his personal responsibility. At the same time it must in fairness be recognised that the Jewish Law was not exclusively

---

[1] Isa. liv. 13.   [2] Acts xv. 10.

ceremonial; it contained moral precepts as well. And one of the results of the new individualism was a decided development of ethical feeling during this age. It was possible for a heart of flesh to exist even under the hard exterior of Jewish legalism,[1] and in the darkest stretches of the centuries immediately preceding the Advent, there were undoubtedly true witnesses for God.

From several points of view we have already seen that Jewish legalism fell below the prophetic ideals. But the latter could not be realised all at once. The actual religious condition of the people made it impossible that there should be an immediate fulfilment of the promise, and so, as St. Paul has emphatically pointed out, the Law came in between as the rigorous school-master of the immature, till the day of Christian liberty should dawn. During this interval the spirit of prophetic religion enshrined itself in the tangible precepts of a positive law determining conduct. In no other way could it become a truly national possession. This implied, however, a certain concession to ceremonialism, and post-exilic times are characterised by an absence of the strong invective directed by the prophets against the hollow pietism of the established ritual. For the latter the priestly code had claimed the authority of the Mosaic revelation, with the result that the ceremonial Law was so intertwined with the ancient belief in Jahweh as virtually to put it beyond the pale of criticism. In this way the cult of the external came to be very strongly entrenched among the Jews of Palestine, and nothing short of the spiritual insight and boldness of Jesus could ever have led an assault against it. Yet

[1] Ezek. xxxvi. 26.

Judaism as consolidated under Ezra and his successors was far from being a mere fossilising of the old prophetic religion. True faith in God could not be altogether stifled by formalism. If there was decided deterioration, there was not absolute petrifaction. Within the hard shell of legalism lay the kernel which was yet to emerge and vitalise the world. Alongside of the resplendent ritual of the Temple there sprang up the simple and edifying worship of the synagogue. " Our houses of prayer in the several towns," says Philo, " are none other than institutions for teaching prudence and bravery, temperance and justice, piety and holiness ; in short, every virtue which the human and the Divine recognises and enjoins." [1] Here were canvassed in the light of Scripture the deepest problems affecting human life, and here was awakened the intense individualism reflected in the literature of the period. To an extent hitherto unknown in Israel, religion now became a personal concern for every man.

We have evidence of this in the Psalms, many of which were the fruit of the synagogue. Without repudiating the Jewish tradition that David was the founder of the Psalter, we must recognise that a large portion of the collection as it now stands cannot be from his pen, for the obvious reason that it embodies the results of the revival of psalmody which marked the restoration from exile. It was the hymn-book of the Second Temple, and although some of the fresh pieces composed for its services may have been adaptations of ancient " songs of Zion," many of them were inspired by the joyous feeling that Jahweh was once more building

[1] *De Vita Mosis*, ii. 168.

up Jerusalem.[1]   In the later books of the collection we
breathe essentially the atmosphere of the synagogue.
The weekly assemblies called forth these songs, and they
were also edified by them.   In Ps. cxix. we have a reflexion of the new devotion to the Law.   While some
psalms express the prayers and feelings of the community as well, others are songs of the individual heart.
In them piety receives an expression so broadly human
that the Psalter remains not only for Jews, but also for
Christians, a hymn-book for all time.   The secret of
this perennial freshness of the Psalms lies in their detachment.   In not a few the element of nationalism is
absent.   For the lyric poets of the Persian and Greek
periods religion overshadowed politics.   They were
concerned not about the destinies of nations, but about
God and the soul.   If in some respects this had a
narrowing effect, it resulted in a singularly keen absorption of the mind in things religious.   Men looked for
salvation not to outward power or influence, but to the
spiritual blessings found in fellowship with Jahweh.   The
same cause led also to the noblest idealism.   Where
shall we find such a beautiful picture of a soul weaned
from worldly ambition and calmly resting on the bosom
of God as that painted in what Dr. Samuel Johnson
reckoned the gem of the Psalter?[2]   And can we imagine
anything loftier in the way of spiritual aspiration than
the prayer of the Psalmist: " Lord, if I have but thee,
there is none in heaven or earth that I desire beside
thee.   My flesh and my heart faileth : but God is the
strength of my heart and my portion for ever ? "[3]

[1] cxlvii. 2.   [2] Ps. cxxxi.
[3] lxxiii. 25 f.   Not, of course, that self-culture, even when carried to the

We have another reflexion of the individualism of the period in the eschatology of the Wisdom literature, to which reference will be made in the next chapter. Meanwhile we must note that as developed in the later Judaism religious individualism was but imperfectly realised. Not only was the detachment of piety from the national life far from complete, but under the new ecclesiastical conditions the religion of the individual was crushed by the weight of tradition. Sufficient scope was not given for the play of individuality, with the result that in the post-Maccabæan age there was an utter lack of outstanding religious personalities. With all this, however, particularly in view of the familiarity of the Jewish people with the doctrine of future retribution, which by that time existed in a highly developed form, some progress had been made in the direction of the pronounced individualism of the Gospel. It needed only the magnetic touch of Jesus to call into active operation what was already dormant in the community.

4. *Conservatism.*—This feature of Judaism goes far to explain the lack of creative originality which character-

---

highest pitch, is the be-all and end-all of religion. The merely contemplative life, however great its depth and compass, is always barren of results for the world. Even the mystical piety reflected in the Psalms could not of itself usher in the gospel of the kingdom. It was an excellent preparation for it, but that was all. It lacked inspirational force. The indispensable element of active and public-spirited endeavour was absent from it—a defect closely connected with the fact that there was no longer any prophet in Israel (1 Macc. ix. 27). Yet the religion of Israel was never without a hue of hope. There remained the expectation that there would certainly arise a faithful prophet who should be the mouthpiece of God to the whole community (1 Macc. iv. 46, xiv. 41). When that time came, and when in the preaching of the Forerunner the deep spirituality of the Psalms allied itself with the social ideals of the prophets, then at length could the proclamation be made : " The kingdom of God is come nigh unto you."

ised our period, and also the lack of great religious
personalities like Moses or Samuel, Origen or Augustine,
Luther or Knox, around whom the life and history of
their own generation revolve. A legal ecclesiasticism
tended to dry up the springs of life. Apart from the
heroism of the Maccabees, and the literature to which
it gave rise, these were virtually frozen. Nor was the
stream that issued even from this source equal in depth
or purity to the rivers which in earlier days had made
glad the city of God. Attention was mainly concentrated upon the development and safeguarding of the
spiritual inheritance transmitted from the past. And
this involved labour at once so mechanical and so all-
engrossing as to preclude the achievement of anything
remarkable either in the way of fresh thought or of
independent action.

But in spite of some unlovely features connected with
it, the extraordinary tenacity with which the Jews clung
to the religion of their fathers compels our admiration.
Neither the subtle influences of Hellenism nor the strong
hand of imperial Rome could break down their devotion.
Under the most difficult circumstances, and at any
sacrifice, they never ceased to observe down to the
minutest detail their religious rites. On this score they
were invincible. Two things in particular attest the
remarkable adherence of the Jews to their ancestral faith,
—their attitude of exclusiveness towards outsiders, and
the formation of the Old Testament canon.

The character of their relations with Gentiles had to
be decided very soon after the Restoration, the question
having been raised in an acute form by the request of
the Samaritans to be permitted to join in the work of

rebuilding the Temple.   These Samaritans were not mere
godless heathen; they had Israelitish as well as Assyrian
blood in their veins.   But the fact that they were a
mixed race led to the declinature of the proffered alliance.
This meant open and implacable enmity on the part of
the Samaritans,[1] and ultimately the erection of a rival
temple on Gerizim.   The point to be noted is that if the
Jews dealt thus with a neighbouring people partly akin
to themselves in race and in worship, there could no
longer be any doubt as to their attitude towards those
who could advance no such claim.   Formerly prone to
idolatry, the Israelites were now firmly set against it, and
endeavoured to isolate themselves as a community
hermetically sealed against all heathen influences whatsoever.   The Hellenistic cities afterwards built in
Palestine formed no part of the strictly Jewish territory.
In their rigid exclusiveness the Jews developed that
bitter hatred and scorn of everything " Gentile," that
pride of race and of knowledge, that Pharisaic self-
righteousness and externalism of worship, which we find
reflected in the Gospels.   The sense of the spiritual
superiority of the Jew to all other men, including his
political masters, continued to grow as the generations
passed.   In the Talmudic writings a Greek philosopher
or a Roman emperor is nothing compared to a Jewish
rabbi.

More or less connected with the religious feeling
which enabled the Jews to maintain their nationality in
face of all disintegrating forces were certain other contributory elements worthy of note.   For one thing, lack
of political independence made them cultivate all the

[1] John iv. 9.

more eagerly the ideal religious fatherland ; as burgesses
of the true Zion they needed no earthly citizenship.
The rite of circumcision, too, kept them apart from
other men, not only through the faith which it
expressed, but also through the ridicule which it
induced. Finally — although this applied to the
Diaspora more than to Palestine—the extent to which
in the post-exilic age the Jews began to busy themselves with trade and money-making had an important
bearing upon the preservation of their separateness as
a race. Then, as now, the wealth and independence
thus secured by individual Jews created a general feeling
of dislike to the race as a whole, and no small measure
even of religious antipathy.

But the most concrete embodiment of the loyalty
of the Jews to their ancient religion is found in "the
Scriptures" of the Old Testament and the collection of
them into an authoritative record of Divine revelation,
occupying as such a plane of its own, and not to be
measured by the standards of ordinary human composition. This provided the Jewish faith with a new
spiritual centre, and facilitated the process of detachment from the State. Israelitish piety was developing
into a Church, and no Church can dispense with a
canon of sacred writings. Difficult questions beset the
subject of canonicity, especially as regards the books
produced during the later stages of the history, but
what concerns us here is neither the precise process by
which the canon was formed, nor the exact date at
which it was closed, but simply the fact that from the
year B.C. 444 onwards Israel did virtually possess a
canon of Holy Scripture in the shape of the new

Law-book introduced by Ezra.[1]   Strictly speaking,
the conception of canonical as contrasted with profane
writings could be crystallised into a definite doctrine
only after the canon was actually closed, but in point
of fact an idea was formed of the difference between
the two categories long before this took place.   The
distinction was equally familiar to the Jews of Palestine
and those of Alexandria.   Although the latter were
less rigid about the admission of new writings, there
was at the time of Christ little difference between the
Palestinian and Alexandrian canons, and the Greek
text was not regarded as less authoritative than the
Hebrew.

Both for Judaism itself, and for Christianity, the
formation of the Old Testament canon was a matter
of the highest moment.   For Judaism itself, inasmuch
as the whole life of the new community centred round
the inspired writings.   These formed the subject of
instruction in schools and the basis of homiletic exhortation in the synagogues.   They engrossed the diligent
labour of numerous copyists.   They were the great
theme of intellectual research on the part of professional
students.   And towards them eagerly turned every
seeker after eternal life.[2]   Nor did the Scriptures
possess less significance for the teaching of Jesus.
Viewing it in this connexion, Wendt speaks of the
formation of the Old Testament canon as "the most
important historical fact of post-exilian Judaism."[3]   The
Gospels make it clear that Jesus had steeped His mind
in the Old Testament.   It was His great controversial

[1] Neh. ix. 13.   [2] John v. 39.
[3] *The Teaching of Jesus*, i. p. 36.

weapon in making good the authority of His teaching. Through His constant appeal to the written word He was able to silence every gainsayer. That the Law was developed in a wrong spirit, and that the living truth was obscured through a mechanical worship of the letter, does not alter the fact that but for the veneration in which, as a fixed and sacred canon, the Scriptures were held, and the consequent care with which they were transmitted, it would have been impossible to preserve unimpaired the spiritual treasure which they enshrined.

Such are the essential features of Judaism.

5. *Religious Syncretism.*—It must not be supposed, however, that it was allowed to develop without a strong admixture of foreign elements. Although after the Exile an effort was made to exclude these from the Jewish community in Palestine, this was in the nature of things an impossibility. When men of different nationalities trade with each other there is necessarily an interchange not only of goods and money, but also to some extent of ideas, opinions, and habits. In the case of Judaism this process was doubtless facilitated by the fact that, while on its guard against laxity of conduct, it had little sense of the danger of intellectual innovation. Moreover, the want of creative originality, the incongruity resulting from the putting of new cloth upon old garments, the tendency to draw from hidden sources, the removal of national particularism, and the universal fusion of religious ideas which characterised the age, all point to the presence of foreign influence in the development of Judaism. As a matter of fact, by the beginning of the second century B.C., it was largely in

touch with the outside world.   It shared in the spread of cosmopolitan ideas, and in its eschatology passed beyond the limits of the older Messianic hopes to the thought of an individual retribution before the Divine judgment-seat.   The allegorising of ancient traditions, along with a transcendental conception of God, brought it more into line with other religions.   Further features which have their analogue in the contemporary life of other nations are the rise of professional teachers and theologians, as well as the reversion to primitive beliefs and superstitions, which marked the Judaism of the period.   All these are probably more than mere parallel developments; they suggest direct influence.

From what quarter, then, can such influence have come?   The religion of Egypt may be regarded as a negligible factor in the case.   At most it can have acted upon Judaism only in the sphere of the magic arts.   It was otherwise too torpid and degraded to have any effect upon a system of belief so immeasurably superior to itself.   The influences really to be taken into account here are the Babylonian, Persian, and Greek.

It is natural to suppose that the Babylonian religion should have influenced the development of post-exilic Judaism, for as a centre of that religion Babylon was scarcely inferior to Jerusalem itself.   Nor is the supposition altogether without confirmation in fact.   In the Old Testament there are certainly traces of Babylonian legends, and the Temple worship was in some respects indebted to Babylonian practice.   Our knowledge of the later development of the Babylonian religion is too slender, however, to enable us to arrive at a clear and accurate estimate of its influence upon Judaism.   After Nebuchadrezzar's empire became subject first to the Persian and then to the Greek dominion, religion sank to a low ebb in the Mesopotamian plain.   Unlike the Jewish, the Babylonian creed called forth no heroism in its defence.   Neverthe-less, it lived on in the schools of the learned, and influenced the West through astronomy and astrology, as well as through the dissemination of popular super-stition and magical lore, in the cultivation of which it rivalled Egypt itself.   Seeing however that the Baby-lonian religion was essentially polytheistic, it could not exert an appreciable influence upon the fundamentals of a monotheistic religion like Judaism.   It affected it only in such secondary matters as ceremonialism, the visionary method as adopted by Ezekiel, and the popular beliefs current at the time with respect to spirits, demons, etc.

The Persian (Iranian-Zarathustrian) influence was more vital.   At this epoch the Iranian religion had spread westwards and attained supremacy in Babylon, where Judaism came into contact with it.   From the first the relations between the Jews and the Persians were of a friendly nature, and it was to a Persian monarch that they owed their restoration.   There were striking affinities between the two peoples in respect of their religions, their laws, and their customs.   Both alike practised monotheism, abhorred idolatry, and valued morality; both alike cared for the poor, believed in the final destruction of evil, and laid stress upon a future judgment.   From being prophetic, both religions became ecclesiastical, with a priestly code considered to have been given to Zarathustra [1] and Moses respectively.

[1] Zoroaster of the Greek historians.

Like the Jews, the Persians had an elaborate system of ceremonial purifications to be observed by those guilty of legal trespass; and their prescriptions with regard to leprosy and other diseases were almost identical with those of the Pentateuch. By both nationalities great honour was accorded to marriage, and great importance attached to family ties. The custom of meeting for worship was common to both. Under such conditions it was inevitable that the two religions should act and react upon each other. Darmesteter maintains that the Persian religion is debtor to the Jews rather than *vice versâ*, but the testimony of Greek writers, including Plutarch, to the priority of Parsism seems conclusive against this view.

What concerns us here, however, is how far Judaism was influenced by Zarathustrianism. The conditions were present for the exercise of such an influence, but what are the facts? Unhappily there are serious difficulties in the way of reaching definite results. For one thing we are unable to attach a date to the various elements that have gone to make up the religion of Zarathustra, although the statements of Plutarch and others favour the view that the ideas of the Zend-Avesta, the sacred book of the Persian religion, of which only fragments are extant, probably for the most part go back to the times of the Achæmenidæ. A scientific investigation of details is still a desideratum, and until this is supplied the extent of the Persian influence cannot be pronounced upon with certainty. Another difficulty is that it can scarcely have been a pure and unadulterated form of the Persian religion which the Jews became acquainted with in Babylon. Bousset is probably right in thinking that it was "perhaps an Iranian religion mixed with Babylonian elements that eventually influenced Judaism." [1]

In what respects, then, may it be reasonably held to have been affected by this Persian or Babylonian-Persian influence? Here we can only map out generally the field on which it made itself felt. It may at once be said that if we except the institution of the Feast of Purim, and the custom of repeating the first prayer (the *Shĕma*) in the Temple at dawn, the Persian religion did not materially affect the outward organisation of the Jewish Church. Still less did its influence tell upon individual spiritual life. Yet it was very manifest in various directions. For some time after the Restoration it was apparently confined to a few isolated points not belonging to the substance of the faith, such as the "seven eyes" of Zech. iii. 9, and the Satan of Job and the Chronicler. But by the third or second century B.C., through the intermediary channel of the Babylonian Jews, Persian ideas had begun sensibly to act upon Jewish beliefs. Not that there was a simple transference of the ideas or doctrines of Zarathustra. There were perhaps a few instances of pure borrowing, such as the apocalyptic divisions of thousands of years, which are older in Persian sources than in the Book of Enoch. But in most cases where the influence of Parsism can be traced, Hebrew religion already contained the doctrines in germ; Mazdeism only stimulated and shaped the course of their development. That it did affect Judaism to this extent, however, is clear from the Palestinian writings of this epoch, especially from the Book of

[1] *Die Religion des Judentums*, p. 457 f.

Daniel, in the Aramaic portion of which numerous Persian words occur.[1] And its influence was most marked in the spheres of mythology, cosmology, angelology, and eschatology.

The Persian influence is clearly traceable in the treatment of primitive legends, which played their part in Judaism as well as in other religions. The stories of the Flood, of the building of the tower of Babel, and others related in Genesis, underwent extraordinary expansion, and were embellished with materials from the Persian religion.[2] In the cosmological conceptions of the Book of Enoch we have another example of Persian influence. Ideas from Iranian and perhaps other sources are here so freely grafted on to the Old Testament account of the creation that naturally the resultant representation is full of incongruity. In the department of angelology the influence of Parsism upon the later Judaism is particularly manifest. It is significant that so great a development of ideas concerning the character and functions of the angelic messengers should have synchronised with the period when the Jews were thrown into direct contact with the Persians, in whose religion a hierarchy of angels played an important part. Doubtless the existence of angels was an accepted belief of pre-exilic Hebraism, but the prominence given to them in post-exilic writings was a direct consequence of the Persian environment, and of the new transcendental conception of the Deity. Hierarchies of good and evil spirits were called in to fill up the gulf between men and God. This is already noticeable in the later

---

[1] A list of these is given in Driver's *Daniel*, p. lvi. f.
[2] See Note 7, p. 370.

portions of the Old Testament, and is a strongly marked feature of the post-canonical writings which have been preserved.[1] Although these intermediary beings bear Hebrew names, at least one of them—that of the evil angel Asmodeus [2]—appears to be simply the Persian *Æshma-Dæva*. It was, however, chiefly in the domain of eschatology that the Persian religion proved to be a real factor in the development of Judaism. While the doctrine of an individual resurrection is properly enough regarded as the ripe fruit of Old Testament religion, there seems no good reason to doubt that its growth into distinctness and maturity was stimulated by the Zarathustrian creed. The fact that in Daniel xii. we have a clearer expression of the doctrines of immortality and the resurrection of individuals than elsewhere in the Old Testament may well have been due to the Persian belief in a future state of happiness in which the faithful, finally victorious over evil, should live for ever in fellowship with Ormazd and his angels. The Persian influence, moreover, is strongly reflected in the Jewish apocalyptic literature, and in the dualistic trend which it gradually assumed. Not that Jewish dualism was ever a mere replica of the Persian : identity is not necessary to prove dependence. But two facts are here of prime importance. The one is that the conception of the devil current in New Testament times was quite foreign to the older Hebraism. The other is the presence in the apocalyptic literature of the Persian doctrine of God's victory over the devil at the end of the world.

[1] Dan. x. 13, 20, xii. 1 ; Tob. xii. 15 ; Enoch xc. 21 f. Cf. Rev. i. 4, viii. 2.
[2] Tob. iii.

With respect to the Greek influence in Palestine, the facts have been more definitely ascertained. On the development of religious thought it was slight. It bore much more upon life and manners than upon doctrine. It is only in Alexandrian Judaism that we detect the impress of the Greek philosophy. Regarding their ancestral faith as the charter of their nationality, the Jews of Jerusalem clung to it with extraordinary tenacity, and viewed with corresponding jealousy all extraneous doctrines and cults. But in other directions Hellenism exerted a powerful influence in Judæa. It stamped itself upon the commercial, social, and political life of the Jewish people, as well as upon their language and literature.

After Alexander's death Palestine became the scene of a keen struggle between Ptolemy I. and Antigonus, two of his successors. In B.C. 320 Ptolemy took Jerusalem, but it passed again oftener than once into the hands of his rival before the slaughter of the latter at the battle of Ipsus in 301 gave the Egyptian king real possession. From this date the process of Hellenisation went on quietly throughout the country, especially in the cities founded by Macedonian soldiers and called by Greek names. Hellenistic Greek became the language of trade and fashion. The non-Jewish section of the population, including the Samaritans, were unanimous in their adoption of Greek manners and customs. Many Jews also were fascinated by the new ideas, attractive habits, and freer morals, alongside of which their own traditional ways of thinking, modes of life, and standards of conduct appeared uncouth, old-fashioned, and provincial. Greek art appealed to the more educated classes, and Greek sports to the populace generally. The amphitheatres and the racecourse were crowded with enthusiastic spectators; gymnasia were multiplied; even the Bacchanalian festivals proved a welcome novelty.

As a sequel to the battle of Paneas in B.C. 198, when Antiochus the Great, king of Syria, defeated the Egyptian general Scopus, the lordship of Palestine passed from the Ptolemies to the Seleucidæ. Although it meant simply a transference from one form of Hellenistic rule to another, the Syrian supremacy was at first hopefully welcomed by the Jews. And they did receive some valuable concessions from Antiochus, but his successors were of a more mercenary spirit, and on the whole the Jews had little reason to be thankful for their change of masters. Indeed they were on the threshold of some of the direst experiences of their history. Antiochus vainly thought to prevent the advance of the Romans in the East. Having been routed in a great battle at Magnesia in B.C. 190, he came under the heel of the new world-conquerors, and in order to pay the heavy indemnity imposed by them, he and his successors were obliged to resort to such desperate measures as the robbing of temples within their own territory. In the year 187 he lost his life while thus occupied in the region of Elymais. According to 2 Macc. iii., an unsuccessful raid was made also upon the Temple of Jerusalem at the instigation of his son Seleucus IV. Philopator (187–176). The contemplated sacrilege was, however, actually committed by the next monarch Antiochus IV. Epiphanes (176–164), under whose reign the conflict between Hellenism and Judaism was destined to reach its height.

At the accession of Epiphanes the pagan propaganda had made considerable progress, and a Greek party had been formed even in Judæa. Although Hellenism had lost its political prestige, its hold upon social manners and customs was in no degree relaxed. Its diffusion still went on. The Book of Daniel, written in Palestine probably during the persecution of Antiochus Epiphanes (B.C. 168–165), contains a few words indisputably Greek, such as κίθαρις, ψαλτήριον, and συμφονία.[1] The employment of foreign terms is in itself an indication of influence exerted from without. But the evidence on this point furnished by the literature of the period is not merely verbal; it extends to ideas and sentiments as well. The presence or otherwise of Hellenic influence in Ecclesiastes is a question still debated among scholars, but in the case of the non-canonical book of Ecclesiasticus it is probably reflected. In the writer's allusions to the danger of associating with women who are public singers,[2] to the artisan who "cuts gravings of signets and . . . sets his heart to preserve likeness in portraiture,"[3] and to "a concert of music at a banquet of wine,"[4] we have some indication that even in Judæa Greek morals, Greek art, and Greek customs had come to be greatly in vogue.[5] Another thing pointing in the same direction is the high repute in which literary ability was then held in Palestine, in common with other countries which were beginning directly to feel the Greek influence. "He that hath applied his soul," says Ben Sira, "and meditateth in the law of the Most High, will seek out the wisdom of all the ancients, and will be occupied in

---

[1] See Note 8, p. 372.   [2] ix. 4.   [3] xxxviii. 27.   [4] xxxii. 5 f.
[5] These features, however, had long been familiar to Egypt and Babylon.

prophecies. He will keep the discourse of the men of renown, and will enter in amidst the subtilties of parables."[1] And perhaps we are to find a further indication of the Hellenic spirit in this author's advocacy of the medical profession, which was evidently rising to a new importance in Israel. In reply to the allegation that the practice of medicine argues a lack of faith in God, he points out that both the skill of the physician and the healing virtue of herbs are in reality creations of the Most High.[2] The significance of his language lies in the fact that the medical science of the Greeks was renowned throughout Western Asia.

By the end of the second century B.C. the entire Mediterranean region had been hellenised, with the single exception of the purely Judæan district. There a stubborn resistance was offered to the progress of the Hellenistic spirit, with the result that it was so far kept at bay. Down to the time of Epiphanes the high priests had been its stoutest opponents. Greek culture had been aggressive, but in connexion with the activity of the scribes Jewish legalism had also been lengthening its cords and strengthening its stakes. A collision between two such antagonistic forces was inevitable. If Hellenism was inexorable in pushing its claims, the adherents of the Law were not less resolute in resisting them. Organising themselves as the Ḥasīdîm or "the pious," they championed the strictest observance of the Law as developed by the scribes. Already in some measure was the prophecy fulfilled regarding the raising up of "thy sons, O Zion, against thy sons, O Greece."[3] And the zeal of the former resulted in keeping the

---

[1] xxxix. 1 f.　　　　[2] xxxviii. 1–8.　　　　[3] Zech. ix. 13.

pagan worship out of Judæa. Like a rocky islet rising proudly out of the sea, the Holy City remained the impregnable citadel of Judaism. By extending its influence so as to embrace outlying districts like Galilee, it did much to counteract the spread of Hellenism during this period. Yet even in Jerusalem, outside of the religious sphere, the tide of pagan civilisation was steadily advancing, and when at last the Greek party succeeded in capturing the priestly nobility, a bold attempt was made to hellenise Jewish life on its *religious* side also. But the excessive severity of the measures employed saved the situation. In decreeing the total suppression of the Jewish religion Antiochus Epiphanes overreached himself. This mad project caused every section of the people to rally in defence of their Law. It led to the revolt under the Maccabees, and for more than two generations effectually arrested the spread of Hellenism in Judæa.

CHAPTER II

PALESTINIAN JUDAISM: PRE-MACCABÆAN

CHAPTER II.

PALESTINIAN JUDAISM: PRE-MACCABÆAN.

THE foreign oppression to which after their return from the Exile the Jews were almost constantly subject could not fail to tell upon the hitherto strongly maintained national unity. From the time of Alexander not only was the way opened up for the introduction of new thoughts and forms, but the people themselves were parted, in respect both of country and of language, into two great divisions. Of these one remained in Palestine and continued to use the Hebrew speech, though they gradually adopted the Aramaic dialect; while the other went abroad and gave up their mother-tongue in favour of the Greek, which was then spoken throughout the region of the Mediterranean. Naturally the home Jews were the more conservative, and they tenaciously adhered to the letter of their ancient polity. Those of the Dispersion, on the other hand, could not avoid being largely influenced by their new surroundings. They were attracted by the Greek culture, and soon to a considerable extent imbibed the Greek spirit. We shall deal first with Palestinian Judaism.

The shock of the Exile had been bewildering to the Israelitish nation. Through the deportation of the

inhabitants the national life had been torn up by the
roots, and had seemed smitten beyond all hope of
recovery.   Yet there were those who could contemplate
the ruins of Jerusalem without despair,—men with that
depth of intellect, strength of piety, and vision of the
future, which went to make up the prophet-statesman so
distinctive of Israelitish history.   To a large extent the
situation was to be saved by the spiritual insight and
sagacity of these noble patriots.   They perceived that
all was not lost, and that there was grace behind the
judgment.   In the destruction of the Holy City they
saw not merely a calamity to be bewailed, but a loud
call to repentance.   They proclaimed it as their firm
conviction that the main cause for lamentation on the
part of Israel lay in their own persistent sin and folly,
and that upon their seeking Jahweh with all their heart
in prayer they would find that His thoughts towards
them were " thoughts of peace and not of evil." [1]   He
would forgive the sins of the past, restore upon the basis
of a new covenant the relation which had been severed,
and write His law upon their heart.[2]   After all, the
Temple was only the material embodiment of the eternal
truth that God had communicated to His people.   It
was not the true Zion.   Its worship was but the
temporary clothing of what was in itself imperishable.
So far therefore from being the death-blow of the chosen
people, the Exile was distinctly a forward movement
in Israelitish religion, and the exiles had only to follow
the counsels of these great prophets—men like Jeremiah,
Ezekiel, Second Isaiah, and Daniel—in order to ensure
the restoration of their national life.

[1] Jer. xxix. 11.   [2] xxxi. 31 ff.

And at least a section of them did so. The truths which had been despised at home found acceptance in Babylon. At the Restoration under Cyrus a great change, amounting to a moral revolution, had been produced in the character of the people. The evil spirit of apostacy had been cast out of them, and the new nationality which they founded was more of the nature of a Church than of a State.

The history of the restored community, although unhappily obscure in many of its details, is as remarkable as it is important. During the six centuries of its existence it passed through many vicissitudes. From being a small struggling colony it grew in strength and self-confidence until on the open field of battle it successfully encountered imperial armies and temporarily regained political independence. It also applied itself with incredible devotion to the study of the Law, which in its completed form probably dates from the post-exilic period. At last it fell on evil days, and on the destruction of Jerusalem by the Romans in A.D. 70 ceased to exist. Our interest in this age of Jewish history is necessarily enhanced by the fact that it contains the key to the proper understanding of the New Testament.

The laws which regulated all civic relations within the Jewish community were based upon possession of "the land," and were specially drawn with a view to securing the preservation of the family and its inheritance. Although agrarian laws were no more able to maintain the economic balance in this instance than in others where the experiment has been tried, and although those enacted were suited only to a small population without political independence, the bond between land and people was particularly strong. It was in fact a religious tie that bound the Jews to Palestine. Not only had their fathers dwelt in it from the days of Joshua until the sack of Jerusalem by Nebuchadrezzar, but the Abrahamic tradition also gave it a special sacredness in their eyes. To them it was already what men have loved to call it ever since—the Holy Land. As such it became the peculiar home and centre of Judaism. It was "Jahweh's land,"[1] inhabited by Jahweh's people.[2] Among the Semites the deportation of a people from its land was viewed as a severance from its god; and for the Hebrews it was one of the bitterest ingredients in their cup to hear the heathen taunt: "These are Jahweh's people, and yet they are gone forth out of His land."[3] But these narrow traditional ideas were gradually dissipated through the monotheistic influence of Old Testament revelation, which, while not dissociating from Palestine the special presence of Jahweh, attributes that presence not to the idea that this is the geographically delimited area over which He holds sway, but to the fact that here is the chosen theatre for God's revelation of Himself to all men. In this latter circumstance lay the real sanctity of Canaan. From the day the Israelites entered this land— the land promised to the patriarchs while as yet they were but strangers and sojourners in it—it became hallowed ground. Not only so; the occupation of Palestine was regarded as indispensable to the national religion, at any rate while the Temple stood. If after its demolition this conception was considerably modified, the restoration of Jahweh's worship on Mount Zion was

---

[1] Hos. ix. 3.   [2] See Note 9, p. 373.   [3] Ezek. xxxvi. 20.

none the less wistfully looked forward to. Even Ezekiel, who repudiates the notion that the forms of a material Temple and an earthly State are essential to the exercise of Jahweh's dominion over the world, does not conceive of His absence from the earthly sanctuary as permanent. For him the presupposition of the establishment of the Divine kingdom is the return both of Israel and of Jahweh to their own land, and their joint re-occupation of it is the seal of the perpetual covenant of peace existing between them. But indeed every son of Israel looked upon "the land" with a religious feeling, and hence the ardour with which it was loved.

But if among the returned remnant there was a warm attachment to the old land and the old faith, there was also in many respects a distinct cleavage with the past. Judaism grew up as a new thing on the ancient soil. It was the embodiment of the altered spirit induced in the people by their new conditions. The freedom and the joyousness which characterised the religion of the ancient Hebrews, the immediate appeal to Jahweh through prophet and priest, the sacrifices offered in person at the various local shrines, ceased with the promulgation of the Deuteronomic Law-book. If the tendency to turn religion into a code of rules had already been pronounced before the Exile, it now became altogether dominant. Every department of life was so penetrated by the religious idea that to a denizen of another country Palestine must have seemed like part of a different world.

The conditions which stimulated the growth of Judaism appeared in the interval between the destruction of Jerusalem by Nebuchadrezzar and the conquests of

Alexander the Great. Perhaps the Jewish mind was unconsciously drawn towards ritualism by contact with the powerful priesthood of Babylon. Be this as it may, the Jews, no longer in possession of a material kingdom, were free to devote their whole energies to religion. They were also at the same time under the necessity of organising their worship upon a non-political basis, and in a form likely to prove a defence against heathenism. Moreover, to many whose faith had received a rude shock by the calamities that had befallen their nation, a system like that of the Priestly Code, embodying the authoritative rules of religion, came as a welcome relief. Finally, the very hatred of the Samaritans, as well as the sympathetic aid of the brethren of the Dispersion, tended to weld the little Jewish community into a body as compactly built together as Jerusalem itself. And it is a remarkable testimony to the solidarity then given to Judaism that to this day it has triumphantly defied every disintegrating and alien influence.

For the starting-point in the development we must go back to the work of Ezekiel, Ezra, and Nehemiah. It was the task of Judaism to attempt to realise Ezekiel's vision of a new theocracy. Its success was only partial. The efforts of the men to whom it fell to undertake this task necessarily bear the impress of their own times. It was not an age of creative enthusiasm, exhilarating prosecution of lofty ideals, and open-minded search after truth, but one of practical skill, laborious energy, and artificial arrangement. The main actors of the period, such as Zerubbabel the prince, and Joshua the high priest, were concerned with carrying out a fixed programme rather than with initiating fresh measures.

They were estimable men, but not born leaders. Neither were the post-exilic prophets Haggai and Zechariah cast in the large mould of the greater prophets who had preceded them. Even Ezra the scribe was only a restorer of former things, and not the pioneer of things new. In some respects Nehemiah may appear to be an exception, but in spite of the dash and decision displayed in his public activity, he never deviated from the course already mapped out before the Restoration. It is certainly significant that, even in presence of this deep-seated tendency to conserve the past, the later Judaism gradually drifted away from the position of the earlier prophets with regard to the relative religious importance of the moral and the ceremonial. So impossible is it to stand still in religion. "Finality is the only heresy." Where there is no normal development, there will be blind deviation into error, or else the fatal stagnation of a petrified orthodoxy.

It was not until the time of the Maccabæan revolt that Judaism received its baptism of power. Previous to that event it had not the energy to accomplish much, but subsequent to the life-and-death struggle which then ensued its labours became as strenuous as its zeal was unquenchable. Both the zeal and the labour were centred in the Law. Jewish legalism appears in two forms, priestly and scribal, "Temple" being the watch-word of the former, and "Scripture" that of the latter. There was a development from the one to the other—from the priestly form to the scribal; and perhaps the Wisdom movement came in between. If the scribe was really the continuation of the "wise," this would shew the irresistible tendency of the age towards legalism.

At first the life and interest of the new community were concentrated in the Temple services.   In so far as it was a restoration, Judaism was a restoration of the cultus.   The sole sovereignty of Jahweh as proclaimed by the prophets was now an unchallenged article in the Jewish creed, but in the absence of political independence something practical had to be done if the sacred remnant was not to perish through absorption by the surrounding heathen.   It was in these circumstances that men bethought themselves of old-established forms and usages as a protecting shield for the religion of Jahweh and the Messianic hopes associated with it.   In spite of the upheaval caused by the fall of the State, the new community established itself accordingly on the old site, and raised up the altar again.   With certain modifications required by the circumstances of the time, the former praxis was restored, all its parts being arranged into one systematic whole, with a view to the proper organisation of the colony as a " congregation" of Jahweh.   Very fittingly the priest and prophet Ezekiel represents the transition stage between the prophets and the Law.[1]

All this meant a great advance in the status of the priesthood.   Even before the Exile, particularly after Josiah's reformation, the priests of Jerusalem, the sons of Zadok, had risen to a position of primacy over their provincial brethren, and the Temple there gained in prestige correspondingly.   But in the post-exilic writings it is everywhere assumed that the constitution of Judaism

[1] As Wellhausen says, " He is by nature a priest, and his peculiar merit is that he enclosed the soul of prophecy in the body of a community which was not political, but founded on the temple and the cultus."—*Prolegomena*, p. 421.

is a hierocracy.[1] By the time of the Chronicler Israel
had become "a kingdom of priests and a holy nation."
A position of unique influence and dignity was accorded
to the high priest, who was virtually invested with kingly
power in addition to the spiritual powers possessed by
him as head of the hierarchy. This was the natural
result of the situation. Israel was now simply a Church
devoting itself to things sacred, all secular and political
affairs having been taken out of its hands. Even under
foreign rule, however, a certain modicum of political
freedom was still granted to the people, and they looked
to the high priest as their natural head. The only
authority he laid claim to was that derived from the
Law, but the position he occupied at the head of the
hierarchy gave him absolute pre-eminence in the nation.
What Horace says of Jupiter's supremacy in the heathen
pantheon—

> Unde nil majus generatur ipso
> Nec viget quidquam simile aut secundum—[2]

might also be said of the high-priestly pre-eminence in
post-exilic Judaism. Evidence of this is afforded by the
glowing description of Simon the high priest in Sirach.[3]
In this unsolicited transference of secular power to the
pontificate there lurked, however, a subtle danger, which
was yet to have disastrous consequences alike for the
high-priestly house and for the Jewish people.

While hitherto there had been only a general distinction between clergy and laity, the priestly order itself

---

[1] The influence of the Priestly Code is very manifest, for example, in the
difference of atmosphere between the Books of Chronicles and the older
Books of Samuel and Kings.
[2] *Odes*, I. xii. 17 f.   [3] l. 1–21.

was now divided into two grades, namely, descendants of Aaron and Levites, the latter being not only officially subordinate to the former, but actually their servants. The Deuteronomic phrase "the priests the Levites" accordingly becomes with the Chronicler "the priests and the Levites." The new hierarchical system was maintained by contributions levied upon the laity, and had its legal basis in the Law-book introduced by Ezra, and accepted by the people as an integral part of the written Law. No better proof could be furnished of the *éclat* to which it had now attained than the enormous crowds which gathered from all quarters to attend the yearly festivals at Jerusalem.

Such was the visible framework provided for the idea of holiness, which was to be the starting-point of a new development for Israel. They reckoned themselves Jahweh's people, holy through separation from the outside world. By a network of ceremonial observances the Jew was singled out from other men. The cultus thus became the waistband of the theocracy. The term "holy" was no longer used in the sense of Divine; it merely meant religious or priestly. The distinction between the sacred and the profane was very sharply drawn, and there was a strong tendency to encroach upon the sphere of the non-religious, until every moment of life was virtually redeemed by the necessity of attending to a Divine precept.

We must not suppose that the restoration of the cultus was a reversion to heathen practices condemned by the prophets, for the sacred festivals no longer possessed their original significance as a recognition of the Deity in connexion with the supply of human needs.

Out of regard to ancient custom, they were revived after the Exile; but they were denaturalised, and transformed into commemorative institutions of supernatural religion. In this way they assumed a purely statutory character. From being a spontaneous tribute designed to please God, worship became a matter of simple obedience to Divine law. To offer sacrifices according to the letter of what was prescribed was the all-important thing. The cultus was based, not upon the inward devotion of the worshipper, but upon the positive command of Jahweh. Formerly it had been the bridge by which Israel too frequently passed over to heathen usages and immoralities, but now that it had become completely divorced from nature, it acted rather as a protection from heathenism, and was the means of preserving the religion of ethical monotheism until it could be embraced by all mankind. In spite of the restoration of the cultus, however, popular piety was at the same time undergoing a process of growing detachment from the Temple and its services. This is indicated by such later developments as the organisation of the Essenes, the universal note in the preaching of Jesus, and the energetic life of Judaism after the destruction of the Temple.

The new prominence given to the Law brought about an important change in the national development. It was drawn up in the interests of the priestly worship, and for some time after Ezra the priests were its custodians and expositors.[1] But its scientific study and interpretation naturally drifted into the hands of a professional class who made this their calling. From

[1] Hag. ii. 11; Mal. ii. 7.

their work as copyists of the Holy Scriptures these men were known as *sopherim* or scribes. They were, however, far from being mere caligraphists ; they were also theologians, Biblical scholars, and exegetes; and they, and not the priests, were henceforth to exercise the controlling influence upon Jewish religious life.

The work of the scribes had necessarily its legal as well as its theological side, for what lay at the very heart of the Law was the administration of justice. They were the jurists of their time. Pentateuchal legislation had to be adapted to the needs of the present, and through the industry of the scribes in this direction there gradually grew up alongside of the written Torah a new law of use and wont, known as *Halacha.*[1] It was their business to deduce from Scripture the proper course to be pursued in any given emergency, and the conclusions thus arrived at all went to swell the traditional Law. Theoretically this could not go beyond the exposition and application of the written Law, but in reality it was a development or expansion of it, and that of such a kind as to push Scripture itself more and more into the background. The importance of the Halacha lay in the fact that it dealt with matters affecting everyday life. At first the new tradition was merely oral, but it was afterwards committed to writing, and so highly was it prized that it was even traced back to Moses. But the scribes did not confine themselves to the sphere of law ; they also busied themselves with the elaboration and embellishment of the narrative and didactic portions

[1] According to Schürer = that which is current or customary ; Levy, *s.v.* "walk, behaviour," law by which life and conduct can be guided.

of the sacred text. And here they had freer scope
for their talents. In order to twist the Law into accord
with practice they were in many instances obliged to
resort to great arbitrariness of interpretation, for they
were bound by the sacred text; but in dealing with
the non-legal parts of the Old Testament they simply
introduced into the text what was necessary in order
to make it reflect the views of their own time. The
Chronicler's treatment of the older history is a case in
point. Even the moral and religious statements of
Holy Writ were modified on similar lines. The product
of this whole department of scribal activity was
designated *Haggada* (narrative). Through the constant
accumulation of oral tradition, and the free manipula-
tion of the Biblical text, the Old Testament itself was
virtually stifled.

The scribes were also the academic teachers of
their day. Their classes met in the porches of the
Temple. As compared with modern usage, their
educational methods were very mechanical. The chief
duties devolving upon their pupils were the faithful
retention in their memory of what they were taught,
and exact adherence to it in their own teaching of
others, the ideal disciple being " like a well of chalk,
which loses not a drop of water." [1] As the work of
a scribe was not paid for, those who practised this
calling combined it with some secular business, unless
they happened to be men of independent means. But
the trade was kept strictly subordinate to the teaching.
" Give thyself a little to thy trade, and much to the
study of the Law," [2] was the rule laid down in this

---

[1] *Pirke Aboth*, ii. 8.   [2] *Ibid.* iv. 10.

connexion. From the severity with which Christ condemns their covetousness, however, it is impossible to
believe in the disinterestedness of the scribes. They
contrived somehow to reap a pecuniary harvest from
their services.[1]

It would be a mistake to suppose that the functions
of the scribes were exclusively professional; they were
judicial as well. In addition to the theoretical system-
atising of the Law itself in oral conference and disputa-
tion with each other, and the instruction of their pupils
in its contents, they were also, latterly, at all events,
called to administer it by delivering judgments in court.
Already in Sirach[2] the scribe is referred to as pre-
eminently fitted to occupy "the seat of the judge"; in
New Testament times the scribes are spoken of as
actually sitting "in Moses' seat;[3] their influence in
the synedrium, as in the synagogue, was paramount.

The scribes were not only a learned order, but also
formed an organised guild with representatives in every
locality. Their headquarters, of course, were at Jerusalem.
In all disputed matters they loyally accepted the
decision of a majority, so preserving uniformity in their
teaching, and retaining power over the people. By the
time of Christ this unity of sentiment seems, however,
to have given way to discord.[4] The title *Rabbi* is a
monument of the universal esteem in which they were
held.[5]

The moral effects of the idea that only through the

---

[1] Mark xii. 40; Luke xvi. 14.   [2] xxxviii. 33.
[3] Matt. xxiii. 2.   [4] See Note 10, p. 375.
[5] From their pupils the scribes exacted a degree of homage greater than
that given to parents. In this respect, indeed, they seem to have levied
universal tribute. Even the priests and the aristocracy bowed to their

toilsome fulfilment of the Law can men win the favour
of God were of that unlovely type disclosed in the
Gospels. There is the greatest possible contrast between
the teaching of the scribes and that of Jesus, who
denounced their habit of subordinating the Word of God
to their own tradition, and so making it void.[1] In
opposition to their artificial externalism He proclaimed
the necessity for a spiritual worship of a spiritual God,
and shewed that religion is not simply a science to be
studied, or an art to be learned, or a manufactured
product, but a disposition and affection of the heart
which will spontaneously find its own appropriate modes
of expression.

authority. Their advice was eagerly sought and implicitly followed by those
in difficulty. This general deference was very agreeable to them. " They
loved the uppermost rooms at feasts, and the chief seats in the synagogues,
and greetings in the markets, and to be called of men Rabbi, Rabbi" (Matt.
xxiii. 6 f.). Thus they had gradually served themselves heirs to the moral
influence of the priesthood.

As the representatives of the Law, the scribes aimed at making real its
supremacy in Israel. Their whole activity and power grew out of the idea
that the Law represented the commandments of God, and that every Jew
was therefore under obligation to obey it in every particular. But rightly to
apprehend from this standpoint the claims of religion, so as to know what was
binding, implied a professional knowledge of the Law. Religion had become
a fine art, and those prepared to shoulder the burden it imposed could not
dispense with the guidance of the expert. A Jew had to reckon not only
with the 613 commandments of the written Law, but also with the inde-
finable number of the unwritten Law or Halacha, said to have been given to
Moses on Sinai, and handed down in regular succession by elders, prophets,
and learned men, till finally embodied in the Talmud. By dint of reasoning
and casuistry the scribes deliberately set themselves to lay down the Law for
every conceivable situation, with the result that the life of the pious was
crushed under an ever-increasing load of legal exactions. Two things have
been clearly established by this great Jewish experiment. One is that no
code of law can take account of everything affecting human life, and the other
is that law does not in itself provide an adequate basis for religion. " The
law maketh nothing perfect " ; its function is simply that of a schoolmaster.

[1] Matt. xv. 6 ; Mark vii. 8 f.

It would, however, be wrong to conclude that, even under this system, there was developed nothing but artificialism in religion. Not to speak of the evidence furnished by the later prophets, the Psalms in themselves afford sufficient proof to the contrary. Many of them were written in the interval between the return from the Exile and the Maccabæan revolt, and so genuine is the spirit of piety pervading them that to this day they remain admittedly the most fruitful and inspiring source of devotional feeling.

What, then, is the essence of piety as reflected in the Psalter?   What, according to it, are the demands made by God upon His people, and what are the forms in which true piety expresses itself?   Here we remark at the outset that piety is based upon the *fear of God*. To serve the Lord with fear and to rejoice with trembling[1] is the one foundation upon which the structure of a godly character can be reared.   Hence the injunction, " Fear him, all ye seed of Israel." [2]   It is significant that the destruction of the wicked is not represented as calling forth joy and gratitude from those to whom deliverance is thus brought, but rather fear: " the righteous also shall see and fear." [3]   The fear of God, however, removes every other fear.[4] He that abideth under the shadow of the Almighty fears neither fowler's snare nor noisome pestilence.[5] That Omnipotence is on the side of the good and against the wicked is a cardinal article of the Jewish creed.

Fear accordingly becomes the mother of *trust*— another of the constituent elements of piety. The congregation of Israel trusts God because it fears Him

[1] ii. 11.   [2] xxii. 23.   [3] lii. 6.   [4] iii. 6.   [5] xci. 3 ff.

alone. Its confidence is not in horses and in chariots, but in the name of the Lord;[1] it trusts not in riches,[2] nor in princes,[3] nor in any son of human kind,[4] but in the mercy of God for ever and ever.[5] As the Divine arm saved their fathers,[6] so is it put forth on their own behalf, and they rely implicitly upon this supernatural aid: " I will not trust in my bow, neither shall my sword save me."[7] God's power and grace are an all-sufficient protection: " Thou hast delivered my soul from death, mine eyes from tears, and my feet from falling."[8] Hence the necessity of trust on the part of every pious Jew.[9] This indeed is represented as the sum of the Divine requirements: " Judge me, O God, for I have walked in mine integrity: I have trusted also in the Lord; therefore I shall not slide."[10] It also becomes a ground of hope in presence of misfortune, both for the individual [11] and for the community.[12] Not that it was always easy for the pious Jew to maintain this glowing confidence in God. Some of the Psalms reveal the inner struggle that frequently went on between faith and doubt. Anguish prompts the question, " Hath God forgotten to be gracious?" But faith answers, " This is my infirmity . . . I will remember the years of the right hand of the Most High."[13] The position of immovable trust can be reached and maintained only through introspection,[14] self-discipline,[15] and prayer.[16]

Another essential element of the piety reflected in the Psalms is that of *humility*. The pious are

---

[1] xx. 7.   [2] lxii. 11.   [3] cxlvi. 3.   [4] cxvi. 11.
[5] lii. 8.   [6] xliv. 3.   [7] xliv. 6.   [8] cxvi. 8.
[9] xxxvii. 3.   [10] xxvi. 1.   [11] xvi. 1, xxxi. 13 ff.   [12] xlvi.
[13] lxxvii. ; cf. xlii. 9 ff.   [14] cxxxi., cxxxix.
[15] xliii. 5, ci. 2 ff.   [16] lxi. 2 ff., lxxiii. 16 ff.

designated "the poor and the needy,"[1] "the poor and
the sorrowful."[2]   In the Psalms these terms are still
more frequently used of Israel itself,[3] while in Zech. ix. 9,
lowliness appears along with justice as an attribute of
the Messiah.   Humility is therefore treated as a root
virtue in religion.   The pious walk humbly before God.[4]
Seeing that He giveth to His beloved in sleep,[5] they are
strangers to an anxious worldliness.   For all needful
provision they look to Him as a servant to his master.[6]
They are "weaned" from worldly ambition and glory.[7]
Intent on the pursuit of peace,[8] they strive to overcome
the natural envy excited by the prosperity of the wicked,
and, perplexing as the situation is, count it bestial folly
to cavil at the ways of Providence in relation thereto.[9]
The attitude of the pious under affliction is one of silent
submission : " I was dumb, I opened not my mouth,
because thou didst it." [10]   They are observant of God's
works in Providence, through which sinners are called to
repentance ere judgment overtakes them.[11]   Conscious
that God is the searcher of hearts, and acquainted with
man's inmost thoughts,[12] they also "walk mournfully
before the Lord of hosts." [13]   The pious man is likewise
alive to the false security induced by prosperity,[14] and to
the necessity of keeping his tongue from evil.[15]   In the
silence of the night he turns his soul inward upon itself
so as to make sure that he is walking humbly with his
God.[16]

[1] xii. 6, xxxvii. 14, cix. 16, 22.   [2] lxix. 29.
[3] xxxv. 10, lxviii. 10, lxxii. 4, etc.   [4] Gen. xvii. 1.
[5] cxxvii. 2.   [6] cxxiii.   [7] cxxxi.
[8] xxxiv. 12, xxxvii. 37.   [9] lxxiii. 22.   [10] xxxix. 9.
[11] xxviii. 5.   [12] cxxxix.   [13] Mal. iii. 14.
[14] xxx. 6 f.   [15] xxxiv. 13, cxli. 3.   [16] iv. 5.

Such being the teaching of the Psalms regarding the inner content of piety, we have next to note the forms in which it finds outward expression. From this standpoint the pious are distinguished from the ungodly above all by their *observance of the Law*. To stand in a right relationship to the Divine will is a vital concern of all who are animated by godly fear, and as the Law is the revelation of God's will, obedience to its precepts is necessarily a leading article of piety. The pious man treasures it in his heart as his most precious possession,[1] and meditates upon it day and night.[2] His one aim is to walk according to its precepts,[3] for God's mercy and truth are peculiarly vouchsafed to such as keep His covenant and are mindful of His commandments.[4] The fulfilling of the Law is the *raison d'être* of all God's goodness to Israel.[5] Not through sacrifice, however, but through the doing of His will and the cherishing of His law in the heart, can they best shew their gratitude.[6]

It is the special province of *worship* to give expression to the inward sense of the Divine goodness. To kneel before the Lord, to give thanks and to sing praises, to shew forth His loving-kindness in the morning and His faithfulness every night,[7] to worship the Lord in the beauty of holiness,[8] is not only becoming,[9] but binding upon Israel, for only thus can all the earth be brought to fear before Him.[10] Such worship is, of course, public, and associated with " the great congregation " as one of its principal duties.[11] The homage

---

[1] xxxvii. 31, xl. 8, xix. 11.   [2] i. 2.   [3] lxxxvi. 11.
[4] ciii. 18, xxv. 10.   [5] cv. 45.   [6] xl. 6 ff.   [7] xcii. 1 f.
[8] xcvi. 9.   [9] cxlvii. 1.   [10] xcvi. 9.   [11] xxxv. 18, xl. 10.

thus rendered to God essentially consists of praise
and prayer, "the free-will offerings of the mouth,"[1]
which are more acceptable to Him than "an ox or
bullock that hath horns and hoofs,"[2] although legal
sacrifices have their own place and function.[3] Every
pious Israelite delights to compass God's altar, in order
to give loud expression to his gratitude and to speak of
God's wondrous works, and loves the habitation of His
house and the place where His honour dwelleth.[4] But
the pious scrupulously practise private prayer also.[5]
It is their wont to kneel in their chambers thrice daily,
and to offer supplication both on their own behalf and
on behalf of the nation.[6] Sometimes the saint's couch is
watered with tears because of the sore chastisement laid
upon Israel ;[7] at other times he is gladdened by the sense
of God's loving-kindness to His people.[8] He is equally
sensitive to the Divine favour and the Divine rebuke, and
makes both the theme of his meditation upon his bed.

Feelings of cordial brotherliness pervaded the circles
of the pious. In the fellowship of religious worship
all true-hearted Israelites were united by a closer tie
than that of blood-relationship.[9] They "took sweet
counsel together, and walked unto the house of God in
company" ;[10] they had discovered "how good and how
pleasant a thing it is for brethren to dwell together in
unity."[11] The pilgrim in Jerusalem felt himself among
brethren.[12] It was usual for those who feared the Lord
to strengthen each other in mutual conference,[13] while

[1] cxix. 108. [2] lxix. 30 f. [3] xx. 7, etc. [4] xxvi. 6 ff.
[5] xlii. 8, cxix. 62. [6] lv. 18 ; cf. Dan. vi. 10. [7] vi. 7.
[8] lxiii. 4 ff. [9] cxix. 63. [10] lv. 14. [11] cxxxiii. 1.
[12] cxxii. 8. [13] Mal. iii. 16.

to offend against the generation of God's children was viewed as a serious crime.[1]

Another form in which the piety of the age expressed itself was that of *witness-bearing*. This assumed the double aspect of faithfulness to God and opposition to the ungodly. Nothing could detach the pious Israelite from God. No extremity of his own could do it.[2] Nor could the world move him, either through its smooth side or through its rough side. To him all its glory was as nothing compared with the proud consciousness of possessing the truth: "I speak of thy testimonies before kings and am not ashamed."[3] In his zeal for God's Law he was also proof against both contempt[4] and persecution.[5] Even when outward events lent no confirmation to his creed, his spirit remained steadfast with God.[6] In view, moreover, of the purity of his prayers,[7] and of the fact that God retained His hold upon him,[8] separation was an impossibility. But if Jewish piety was distinguished by loyalty to God, it was no less so by opposition to the godless world. It was the business of a good man to eschew evil.[9] His hatred and avoidance of evil were in inverse ratio to his zeal for God's house.[10] To avoid the sins of the fathers was at first the ruling idea in the mind of the restored community, but afterwards what chiefly exercised the pious was the ungodliness with which they were daily confronted. For among Jews themselves there had arisen an irreligious party who complained that they had served God and kept His

---

[1] lxxiii. 15.   [2] lxi. 2.   [3] cxix. 46.   [4] cxix. 141.
[5] cxix. 164.   [6] lxxviii. 8, 37.   [7] lxvi. 18; cf. Job xvi. 7.
[8] lxxiii. 23.   [9] xxxiv. 14; Job i. 1.   [10] lxix. 9.

ordinances in vain.[1] Those too who took this attitude were in the majority; they were rich and prosperous;[2] they were proud, violent, and corrupt;[3] they hated instruction, and forgot God.[4] The pious, on the other hand, kept their hands clean and their hearts pure,[5] and set their hope in God.[6] There came thus to be two keenly antagonistic parties in Israel. The question at issue was neither more nor less than that of the supremacy of the Law. It was the aim of the pious to bring the whole community into subjection to the will of God, and to make the Law effective throughout the entire range of public and private life. Their hatred of evil soon became hatred of evildoers. They hated the wicked as the enemies of God;[7] they despised and shunned them;[8] they ardently desired their destruction.[9] In their whole philosophy of life they were diametrically opposed to the wicked.

Although in the conflict thus induced they certainly reaped some spiritual advantage, and in particular "learned in a high degree what faith and duty were,"[10] the very fact that piety was made a matter of party strife was fraught with serious dangers. For thereby it inevitably took on an element of unreality. Zeal for the cause of God and purity of heart are by no means synonymous terms; religiosity is not religion. A Jew might devote his life to fulfilling the obligations of the Law, and yet never attain to the righteousness required by the prophets. The outward ordinance may be satisfied, and God's will yet remain undone. This is

---

[1] Mal. iii. 14.   [2] xlix. 7, xxxvii. 7.   [3] lxxiii. 6, 8.
[4] l. 17, 22.   [5] xxiv. 4.   [6] lxxviii. 7.   [7] cxxxix. 21 f.
[8] xv. 4, i. 1.   [9] xxviii. 4, cix. 8.   [10] Smend, *Alttest. Rel.* p. 451.

what actually happened in the case of Jewish piety. It tended more and more to become external, and to substitute legal enactment for the homage of the heart. This tendency was strengthened by the fact that it was no longer customary to see the Divine glory and activity through the medium of historical events. Such an outlook proved a safeguard to the older Judaism; now that it was abandoned, piety speedily degenerated into a mere matter of conformity to a book.

There is another remarkable movement which probably might be assigned to this time, namely, the Wisdom movement. The "Wisdom literature" is the name applied to a group of writings represented in the canonical Scriptures by Proverbs, Job, and Ecclesiastes, and in the Apocrypha by Ecclesiasticus and the Wisdom of Solomon. With the exception of the last-mentioned, which reflects throughout the influence of Greek culture, these books are all distinctly national in their type, and set forth the teaching of "the wise" in its purely Palestinian form.

For the historical origin of the Wisdom movement, which ultimately became a great intellectual force in the life of the nation, it has been usual to go back to the days of Solomon, who, as the father of proverbial Hebrew poetry, is supposed to have laid its first foundations in Israel. From the time of that king, at whose court a band of sages was thought to have already gathered, the Ḥăchāmîm, or "the wise," formed, it is said, an important element in Israelitish life. According to this view the Wisdom is not the product of any particular age of Jewish history, but the accumulated literary outcome of the cogitations of a succession of sages who had their prototype in Solomon, and who ultimately formed themselves into an organised body of professional teachers. The strong point about this theory is that it explains the tradition which assigned at least half of the entire Ḥokhma literature to the wise king. At the same time it is quite possible that the ascription of these books to Solomon was merely an example of the tendency to pseudepigraphy which became so pronounced in the case of Jewish apocalyptic writings, and the view which has hitherto been commonly accepted is not shared by recent scholars like Smend, N. Schmidt, Toy, and Bousset, who think that in view of its common features the Wisdom literature is the monument of an intellectual movement confined to a certain period in the history of Jewish religion. Just as it was preceded by an age of prophecy, and an age of legalism, and followed by an age of apocalyptic, so, it is suggested, there may have been an age of Wisdom —a period during which its special point of view was the prevailing one, and during which it powerfully influenced the development of Judaism. Assuming that this hypothesis is correct, there is clearly only one period to which the movement can suitably be assigned, namely, that immediately prior to the Maccabæan revolt, the recognised watershed of post-exilic Judaism. As the date of Ecclesiasticus is known to be *c.* B.C. 180, or little more than a decade before the outbreak of the rebellion against Antiochus Epiphanes, this may be taken as the inferior limit in estimating the time when such a movement might have flourished. Working back from this, we may perhaps reckon Ecclesiastes as the next in order of priority; and the other books belonging to the Wisdom category need not have preceded it by more than a century and a half or thereabouts. The golden age of the Hebrew Wisdom would thus be the century and a half or two centuries preceding B.C. 180. In the development of Judaism during these years there is certainly nothing inconsistent with this theory. On the contrary, it seems to derive some support from the fact that the vital changes which they witnessed in the inner life of the Jewish nation, and which have already been enumerated in the previous chapter, all coincide with the spirit of the Wisdom movement. During this period, moreover, Greek influence was at its height, and may have been a factor in moulding the peculiar type of thought which characterises the Wisdom books. It is also conceivable that other cosmopolitan influences had an even greater share in the shaping of this form of literature. As yet, however, this whole theory has only reached the stage of discussion, and cannot be regarded as proved. Another interesting question raised with regard to the Wisdom movement is whether it was peculiar to Israel, or merely the Hebrew aspect of a great Oriental wave of thought which swept over other civilised nations as well, and found among them parallel developments.[1] As this also, however, still awaits solution, we cannot enter upon the discussion of it here, but must proceed to describe positively the nature and characteristics of the Hebrew Wisdom.

[1] Cf. 1 Kings iv. 29-31 ; Prov. xxx. 1, xxxi. 1 ; Jer. xlix. 7 ; Obad. ver. 8 ; and see the very suggestive discussion of this question in an article by Principal Skinner, of Westminster College, Cambridge, on "The Cosmopolitan Aspect of Hebrew Wisdom," in the *Jewish Quarterly Review* for January 1905.

6

In this connexion we may remark first of all that the Hebrew sage, in his treatment of nature and human life, occupies a different standpoint from that of the Greek philosopher. The wisdom he cultivated was of no recondite, academic type; it found expression in the most public resorts.[1] Without being an expert in physical science, as some have inferred from 1 Kings iv. 33, he sought to arrive at a philosophy of life through the free contemplation of nature and man, of religion and morals. The " sacred " philosophy of the Hebrews knows nothing of metaphysics, and is essentially religious and practical in its aims. It is not concerned to prove the existence of God, for this is assumed to start with; only a fool can say in his heart, " There is no God." [2] The Hellenic philosopher seeks to read the riddle of the universe by the investigation of natural phenomena; the Hebrew philosopher already holds in his hand the key of revelation, and with the help of this aims merely at a clear understanding of the ways of God and the duty of man. His theme is not the theocracy, but the cosmos ; not the history of Israel, but the moral relations of men. Although Wisdom did not, like the Law and Prophecy, concern itself with the theocracy, there is no reason to suppose that its votaries took up an attitude of antagonism towards the legalised worship.[3] They were independent thinkers, but not free-lances.

In the Old Testament the Wisdom is presented both in a Divine and in a human aspect. It is objectively viewed as the skilled artist who, as His

---

[1] Prov. i. 20 f.   [2] Ps. xiv. 1.
[3] So Bruch, *Weisheitslehre der Hebräer*, 1851.

workman and fellow, consciously moulds the universe
in accordance with the will of God, so that it is at once
the expression of the Divine intelligence, the reflexion
of the Divine character, and the unfolding of the Divine
purpose. As the Divine agency in the creation of the
world, and the principle of revelation, it occupies the
same position in later Judaism as the Spirit and Word
of God in the older Hebraism. But Wisdom also makes
her appeal to men, and "the wise" are those who listen
to it, and recognise the fulfilment of God's design in the
events of human life as well as in the phenomena of the
material world. In everything they seek first to
discover, and then to carry out, God's purpose. Wisdom
thus assumes a human and subjective as well as a Divine
and objective form, and from this standpoint, theoretically
and practically, "the fear of the Lord is the beginning
of wisdom." Moral and intellectual wisdom are scarcely
distinguished ; to be righteous is to be wise, and to be
a worker of iniquity is to be a fool.[1]

Now that religion was no longer merely a national
custom, but the concern of the individual, men naturally
began to reflect upon it, and the result lies before us
in these "Books of Wisdom." They deal in didactic
fashion with the problems of moral and religious
philosophy. With the exception of some strains of
meditation in Sirach, they are characterised on the one
hand by their freedom from nationalism, and on the
other by their cold intellectualism. In their setting
forth of moral and religious truth they deal in abstract
propositions of general application, and exhibit a cosmo-
politanism hitherto absent from Hebrew literature. As

[1] Ps. v. 5.

compared with the Psalms and prophetic writings, they are marked by a lack of religious fervour. In the form of aphorisms or proverbs (מְשָׁלִים, *m*e*shālîm*) they contain the distilled utterances of sages whose meditative instincts have been awakened by revelation. These books are not to any great extent the expression of a living experience of religious truth, but represent rather an attempt to clear up difficulties connected with facts of human history which seem irreconcilable with the Mosaic doctrine of retribution. They constitute, in short, a religious philosophy in which the ruling principle is the Law, God being abstractly conceived as existing in remote majesty above and away from the world.

Two important theologoumena emerge from the speculations of the sages — the conception of the hypostasis of Wisdom, and the doctrine of rewards and punishments.

The former, besides constituting the link between the Palestinian and the Hellenistic development of Judaism, represents the contribution made by the Wisdom literature to the Christology of the Old Testament, and has greatly influenced Christian theology. In Proverbs Wisdom is conceived as something intermediate beween God and the world. She is virtually an attribute of God, and yet a separate subsistence, called into being by Him, and existing alongside of Him as His workman in creation.[1] A projection out of the Divine mind, she is something more than an attribute, and something less

---

[1] If, however, as Gunkel and other scholars maintain, the real meaning of the word אמון be *nursling*, the part played by the Wisdom would require to be regarded as merely that of an interested spectator.

than a hypostasis—" a little more than kin and less than kind." As a public teacher she leads men to a God-fearing life,[1] and as the substratum of intelligence and piety imparts herself to them that love her. The most striking personifications of Wisdom are contained in Prov. viii. 22 ff. and Ecclus. xxiv.[2] In the Revised Version the former passage (with omissions) is thus rendered : " The Lord possessed me in the beginning of his way, before his works of old. I was set up from everlasting, from the beginning, or ever the earth was. . . . When he established the heavens, I was there : when he set a circle upon the face of the deep . . . when he marked out the foundations of the earth : then I was by him, as a master workman : and I was daily his delight, rejoicing always before him ; rejoicing in his habitable earth ; and my delight was with the sons of men." The remarkable thing about the presentation of Wisdom in Sirach is that she is represented as taking up her abode in Israel, and as incorporated in the Mosaic Law.[3] In this we may detect a reversion from the universalistic standpoint to the local and national, which seems to foreshadow the practical extinction of the Wisdom movement as a separate factor in Jewish life. A section of Baruch [4] is devoted to the praise of Wisdom, which is described as unattainable by man, and as nevertheless appearing upon earth and being conversant with men.

[1] viii. 1–3.

[2] Cf. Job xxviii., where, however, there is no personification.

[3] xxiv. 8 ff. This latter point, however, is expressed in such a form as to lead to the suspicion of interpolation. In any case, this is probably the earliest trace in Jewish literature of that cardinal dogma of rabbinical Judaism—the pre-existence and Divinity of the Law. It is also reflected in Baruch.

[4] iii. 9–iv. 4.

The passage is noteworthy because of the identification
of Wisdom with the Divine Law: " This is the book of
the commandments of God, and the law that endureth
for ever." We have here a good illustration of the fact
that even in theoretical speculations Palestinian Judaism
always had an eye to the practical.[1]

As regards the second point mentioned above, we
have to note that, according to the Book of Proverbs,
great blessings accompany the possession of wisdom.
In his own personal life the wise man who follows after
righteousness enjoys the peace of one who is well-pleasing
to God. Length of days, riches, and honour are his
portion.[2] Earthly possessions, however, are of value only
when conjoined with righteousness.[3] The moral good
accruing to the wise extends to his domestic life also,
the Divine favour being betokened in the gift of a good
wife,[4] and the sight of children's children.[5] As a member
of the community he will command respect, and be
listened to in the gate.[6] Since kings are guided by
wisdom,[7] and nations exalted by righteousness,[8] many
directions are given to rulers.[9] What the Jewish thinker
delights in is the idea of life as a whole working out the
Divine plan. When the wise are plunged into adversity,
this is by way of discipline for their good, " for whom
the Lord loveth he correcteth." Even for evil itself a
place is found in the teleology of Him who shall judge it
at the last: " Jahweh hath made all things for himself,

---

[1] The figure of the Wisdom is also known to the Book of Enoch (xxx. 8,
xxxiii. 4, xlii. 1 f.; cf. xci. 10). Speculation on the subject was naturally
rife among the Alexandrian Jews. See Chapter VII.

[2] iii. 16.   [3] xi. 28.   [4] xviii. 22.
[5] xvii. 6.   [6] xxiv. 7.   [7] viii. 15.
[8] xiv. 34.   [9] xxix. 12, 14.

yea, even the wicked for the day of evil."[1] The stand-point of Ecclesiasticus is practically that of Proverbs, although rather more subtly worked out. Having drawn the picture of wisdom's reward from Proverbs, we may hear Ben Sira regarding the retribution reserved for the sinful contempt of wisdom. " Wisdom will forsake the man that goes astray, and will give him over to his fall ;[2] the Lord's indignation will rest upon sinners ;[3] in one sin thou shalt not be unpunished ;[4] envy not the glory of a sinner, for thou knowest not what shall be his over-throw ;[5] the Most High also hateth sinners, and will repay vengeance unto the ungodly ;[6] as his mercy is great, so is his correction also: he judgeth a man according to his works ;[7] think upon the wrath that shall be in the days of the end, and the time of vengeance when he turneth away his face ;[8] the congregation of wicked men is as tow wrapped together, and the end of them is a flame of fire ;[9] the ungodly shall go from a curse into perdition."[10]

The great problem dealt with in the Wisdom litera-ture is the reconciliation of the facts of experience with belief in the government of the world by a righteous God. So long as the matter was regarded merely from the general standpoint of the national welfare, the question did not press for solution ; indeed the older Hebraism is hardly conscious of it. But with the individualisation of religion, and the new consciousness of personal relation-ship to God, and of each man's accountability for his own actions, it became acute, and formed the standing

---

[1] xvi. 4. [2] iv. 19. [3] v. 6. [4] vii. 8.
[5] ix. 11. [6] xii. 6. [7] xvi. 12. [8] xviii. 24.
[9] xxi. 9. [10] xli. 10.

enigma of religious life.   As the fundamental aim of the
Wisdom movement was to base religion and morality on
observation, the doctrine of Providence was for it of
supreme consequence, and its devotees tried to maintain
that doctrine in spite of everything that seemed to
invalidate it.   They generalised, and said, the righteous
man is pleasing to God, and therefore will be prosperous
and happy ; and *vice versâ* in the case of the unrighteous
man.   The application of this principle to the providential
government of the world and of the lives of individual
men necessarily caused that collision between theory and
facts which for generations exercised the minds of
religious thinkers in Israel.

   We have now to glance at the attempts made to
solve this mystery.   At first indeed there was a disposition simply to assert the wise man's conception of
God's method of government, and to take no account of
exceptions.   This is still the point of view in Proverbs ;
outward circumstances illustrate the principles of the
sage.   " There shall no evil happen to the just ; but the
wicked shall be filled with mischief." [1]   " Evil pursueth
sinners ; but to the righteous good shall be repaid." [2]
Soon, however, there shewed itself a disposition to find
some explanation of the problem in the recognition of
the disciplinary value of suffering.   This comes out in
Proverbs : " My son, despise not the chastening of the
Lord ; neither be weary of his correction " ; [3] in Job,
where Eliphaz is made to say, " Behold, happy is the
man whom God correcteth ; therefore despise not thou
the chastening of the Almighty " ; [4] in Sirach, who says,

[1] xii. 21.   [2] xiii. 21.
[3] iii. 11.   [4] v. 17.

" He that feareth the Lord will receive his discipline " ; [1]
and in some of the psalms, for example the hundred and
eighteenth, " The Lord hath chastened me sore, but hath
not given me over unto death." Closely connected with
this attitude of mind is the view put forward in Sirach
that temptation is the test of a man's character. " My
son, if thou comest to serve the Lord, prepare thy soul
for temptation, etc." [2] " He that giveth ear unto her
shall judge the nations ; and he that giveth heed unto
her shall dwell securely. If he trust her, he shall inherit
her ; and his generations shall have her in possession.
For at the first she will walk with him in crooked ways,
and will bring fear and dread upon him, and torment him
with her discipline, until she may trust his soul, and try
him by her judgments : then will she return again the
straight way unto him, and will gladden him, and reveal
to him her secrets." [3] Neither of these two views, it
should be observed, carries us outside the principle of
retribution in this life. But the solution began to be
pushed still further back through the assertion that the
moral character of a man is revealed in the fate of his
children.[4] The same idea occurs also in Job. " His
children are far from safety, and they are crushed in the
gate, neither is there any to deliver them ; [5] his children
shall seek to please the poor, and his hands shall restore
their goods ; [6] God layeth up his iniquity for his children ;
he rewardeth him, and he shall know it ; [7] if his
children be multiplied, it is for the sword, and his off-
spring shall not be satisfied with bread." [8] The last
attempt to find a solution of the mystery within the

---

[1] xxxii. 14. [2] ii. 1–6. [3] iv. 15 ff. [4] Ecclus. xi. 28.
[5] v. 4. [6] xx. 10. [7] xxi. 19. [8] xxvii. 14.

limits of this present life is represented by a passage in
Sirach which is a refinement upon all that went before.
In the event of the contradiction between the fact and
the requirements of justice for the individual lasting all
his lifetime, the writer suggests that even on the day of
his death God can still redress the inequality.   " For it
is an easy thing in the sight of the Lord to reward a
man in the day of death according to his ways.   The
affliction of an hour causeth forgetfulness of delight; and
in the last end of a man is the revelation of his deeds.
Call no man blessed before his death." [1]   This is a somewhat desperate solution, no doubt, but it illustrates the
earnestness with which the problem had been studied.

It is in the Book of Job that we have the grandest
effort to grapple with the difficulty.   The writer represents the pious upright Job as overtaken with sore
calamity, which his friends, as adherents of the traditional
theory that suffering is in every case the just punishment
of sin, attribute to the hidden guilt of the sufferer.
Against this Job protests with all the fervour of conscious
innocence, and finally obtains God's verdict in his favour.
He entirely undermines the position taken up by his
friends, and shews that there is no absolute connexion
between suffering and the merits of the sufferer.   In the
interests of the religious life he discards the time-honoured
explanation of the wise as pushing the ethical idea of
God to a one-sided extreme.   The wisdom of which the
book speaks is traditional, not scholastic.   It is thus not
so much a product of the Wisdom as a spirited revolt
against the Wisdom theory, which it plucks up by the
roots.   While, however, the ordinary explanation is proved

[1] xi. 26 ff.

to be untenable, no positive solution is substituted for it.
The poem does not go beyond the suggestion that it
behoves frail man to resign himself in presence of the
mysterious ways of God.   In the epilogue, indeed, which
represents Job as receiving ample compensation for his
sufferings, there is a return to the general principle of
retribution.   It is impossible to be certain what answer
the writer intended to give, or even whether he had the
problem in mind at all; but at any rate the tendency to
postpone the solution had at length the effect of pushing
the difficulty beyond the present life altogether, until the
Wisdom grew into an eschatology.   Towards this an
important contribution is furnished by the great poem of
the Wisdom.   Job after all is still sure that he is right
with God.   But, as a late revered teacher of our Church
has remarked, " If this consciousness refused to deny
itself, it must postulate something after death which
would be its verification.   This appears to be the meaning of Job xix., ' But I know that my Redeemer liveth
. . . and after this my body is destroyed, I shall see
God.'   We may not attribute to Job belief in what we
call a future life, only an assurance of some point or
event after death, which would verify the reality of
religion and of his religion, and shew to him and men
that the pious consciousness of God is true possession of
God." [1]

   This idea did not find congenial soil in Palestine.
It is discarded by Ecclesiastes, which is more of a philosophical work than any other book of the Old Testament,
as an idle speculation.[2]   It exhibits a strain of Epicure-

---

[1] A. B. Davidson, *Biblical and Literary Essays*, p. 285.
[2] iii. 21.

anism and a sceptical pessimism which suggest the possible pressure of Hellenic influence. The writer is without an ideal either for the present or for the future, and so for him life loses its moral significance. As all share the same fate—the wise man and the fool, the righteous and the wicked—he concludes that " all is vanity." Such pessimism is but the logical outcome of a conception of the world according to which everything is regarded from the standpoint of the happiness of the individual. The author, however, is no atheist; he does not renounce belief in an Almighty God, without whose will nothing happens. At the same time it is clear that anything like a general diffusion of the sceptical mood indulged in by him must have led to a rejection of the very belief in God's existence. Such a result was averted, however, through the check given to the progress of Hellenism by the Maccabæan revolt. The author of Ecclesiastes stood upon the confines of two religious worlds. Ancient Hebraism had become effete, and the new impulse given to religion by the revival of patriotic sentiment under the Maccabees was still a thing of the future. Clouds had overcast the sky; the spiritual atmosphere was one of fog and mist; Koheleth, standing on the edge of a dark abyss, could discern no means of reaching the further brink.[1]

But if the eschatological aspect of the Wisdom remained undeveloped in Palestine, it took deep root and flourished in Alexandria. This is evident from the Book of Wisdom, to which attention will be directed later on, in connexion with Hellenistic Judaism.

[1] Reuss.

CHAPTER III

THE HISTORY OF THE MACCABÆAN STRUGGLE

CHAPTER III.

The History of the Maccabæan Struggle.

By the beginning of the second century B.C. that Hellenic culture, in the interests of which Alexander the Great undertook his world-wide campaigns, had taken firm hold upon Palestine. Even in the strictly Judæan district the Greek life was fast commending itself. The upper classes in particular, with the priestly aristocracy at their head, became enthusiastic Hellenists. They spoke the Greek language, cultivated Greek art, and adopted Greek customs. Under the magic spell of the gymnasium and the theatre some even went the length of renouncing Judaism altogether.

In other circles, however, a strong reaction set in against the fashionable Hellenism. Many felt that they could not embrace it without being traitors alike to their past history and to their religious faith. These now stood forth as determined opponents of Greek innovations, and as uncompromising champions of the Jewish Law. Their ideals were those of the scribes. If they were drawn chiefly from the ranks of the poor, they were at all events a spiritual aristocracy. The better to effect their purpose of checkmating Hellenism, they organised themselves into a corporate society known as the

Ḥasîdîm, *i.e.* "pious" or "tender" ones.   They devoted
themselves to the study and practice of the Law, and
were ready to lay down their lives if necessary for its
sake.

So far there seemed to be a plain issue between the
opposing parties.   The question was whether Judaism
or Hellenism was to prevail in Judæa.   Owing, however,
to the financial embarrassments of the Syrian government, and the opportunity for intrigue thus afforded to
unpatriotic men in Jerusalem, curious complications
ensued.   The Ḥasîdîm had not only to fight against
Hellenism, but against the grasping covetousness of the
Seleucid court and the corrupt ambition of unscrupulous
magnates in Judæa.   For some time the road to success
and political favour had been barred for all who refused
to conform to Greek habits.[1]   In Onias III. the Jews
had still, it is true, a worthy and godly high priest at
the head of the national party, but his influence was
undermined by the machinations of Simon, an ill-
conditioned priest belonging to the family of the
Tobiadæ.   Not without hopes of self-preferment, and
out of malice towards Onias, this man informed
Apollonius, the governor of Cœle-Syria, that vast
treasures lay stored up in the Temple at Jerusalem,
with the result that the impecunious Seleucus IV., who
had inherited from his father Antiochus the Great the
burden of the war indemnity imposed by the Romans
after the battle of Magnesia, sent his minister Heliodorus

---

[1] It was correspondingly open to men like the knavish tax-collector
Joseph, son of Tobias and nephew of the high priest Onias II., who under
somewhat difficult conditions adroitly wormed himself into favour with
Ptolemy III. Euergetes.—Josephus, *Ant.* xii. 4. 2-4.

to appropriate "the foresaid money."[1]   At the Syrian
court Simon represented that the failure of this project
was due not to supernatural interference as was supposed,
but simply to the cunning contrivance of the high priest.
As he was also stirring up mischief at Jerusalem, Onias
decided to go to Antioch and interview the king in
person; but there was no royal smile for one who
asserted the inviolability of the sacred treasures.

At this stage there appears on the scene a personage
who for more than a decade was to play a leading part
in the struggle between Hellenism and Judaism. I
refer to Antiochus IV. Epiphanes, the occupant of the
Syrian throne from B.C. 175–164.[2]

It is not easy to figure to ourselves the strange
personality of Antiochus.   He was a puzzle even to his
contemporaries.   "Rational people," says Polybius,
"were at a loss what to think about him. Some
regarded him as a simple and homely man, others
looked upon him as crazed."[3]   The former estimate was
based upon his tendency to fraternise with any sort of
people whom he chanced to meet; the latter found
expression in the popular parody of the surname
Epiphanes into Epimanes (the Madcap). He was
certainly a successful soldier and an acute diplomatist,
and if he had many eccentricities, these were so amply
atoned for by his kingly munificence as to secure for

---

[1] 2 Macc. iii. 4 ff.

[2] Just before the assassination of his brother Seleucus IV. by Heliodorus in
176, his place as a hostage at Rome had been taken by Demetrius, the son of
Seleucus. In the absence of the true heir, and with the assistance of the king
of Pergamos, Antiochus prevented Heliodorus from reaping the expected
truits of his crime by himself seizing the kingdom.

[3] *Hist.* xxvi. 10.

7

him considerable popularity.[1] But to his character
there was a darker side also. It is clear from his treatment of the Jews that there was an element of savagery
in his composition. We can scarcely account for this on
the theory of insanity pure and simple, although previous
to his death he appears to have suffered from serious
mental aberration. Whatever he was, Antiochus was
not a mere maniac. Possibly his officers were responsible for much of the barbarity inflicted on the Jews;
but assuming that it must be credited to himself, how
are we to explain it? First of all probably by the
circumstance that in its various forms Hellenism
appealed strongly to the imagination of this monarch,
who was a lover of ceremonies, pomp, and colour; and
then by the further fact that it was a necessity of his
passionate nature that whatever idea took possession of
his mind should speedily assume concrete form. The
idea of restraining his passions was utterly foreign to
him; he gave free play to his impulses in whatever
direction they led him, that of vengeance not excepted.
He could brook no interference with his plans, and
could not allow anything to stand in the way of their
realisation. Beneath all his good-natured frolics, lavish
generosity, and odd eccentricity, lay the self-willed
tyrant. It thus becomes possible to view his inhuman
conduct towards the Jews as his natural treatment of
men who were unfortunate enough to be an obstacle in
his path rather than as affording evidence of a deliberate
delight in cruelty.

The public policy of Antiochus was as transparently
clear as his character is psychologically puzzling. He

[1] I Macc. vi. 11.

III.] *Maccabæan Struggle*

aimed at the unification of his empire on the basis of
Hellenic culture and local self-government. This ideal
of the combination of the freedom of individual cities
with the uniting bond of a universally established
religion proves him to have been a man by no means
destitute of political insight. So far as the conception
itself is concerned, it was rather to his credit than othei-
wise. In Antiochus Epiphanes, however, the instincts
of the statesman were subordinated to vanity. Not
content to receive and rate at its proper value the official
worship commonly offered to kings in those days, he
followed the unhealthy example set by his predecessors
of proclaiming his divinity upon his coins. These bore
the high-flown inscription :—

ΒΑΣΙΛΕΩΣ ΑΝΤΙΟΧΟΥ ΘΕΟΥ ΕΠΙΦΑΝΟΥΣ ΝΙΚΗΦΟΡΟΥ
(of King Antiochus, God Manifest, Victory-bearer).

Nothing could have better served the interests of
Hellenism at Jerusalem than the accession of such a
prince. From the first he was the ardent partisan of
everything Greek. The good Onias was quickly superseded by his brother Joshua, who as leader of the
Hellenistic party altered his name into Jason, and bribed
the new monarch to bestow upon him the sacred office,
as well as liberty to set up a gymnasium in Jerusalem.
The state of matters which thus prevailed is graphically
described in the Books of Maccabees.[1] There was a
rush upon places of public entertainment. Jewish
youths wearing the Greek chlamys and broad-brimmed
hat formed themselves into a company of ephēboi.
Many tried to make it appear that they had not been
circumcised. Even the priests neglected their official

[1] 1 Macc. i. 11–15; 2 Macc. iv. 10–15.

duties in order to join in the games. Inhabitants of Jerusalem were enrolled as citizens of Antioch. From all this it is evident that the Tobiadæ, the wealthy descendants of Joseph, and now the leaders of the Hellenistic party, were strongly contending for the removal of the wall of partition between the Jews and the pagan world as a measure fitted to promote the best interests of the community. And they had succeeded so well that a majority of the people were in sympathy with the Hellenistic movement. The Holy City had apparently exchanged its attitude of aloofness for an enthusiastic adoption of Greek customs and ways. Hellenism had at last got control of the Temple, and Judaism, driven from its stronghold, seemed to have become practically extinct. Jason even sent gifts to grace the festival of Hercules at Tyre, but the bearers, out of very shame, handed them over for behoof of the royal navy.

To witness Jerusalem so much given over to heathen frivolity must have been very galling to the Ḥasīdîm. We may wonder indeed why the wearing of Greek hats and a fondness for athletics should have proved a stumbling-block to any, but to the "tender" ones of Israel in the Maccabæan age these things were abhorrent from the very fact that they were foreign. There was nothing essentially wicked in the practices referred to; yet there can be no doubt that the flower of Jewish piety was to be found outside the palæstra, and among those who scorned to wear the Greek costume. We may smile at their prejudices; we dare not minimise their services. To them, and not to the Hellenistic faction, we owe the preservation and transmission of the spiritual heritage granted to Israel in trust for the world.

Although buttressed by the imperial power, the Greek party contained within itself the seeds of dissolution. It had no ethical foundation on which to build. Its adherents were actuated by no lofty patriotism, moral ideal, or religious enthusiasm. Selfish motives led them to seek every man his own aggrandisement. They were untrue to one another. Jason, who had supplanted Onias, had held office for only three years (B.C. 174–171), when he was himself in turn supplanted by the Benjamite Menelaus, who outbade him by three hundred talents. In order to meet this financial obligation, Menelaus did not hesitate to despoil the Temple. When the exiled Onias III. denounced the impious deed, the base Benjamite contrived that he should be treacherously murdered. An attempt to impeach Menelaus before the king at Tyre was frustrated through bribery, while his righteous accusers were put to the sword. These things won for him the bitter hatred of the Jews; but by openly renouncing Judaism he obtained imperial help against Jason, who was compelled to retire to the east of the Jordan. Emboldened by a false rumour that Antiochus had died in Egypt while making war on Ptolemy VI. Philometor, Jason marched upon Jerusalem, forced Menelaus to entrench himself in the citadel, and slew many citizens who were on the side of the Syrian government.

On his return from Egypt in B.C. 170, Antiochus visited the Jews with condign punishment for what he regarded as a wanton revolt. Advancing on Jerusalem, he ordered his troops to slaughter the inhabitants irrespective of age or sex. Thousands perished, and many were sold as slaves. Led by the traitorous

Menelaus, he then sacrilegiously entered the sanctuary seized its remaining treasures, and carried off the holy vessels to Antioch. The whole Jewish nation was stunned by the terrible blow. These measures were mild, however, in comparison with what followed. Two years later, Epiphanes was returning a baffled man from another Egyptian campaign. His plans had been upset by the intervention of Rome. This made him all the more determined to have his own way in Judæa. An army, led by Apollonius, was sent against Jerusalem. Deceitfully on a sabbath-day that "lord of pollutions" let loose his soldiers to plunder and slay in the defence-less city, which was then given to the flames. The sanctuary was laid waste, and a Syrian garrison quartered in Akra, a fortress which overlooked the Temple, and which for more than a quarter of a century remained the stronghold of Hellenism, and " an evil adversary to Israel." [1] Not even yet was the scope of the royal commission exhausted. Apollonius had instructions to extirpate Judaism and force the adoption of Greek manners and customs at the point of the sword. An edict was issued prohibiting under pain of death all distinctively Jewish observances and requiring the Jews to conform to heathen rites. The Temple was dedicated to Zeus Olympios, and in every township Jews were commanded to sacrifice to idols animals which they reckoned unclean, and then eat their flesh. All obtainable copies of the Law were destroyed, and the study of it proscribed. Certain women with the children they had circumcised were flung down from the city wall. It was made compulsory to observe the feast of Bacchus. By means of a monthly

[1] I Macc. i. 36.

inquisition care was taken to see that the king's commands
were strictly carried out. The penalty of disobedience
was death. In Chislev (December) B.C. 168 the height
of sacrilegious oppression was reached. An idol altar
("the abomination of desolation"[1]) was erected on the
site of the great altar of burnt-offering, and sacrifice
made in Greek form to Zeus.

To all appearance Antiochus had achieved his object,
and Jerusalem had become a pagan city.[2] It had a
heathen governor,[3] a heathen garrison, and a heathen
temple. Leading apostates acted as spies, and reported
cases of contumacy. To save their lives, others re-
luctantly renounced their religion. Yet in reality the
Syrian despot had failed. There were many not to be
moved by torture or death. Rather than conform,
multitudes fled the country or hid themselves in the
wilderness. Thus it came to pass that a people insignifi-
cant in number, but invincible in spirit, now defied the
proud Hellenism which no other nation could withstand.
In disappointed rage Antiochus increased the severity
of his persecutions, but only to discover that by his
extreme and cruel measures he had alienated even those
who sympathised with the Hellenistic movement and
given to the Jewish opposition a solidarity which nothing
could overcome. As a nation they could endure much,
but they could not, and would not, abandon their Law.

It was none the less a fearful ordeal through which
the Jews had to pass. "The noble army of martyrs"

[1] Dan. ix. 27.
[2] According to Schrader (*Die Keilinschriften*,[3] p. 303), it was given a
new name—'Ἐπιφάνεια—in harmony with the new cult of θεὸς ἐπιφανής.
[3] 2 Macc. vi.

drew from them its first recruits. Many bore untold agonies rather than dishonour the Law of their God. Typical instances fondly remembered in Israel were those of the aged priest Eleazar, and of the seven brethren and their mother who were tortured to death for refusing to defile themselves by eating swine's flesh.[1] Even in the rhetorically coloured narrative of 2 *Maccabees* we can find proof of deep suffering nobly endured for the sake of God and religion.   Such examples were an inspiration to multitudes.

That the sympathy of heathendom in general was with Antiochus may be gathered from the remark of Tacitus that he " endeavoured to root out the Jewish superstition, but was hindered by a Parthian war from reforming this vilest of peoples." [2]   But there was more than the Parthian war to prevent the execution of his designs. Just when their outlook was of the blackest, when the cherished doctrine of the happy end of the righteous seemed utterly discredited, when fellowship with Jahweh appeared absolutely broken off through the cessation of the daily sacrifice, a welcome ray of light shot through the cloud to gladden the hearts of the bewildered Jews. More clearly than ever before, they saw the vision of the New Jerusalem. To some extent the resurrection was probably by this time a current article of belief, but it had never yet been to them as a nation the strong consolation that it now became with the issue of the Book of Daniel. The narratives with

[1] In the church of Santa Felicita, Florence, there is a great painting by Professor Antonio Ciseri, representing " The slaughter of the Seven Martyr Children and their Mother " at Jerusalem. For a photograph by Alinari see the Frontispiece to 1 and 2 Maccabees in the *Temple Bible*.

[2] *Hist*. v. 8.

which this book opens furnish exalted ideals of piety
and endurance from Israel's past; the series of apocalyptic
visions with which it closes indicates that deliverance is
near.   Not only will the righteous be rescued from the
terrible trials to which meanwhile they are subject; the
holy dead will also rise to share their blessedness.   This
clear proclamation of the doctrine of the resurrection
marks an epoch in the religious history of Israel.   Face
to face with torture and death, they were led to grasp as
never before the great truth respecting the future destiny
of man.   In another life the righteous would awake to
everlasting honour, the wicked to everlasting contempt.
This conviction nerved the martyrs to endure, and, coupled
with the moral strength of their leaders, enabled the
Jewish patriots to prove themselves more than a match
for their adversaries.   It soon became plain that no
human power could make them abjure their religion.

At first the persecuted Jews offered only a passive
resistance, but this attitude was suddenly changed into
one of open defiance.   What brought matters to a crisis
was the enactment of Antiochus that heathen altars
should be set up in every township of Palestine, and the
appointment of commissioners to see that sacrifices were
offered upon them in heathen fashion.   The pioneer of
Jewish rebellion was found in Mattathias, an aged priest
of the house of Hashmon.   Under stress of persecution
he had retired to his native town of Modin, between
Joppa and Jerusalem.   Called upon to offer the first
pagan sacrifice, he refused, at the same time declaring
that he and his family would never forsake the Law and
the ordinances.   When a renegade Jew was about to
conform, Mattathias slew both him and Apelles th'

king's officer, and pulled down the altar as a defilement
to the holy land.   Summoning all the faithful to follow
him, he then with his five sons fled into the mountains
and raised the standard of revolt.   Many sought an
asylum in the wilderness, but even there the imperial
officers followed them up, and required them to yield or
die.   Rather than desecrate the sabbath by fighting, a
thousand fugitives tamely submitted to be slain; but
Mattathias and his followers decided to repel hostile
attacks even on the sabbath.   Approving of this policy,
the Ḥasīdîm and many others joined them.   Emboldened
by numbers, the insurgents raided the country, slaying
apostates, destroying pagan altars, and enforcing the
observance of Jewish rites.   Mattathias lived only
to see the movement for religious freedom inaugurated.   He died in B.C. 166, after charging his sons to be
zealous for the Law, and advising that Judas, surnamed
Maccabæus or "Hammerer,"[1] should assume the
leadership.[2]

The rare personality of Judas at once lifted the
Jewish revolt into prominence.   Possessed of every
soldierly quality, he was the idol of his friends and the
dread of his foes.   His generalship was superb.   Although
it was no disciplined army that he led, Judas soon worsted
the provincial troops of Syria under Apollonius and
Seron.   The defeat of both of these generals in the
first year of his leadership laid the foundation of his

[1] On the derivation of the name, see Kautzsch, *Pseudepigr. d. AT.* p. 24;
the art. "Maccabees" in Hastings' *Bible Dict.*, or the Introd. to I Macc.
in *Cambridge Bible for Schools.*

[2] Hence the name Maccabees, as applied not only to the kinsmen and
adherents of Judas, but even to all who withstood the tyranny of the
Seleucidæ.

fame: "every nation told of the battles of Judas."[1]   In
Jerusalem itself the effect was extraordinary :—

> And soon the city rose,
> As at the touch of an enchanter's wand,
> To her old glories, and through all the land
> Rose a glad shout of happiness, for now
> The gloom was fading, and o'er Judah's hills
> Dawned a new day of freedom, hope, and peace.[2]

It was only anxiety regarding his eastern provinces,
which had been withholding tribute, that kept Antiochus
from avenging in person these disasters in Judæa.   As
it was, he commissioned his kinsman Lysias to employ
half of the imperial army in suppressing the rebellion.
In B.C. 166–165 a strong force was accordingly dispatched against Judæa under three experienced generals
—Ptolemy, Nicanor, and Gorgias.   The result was
considered so little doubtful that slave-dealers were in
attendance to buy up Jewish captives.   By observing a
day of prayer and fasting at Mizpeh, and by such military
organisation as was practicable, Judas prepared his men
for battle.   The two armies met at Emmaus,[3] on the
border of the hill-country.   With a detachment of six
thousand men Gorgias thought to surprise the Jews by
night, but, warned in time, Judas promptly attacked and
defeated the main army under Nicanor.   Finding only
a deserted camp, Gorgias vainly searched for his foes
among the hills.   At daybreak he saw the Syrian camp
on fire, and the Jews ready for battle.   This fairly un-

---

[1] 1 Macc. iii. 26.

[2] The Seatonian Prize Poem ("Judas Maccabæus") for 1877.

[3] It has been alleged that "the stratagem of Judas at Emmaus was
imitated by Bonaparte.   If this is so it gives additional point to Professor
Shailer Mathews' neat description of Judas as a 'Miniature Napoleon.'"
—*International Journal of Apocrypha* for July 1908, p. 20.

nerved his troops, and he withdrew, leaving to the Jews
enormous spoils.   The year following, Lysias himself led
a still larger army against them.   Avoiding the danger-
ous northern passes, he entered the country from the
south, and engaged the insurgents at Beth-zur, but only
to meet with another crushing reverse, in consequence
of which he decided to return to Antioch and recruit his
forces on a scale which would render further resistance
on the part of the Jews hopeless.[1]

During the breathing-space thus afforded them the
Jewish patriots reverently restored the Temple worship.
They were deeply moved at sight of the deserted
sanctuary and desecrated altar.   Unable to capture the
citadel, Judas took means to prevent annoyance from the
Syrian garrison while "blameless priests . . . cleansed
the holy place, and bare out the stones of defilement."[2]
A new altar and new vessels having been provided, the
Temple was re-consecrated by the offering of the legal
sacrifice on the third anniversary of its first pollution.[3]
The Feast of the Dedication lasted for eight days, and
became a statutory observance in Israel.[4]   As a protection against the Syrian garrison and the Idumæans

[1] Such is the account given in 1 Macc. iv. 26 ff.   But even if five
thousand Syrians fell, Lysias would still have had sixty thousand men according to the statement of ver. 28—an ample force for his purpose. Possibly the
numbers are patriotically falsified. Bevan (*Jerusalem Under the High Priests*,
p. 89 f.) thinks the withdrawal of Lysias was due to the change in the general
situation caused by the news of the death of Antiochus, but this event does
not seem to have occurred until B.C. 164, whereas the battle of Beth-zur was
fought in the autumn of B.C. 165.

[2] 1 Macc. iv. 42 f.   [3] 25th Chislev (December), B.C. 165.

[4] It is still observed in Jewish synagogues under the name of *Hannukkath-
habbaith* (=Consecration of the House), or the Feast of *Lights*, in allusion to
the illumination of the houses, which formed part of the celebration (John x.
22).   For further particulars regarding this festival see note on 1 Macc. iv. 59
in *Cambridge Bible for Schools*, and Stanley, *Jewish Church*, iii. p. 343 ff.

respectively, Judas now proceeded to fortify the Temple mount and the frontier city of Beth-zur. This ends the first chapter in the history of the wars of the Maccabees. As yet their arms had been victorious.

The surrounding heathen tribes were much chagrined at the success of the Maccabees, and shewed their resentment by persecuting the Jews resident within their borders. A league was formed against "the race of Jacob," but Judas immediately took the aggressive and severely chastised the Edomites, Ammonites, and others who were parties to it. Relief expeditions were also organised on behalf of oppressed Jews in Gilead and Galilee. Simon marched into Galilee with three thousand men, and Judas into Gilead with eight thousand. In both cases a rescue was effected, and the Jewish population brought back to Judæa. This not only secured their safety, but helped to strengthen the Jewish power at the centre. Obviously these wars were conducted with all the cruelty of religious fanaticism. At Bosora, Mizpeh, and Ekron all male inhabitants were slain. Jewish writers record these atrocities with evident satisfaction. In the case of one place which fell into the hands of Judas, the narrative runs thus: " Having taken the city by the will of God, they made unspeakable slaughter, insomuch that the adjoining lake, which was two furlongs broad, appeared to be filled with the deluge of blood." [1] Goaded into rebellion by the barbarities they suffered, the Jews themselves displayed a spirit of ferocity about equal to that shewn by their oppressors.

Freed meanwhile from the necessity of protecting the Jewish religion, the Maccabees now assumed the

[1] 2 Macc. xii. 16.

offensive, and by their raids against the Philistines and others made it clear that they were aiming at nothing less than political independence. The unexpected tidings that Antiochus Epiphanes had died in the far East (B.C. 164) added fuel to the fire of ambition already kindled in their hearts, while at the same time it led to disorder in Syria. Before his death Antiochus had appointed Philip, one of his "Friends," regent and tutor to his young son Antiochus V., but Lysias set up the latter as king, with the surname of Eupator. In the following year Judas made a bold attempt to capture the Akra, so as to secure free access to the Temple on the part of worshippers. The situation was fast becoming critical for the Hellenists of Jerusalem, who now represented to the court at Antioch the urgent need of imperial intervention, if the friends of the government were not to be placed at the mercy of its enemies. In response to this appeal Lysias and his ward advanced with a huge army against Beth-zur. For the first time the Jews saw themselves confronted by elephants trained for war. Raising the siege of the Akra, Judas marched to the relief of the southern fortress, and encountered the king's forces at Beth-zacharias, eight miles nearer Jerusalem. Here for the first time he suffered defeat. His brother Eleazar, who had greatly distinguished himself in the battle, having courageously fought his way to what appeared to be the royal elephant, stabbed it from beneath, but was himself crushed by its fall. After reducing Beth-zur, the Syrians had almost captured Mount Zion also, when its defenders were surprised by sudden deliverance. Partly in order to have a free hand against Philip, who had seized Antioch, and partly from a feeling that Epiphanes had been misled by the aristocratic party in Judæa, Lysias quickly came to terms with the Jews, and granted them by treaty the spiritual independence for which they had so bravely fought. Though still politically subject, they were to be free to "walk after their own laws as aforetime." As the formal repeal of the policy of religious coercion, this concession marks the second stage in the Maccabæan struggle. In its further developments it was no longer a religious war, but a contest between the stricter and the hellenising parties for civil supremacy. Henceforth it was carried on primarily within the nation, the aid of the Syrians being given now to the one side and now to the other.

Lysias soon overcame Philip, but his rule became unpopular, and when Demetrius I., who had been a hostage at Rome, escaped and landed in Syria, the country supported his claim to the throne. He began his reign in B.C. 162 by putting Lysias and Eupator to death. The new political situation helped to precipitate the struggle between the rival parties in Judæa. Led by one Alcimus, who desired to be reinstalled as high priest,[1] the Greek party complained to the new king that they were being oppressed by the Maccabees, whom they also represented as fierce enemies to the government. Demetrius accordingly dispatched Bacchides with an army to instal the ungodly Alcimus in his office, which he did. This action, of course, had nothing to do with the revival of paganism; it was simply in the interests of the Hellenisers.

[1] According to 2 Macc. xiv. 3, 7, he had been deprived of the office on account of his pagan proclivities.

At this point we meet with a fact of deep significance in connexion with the Maccabæan movement. It
was no longer a united patriotic party that carried on
the struggle. Judas and his brethren now lost the
sympathy and support of the Ḥasīdîm, who, having no
objection to the Syrian supremacy as such, were content
to receive Alcimus as an Aaronic high priest, whose
blood and office alike were a guarantee of his good faith.[1]
But though he spoke them fair, they soon found their
confidence misplaced, for in one day he treacherously
slew sixty of them. This and a similar outrage
committed by Bacchides not only alienated the Ḥasīdîm,
but also did much to rehabilitate Judas and his
adherents in the national esteem. But for the stupid
vindictiveness of Alcimus there might ere long have been
open strife between the Ḥasīdîm and the Maccabees,
who now took the ground that their religious interests
could never be safe under a foreign yoke.

Having established the Greek party in power,
Bacchides returned to Antioch. Judas, however, soon
made things impossible for Alcimus, who once more
invoked the aid of Syria. Demetrius accordingly sent a
fresh army under Nicanor, but this general failed either
to secure the person of Judas or to worst him in battle.
Falling back upon Mount Zion, he insulted the priests,
and blasphemously threatened to burn the Temple unless
Judas was delivered into his hands. His threats,
however, effected nothing, and in a further battle at
Adasa, on the 13th Adar (March), B.C. 161—afterwards
known as "Nicanor's Day"—his troops were routed,
and he himself slain. On the principle that sin and its

[1] See Note 11, p. 376.

punishment should exactly correspond, the hand so impiously " stretched out against the holy house of the Almighty," together with the head of the blasphemer, were hung up in the vicinity of the Temple.[1]

At this juncture Judas, realising that in the end he could not cope with imperial armies, applied to the Roman Senate for protection against Syria.[2] A treaty was concluded, but never became operative. Within two months of Nicanor's defeat fresh troops under Bacchides were poured into Judæa. Only eight hundred stalwarts consented to face the imperial host, and even of these some counselled a prudent retreat. But the foe did not exist on whom Judas Maccabæus would turn his back. And so Elasa became " the Jewish Thermopylæ." Battling against overwhelming odds Judas fell, and for the time Hasmonæan hopes were quenched.

That Judas shewed military genius of a high order is beyond dispute. But is he entitled to rank as a high-souled hero? Some doubt this, not so much because of the ferocity of his reprisals, which was a characteristic of his times, as because of the half-hearted allegiance of the Ḥasīdîm, and the subsequent history of his house. Would " the pious," it is asked, have latterly hesitated to follow him had his own piety been above suspicion? And did not the Jewish nation suffer spiritually from being led to abandon their position of political detachment and exclusive devotion to the Law for " a career of carnal strife "? It will, however,

---

[1] Gorionides says: " They hung them up in front of the (Eastern) gate. Therefore that gate is called the Gate of Nicanor to this day."

[2] See Note 12, p. 376.

8

scarcely be contended that to fight for independence is incompatible with real piety, particularly where religious interests are imperilled by political subjection. Apart from this, the portraiture of Judas drawn in 1 Maccabees decidedly favours the view that he was both a saint and a patriot, and bears out Chaucer's description of him as "goddes knight." [1] He and his brethren "fought with gladness the battle of Israel . . . and salvation prospered in his hand." [2] His preparation for battle at Mizpeh was religious as well as military, and not that of one lacking in piety or purity of motive. To him death was more welcome than to witness the dishonour of the holy place, and he was content to leave the result in the hand of God.[3] The principle on which he uniformly acted, that "with heaven it is all one to save by many or by few," was the practical application to his own circumstances of the great foundation truth that "the just shall live by his faith." As regards the other contention, that the worldliness of the later Hasmonæans is a reflexion upon the character of Judas, it is enough to remark that a man cannot be held responsible for the misdeeds of his successors. A recent suggestion, that perhaps his title to fame is on a level with that of "the Mahdists of the Sudan," [4] prompts the question whether in view of all the facts Judas may not more fitly be compared with their most illustrious opponent—General Gordon. Or perhaps we might say that he was a kind of Cromwell, who identified the good of the country with the good of his own house. At all events he was a bigger man than any of the

---

[1] *The Tale of Melibœus.*
[2] iii. 2, 6.
[3] iii. 59 f.
[4] Bevan, *op. cit.* p. 99.

Ḥasīdîm. Like Alfred of England, Judas Maccabæus
is the very embodiment of the Happy Warrior so finely
described by Wordsworth—the warrior

> Who, if he be called upon to face
> Some awful moment to which Heaven has joined
> 'reat issues, good or bad for human kind,
> ،s happy as a Lover; and attired
> With sudden brightness, like a Man inspired;
> And, through the heat of conflict, keeps the law
> In calmness made, and sees what he foresaw: . . .
> Who, whether praise of him must walk the earth
> For ever, and to noble deeds give birth,
> Or he must fall, to sleep without his fame,
> And leave a dead unprofitable name—
> Finds comfort in himself and in his cause;
> And, while the mortal mist is gathering, draws
> His breath in confidence of Heaven's applause:
> This is the happy Warrior; this is he
> That every Man in arms should wish to be.

The cause of the Jewish nationalists seemed irretriev-
ably lost. Their leader was dead, and the country in
the hands of the Hellenistic party. Bacchides fortified
and garrisoned the strongholds, imprisoned the sons of
leading men as hostages in the Akra, and oppressed
the friends of Judas. Yet, owing to the internal
divisions of Syria, the Hasmonæans were soon to attain
a height of power undreamt of. Jonathan, the younger
brother of the fallen leader, was chosen as his successor,
and for a time could only maintain himself as a freebooter in the wilderness of Tekoah. On one occasion,
while returning from Medaba, whither he had gone to
chastise a robber tribe for cutting off his eldest brother
John, he suddenly found himself intercepted by Bacchides
at the fords of Jordan, and with difficulty contrived to
cross to a place of safety. Thereafter the tide began

to turn. The death of Alcimus in B.C. 160 was viewed as the judgment of heaven upon his sacrilegious interference with the wall of the inner court of the Temple.[1] Presently Bacchides returned to Antioch, but within two years the Syrian party had again to invoke his aid—so rapidly had the strength of the Maccabees increased. No success, however, attended the campaign, and so chagrined was Bacchides at the Hellenisers who had undertaken to deliver Jonathan into his hands, that he slew many of them, accepted proposals for peace, and vowed that he would never again trouble Judæa. Possibly the Roman alliance may have prompted this decision. At any rate " the sword ceased from Israel." [2] Excluded as yet from the capital, Jonathan dwelt for four years at Michmash, " judging" the people, keeping the Hellenisers in check, and in general establishing his power. Now that there was no longer any religious coercion, the mass of the people shewed unabated loyalty to the Law. The cause for which the Maccabees took up arms had been won, but they had begun to dream of new conquests. Formerly they had fought to secure religious liberty for their nation ; now they were bent upon the aggrandisement of their own house.

The goal of Jonathan's ambition was the high-

---

[1] " Either the boundary which divided the priests' court from the space to which all Jews had access, or more probably the so-called Soreg—a low breastwork—which separated the court of the Jews (*i.e.* the inner court) from that of the Gentiles. See Schürer, *HJP*, 1. i. p. 237. In any case the offence consisted in the attempt made by Alcimus to destroy the lines of demarcation between the "holy" space of the court and the unholy outer space, and thus to admit the Gentiles freely within the court" (*Cambridge Bible for Schools*, note on 1 Macc. ix. 54). Wellhausen thinks Alcimus only intended to rebuild it on a more splendid scale (*Isr. und Jüd. Geschichte*, p. 216).

[2] 1 Macc. ix. 7.

priesthood, or rather the secular authority which this office carried with it, for he was not essentially a religious man like Judas. In his hands the struggle was frankly continued in the interests of the Hasmonæan supremacy as against the old aristocracy, and the means he employed were of a purely worldly sort. He was, above all, an astute diplomatist, and had frequently the pleasure of seeing his power advanced by those who thought to make use of him. Two things in particular helped Jonathan to achieve his purpose. One was the vacancy in the high-priesthood. No successor to Alcimus had been appointed by the Syrians, who were weary of giving military protection to their nominees, and to whom it mattered little which party was uppermost in Judæa, so long as tribute was paid. The other favourable circumstance was the contest which arose in B.C. 153 for the Syrian crown between Demetrius and Alexander Balas, a pretended son of Antiochus IV. Epiphanes. Both courted the friendship of the Hasmonæans. Jonathan had now the game in his hands, and he played it well. He might have said with Pericles in Shakespeare's play :—

> Thanks, Fortune, yet, that after all my crosses
> Thou giv'st me somewhat to repair myself.[1]

Demetrius was the first to negotiate. He authorised the Maccabee to raise an army, and sent an order for the liberation of Jewish hostages. Nothing loth, Jonathan at once re-entered the city, strengthened the fortifications, and drove out the Hellenisers, whose only places of refuge now were the Akra and Beth-zur. But

[1] Act ii. Sc. I.

Balas resolved to outbid his rival. He appointed Jonathan high priest, conferred on him the distinguished order of "King's Friend,"—something analogous to our orders of the Garter and the Bath,—and sent him a purple robe and a diadem, the insignia of royalty. Without hesitation Jonathan went over to his side. Not only were his terms more alluring than those of Demetrius, but he had the powerful support of the Romans. At the Feast of Tabernacles, B.C. 153, "by the grace of Balas" Jonathan donned the sacred vestments and officiated as high priest. He was the first of the Hasmonæans to fill that office.[1] Demetrius now hastened to offer much larger concessions, but in vain. Jonathan had no belief in his sincerity, and chose to adhere to the worthless Balas. This decision was fortunate, for in a battle between the rivals Demetrius was defeated and slain. Nor did Balas fail to reward his faithful ally. At Ptolemais, where in B.C. 150 he married Cleopatra, the daughter of Ptolemy VI. Philometor, he accorded him a splendid reception, while at the same time refusing to listen to the complaints of the Hellenisers. He also raised him to the rank of a "Chief Friend," and "made him a captain and governor of a province,"[2] thus conferring on him, subject, of course, to the Syrian suzerainty, the military and civil, as well as the spiritual lordship of Judæa. No wonder that "Jonathan returned to Jerusalem with peace and gladness."[3] One eyesore, however, remained—the Akra with its Syrian commander.

When, three years later, Demetrius II. came from Crete as the avenger of his father, Apollonius, governor

---

[1] See Note 13, p. 378.   [2] 1 Macc. x. 65.   [3] 1 Macc. x. 66.

of Cœle-Syria, supported his claim to the throne. But Jonathan stood loyally by Balas, and after making himself master of Joppa, defeated Apollonius at Ashdod, which, with the temple of Dagon, was given to the flames. A like fate befell the neighbouring cities; only Ascalon saved itself by timely submission. In appreciation of these services Balas promoted Jonathan to the highest order of all, that of the "Kinsmen" or princes of the blood, and gave him the city of Ekron and its lands in perpetual possession. But not even Jonathan's steady allegiance could save the cause of Balas after his father-in-law Ptolemy Philometor became the ally of Demetrius II. Defeated in battle, Alexander fled to Arabia, where he was murdered by his own escort. Ptolemy had himself been seriously wounded, and died soon after being shewn the severed head of his former son-in-law, transmitted probably by Demetrius, who now became king (B.C. 145).

Deeming the time opportune, Jonathan laid siege to the Akra, and was summoned to Ptolemais to answer for himself before the king. Although his enemies tried to use the occasion against him, he was tactful enough to win the favour of Demetrius, who, so far from treating him as a rebel, "gave him pre-eminence among his Chief Friends." [1] He also confirmed him in the high-priesthood; and in view of a payment of three hundred talents, granted him most of the concessions which his father had vainly offered six years before. All this meant a considerable step in the direction of Jewish independence, although Jonathan probably undertook to desist from his attack upon the Akra. It was

[1] 1 Macc. xi. 27.

not long before he rendered important service to
Demetrius by sending three thousand men to help in
quelling an insurrection in Antioch, where the people
were seeking to free themselves from a tyrannical yoke.
Strange work this, it may be thought, for Jews who
were themselves struggling to be free! Perhaps so,
but it is fair to remember that they were not there
primarily at least as the champions of oppression, but
as parties to a contract. Jonathan had agreed to assist
Demetrius against the rebels on condition that the
Syrian garrisons should be removed from the Akra
and other fortresses—an object almost as dear to the
Maccabees as life itself. But although the Jewish
forces admittedly turned the scale in his favour
at Antioch, Demetrius failed to keep his word.
Jonathan accordingly went over to the side of Tryphon,
a former Syrian general who had set up Antiochus VI.,
the infant son of Alexander Balas, as king at Apamea,
and who not only confirmed the high priest in all his
dignities, but also appointed his brother Simon commander of the Mediterranean coast.

Jonathan, now a Syrian officer, soon brought the
whole region between Jerusalem and Damascus into
subjection to Antiochus VI. Having captured Gaza,
he marched to Galilee to meet the generals of Demetrius,
whom after a slight reverse he routed on the plain of
Hazor. He also chastised the Zabadæans, an Arab
tribe on the Antilibanus, and occupied Damascus, before
returning to Jerusalem, where he set about strengthening
the walls and isolating the Akra. Simon, on his part,
had been equally active, and had succeeded in reducing
Beth-zur and Joppa, in both of which he placed Jewish

garrisons.   He now also fortified Adida, on the Philistine
frontier.   But as in thus ostensibly furthering the interests
of the new claimant the Maccabæan brothers were at the
same time clearly working for their own hand, Tryphon's
distrust was aroused.   If, as stated in 1 Macc. xii. 1–23,
treaties were actually concluded with Rome and Sparta,[1]
this was certainly not for the benefit of Syria, and the
practical outcome of the intervention of the Maccabees
was that in the name of the Syrians they had driven the
Syrians out of Palestine.   Too astute not to perceive this,
Tryphon resolved to be rid of the Jewish high priest,
whose growing power might militate against his own
plans.   Afraid to encounter Jonathan in open battle,
he decoyed him into Ptolemais, where he was treacherously made a prisoner, and had his escort slain.   That
the wily Maccabee should have been so easily deceived
is one of the surprises of history, and a striking illustration of the irony of fate.   His indiscretion cost him
dear, for it put a period to his public life.

Although the character of the struggle had already
changed under Judas, and from being religious had
become political, the attitude of the great Maccabee
remained one of pious patriotism.   He took a genuine
pride in the Law as the palladium of the Jewish people.
With Jonathan it was otherwise.   From the first he

---

[1] The historicity of the statement is accepted by Schürer, but denied by
Wellhausen, who rejects the entire passage as having no proper connexion
with the narrative (*Isr. u. Jüd. Gesch.*[3] p. 266, n. 3).   Kautzsch thinks
Jonathan's letter to the Spartans (xii. 6–18) quite apposite if the intention
was to make clear to Jewish readers the true theocratic standpoint with
reference to treaties with the heathen (*Apok. u. Pseudepigr. des AT.* i. p. 29).
In any case it must be recognised that the document is one which may very
well have been in the hands of the original author.   See note on 1 Macc. xii.
1–23 in *Cambridge Bible for Schools.*

fought a purely partisan fight, in which he displayed the courage of the desperado and the freebooter, but nothing of high-souled heroism. His favourite weapons were those of the diplomatist — flattery and gifts. Although a high priest of Israel, his *morale* is scarcely superior to that of a Hellenistic Jew at the court of the Ptolemies. He valued the sacred office only for the sake of the power and prestige connected with it. But if he did nothing to shed lustre on the high-priesthood, he certainly achieved much both for himself and his party. His effectiveness was due to the cleverness with which he exploited the rival factions in Syria. Few men have been more favoured by circumstances than Jonathan Apphus; fewer still have shown themselves so dexterous in the art of taking occasion by the hand and making full use of their opportunities.

The news of Jonathan's capture caused consternation at Jerusalem. But there was still left one of the sons of Mattathias to guide the national movement. Gallantly stepping into the breach, Simon roused the enthusiasm of the people, who formally chose him as their leader. His first care was to forward the work of fortifying Jerusalem, and to annex the seaport of Joppa. The latter operation marks a distinct change in tactics as compared with the time when, twenty years before, Jews were drafted into the capital from the outlying districts of Galilee and Gilead. Then the path of wisdom seemed to lie in the direction of centralisation; now it was deemed advisable to aim at colonisation.

Tryphon soon marched against Judæa, but Simon awaited him in force at Adida. Thereupon he offered to release Jonathan on receiving a ransom; but though

his demands were satisfied he broke his promise. After
this he tried to reach Jerusalem by way of Adasa, but
found himself completely checkmated by Simon. Just
as Fabius Maximus kept alongside of Hannibal, but
always on the mountains, so Simon moved his forces
along the mountain paths, with the result that they
were always between the invader and Jerusalem.
Equally unsuccessful was Tryphon's attempt to convey
supplies to the starving garrison in the Akra; a heavy
fall of snow made the wilderness impassable for his
cavalry. Advancing into Perea, he meanly revenged
himself by putting Jonathan to death (B.C. 143). The
bones of the murdered Maccabee were carried to
Modin, and laid in the family grave, over which Simon
afterwards erected a magnificent monument which was
visible from the Mediterranean. While it stood, this
stately pile, with its seven pyramids and sculptured
pillars, would inspire the sons of Israel with a patriotic
spirit by filling them with a grateful admiration for the
men who saved their religion and (ultimately) won
independence for their country.

About this time Tryphon put to death the boy-king
Antiochus VI., and contested the Syrian throne with
Demetrius II., whose eastern provinces were being
menaced by the Parthians. Although taking no part
in these struggles, Simon seized the opportunity to conclude an alliance with Demetrius on the footing that
Judæa should be wholly exempt from taxes. The
political independence of which the Maccabees had
dreamed, and for which they had planned and fought,
was thus at length actually achieved and formally
recognised. If the Jews had still to own the suzerainty

of Syria, they were freed from all oppressive burdens. The writer of 1 Maccabees proudly records that " in the one hundred and seventieth year (*i.e.* of the Seleucid era = B.C. 143–142) was the yoke of the heathen taken away from Israel." To signalise an event so glorious, they made it the commencement of a new era, all documents being henceforth dated according to the year of Simon as high priest and ethnarch of the Jews.[1]

While the two rival kings of Syria were occupied in fighting each other, Simon took care to strengthen still further his position in Palestine. In particular, he aimed at reducing the fortresses of Gazara and Jerusalem. The former was of great strategic importance as commanding the mountain passes and covering Joppa, which had already been made the port of Jerusalem; without the capture of the latter there could be no real Jewish independence. In both cases Simon was successful. Having expelled the heathen population of Gazara, he entered the city in triumph, placed in it loyal adherents of the Law, and appointed his son John resident governor. By reducing the garrison to starvation he also made himself master of the Akra; and after it had been duly cleansed, triumphantly entered the long-coveted citadel on the 23rd Iyar (May), B.C. 142. This was one of those glad days in the history of Israel which were ordered to be commemorated by a yearly festival.

Simon could now devote his energies to the congenial task of internal administration. He proved himself an ideal ruler. Under his fostering care the

---

[1] Although a year or two elapsed before he got formal permission to do so, Simon seems to have lost no time in issuing Jewish coins. See Note 14, p. 379.

country became a hive of peaceful industry. Trade and
agriculture flourished; the fortresses were provisioned,
and the young men exercised in military drill; a spirit
of respect for law and religion was evoked. No rallying
point was left for the Syrians, and every Jew sought the
common weal. The charming picture drawn in 1 Macc.
xiv. 4–15 shews that both morally and materially the
nation was now prosperous to a degree unparalleled in
its post-exilic history. " The land had rest all the days
of Simon : and he sought the good of his nation ; and his
authority and his glory was well-pleasing to them all
his days. . . . And they tilled their land in peace, and
the land gave her increase, and the trees of the plains
their fruit. The ancient men sat in the streets, they
communed all of them together of good things, and the
young men put on glorious and warlike apparel. He
provided victuals for the cities, and furnished them with
all manner of munition, until the name of his glory was
named unto the end of the earth. He made peace in
the land, and Israel rejoiced with great joy : and they
sat each man under his vine and his fig tree, and there
was none to make them afraid : and there ceased in the
land any that fought against them : and the kings were
discomfited in those days. And he strengthened all
those of his people that were brought low : the law he
searched out, and every lawless and wicked person he
took away. He glorified the sanctuary, and the vessels
of the temple he multiplied."

The fortunes of the Hasmonæan house had vastly
improved since Judas fell at Elasa. Only twenty years
had passed, yet now it was troubled neither by rivals
within the nation nor by despots without. But as it was

represented by the last survivor of the sons of Mattathias, the question as to the succession to the chief power had to be faced. It was settled favourably for the Hasmonæans, and on the basis of national gratitude. At a great public assembly held on the 18th Elul (September), B.C. 141, Simon was formally appointed high priest, military commander, and ethnarch; and it was further ordained that these offices should be hereditary in his family until "a faithful prophet" should otherwise direct.[1] The decree to this effect was engraved on tablets of brass and hung up in the Temple. And so Simon became the founder of the Hasmonæan dynasty. He no longer held his position by the authority of the Syrian king, but by the expressed will of the people. The arrangement was provisional, however, in so far as it was subject to a fresh revelation through a trustworthy prophet.

After some peaceful years, during which Simon renewed the fatuous alliance with Rome which was yet to cost the Jews so dear, he was once more caught in the meshes of Syrian politics. Tryphon was now being opposed by the energetic Antiochus VII. Sidetes, younger brother of the weak Demetrius II., who had been taken prisoner by the Parthians. While the contest was still doubtful, Antiochus wrote to Simon confirming to him the privileges granted by Demetrius, including the possession of the strongholds, and also conferring on him the right to coin money in his own name. But when, in B.C. 139, he succeeded in getting the better of Tryphon at Dora, he perfidiously demanded the cession of Joppa, Gazara, and the Akra, or, in default of this, payment of a thousand talents. To Simon's offer of a hundred

[1] 1 Macc. xiv. 41.

talents his only reply was to dispatch Cendebæus, governor of the Philistine coast, with an army against the Jews. As he was now too old to undertake the campaign himself, Simon entrusted the conduct of it to his sons Judas and John. After a keen battle, in which Judas was wounded, the Syrians were routed near Modin. This victory freed the Jews from further molestation at the hands of Antiochus all the days of Simon. These, unhappily, were almost numbered. Within two or three years after the defeat of Cendebæus he came to a tragic end. Ever solicitous for the welfare of his country, he was engaged in visiting officially the several townships of Judæa. In February, B.C. 135, accompanied by two of his sons, he came to Jericho, over which Ptolemy the son of Abub, and Simon's own son-in-law, was governor. This man, who secretly coveted the supreme power, invited them to a banquet in the castle of Dôk, and caused them to be treacherously murdered while they were heavy with wine. Ptolemy's ambitious designs were foiled, however, owing to the prompt action of John Hyrcanus, Simon's third son, who not only contrived to elude assassination at Gazara, but also forthwith to occupy Jerusalem, where he was installed as high priest and prince of Judæa. At once he had to defend Jerusalem against Antiochus VII. Sidetes, who laid siege to the Jewish capital, and forced it to capitulate after a stubborn resistance of about twelve months. Thus, having enjoyed only eight short years of political independence, Judæa had once more to bear the Syrian yoke.

Simon was the last, but not the least, of the five brethren. His was in many respects a noble career. Possessing in no small degree the soldierly ability of

Judas and the shrewdness of Jonathan, he excelled also as a far-seeing statesman and a worthy priest. Some scholars think the glowing eulogy of Ecclus. l. 1–21 is best applied to him.[1] If he sought to promote the honour and advantage of his own house, he was not less concerned for the social and moral well-being of his subjects.

The elements
So mix'd in him, that Nature might stand up
And say to all the world, ' This was a man ! '

It was now two and thirty years since, at Modin, Mattathias had thrown down the gauntlet in defence of freedom to worship God. All his sons had fulfilled his solemn charge to give their lives for the covenant of their fathers. One after another they had died for their country and their Law. In the course of the conflict other and less worthy aims and ambitions had indeed weighed with them, but, at all events, they had re-habilitated the Jewish nation. Under their valiant leadership the old spirit of independence had been re-kindled, and in the popular mind there had been created a fresh appreciation of the worth of their religion. Generally speaking, the Maccabæan movement was of supreme importance for post-exilic Judaism. It is the watershed of those centuries. Before it, both politically and religiously, Israel was weak and lifeless. The Diaspora had not yet got beyond the stage of feeble beginnings. There had also set in a deadly decay of self-consciousness in Israel. The nation was fast losing its distinctiveness ; as a whole it was torpid and depressed. This apathy had already shewn itself in the days of Haggai and Zechariah, who had difficulty in persuading

[1] See Note 15, p. 380.

the returned exiles to rebuild the Temple; and the later
Jewish literature of the pre-Maccabæan age, as represented by the wisdom books, bears witness to the
prevalence of the same sluggish, moderate, rationalistic
spirit. The Maccabæan crisis altered all this completely.
It gave a mighty impulse to Judaism. And the remarkable renaissance in Palestine synchronised with a no less
remarkable expansion abroad. " Once again Israel has
a history, its religion puts forth a fresh blossom." The
intensification of the national consciousness and the
newborn enthusiasm called forth by the Maccabæan
revolt are reflected in the apocalyptic literature, which
originated in this period. These books mark the revival
in a modified form of the old prophetic ideal of a future
Messianic kingdom, characterised by righteousness and
happiness, having Jerusalem for its centre, and thence
extending to the whole world. All this was no doubt
of the nature of an aftergrowth, yet historically and
spiritually it has a deep significance as forming the
immediate background of the Gospels.

In concluding this chapter we may advert to the
vexed question of Maccabæan psalms. The Psalms of
Solomon, written a century after the Maccabæan crisis,
shew that although prophecy had ceased,[1] the revived
national sentiment did not fail to find poetical expression,
and the question arises, do any of the canonical psalms
reflect the circumstances of the Maccabæan period?
Two extreme views have been held,—the one, that of
those who, on the ground that the canon was already
closed, deny the possibility of the existence of such

_____
[1] 1 Macc. iv. 46.

9

psalms in the Psalter at all; the other, that of those who maintain that from Ps. lxxiii. onwards the collection is mainly or even wholly Maccabæan. Neither of these pronouncements can be regarded as satisfactory. Our knowledge respecting the formation of the Psalter and the history of the canon is insufficient to establish the former; and in view of the fragmentary character of the post-exilic history, and of the lack in so many of the psalms of anything like a definite historical background, it is scarcely possible to accept the latter. The question is really one of exegesis, and hitherto opinion has widely differed. Theodore of Mopsuestia already set down seventeen psalms as (prophetically) Maccabæan. Calvin ascribes to this period Pss. xliv. and lxxiv., and considers Ps. lxxix. at least as applicable to it as to the destruction of Jerusalem by the Chaldæans. Most modern scholars accept as Maccabæan Pss. xliv., lxxiv., lxxix., and lxxxiii. To these Bousset would add Pss. lxxvi.–lxxviii., lxxx., lxxxv., lxxxix., and in the later books Pss. cviii. (= lx. B), cx., cxviii., and cxlix. Baethgen thinks Pss. ii., lxix., cx., and cxlix. most probably Maccabæan, and Pss. lxxv., cii., cviii., and cxliv. possibly so. Hitzig, Olshausen, Reuss, and Duhm go still further in the same direction. Cheyne also at one time (1891) set down twenty-seven psalms as Maccabæan, but in 1895 withdrew this opinion and supported the view of Robertson Smith, that Pss. xliv., lxxiv., lxxix., and lxxxiii. are best referred to the time of Artaxerxes Ochus, not because of their contents, which fit the Maccabæan period well, but because of their position within the first three books of the Psalter. On the other hand, the presence of Maccabæan psalms in our Psalter is disputed by

Gesenius, Ewald, Dillmann, Hupfeld, Bleek, Ehrt, and
Kirkpatrick. Although we are here manifestly on very
debatable ground, the prevailing trend of modern critical
opinion is towards the ascription of practically the whole
Psalter to the post-exilic period, and of a considerable
portion of it to the Maccabæan age. Thus Wellhausen
epigrammatically says: "Since the Psalter belongs to
the Hagiographa, and is the hymn-book of the congregation of the second Temple . . . the question is not
whether it contains any post-exilic psalms, but whether
it contains any pre-exilic psalms."[1] The recognition of
the element of truth expressed here has led, however,
to extravagance in the reference of psalms to the
Maccabæan period. Such a reference is often mere
guesswork; and even where the cumulative impression
derived from the presence of various contributory factors
constrains us to regard this as the probable date of
composition, there are also considerations opposed to
such a conclusion. But to regard the latter as
warranting the denial *a priori* of the Maccabæan origin
of any of the psalms included in the Psalter, is to be
guilty of equal extravagance in an opposite direction.

The following are the arguments adduced against
the possibility of such late additions :—

1. Among psalms ostensibly Maccabæan several
are ascribed to David; but if they were written so
shortly before the close of the canon, such a mistake
would be inexplicable.

This is not decisive. Ps. cviii. is certainly late, and
yet is ascribed to David; a Davidic authorship is likewise assigned to 1 Chron. xvi. 8 ff., which is composed

---

[1] In Bleek's *Introduction*, p. 507, ed. 1876.

of post-exilic pieces. The fact that in the Septuagint several psalms are ascribed to David which in the Hebrew text are anonymous, shews that there was a tendency to attach a name to psalms bearing none; but we have no means of judging as to when the inscription לדוד was affixed to any particular psalm. That the Septuagint translators recognised the composition of psalms in the post-exilic period is clear from the fact that they ascribe Pss. cxxxviii. and cxlvi.–cxlviii. to Haggai and Zechariah. Naturally, however, they were not informed with respect to Maccabæan psalms.

2. Since Ps. lxxix. 2 f. is quoted in 1 Macc. vii. 17 (*c.* B.C. 90) as Scripture, the Psalter must have been closed at a considerably earlier date.

But half a century would suffice to give canonical weight to a song which had been admitted into the hymnary. This would take us back to B.C. 140 as an approximate date for the closing of the canon. On this basis it only follows that Maccabæan psalms incorporated in it cannot have been very numerous; the question of their possibility is not affected.

3. Nearly all the psalms supposed to be certainly Maccabæan are in the Elohistic collection, and not in the later collection contained in Books IV. and V.

This is no doubt a real difficulty; but the Psalter as we have it is the final result of a process extending over centuries; and if poems by other writers were admitted into the Davidic collection, Maccabæan psalms may also have been subsequent additions to the Elohistic group. " We are bound to admit that Simon the Maccabee, as high priest, had power to deal as he thought best with the provisionally closed temple hymn-book." [1]

[1] Cheyne, *Origin of the Psalter*, p. 457.

4. From the supposed quotation of the closing doxology of Book IV.[1] in 1 Chron. xvi. 36*a*, it has been inferred that by the time of the Chronicler the Psalter was already arranged into five divisions.

It is by no means improbable, however, that the words in question were really "liturgical formulæ" in common use. But even if a fivefold division did then exist, this is no proof that fresh psalms could not still have been inserted.

5. From the prologue to Ecclesiasticus it appears that in B.C. 180 there was a threefold canon of Scripture ("the law and the prophets and the other books of our fathers"), and that this had been translated into Greek before B.C. 132. Obviously, therefore, it is argued, the collection in its Hebrew form must have been completed at latest by B.C. 140. Moreover, in the recently recovered portions of a Hebrew text of Ecclesiasticus there occurs (after ch. li. 12) a psalm of fifteen verses containing many phrases derived from psalms in Book v., *i.e.* from some of the latest psalms in the Psalter.

All this may be conclusive enough against the extreme views of Hitzig and others, but it is not so against the existence of *some* canonical psalms dating from the Maccabæan period. For the question remains, was Sirach's Psalter commensurate with ours? May it not have been supplemented in Maccabæan times? That the collection of the Kethubim was not closed at the time of Ben Sira is proved, if not, as Dillmann thinks, by the Prologue to Sirach, at all events by the subsequent admission of the Book of Daniel; and instead of inferring the impossibility of Maccabæan psalms owing

[1] Ps. cvi. 48.

to the canon having been previously closed, it would seem more reasonable to argue that because of the presence of such psalms in the Psalter the canon cannot have been finally fixed at the date of the Maccabæan revolt (B.C. 167).

6. The statement that Judas Maccabæus followed up the work of Nehemiah in forming a collection of the national literature [1] is held to attest the then existence of the Psalter (τὰ τοῦ Δαβίδ) in its present form.

In point of fact it is rather fitted to suggest that it was at that time enriched by some additions. But in any case the passage has no historical value.

Our conclusion is that if the history of the canon does not favour, neither does it preclude, the view that some Maccabæan psalms were received into the Psalter. On the question as to how many, and which, of the psalms are really Maccabæan, opinion will probably always vary.

[1] 2 Macc. ii. 13.

CHAPTER IV

PALESTINIAN JUDAISM: POST-MACCABÆAN

CHAPTER IV.

PALESTINIAN JUDAISM: POST-MACCABÆAN.

THE age of the Maccabees is interesting in itself as the most heroic chapter in Israelitish history. To the student of Christianity it is still more interesting and significant as that to which we are to look for the formative influences which went to mould Jewish character and beliefs in the period immediately preceding the Advent of our Lord. These influences are chiefly associated with the names of the rival parties of the Pharisees and the Sadducees, but also subordinately with those of the Zealots and the Essenes.

The Pharisees may be broadly characterised as the party of the scribes. Not that the two terms are convertible, for all Pharisees were not scribes, and some scribes were not Pharisees.[1] Historically also the scribe represents an older factor in Israelitish life than does the Pharisee. Yet from the way in which "scribes and Pharisees' are usually linked together in the Synoptic Gospels it is evident that they formed practically one party, and that the tendencies developed by the scribes at an earlier date became, later on, the shibboleths of the distinctively Pharisaic party. The aim of the

[1] Mark ii. 21*b*; Acts xxiii. 9.

Pharisees was the complete and exact fulfilment of the
Law as interpreted and built up by the scribes.   Under
the latter the nation "became a school, and its heads
were the schoolmasters."   They sedulously imbued it
with their own ideas, and laboured to bring the prophetic idealism concerning the supremacy of God to
actual realisation.   But the system of rules drawn up
by them for the regulation of conduct was so elaborate
that the great mass of the people could not even become
acquainted with it, much less put it into practice.[1]   No
one could realise the ideal of the scribes without devoting his life to the task.   The Pharisees were those who
were prepared to do this.   As their name signifies, they
were separatists, "those who set themselves apart," not
only from the surrounding heathen, but also from the
great mass of their own nation.   Probably it was their
enemies who first called them *Pĕrūshim*; their own
designation was *Ḥăbērim* (brethren).   In their view the
true Israel did not extend beyond their own ranks.
The Pharisees were therefore "simply Jews in the
superlative," an *ecclesiola in ecclesia*, a select circle of
the pious such as never fails to form itself in connexion
with Church life.   They represented in its extreme form
the old antagonism of the pious to the ungodly which
already shewed itself in the time of Ezra and Nehemiah,
and which is also so clearly reflected in the Psalms and
in Ecclesiasticus.   That this opposition became keener
during and after the Maccabæan crisis is apparent from
the later literature, especially the Book of Enoch and
the Psalms of Solomon.   Regardless of consequences,
the Pharisees set themselves to embody in practice the

[1] John vii. 49

strictest demands of the scribal deductions from the Law as the expressed will of Jahweh. Legally to fulfil all righteousness, and to attain complete separation from everything that defiled;—this they conceived to be the one concern of the Jewish nation, the one thing needful in order to inherit the promises, and therefore the one thing worth doing. The tenacity with which they held their principles is illustrated in their reply to Petronius with reference to the proposed erection in the Temple of a statue to the Emperor Caius: " We shall die rather than transgress the Law."[1] As a party the Pharisees simply stood for strict legalism. They were not a sect representing any special religious tendency. Their standpoint was that of orthodox Judaism. They adhered to the current belief in the existence of angels and spirits; they believed in the resurrection of the body, and in a future state of rewards and punishments.[2] According to Josephus,[3] they held the doctrine of pre-destination, while at the same time maintaining the freedom, within certain limits, of the human will. But it is scarcely safe to estimate their attitude on these points from the statements of a writer who tries to represent to his pagan readers that the Pharisees were a philosophical school akin to the Stoics, while the Sadducees and Essenes corresponded respectively to the Epicureans and Pythagoreans. If the Pharisees were not a sect, as little were they a political party. Properly speaking, they took no account of politics at all. It is true that they were sometimes involved in political struggles, but only in so far as they found it

---

[1] Jos. *Ant.* xviii. 8. 3.
[2] Acts xxiii. 9.
[3] *Ant.* xiii. 5. 9; *B. J.* ii. 8. 14.

necessary to fight for freedom to obey the Law. This
was their one objective. In the cause of legal piety
they were ready to suffer and even to die. They
believed in its ultimate triumph. " God is superior to
Caius," and " will stand on our side "—this was the
motive power behind their action, and was, in fact, a
form of the Messianic hope.

Already in the Ḥasīdîm of the days immediately
preceding the Maccabæan rebellion the Pharisaic party
existed in germ. These men were zealous for the Law,
and opposed the hellenising movement under Epiphanes.
Although they were well organised,[1] many of them, as
we have seen, let themselves be butchered rather than
fight on the sabbath. Even afterwards, when they had
joined the Maccabæan warriors, it was not the political,
but the religious element in the struggle on which they
laid stress. They were not patriots fighting for independence, but were content to live under a foreign yoke
so long as they were free to observe the Law. As soon
as they thought this had been secured they came to
terms with Alcimus, and parted from their Maccabæan
allies. So also later on as Pharisees they endured the
dominion of Herod, and even of the Romans, although
they hated the latter for their " anti-legal exactions."

Amid the confusion created by renewed wars
between rival claimants for the throne of Syria, the
Jewish State enjoyed unbroken freedom until the conquest of Palestine by the Romans in B.C. 63. John
Hyrcanus took advantage of the situation to extend
his territory. In the worldliness of his policy he even
surpassed Jonathan his uncle, inasmuch as he employed

[1] 1 Macc. ii. 42, vii. 13.

mercenary troops, and paid them with treasure taken from the graves of the ancient kings. Thus equipped, he first marched to the east of Jordan and captured Medaba; then subdued the Samaritans, and destroyed the temple on Gerizim; and finally, turning to the south, he forced the Edomites to embrace Judaism on pain of expulsion from their land. Although they chose to comply, so that at last the breach between Jacob and Esau seemed to be healed, these Edomites and their descendants proved a discordant element in the congregation of Israel, and continued to be regarded as Jews of an inferior caste. Towards the close of his reign Hyrcanus laid siege to Samaria, in order to avenge the injuries inflicted by the inhabitants upon the Jewish colony of Marissa. After seeing the city invested, he left his sons Antigonus and Aristobulus to carry on the siege. The Jewish legends relate that while Hyrcanus was officiating in the Temple a voice announced to him the victory of his sons. This gained for him the reputation of a seer, and shed on his high-priesthood the lustre of special sanctity. We have here, however, not so much the record of a fact as an indication of the wistful yearning for the restoration of the prophetic gift. John died in B.C. 105 after a prosperous reign of thirty-one years. He was the first Jewish prince to have his name engraved on the coins. The fortunes of the Hasmonæans had been steadily rising. Religious liberty, the displacement of the ancient priestly line, and independence of the Syrian supremacy, mark the successive steps by which they had risen to power.

But if John's reign was characterised by outward

splendour, it was no less marked by internal discord. It was at this time that the deep-rooted antagonisms represented by the terms Pharisees and Sadducees first crystallised and took definite form in party organisation. The consolidation of two rival parties under those names was really an outcome of the Maccabæan movement. It was upon the establishment of the Hasmonæan dynasty that matters came to an open breach, and that a section of the scribes were first called Pharisees. These were virtually identical with the Ḥasīdîm. According to the obviously somewhat legendary account of Josephus, Hyrcanus, called upon to "lay down the priesthood and content himself with the civil government of the people," replied by forsaking the Pharisees and joining their opponents the Sadducees. What is certain is that a ruler who had come to regard the aggrandisement of his own house as of greater importance than a scrupulous fulfilment of the precepts of the Law, could not continue in close association with the Pharisees. His natural affinities were necessarily with the aristocratic party, who saw nothing amiss in the arrangement according to which the royal and the priestly power were vested in the same person, and not with the men who had the spiritual insight to perceive that herein lay a lurking danger to all that they held most sacred. The cleavage between the two opposing parties increased until under Alexander Jannæus, the second of the sons of Hyrcanus to occupy the throne, the country was plunged into the miseries of a civil war. The Sadducees were on the side of the king; the Pharisees and the mass of the people fought against him. Long and bitter was the feud, but after six years

it ended in a victory for Jannæus. After his death a
new situation was created through the reversal of his
policy by his widow and successor Alexandra. Her
alliance with the Pharisees enabled them to gain an
absolute ascendancy over the popular mind, while it
correspondingly weakened the influence of the Sadducees.
The latter received their death-blow as a political party
when, in B.C. 63, the Romans chose as their vassal-king
the Pharisaic Hyrcanus, son of Alexandra, in preference
to his Sadducean brother Aristobulus.

The Pharisees were the pious of their time, and in
them ecclesiastical piety reached its full maturity. In
one important respect, however, the whole position and
character of the pious had changed since pre-Maccabæan
days. They were no longer the oppressed, but the ruling
party in Israel. Formerly the power had been in the
hands of their enemies, now it was in their own. They,
and not the priestly nobility, were the real leaders of the
people in the Herodian age. In the time of our Lord
the scribes and Pharisees, as the pre-eminently pious,
enjoyed the highest esteem, and exercised the greatest
authority. They " sat in Moses' seat," and controlled
the internal life of the nation. As the head of the
State the high priest represented the supreme external
authority, but the inner springs of the national life
were directed by the scribes and Pharisees. Their
ascendancy, however, was moral, not official ; the Divine
Law was the sole basis of their power. It is true
that the Sanhedrin, which was the Jewish parliament
and metropolitan town council in one, shared the highest
power with the ethnarch and high priest, and that it
included scribes among its members ; but they were in

a minority, and could exert only a moral influence upon
its decrees.

The question regarding the composition of the
Sanhedrin has an important bearing upon that regarding
the place occupied by the scribes and Pharisees in the
Jewish community. Under the Maccabees the powers
of this court had been practically unlimited, and under
the Romans it was subject only to the supreme jurisdiction
of the procurators. Its prestige is proved by the fact
that Herod deemed it " as necessary to slay the Sanhedrin
as Antigonus." He had once been cited to appear before
it for having exceeded his powers; but after his cruel
slaughter of many of its members, it dared in nothing to
thwart the will of its master. According to the New
Testament the Sanhedrin was composed of chief priests
(ἀρχιερεῖς), elders (πρεσβύτεροι), and scribes (γραμματεῖς).
The first category probably includes not only those who
had been high priests, but also high-priestly families.
These "chief priests" constituted the most important factor
in the council,—of which, at all events after the death
of Hillel, the high priest was president,—and appear to
have sided with the elders against the scribes.[1] While
the statements of Josephus agree with those of the New
Testament, the Sanhedrin is represented in the Mishna
as a mere assembly of scribes, in which the high priest
could not sit, far less preside, unless he were also a scribe.[2]
The names are given of those pairs (*zūgoth*) of learned
men who acted as president (*Nasi*) and vice-president
(*Ab-bêth-din*) respectively, from the times of the Maccabees downwards. But it is impossible to accept this
Talmudic version as the true one. Scribes are not

Acts iv. 23, xxiii. 14.   [2] See Note 16, p. 381.

ranked as members of the great politico-ecclesiastical
assembly of 1 Macc. xiv. 28, and it is safe to conclude
that previous to that date (B.C. 141) they had no such
professional standing.   Still more important is the fact
that in the Torah no official position is assigned to the
scribes, as to the priests and elders.   The second
theocracy was based not upon learning, but upon holiness.
The high priest was the head alike of the Church and of
the State.   Moreover, the entire history of post-exilic
Judaism circles round the high priests.   It is especially
significant that by the accession of Alcimus to the
high-priesthood the Maccabees became a mere rump
known as " the friends of Judas," and that it was only
through obtaining the high-priesthood that Jonathan was
able to become prince of the Jews.   Even after the
succession was declared hereditary in Simon's family,
the throne of the Maccabees was rendered insecure by
the fact that they were not the legitimate high priests.
Their retention of the office was, however, essential to
their position as national kings.   Herod saw clearly that
the sovereign power was bound up with it, and because
he could not hold it, did his best to discredit it.   The
Romans themselves looked somewhat askance upon the
office.   The Sanhedrin of the Talmud, then, is not that
of Jewish history.   This is not to deny that sometimes
the moral weight of the scribes may have influenced the
decisions of the council, but it is out of the question to
suppose that mere doctrinaires such as they were should
have actually carried on the public business of the Jewish
State until it came to an end in A.D. 70.   After that
date the scribes enjoyed undisputed leadership in
Palestine.   They captured not only the Sanhedrin, but

10

also the titles of its officials and members. What has been said of the relation of the scribes to the Sanhedrin holds good also with regard to the Pharisees. For the Synoptists the scribes form the third class of Sanhedrists, and though not yet called Pharisees, must be regarded as such. In the Acts of the Apostles, however, Gamaliel is introduced as a Pharisee, his special rôle as a teacher of the Law receiving only subsidiary mention. Josephus, in whose time the political power formerly possessed by the scribes had passed into the hands of the Pharisees, scarcely uses the term scribes at all, even with reference to the earlier history.[1]

The revolution which had taken place in the lot of the pious had not been effected suddenly; it was the outcome of a historical development covering the centuries between Ezra and the Maccabees. Particularly noteworthy in this connexion is the fact that during that period the conceptions of piety and wisdom gradually coalesced, until the pious sage ("wise man") virtually took the place of the quondam prophet. This was inevitable in the circumstances of post-exilic Judaism, which centred so entirely around the written Law as greatly to increase the prestige of the learned. Already for Malachi the true priest has taken on the aspect of the scribe.[2]

[1] " The chief consideration here, however," as Wellhausen has said, "is not the positive one, that the Pharisees were represented in the synedrium, but the negative one, that they formed there the minority as *homines novi*, intruders into a sphere not properly theirs. The peculiar seat of their supremacy was not the synedrium, but the school (Joh. ix. 22), and life. What has been said of the scribes is applicable to them : they were private persons without official character ; their power rested upon no difference in office or rank as between them and the ordinary members of the theocracy, but upon the fact that they brought home to the Jew what manner of man it behoved him to be."—*Die Pharisäer und die Sadducäer*, p. 43.

[2] ii. 6.

Learning not only came to have an extraordinary value for piety, but to be actually identified with it. For Sirach the scribe is the "wise," who has acquired his wisdom by foreign travel, and whose counsel is sought by rulers and great men. Through intercourse with men of renown he can interpret the subtlest parables.[1] A master of etiquette, he will also instruct his own people, win their confidence, and make for himself an everlasting name.[2] In the popular assembly he shall mount on high, and sit on the seat of the judge.[3] But no one can attain such wisdom apart from the knowledge of the Law, which is the embodiment of the Divine creative wisdom itself.[4] To fear the Lord is the beginning of wisdom;[5] therefore "if thou desire wisdom, keep the commandments, and the Lord shall give her unto thee freely; for the fear of the Lord is wisdom and instruction."[6] For the writer, education and piety are convertible terms; and so also are ignorance and ungodliness. "A wise man will not hate the law,"[7] and "the knowledge of wickedness is not wisdom."[8] True wisdom is inseparable from piety. This new idea, that piety is culture, and therefore a thing capable of being taught and learned, was pregnant with great issues for Judaism. It led to supreme importance being attached to education and upbringing. And here the main object always was to secure a proper atmosphere by shunning fools and associating with the wise. According to Sirach, the wise man has stepped into the place of the prophet as the true leader of the people. "If the great Lord

---

[1] xxxix. 2 ff.   [2] xxxvii. 23, 26.   [3] xxxviii. 33.
[4] xxiv. 10.   [5] i. 14.   [6] i. 26 f.
[7] xxxiii. 2.   [8] xix. 22.

will, he shall be filled with the spirit of understanding."[1] And Wisdom herself is represented as declaring that she will yet pour out doctrine as prophecy.[2]   Whether the thought originated with him or not, the influence of Sirach must be regarded as a powerful factor in producing among the Jewish people the conviction that piety is something to be learned, and that the learned are its peculiar representatives.   Although for this writer the Law was certainly the centre of wisdom, and as such had profound ethical significance, wisdom is not yet regarded as confined exclusively to the knowledge of the Law.   In his proverbial sayings it has a much wider range, and denotes man's susceptibility to the Divine reason which rules the universe.   But soon afterwards there set in the narrower conception, according to which wisdom is simply knowledge of the Law, and the Law is essentially ceremonial.   Naturally it took some time for this tendency to develop, but ultimately it reached its logical issue in the banning of the Greek language and of all secular literature, and in the limitation of every Jewish boy's education to instruction in the Law.   At the time of Christ no one who did not know the Law was accounted wise, nothing beyond the knowledge of the Law was reckoned essential to wisdom, and the dictum of Hillel, that " an ignorant man cannot be pious," found general acceptance.   But it was not until the post-Maccabæan age, when the land had comparative rest from the turmoil of war, that the alliance between piety and theology began thus to dominate the life of Judaism.   Even in Maccabæan times Jewish writings were still entirely free from the spirit of professionalism.

[1] xxxix. 6.   [2] xxiv. 33.

In Enoch, for example, the pious are proud of their esoteric knowledge, but not with the pride of a learned caste.   During the Herodian period all this was changed. Learning and piety, " scribes and Pharisees," began to be inseparably linked together.

The real character of the Pharisaic development is best illustrated by its opposition on the one hand to the Sadducees, and on the other to the uneducated masses— the Amhaarez.

In the post-Maccabæan age the Sadducees formed a majority of the Sanhedrin.   They were the representatives of the old priestly aristocracy, and controlled the Temple ritual.   It is difficult to trace the historical origin of the party, which seems to have arisen gradually as a conservative bulwark against the inroads of liberal theology as represented by the more democratic scribes and Pharisees.   The old nobility could not see their leadership undermined without their hostility being aroused.   If the antagonism existed in pre-Maccabæan times, it did not express itself in definite party organisation until the days of the Hasmonæans.   But indeed the strife which then broke out so virulently cannot be regarded as simply the continuation of an older quarrel.   The Maccabæan rising had changed everything.   Neither the internal nor the external relations of the Jewish community were what they had been previous to the war of independence.   To quote Wellhausen, " The beginning, and foundation, and content of that inner discord must lie within the new development of things itself.   Only the Hasidæans as the one pole of the hostile relationship are taken over from the earlier period, being now in their present position named Pharisees; on the other hand, the Sadducees are certainly in possession of political supremacy like the sons of Zadok before them, but they are other people with other tendencies, and the quarrel is about other things. The oppositions can well be compared, but can only be compared."[1] The same writer has shewn that little light upon the origin and nature of the cleavage is to be derived from the disputes which according to rabbinic tradition were carried on between Pharisees and Sadducees,[2] and that but for the idea of Geiger and others that Sadduceeism was equivalent to priesthood, no one would ever have traced the purely theoretic minutiæ discussed in the Talmud to the conflict between the general and the special priesthood. Jewish history alone can supply the key to the genesis of the cleavage, and its real character can be estimated only from its bearing upon the national life and destiny. The root of the enmity is probably to be found in the essential difference of view which led the Ḥasīdîm to withdraw from the Maccabees. For them the supreme concern was the Law, not the cause of the nation and of the Hasmonæans. From the first they had no sympathy with the pretensions of the latter; and even when the high-priesthood was made hereditary in Simon's house, the arrangement was only provisional.[3] Many never ceased to contest the legitimacy of the Maccabæan succession to the sacred office. As we have already seen, the first historical trace of hostility between the two parties dates from the reign of John Hyrcanus. The Ḥasīdîm could not bear to see a spiritual theocracy

---

[1] *Die Pharisäer und die Sadducäer*, p. 89.
[2] See Note 17, p. 384.   [3] 1 Macc. xiv. 41.

changed into an ordinary kingdom of this world, while yet a vain pretence was made of adhering to the old sacred polity. In their opposition to the Hasmonæan princes they became Pharisees, and in their opposition to the Pharisees the Hasmonæans and their supporters became Sadducees. The Pharisees, then, are essentially the party of the Law, and the Sadducees the functionaries and champions of the new State which was the fruit of the Maccabæan struggle. As, however, the fundamental idea of Judaism was "not the earthly fatherland, but God and the Law," the Pharisees were able in the long-run to secure the adhesion of the multitude, who at first had been caught in the enthusiasm of the national movement, and by wrecking the Hasmonæan State undoubtedly saved Judaism.

No satisfactory explanation of the name Sadducee has yet been given. The most likely derivation is that from the proper name Zadok ; and here again the most probable reference is to Zadok the high priest in the time of David and Solomon. Although Josephus refers to it as having been already current in the time of the Hasmonæan kings, the first actual occurrence of the term Sadducee is in the Synoptic Gospels. So far as can be gathered from the sources, it was theological, not political, in its application. It seems to have been applied in a depreciatory sense to the adherents of the aristocratic party, which, however, was essentially political. Perhaps it was a nickname.[1]

---

[1] So Wellhausen: "Es sollte damit gesagt werden, die jetzigen Herrscher, die vielleicht gar nicht zum geschlechte Zadok's gehörten, seien nicht besser als ihre dem Heidenthum zugeneigten Vorgänger, auf die sich der ganze Hass und die Verachtung des Volks gesammelt hatte" (*Op. cit.* p. 94).

If the Sadducees were not numerous, they were influential, and held, in fact, the highest offices. They were rulers, and elders, and associates of the high priest.[1] As an aristocracy they did not include the ordinary priests. It was not the priestly, but the worldly position of the Sadducees that gave to the party its peculiar complexion. High-priestly lineage was valued chiefly for the heritage of political power which it carried with it. The Sadducæan party, therefore, was not confined to officiating priests; it embraced the aristocracy in general. If the high priests constituted its most influential section, this was due more to their secular power than to their ecclesiastical standing. The genius of Sadduceeism was distinctly political. While the Pharisees did not understand politics, this was the sphere in which the Sadducees were at home. Josephus, however, is scarcely exact in representing them always as a definite political party. The truth is they were distinguished from the mass of the people by their entire philosophy of life, and it was this rather than the mere fact of their being the ruling class that made them a party. They stood for practical politics in opposition to the purely religious life of the Pharisees. Like the ancient kings of Israel and Judah, the Sadducees were pleased to form alliances, erect fortresses, and maintain troops; like the prophets, the Pharisees believed in attending to the requirements of religion and leaving everything else to providence. The one party refused to think that God would commit to them the internal, and deprive them of the external, management of the State; the other regarded all statecraft as a usurpation of the functions of the

[1] Acts iv. 5, v. 17.

Almighty.   The Sadducees were men of this world, who
looked with a kindly eye on the general culture of the
age; the Pharisees cared for nothing but the Law, and
looked for the future Messianic deliverance.   Now it is
not in virtue of their official positions, but in virtue of
their well-marked spiritual tendencies, and as enemies of
the Pharisees, that the Sadducees are so named in the
sources.   The Pharisees had no quarrel with the sanctity
of the priestly office; what offended them was the
degenerate character of the priestly nobility, and the
antagonistic attitude taken up by them towards their
own doctrinal beliefs.   Yet it was not any mere theological difference that caused such a rift in the life of
the Jewish people.   As Wellhausen says, " It is the
opposition between a prevailingly political and a prevailingly religious party in a community more spiritual
than worldly." [1]

The general doctrinal position of the Sadducees was
the natural result of their view of the world.   Having
no mind to be dragged at the tail of Pharisaic opinion,
they strenuously disavowed the new ecclesiastical faith.
According to Josephus,[2] they accepted only the written
Law, rejecting tradition.   It was, however, merely the
later development of the Law which they rejected; no
question appears to have been raised with reference to
any tenet of Judaism recognised prior to the Greek
dominion.   Their great weakness was that they had
recourse to barren negation and cavilling opposition;
they stood for nothing positive.   All the labours of the
scribes and Pharisees in adapting the Mosaic Law to
altered circumstances met with their scornful disapproba-

---

[1] *Op. cit.* p. 56.   [2] *Ant.* xviii. 10. 6.

tion. Nor were the eager aspirations of the poor and the distressed after a future state in which the wrongs of the present should be redressed shared by the Sadducees, who formed a select oligarchy of the well-to-do. Believing that soul and body die together, they denied the doctrine of the resurrection and a future judgment. In this particular they refused to move beyond the standpoint of primitive Judaism. Their materialism led them also to deny the existence of angels, spirits, and demons. How they reconciled this negative attitude as to intermediaries between God and men with the Pentateuch we do not know. It was, of course, in pronounced contrast to the extraordinary Pharisaic development of angelology and demonology which characterised post-Maccabæan times. According to Josephus, the Sadducees also denied fate, and asserted within certain limits the freedom of the human will. The idea of predestination was as unwelcome to them as that of future retribution. Sheer worldlings at heart, they were also reactionaries and conventionalists in religion.

The views already expressed as to the origin and nature of the conflict between the Pharisees and Sadducees are confirmed by the state of the party relations under the Hasmonæan dynasty. These have already been briefly indicated; but in order to a clear understanding of the situation, it will be necessary to trace the external history somewhat in detail.

At the death of John Hyrcanus there was nothing to distinguish the Hasmonæans from other earthly potentates, except that as yet none of them had actually assumed the title of king. This sole point of difference was now to disappear. John had made

over the civil government to his wife, and the high-
priesthood to his eldest son Judas—better known by
his Greek name Aristobulus.   Dissatisfied with this
arrangement, the young prince imprisoned all his
relatives except his favourite brother Antigonus, and
assumed the diadem.   He did not, however, venture
to inscribe the title of king on the coins; these bore
the simple name, "Judas, high priest."   Aristobulus
was in full sympathy with the revival of Greek culture
which had set in with the rise of the Sadducæan party.
If he was not actually called Phil-Hellen,[1] the term
expresses accurately enough the general bent of his
inclinations.   So strangely had the Hasmonæan princes
drifted away from the ground taken up by the early
Maccabees.   Their Greek tastes did not, however,
prevent them from acting as champions of Judaism.
In the north of Palestine, Aristobulus took the field
against the Ituræans, annexed a large portion of their
territory, and forced them to accept the Jewish Law.
Everything points to the interesting conclusion that
the tract thus subdued and judaised was practically co-
extensive with the Galilee of the Gospels—a region
characterised at once by Jewish faith and Gentile blood.
Great significance is thus lent to the expedition against
the Ituræans, particularly in view of the fact that some
of our Lord's apostles were of Galilean extraction.[2]

Although Aristobulus shared his kingdom with his
brother Antigonus, his jealousy was so roused by a

---

[1] The words of Josephus (*Ant.* xiii. 11. 3) are χρηματίσας μὲν φιλέλλην.

[2] "This part of the work of the Hasmonæan dynasty, preparing as it did
the field for Christ, was perhaps, of all that they did in the world, the thing
of most durable consequence for the history of mankind."—Bevan, *Jerusalem
under the High-Priests*, p. 116.

deceitful plot hatched during his illness, that the innocent
Antigonus was slain by the royal bodyguards as he
was entering the citadel. Remorse for this crime is
said to have hastened the king's death, which took
place in B.C. 104, after he had reigned only one year.
It is difficult to form a true estimate of the character
of Aristobulus. If he was cruelly betrayed into giving
the order for the slaughter of his brother, what excuse
can be offered for the atrocity of starving his own mother
to death in prison? As he was a Sadducee, and a
friend of the Greeks, it is, of course, possible that what
is recorded as to his cruel treatment of his relatives is
the malicious invention of the Pharisees. Some confirmation is given to this view by the fact that classical
writers represent him in a favourable light as " a man
of candour, and very serviceable to the Jews." [1]

On the death of Aristobulus his childless widow
Salome, whose Greek name was Alexandra, released
his three brothers, and made the eldest of them,
Alexander (called in Hebrew Jonathan = Jannai,
Jannæus), king and high priest. Following the Hebrew
custom, she also gave him her hand in marriage. After
ridding himself of that one of his two still surviving
brothers from whom he apprehended danger to his
throne, Jannæus set himself to complete the work of
Palestinian conquest initiated by his father. This was
a task thoroughly congenial to him as a man of war,
and he was able to devote himself to it with but little
interference from Egypt or Syria, whose rulers were
engrossed with their own interminable quarrels.

---

[1] Strabo in the name of Timagenes, according to Josephus, *Ant.* xiii.
11. 3 : ἐπιεικής τε ἐγένετο οὗτος ὁ ἀνὴρ καὶ πολλὰ τοῖς Ἰουδαίοις χρήσιμος.

Although Alexander's efforts were not uniformly successful, the whole country felt the power of this savage chieftain. Along the coast of Philistia, from the Ladder of Tyre to the borders of Egypt; to the north, as far as Lake Merom; and among the Hellenistic cities east of the Jordan, he enlarged the scope of his dominions until he reigned over a territory equal to that of the ancient Davidic kingdom. Although certainly at first a supporter of Hellenism, even to the extent of having a bilingual inscription stamped upon the coins, his wars were not waged in the interests of Greek culture. The hellenised city of Gaza he completely destroyed, while a similar fate befell Pella, and presumably other cities, for refusing to adopt Jewish customs and rites. What had been flourishing towns were represented only by piles of ruins, and nothing in the way of reconstruction was attempted until the times of the Roman occupation.

In view of the devastation thus produced, Alexander's was after all but a barren victory. And it was secured at a great price, for his territory had been enlarged at the expense of civil and religious unity. Party feeling ran high even in the days of Hyrcanus; but during the reign of Jannæus, Judæa became a prey to internal strife. His employment of foreign mercenaries, and his Sadducæan sympathies, alienated his subjects, who increasingly adhered to the Pharisees. Time had been when under the glamour of the victories won by the early Maccabees the populace paid little heed to the extreme party of the Law as represented by the scribes and the Ḥasīdîm. But already under Hyrcanus the tide had turned, and now under Jannæus it flowed steadily in the opposite direction. God and the Law, it was perceived, were more to Judaism than an earthly kingdom maintained by force of arms. Not only so, the very existence of the latter was a menace to the due cultivation of the former in Temple and synagogue. The priesthood was being made a mere secondary thing, and the theocracy was being brought into contempt. Many began to witness with impatience the performance of the high priest's sacred duties by a red-handed warrior like Alexander Jannæus. At length, on his return from Gaza, the crisis came. During the Feast of Tabernacles, as he stood at the altar in his priestly robes, and was about to offer sacrifice, the people pelted him with citrons from the green branches which according to custom they carried. They also repeated the taunt directed against his father, that as the son of a woman who had been a prisoner of war he was not a fit and proper person to act as high priest. Jannæus could not sit quietly under an insult so gross, and found an instrument of vengeance to hand in his mercenaries,—fierce highlanders from Cilicia and Pisidia,—who slew six thousand of the offending Jews. Although cowed by this cruel punishment, the people were also embittered by it, and eagerly waited for an opportunity to revolt. This soon came. At the close of an otherwise successful campaign in Peræa, Jannæus met with a serious reverse while fighting against Obedas, king of the Arabian Nabatæans, at Gadara, and with difficulty contrived to escape to Jerusalem. There he had to face open rebellion, and for the next six years (B.C. 94–89) the country was steeped in the horrors of a civil war. The king was supported by the Sadducees, as well as by his mercenary troops; the Pharisees, and the great mass of the Jewish people, ranged themselves against him. Persistent fighter as he was, even Jannæus became weary of the strife, and endeavoured to come to terms with his opponents. But they were irreconcilable. When he asked them what he could do to appease them, they advised him to kill himself, and at the same time invoked the aid of Demetrius III. Eukairos, then reigning over a part of Syria at Damascus. Demetrius accordingly marched into Palestine with a large force, effected a junction with the insurgent Jews, and pitched his camp near Shechem. A battle was fought, and Alexander, having sustained a crushing defeat, fled to the mountains. At this stage things took an unexpected turn. Fearing fresh subjection to the Syrian yoke, and out of pity for the sad plight of the heir of the Maccabees, six thousand Jews deserted from Demetrius and attached themselves to Jannæus. This revival of patriotic sentiment led Demetrius to withdraw to Damascus, and enabled Alexander to suppress the revolt. Having obliged his opponents to shut themselves up in a fortress, he captured it, and carried them as prisoners to Jerusalem. There, while feasting with his courtesans, he had eight hundred crosses erected and a victim nailed to each, and ordered their wives and children to be butchered before their closing eyes. As an instance of fiendish revenge this would be difficult to match in history. His horror-stricken adversaries, to the number of eight thousand, fled away by night, and remained in exile until the day of his death. Thus at length the Pharisees were crushed. This protracted struggle sets the position of the opposing parties in a clear light. It shews what the Pharisees fought for, and what they resisted; it reveals the Sadducees as nothing more nor less than the adherents of Alexander; it proves that the sympathies of the people were with the Pharisees.

After Alexander's death in B.C. 78 a sudden transformation was wrought in Judæa. The widowed queen, Salome Alexandra, who succeeded to the government, entirely reversed the policy pursued by her husband. While Jannæus detested the Pharisees, she cultivated friendly relations with them, and delighted them by announcing her desire to rule in accordance with their ideals. It is difficult to accept the statement of Josephus, that in taking her stand on the side of the Pharisees Alexandra was acting upon the advice given her by Jannæus on his deathbed. If this was so, however, he must either have been seized with compunction for the enormities he had committed, or have become convinced of the inability of the Sadducees to carve out any sort of tolerable future for the nation. What is certain is that Alexandra was so completely in the hands of the Pharisees that they became the real rulers of the country, at least as regards internal administration. The Pharisaic ordinances suppressed by Hyrcanus were legalised anew. There is, however, no reason to suppose that the Sanhedrin was at this time converted into a mere college of scribes. All that can be said with safety is that the action of every public official was controlled by the Pharisaic spirit. Even the Sadducean priests had in matters of ritual to obey the directions of the Pharisees. Rabbinic tradition looks back upon the times of Alexandra as a golden age of miraculous fertility. Rain used to fall periodically on the eve of the sabbath when no one might be out of doors, "so that the grains of wheat became as large as kidneys, those of barley as large as olives, and the lentils like gold denarii."[1]

Alexandra's elder son Hyrcanus, a feeble creature who could be relied upon not to intermeddle with politics, was appointed high priest, while her younger son Aristobulus, who was brimful of energy and courage, was held in strict control. As regards foreign policy, she kept the reins in her own hands. Peace was maintained by means of a strong army of Gentile troops. Jannæus had employed mercenaries as an auxiliary to his own forces, but Alexandra made them the staple element in her army. In this way her soldiers were not hampered by the restrictions of Judaism, and might disregard the Law without protest from the Pharisees. Her sagacity is attested by the fact that neighbouring rulers gave hostages to Judæa, and that money found its way into the treasury. Beneath all this outward calm, however, the fires of Pharisaic revenge were smouldering, and ready to burst into flame. The queen was pressed to punish with death the instigators of the crucifixion of the eight hundred. But when a beginning was made in this direction, the Sadducæan party lost patience. Led by her own son Aristobulus, a deputation waited on the queen and sought redress. After a pathetic reference to their services to the State, they begged to be placed in the fortresses, where they might live privately and unmolested. A more insolent tone was adopted by Aristobulus, who declared that they had been themselves the creators of their misfortunes in permitting "a woman

---

[1] *Ta'anîth* 23ᵃ, in Derenbourg, p. 111.

mad with ambition to rule over them, when there were
sons in the flower of their age fitter for it." [1]   Alexandra
was obliged to yield.   The fortresses were entrusted
to the Sadducæan leaders, and Aristobulus sent on a
fruitless expedition against Damascus.   Soon after, the
oppressed Sadducees were roused to new activity by the
prospect of Alexandra's death.   Within a fortnight
Aristobulus secured the adherence of more than twenty
strongholds.   He quickly found himself also at the head
of a large army.   The alarmed elders, along with
Hyrcanus, surrounded the queen's deathbed asking for
advice.   But it was now vain to look for help in that
quarter.   In B.C. 69, while the rebels bore down upon
Jerusalem, she died after reigning for nine years, the
only woman since Athaliah who had wielded the Jewish
sceptre.

Aristobulus II. lost no time in directing his military
power against Hyrcanus II., who now assumed the civil
government in addition to the high-priesthood.   Defeated
near Jericho, Hyrcanus fled to the citadel of Jerusalem,
where, perhaps fortunately for him, the family of
Aristobulus were still imprisoned.   An agreement was
arrived at between the two brothers, in terms of which
Hyrcanus, although the elder, was to abdicate in favour
of Aristobulus, and to live as a private citizen in the
peaceful enjoyment of his wealth.   This meant the
return of the Sadducees to power, and a corresponding
eclipse of the Pharisaic influence.   Although less
prominence was thus given to the religious element,
there was an absence of the extreme friction which
marked the times of Alexander Jannæus.

---

[1] Josephus, *Ant.* xiii. 16. 3.

Trouble was imported, however, from an unexpected quarter. Hyrcanus probably entered into the compact with Aristobulus in perfect good faith, but he now came under the sinister influence of one who made it his business to stir up jealousy and strife between the brothers, with a view to the furtherance of his own designs. This was the Idumæan adventurer Antipater, who, together with his son Herod the Great, was to dominate Jewish politics down to the Advent of Christ. His genealogy is doubtful, but it seems not unlikely that he sprang from one of those families upon whom Judaism, to its own ultimate detriment, had been forced by John Hyrcanus. Called by the same name as his father, who as governor of Idumæa under Jannæus had curried favour with the surrounding tribes, the young Antipater shewed himself equally possessed of the diplomatic genius. Disappointed at the retirement of the weak Hyrcanus, from whose régime he had hoped to reap much advantage to himself, he resolved to bring about, if possible, his restoration to power. To Hyrcanus himself, as well as to influential Jews, he represented the injustice of his ejection by Aristobulus, regardless of the prerogative of birth. Working upon his fears, he also induced him to throw himself upon the protection of the Arabian king Aretas, who in return for the cession of twelve cities wrested from him by Jannæus, undertook to reinstate Hyrcanus. The defeat of the usurper in battle caused many of his troops to desert him for Hyrcanus, to whom the Pharisees and the people generally also adhered. Only the Jerusalem priests stood by Aristobulus, who was obliged to entrench himself on the Temple hill, where he was besieged by the united forces of Aretas and Hyrcanus. Such was the situation in B.C. 65, two years after the death of Alexandra.

The glory of the Hasmonæans was now upon the wane. Although they had in succession secured the civil supremacy, the high-priesthood, the status of kings, and the extension of Jewish territory, all this was largely due to the dissolution of the Syrian empire, and to the opportunity thus afforded for free development in Judæa. But now the situation was on the point of being radically altered. The Romans were steadily pushing their dominion eastwards, and Palestine began to be affected by the convulsions incidental to the process that led up to the enthronement of the Cæsars. As a result of the new conditions, the Hasmonæan dynasty came to be superseded by the Herodian, the downfall of the one being closely connected with the rise of the other. The relations between the two great Jewish parties were also materially influenced by this important turn of the wheel of fortune. It was while Aristobulus was being besieged upon the Temple mount that the Jewish people first came into actual contact with Rome, one of three competitors for the now disintegrated Seleucid kingdom. The other two were Armenia and Pontus. In B.C. 65, Pompey received the submission of the Armenian king Tigranes, and vanquished Mithridates, King of Pontus. Rome thus served herself heir to Alexander's dominions as far as the Euphrates. The year following, Pompey sent his legate Scaurus into Syria. Synchronising as it did with the peculiar situation in Jerusalem, this event had a supremely important significance for the subsequent history of the Jewish State. On hearing at Damascus of the strife between the rival princes, Scaurus hastened to Judæa so as to reap the fruit of it for Rome. Both parties sent envoys to meet him. Not desiring to promote the lordship of the Nabatæan Arabs over Palestine, Scaurus took the side of Aristobulus, and ordered Aretas to withdraw, on pain of being declared an enemy to the Romans. The oracle had spoken, and the siege was raised. After inflicting heavy losses upon the retreating army, Aristobulus returned to Jerusalem and fancied himself king.

The arrival of Pompey himself in the spring of B.C. 63 was made the occasion for a threefold deputation from Jerusalem. In addition to the ambassadors of the rival claimants were representatives from the Jewish people, *i.e.* the Pharisees, urging the abolition of the kingly power altogether as alien to the spirit of the ancient theocracy. This deputation had great significance. Although the Pharisees sided with Hyrcanus, they were thereby only playing into the hands of Antipater. The consciousness of this, and the fact that the quarrel was really no special concern of theirs, led them to approach Pompey with a request which was only the logical sequence of the attitude previously taken up by them towards John Hyrcanus and Alexander Jannæus. Their grievance was that the present high priests were kings rather than priests, and they petitioned for a return to the former condition of things, in which the high priests were high priests first, and only incidentally heads of the community generally. In other words, they welcomed foreign dominion as a security for the maintenance of the theocracy in all its ecclesiastical purity.[1]

Although Aristobulus had sent a costly gift to Pompey, the latter postponed his decision, and meanwhile marched against the Nabatæans, accompanied by Aristobulus, who, however, becoming suspicious, suddenly departed from Dium and secured himself in the fortress of Alexandrium. Pompey at once suspended his Nabatæan campaign and turned against him; whereupon at the instigation of his friends he surrendered the fortress, but retired in wrath to Jerusalem. When Pompey promptly appeared before the walls, Aristobulus lost courage and sued for peace, offering to pay a sum of money and to open the city gates; but when Gabinius was sent to exact the fulfilment of these promises, he met with a rebuff at the hands of the king's troops. Irritated at this vacillation, Pompey then made Aristobulus a prisoner, and proceeded to attack Jerusalem. No resistance was offered by the party of Hyrcanus, or rather of Antipater, whose guiding principle it ever was to adhere to Rome. But the supporters of Aristobulus entrenched themselves in the Temple mount, and for three months withstood the efforts of the Romans to effect an entrance. Even then it was possible for Pompey to succeed only by utilising the opportunities presented by the Jewish observance of the sabbatic rest.[2] In the autumn of the year 63 a breach was

---

[1] Hence the joy expressed when the Hasmonæan State was abolished by Gabinius : "The people were glad to be thus freed from monarchical government, and were governed for the future by an aristocracy."—Josephus, *B. J.* i. 8. 5.

[2] The decision of the Maccabees to defend themselves on the sabbath was

made in the wall, and the stronghold was carried by storm. Twelve thousand Jews were slaughtered, and many priests, who calmly went on with their sacred duties as if nothing were happening, were hewn down at the altar. Hoping to discover "some visible symbol of the mysterious Eastern cult," the Gentile conqueror sacrilegiously forced his way into the Holy of Holies; but to his surprise he found nothing at all. In spite of this outrage upon Jewish feeling, however, Pompey neither attempted to despoil their Temple of its treasures nor to suppress their religion, as Antiochus Epiphanes had done. He even made provision for the continuation of the legal sacrifices, and reinstated Hyrcanus II. in the high-priesthood, but without the title of king. All the territory annexed by the Hasmonæans was taken away, and the jurisdiction of Hyrcanus confined to Judæa proper, which was made tributary to the Romans. After beheading the ringleaders in the war, Pompey set out for Rome, where Aristobulus and his family,—with the exception of his elder son Alexander, who made his escape on the way,—and many other Jews, helped to grace his third triumph in September, B.C. 61. On their release, the captives settled in Rome and founded the Jewish community so well known to us from Roman literature as well as from the writings of St. Paul.

The loss of the independence achieved under the Maccabees Josephus properly enough ascribes to the internecine quarrels raised by the Hasmonæan princes,

not regarded as covering a case like the present, where the enemy took care to do nothing on sabbaths beyond *preparing* for such direct attack as might at any time be resisted. Cf. Josephus, *Ant.* xiv. 4. 2.

and to the fatal step of calling in the interference of strangers. Besides lacking the nobler qualities of their ancestors, these men were possessed by the spirit of stupidity, and simply played into the hands of Rome. Not only had the Jews now to mourn the loss of their liberty, but their lives were also embittered by severe oppression. So different did the reality prove to be from the anticipations cherished as to the " friendship " of the Romans ever since the days of Judas Maccabæus.[1] Instead of a strong ally they had found a hard task-master, towards whom they began to entertain a hatred so deadly and so unanimous as virtually to quench their own party strifes, now that the vexed question of the temporal sovereignty had been settled. Accordingly, the extinction of the Hasmonæan dynasty marks the close of the first and main stage in the conflict between Pharisees and Sadducees. Through the abolition of the kingship the Pharisees had gained their end, and the Sadducees had become a spent force. With the intervention of Rome there had entered into the situation a new and potent factor which could not fail to affect party relations in Judæa. Henceforth the strife between Pharisees and Sadducees was little more than the back-wash of the earlier feuds.

What, then, it may be asked, was the position of the Jews in general, and of the Pharisees and Sadducees in particular, during the first quarter of a century of Roman supremacy? Most noteworthy, as regards the spirit of the people, is the revival of patriotic feeling. Greatly as they revered the Law and its doctors, they rated at a still higher value their freedom and their

[1] 1 Macc. viii. 1, 12.

fatherland. Hatred of foreigners led them to support repeated attempts to remove Hyrcanus from the throne. Although still obeying the Pharisees in matters ecclesiastical, their growing nationalism caused an inward estrangement between them and that party. So far from being destroyed by the fall of the Hasmonæans, patriotism now became the popular religion.[1] It was along this path that the Jews began to look for the realisation of their Messianic hopes. To rebel against Rome was conceived to be a religious duty and a work of faith which, performed upon a national scale, would be accounted to them for righteousness. And so there was formed that idea of a political Messiah, who would restore the earthly kingdom to Israel, which is so clearly reflected in the New Testament.

In some respects the Pharisees could not deplore the results of Roman intervention. Although of no political party themselves, they must have been grateful to the new masters for espousing the cause of Hyrcanus against Aristobulus. Freed, moreover, from the necessity of opposing the Hasmonæans, they could now devote all their energies to the sacred cause of the Law. But it was impossible for them to forget Pompey's desecration of the Temple, and this in itself was enough to fill them with undying hatred of the Romans. This feeling was afterwards to find expression in the efforts of the Zealots, a fanatical section of the stricter Pharisees.

It was the Sadducees who suffered most from the advent of Pompey upon the scene. Now that Hyrcanus had been reinstated in office, they were obliged to accept him as their head, although between them and him there

---

[1] Wellhausen, *Isr. u. Jüd. Gesch.*[3] p. 307.

was no real bond of sympathy.   As they watched him
become increasingly the pliant tool of Antipater and the
Romans, they made it their chief concern to conserve
their own position in face of the menacing attitude of
the Idumæan house.   During the earlier decades of the
Roman period, Jewish history was consequently little else
than a series of futile attempts under Sadducæan auspices
to restore the Hasmonæan rule.   The first revolt was led
by Alexander, the son of Aristobulus, in the year 57.
He soon got the better of Hyrcanus, but was defeated
by Gabinius, proconsul of Syria, who stripped the Jews
of the last shred of political freedom by restricting
Hyrcanus to his priestly functions and dividing Judæa
into five fiscal or juridical districts (σύνοδοι or συνέδρια),
each with its own council or sanhedrin.   Although the
change from a monarchy to "an aristocracy" was
acceptable enough, particularly to the Pharisees, it had
no disintegrating effect upon the national unity, and
failed even appreciably to lessen the importance of
Jerusalem, which, while the Temple stood, remained the
premier centre of influence.   The new arrangement,
indeed, was of short duration.   "By the ordinances of
Cæsar it was again wholly set aside."[1]   The probability is that the placing of four other cities on a
level with Jerusalem was highly provocative of rebellion
on the part of the Jews.   But not even yet was
their proud spirit broken.   The defeat of the Romans
at Carrhæ was the signal for another Jewish rising,
which, however, was promptly suppressed by the
quæstor Cassius.   But for the help rendered him by
the Romans, the Sadducæan party would no doubt have

[1] Schürer, *HJP* I. i. p. 374.

crushed Antipater; as it was, the fawning Idumæan remained on the crest of the wave.

The year B.C. 49 marks the outbreak of the civil wars, through which Rome was transformed from a republic into an empire. After Pompey and the senate had fled "beyond the Ionian sea," Cæsar released Aristobulus from prison with the view of utilising him against Antipater, who in common with the entire Orient had declared for Pompey. Not only did the scheme fail, however, through the poisoning of Aristobulus by those friendly to Pompey, but about the same time his son Alexander was beheaded at Antioch. There now remained only his son Antigonus to contest with Antipater the chieftainship of Judæa. After the defeat of Pompey by Cæsar at Pharsalia in B.C. 48, the astute Antipater at once went over to Cæsar's side and rendered him effective service, which the great Roman did not forget to reward. Hyrcanus was confirmed in the high-priesthood; Antipater was raised to the rank of a Roman citizen, and was granted immunity from taxation. The prospects of the Sadducees were now of the gloomiest. An appeal by Antigonus to have the government conferred upon himself, Cæsar answered only by showering fresh privileges upon his opponents. Hyrcanus was appointed hereditary ethnarch of the Jews, with the civil jurisdiction which he had possessed prior to the "aristocracies" of Gabinius, and got permission to rebuild the walls of Jerusalem; while Antipater was made procurator of Judæa, Samaria, and Galilee. Many privileges were also conferred upon the Jews generally. They were freed from military service, and empowered to manage their own affairs.

Joppa and other Palestinian towns were restored to them, and throughout Asia Minor they were guaranteed full religious liberty.

Although Antipater had been largely instrumental in securing these advantages, and had in consequence earned great popularity, " the principal men among the Jews," *i.e.* the Sadducees, looked askance upon his growing wealth and power. They sought to rescue Hyrcanus from the position of a mere puppet in the hands of the Idumæan, who now shewed that he had an eye to the future by appointing his eldest son Phasael governor of Jerusalem, and his second son Herod governor of Galilee. The latter, a young man of twenty-five,[1] ingratiated himself with the Syrians and with the Roman governor Sextus Cæsar by his summary execution of a robber chief named Hezekiah. But this action brought him into collision with the Sanhedrin, to whom alone it was competent to pronounce a death sentence. At the instigation of the Sadducæan aristocracy, Hyrcanus summoned Herod to appear before that august body to take his trial. This he did, not, however, in garments befitting a culprit, but arrayed in purple, and attended by a bodyguard. Then was seen " the powerlessness of the party which was built upon power." Herod's judges were so overawed that silence prevailed in the assembly until Sameas (? = Shemaiah) made a fearless protest in the name of justice. Poor old Hyrcanus, who had received a

---

[1] The text of Josephus (*Ant.* xiv. 9. 2) reads " fifteen " ; but this is clearly wrong, since at his death, some forty-five years later, Herod was about seventy years of age (*Ant.* xvii. 6. 1). At fifteen, moreover, he could not have filled the position of governor.

threatening letter from Sextus Cæsar, then adjourned
the sitting and urged Herod to flee. On withdrawing
to Damascus the latter was appointed governor of Cœle-
Syria, and soon appeared again before the gates of
Jerusalem with an army to avenge what he chose to
regard as an insult, but was prevailed upon by his father
and brother to abstain from violence, and content himself
with having shewn his power. The episode was
ominously significant in view of Herod's possible future
elevation to the Jewish throne. Indeed the downfall of
the Hasmonæans was no longer doubtful. Sameas
truly told the Sanhedrin that although, according to the
Law, Herod was punishable with death, they had been
too late in putting a proper restraint upon him, and that
from a political point of view he was less blameworthy
than they. After this it is not surprising that the
Herodians began to distinguish between Hyrcanus and
his "evil counsellors!"[1] The assassination of Julius
Cæsar in B.C. 44 led the Jews to chafe more than ever
under the yoke of the Idumæans. Accordingly, when
the crafty Antipater embraced the republican cause,
and became tax-gatherer for the triumvir Crassus, one
of his protégés, Malichus by name, with a view to
preserving Judæa for the Jews, had him cut off by
poison (B.C. 43).

　　After the defeat of Brutus and Cassius by Antony
and Octavian at Philippi in B.C. 42, the position of
the Sadducæan aristocracy became hopeless. As an
opportunist Herod was the apt pupil of his father,
and succeeded in securing the favour of Antony, the
new lord of the East. More than one delegation of

---

[1] Josephus, *Ant.* xiv. 9. 5.

influential Jews appeared before Antony to complain of Phasael and Herod; but so far from paying them any heed, he appointed the sons of his old friend Antipater[1] tetrarchs of Judæa (B.C. 41). Hyrcanus still remained nominally ethnarch as well as high priest; but in reality all political authority was now given into the hands of Phasael and Herod. The latter had already received from Cassius the assurance that he would be made King of Judæa, but he had to pass through a severe ordeal before attaining to this position. There was still another claimant to the throne—Antigonus, the son of Aristobulus II. Realising that the interests of Rome and of Herod were inseparable, and stung by the treatment it had received at the hands of Antony, the Sadducæan party in concert with Antigonus made a last desperate effort to retrieve its fortunes. Two things favoured the attempt—Antony's absence in Egypt, where he was spell-bound by Cleopatra, and the simultaneous invasion of Syria by the Parthians in B.C. 40. With such a situation Herod and Phasael were unable to cope. The former had already defeated Antigonus and his allies, Ptolemy Menneus of Chalcis and Marion of Tyre, but now that the Parthians were at his back the Idumæans were no longer a match for him. The Jews generally supported him as an enemy of Rome. Phasael and Hyrcanus were thrown into prison; and Herod, after securing his family and his belongings in the fortress of Masāda, fled to Rome, where he was declared King of Judæa by the senate. Meanwhile the Parthians had set up Antigonus Mattathias as king and

---

[1] Antony and Antipater had become friends when the former served in Syria under Gabinius, about fifteen years previously (B.C. 57–55).

high priest, and handed over Hyrcanus and Phasael as
his prisoners. Hyrcanus was deported to Babylon, his
ears cropped, so as to disqualify him from ever again
acting as high priest; Phasael gleefully committed
suicide on learning that his brother had escaped. But
although for three years (B.C. 40–37) Antigonus had a
semblance of power, his position was a precarious one.
So soon as the Roman general Ventidius had driven the
Parthians out of Syria, the Hasmonæan king had to
purchase the leniency of the conqueror. A certain
obstacle was thus put in the way of Herod when, in
B.C. 39, he landed at Ptolemais to make good his title to
the kingdom. The support given him by the local
representatives of Rome was so half-hearted that no
headway was made against an opposition that was at
once fanatical and bitter. For two years the war had
dragged on without decisive result, when, in consequence
of a personal interview between Herod and Antony at
the siege of Samosata, the Roman legions under Sosius
were sent against Jerusalem. In B.C. 37 siege was laid
to the capital. While engines of attack were being
prepared, Herod celebrated his marriage with Mariamme
at Samaria, probably deeming it politic under the
circumstances to consummate a union with that beautiful
and high-spirited daughter of the Hasmonæan house.[1]
Returning to Jerusalem, he joined Sosius in his assault
upon the city, which, after a further stubborn resistance
of about two months, fell on the twenty-sixth anniversary
of its capture by Pompey. So ruthless was the slaughter

---

[1] Mariamme, to whom Herod had been betrothed for five years, was the
granddaughter of both Hyrcanus and Aristobulus, and thus represented the
two opposing branches of the Hasmonæan house.

that ensued, that Herod felt constrained by lavish gifts to induce the Romans to depart. Antigonus threw himself at the feet of Sosius, who scornfully called him Antigon*e*, and carried him a prisoner to Antioch, where at Herod's instigation Antony ordered him to be beheaded. Never before had the Romans so dealt with a king. The fall of Antigonus necessarily involved that of the Sadducæan aristocracy which had linked its fortunes to his. With this we reach the end of the second stage in the history of the two great Jewish parties. Herod now assumed the kingdom, and the rule of the Hasmonæans was at an end.

CHAPTER V

THE HERODIAN AGE

CHAPTER V.

The Herodian Age.

IT is impossible to admire the character of the Idumæan Antipater, whose son now occupied the throne of Judæa. He was an obsequious and self-seeking opportunist. Yet it may be truly said that in the peculiar circumstances of the Jews in his time, he did them a far greater service than the aristocratic party opposed to him. Antipater had at least the discernment to see that the struggle against Rome was a hopeless one, whereas his antagonists by their constant and futile insurrections brought much misery upon Palestine.[1] In spite of its obvious advantages, however, the Idumæan dynasty was scorned and detested by the Jewish people. This, indeed, is a leading feature of the historical situation reflected in the Gospels. At the beginning of his reign, Herod had to face the fact that, although controlled by the Pharisees, the great mass of the people viewed his dominion with suppressed indignation. It was therefore necessary for him either by austerity or by politic concession to secure their allegiance.

---

[1] Moreover, " by their opposition to the Romans they were in reality throwing themselves across the path of the Divine purpose, which was working itself out in history by binding the Mediterranean peoples under one form of civil rule, as a preliminary to the advent and propagation of the Christian faith."—Morrison, *The Jews under Roman Rule*, p. 56 f.

He began in true Roman style by proscribing the
leading men of the party opposed to the Idumæan
usurpers. Forty-five Sadducæan nobles were led to the
block, and their property confiscated. The high-priestly
office was shorn of its hereditary character, and put
under the heel of the secular power. Nobodies from
Babylon and Egypt, who could be shifted like pawns
upon a board, were set up and removed at will. Cut
off in this way from the political sphere, the Sadducees
were deprived of what was to them the very breath of
life. To wrangle with the Pharisees about points of
doctrine and ritual was for minds constituted as theirs
were a poor substitute for the high game of politics.
But while Herod lived they had no choice. He was
resolute in his determination to drive back the national
life into the narrow ecclesiastical groove out of which it
had been diverted under Maccabæan auspices. The
third and last stage in the history of the rival Jewish
parties was marked, therefore, by a growing decadence
of the Sadducees, and a corresponding accession of strength
to the Pharisees, who remained unaffected by political
changes. Herod could never hope to win the friendship
of the Sadducees, whose leaders he had slain and superseded by his creatures. He accordingly threw himself
into the arms of the Pharisees, although their leaders,
Polion and Sameas, in counselling the surrender of the
city, had only recommended acceptance of his rule as a
Divine judgment to which it was necessary to submit.
Antipater's son had the shrewdness to perceive that there
was no other course open to him, and that only by
humouring the Pharisees could he hope to sit securely on
his throne. Profiting by the experience of Pompey, he

had accordingly on the capture of Jerusalem restrained
the Roman soldiers from desecrating the Temple. This
consideration for the religious susceptibilities of the Jews
was, however, a mere matter of prudence; it was simply
the price he was ready to pay in order to have a free
hand politically. It did not at all proceed from conviction. Nor did Herod's good understanding with the
Pharisees imply that he shared their fellowship. In
point of fact he held paganism in quite as high esteem as
Judaism. The force of circumstances, however, made it
politic for him to cultivate the friendship of the Pharisees
and Essenes. If many of these refused to take the oath
of allegiance to him, this meant no special antipathy
to Herod; it represented their religious attitude towards
all human supremacy. That Herod should have been
willing in their case to dispense with the act of fealty
may certainly be interpreted as a mark of esteem. At
the same time, had he apprehended that in their refusal
of the oath there lurked the least political danger, their
religious scruples would not have had for him the weight
of a feather.

It took Herod more than a decade to establish his
power. In his general policy of confining Jewish national
life to the sphere of religion he had, of course, the approval
of the Pharisees, who eschewed politics altogether. Still
in the popular estimation he was regarded with a grudge
as the destroyer of the Maccabæan sovereignty, and of
the liberties enjoyed under it. After having tasted the
sweets of freedom, the Jews were in no mood to endure
a foreign yoke; and this was virtually what they had to
bear, for what was Herod but the minion of the Romans?
Besides the dislike of the populace, he had to reckon

with the hostility of the Egyptian Cleopatra, who not
only assisted his mother-in-law Alexandra in securing
the high-priesthood for Aristobulus, but also induced
Antony to make over to her some of the choicest portions
of Herod's dominions, including the rich and fertile
region of Jericho.   But Herod's position was chiefly
imperilled by the still surviving members of the Hasmonæan house, on whom the national hopes were
evidently set.   His marriage with Mariamme, and the
honour paid to Hyrcanus, who had returned from exile,
failed to reconcile all parties to his rule.   These politic
steps could not alter the fact that he had supplanted the
dynasty.   During the first twelve years of his reign he
gave full vent to his jealousy by handing over its remaining representatives—the youthful Aristobulus III.,
the aged Hyrcanus II., his own wife Mariamme, his
mother-in-law Alexandra, the daughter of Hyrcanus II.,
and the sons of Babas—one after another to execution.
Herod had thus at length consolidated his power by the
extermination of all possible rivals.   Except in so far as
it was still represented in his own children, the Maccabæan
line had become extinct.   For the rest, he had secured
his fortunes by promptly espousing the cause of the
conqueror after the victory of Cæsar (Augustus) over
Antony at the battle of Actium.   In spite of his outward success, however, he was made miserable by the
jealousies and hatreds which permeated his own household.

When he had obtained a free hand, Herod shewed
himself no common ruler.   But although in his day he
was " the brain of the East," the task devolving upon him
—that of pleasing at once his imperial masters and his

Jewish subjects—was a hopeless one. He was placed
on the horns of a dilemma; it was impossible to gratify
Augustus without offending his own subjects. As the
patron of heathenism he could not at the same time be
the friend of Judaism. By effectually maintaining peace
and order, and by doing his utmost to introduce Western
civilisation into Palestine, Herod gave satisfaction to his
Roman master, and ensured the external stability of his
kingdom; but he found it a much harder thing to please the
Jews. To a certain extent, indeed, he outwardly conformed
to the Law. He could rank himself among the circumcised; he abstained from eating swine's flesh; he avoided
the use of graven images on his buildings and coins. The
projected marriage of his sister Salome to the Arabian
Syllæus was abandoned because the latter declined to
conform to the Jewish customs. But all this did not
constitute him in reality a Jew. The people hated him
as a double-dyed alien who in his own person represented
at once the untitled vassal of a foreign power and the
upstart "slave of the Hasmonæans."[1] He had therefore
to rule by coercion, by nepotism, by extortion, and by
espionage. His own creatures and relatives made up to
him for the counsels of the elders, his policy from the first
having been to weaken the Sanhedrin, and to make public
officials, from the high priest downwards, entirely dependent on his own caprice. It was, of course, on the
religious side that the keenest friction was apt to be generated. On one occasion loud protests were made against
the imperial trophies which he placed in the theatre
at Jerusalem. These simple suits of armour hung upon
wooden frames the people mistook for statues, until they

[1] So described in the Talmud.

were disillusioned by ocular demonstration of their real
character.   Although the public indignation was thus for
the time dissolved in laughter, many continued to resent
the introduction of heathen innovations.   Ten citizens
banded themselves together to kill Herod in the theatre;
but the plot was discovered by one of his spies, and they
were executed forthwith.   The lynching of the informer
shortly thereafter was a plain intimation that his escape
from death was viewed as a public calamity.   But the
restiveness of the people only added to the despotism
of his rule.   Not that he wished to institute a reign of
terror pure and simple.   Even had he been disposed to
emulate the persecuting violence of Antiochus Epiphanes,
Hellenisation by force was no longer practicable in view
of the ardent national sentiment which had now grown
up among the people.

While, therefore, his rule was essentially despotic,
he strove to commend himself to the Jews by laying
them under special obligation to him in various directions.
In times of acute distress he remitted part of the burden
of taxation under which they groaned.   During a famine
he sold his plate and furniture in order to feed and
clothe the poor, and to supply them with seed-corn.   To
northern Palestine, which was infested with robber
bands, he restored security and order by assailing the
marauders in their most inaccessible fastnesses, and so
"prepared in the wilderness a highway for the Christ."
His influence with the Roman court was steadily used
for the protection of the Jews of the Dispersion.   By the
construction of the commodious haven of Cæsarea he
gave an impetus to trade and to the material prosperity
of Palestine.   But his crowning service to the Jewish

nation was the rebuilding of the Temple at Jerusalem. Only specially trained priests were employed upon the work, which was begun in B.C. 20, and was still going on in the days of our Lord.[1] Its beauty was proverbial, and impressed all beholders. Numerous Corinthian pillars, with sculptured chapiters, lent an aspect of grandeur to the entire structure. " Master," said one of the disciples of Jesus, " see what manner of stones and what buildings are here." [2]

These benefactions certainly did much to temper the hatred with which Herod was regarded by his subjects. Deeply sensible of what the Jewish nation owed to a prince who had raised it to a position of influence by securing for it the steady support of Rome, some even fancied that in him they saw the Messiah Himself, the Deliverer promised of old to Israel,—a theory which seemed to gain support from the fact that the date chosen for the dedication of the Temple was the anniversary of his own coronation. Such a view, of course, emptied the work of the Messiah of all spiritual significance. But as a purely political party the Herodians, as they were called, considered that, broadly speaking, the Messianic aspirations of the Israelitish people were sufficiently met by the Herodian dynasty. They were satisfied with " the leaven of Herod." The spirit of his kingdom, as a combination of Hellenism and Judaism fitted to enable Jews to make the best of both worlds, strongly appealed to them. But these sentiments could not prevail in Israel. Although Herodians and

---

[1] " Then said the Jews, Forty and six years was this temple in building, and wilt thou rear it up in three days?"—John ii. 19.

[2] Mark xiii. 1.

Pharisees might agree in their opposition to Roman rule, they had little else in common. Nothing could ever induce the populace to look with favour upon the man who had risen to power by crushing and exterminating the beloved Maccabæan line, who degraded the high-priesthood by bestowing it upon puppets of his own, and who even while conferring upon the Jewish nation an enormous boon in the rebuilding of the Temple, insulted them by erecting over the great gate a golden eagle. Thus all Herod's efforts to win popularity failed in the end. As a ruler he never knew the luxury of a people's love. Having wooed the Jews in vain, he could only fall back on the resources of the tyrant. As it was, many refused to take the oath of allegiance which he sought to impose, and in the heart of the nation there grew up a silent but deep antagonism to the king.

During the latter part of his reign Herod was kept mentally on the rack by the intrigues of his household. These overshadowed everything else, and were of the most sensational Oriental type. A man who had married ten wives could scarcely expect his domestic atmosphere to be perfectly calm; but Herod's court became the scene of diabolical slanders and plots which issued only too surely in storm and bloodshed. His jealous nature exposed him in a singular degree to the operations of the traducer and backbiter, with the result that he was made to drink the cup of misery to the dregs. All along, not unlikely, he had been troubled with misgivings lest the murder of Aristobulus should prove only the first step in a fateful course. This is

[1] Cf. Matt. xxii. 16; Mark xii. 13; and see Note 18, p. 386.

finely brought out in Qhe drama of Mr. Stephen
Phillips :—

> Dimly I dread lest having struck this blow
> Of my free will, I by this very act
> Have signed and pledged me to a second blow
> Against my will. What if the powers permit
> The doing of that deed which serves us now;
> Then of that very deed do make a spur
> To drive us to some act that we abhor?
> The first step is with us; then all the road,
> The long road is with Fate. O horrible !
> If he being dead demand another death.

At any rate, Herod reaped only what he had sown. In
its melancholy close his reign inevitably corresponded to
its evil beginning. The executioner of the Hasmonæans
became the executioner of his own sons, and only discovered when too late that he had been duped.

If the closing years of Herod's reign were characterised by domestic misery and by remorse for the slaughter
of his innocent sons, they also witnessed a change in his
attitude to Judaism. This became one of increasing
disregard. Neither the Law nor the customs of the
Jews received the same consideration at his hands as
formerly. He seems to have conceived a dislike of
everything Jewish, and did not hesitate wantonly to
outrage Jewish feeling, as in the matter of the golden
eagle. In this way he came into collision even with the
Pharisees. It was not merely the fact that six thousand
of them refused to swear allegiance to him that caused
his mistrust ; he knew that this was due to religious
scruples, and had no political significance. The crux of
the situation lay in the influence which the Pharisees
exercised at court. This continued undiminished. Consequently they were, as Josephus puts it, "in a great

capacity of opposing kings," and by " inveigling a set of women " in Herod's household contrived to thwart his designs. The strength of their influence may be inferred from the rigorous measures which he adopted against them : " Herod slew such of the Pharisees as were principally accused."

With all this it is still the case that the reign of Herod was the golden age of Pharisaism. It was doubtless owing to his goodwill that the representation and influence of the scribes and Pharisees in the Sanhedrin increased. At the time when he had himself defied it under Hyrcanus II., their spokesman Sameas did not possess the commanding influence which the scribes, as members of the chief council, enjoyed at the time of Christ. It was during Herod's reign that they gained complete ascendancy over the religious life of the people. This period is therefore of epoch-making importance for the development of legalistic Judaism. Under the impulse derived from the Maccabæan age it now began with a quiet but fierce intensity to grow up into a detailed and elaborate system. With the possible exceptions of Simon the priest in the time of Jesus Sirach, and of Simon ben Shetach in the days of Jannæus and Alexandra, almost nothing is known of the scribes who lived before the Herodian period. Then, however, certain individual scribes come significantly to the front. Among these the most famous are Hillel and Shammai, who, shortly before the Advent of Christ, founded rival schools. While this proves their import-ance for the development of Jewish law, it does not imply that much is known with certainty about their personal life. Apart from legendary material, our knowledge regarding Hillel is practically limited to this—that he was the most famous scribe of his age, and was marked by a singularly kind and gentle disposition. We have a reflexion of his character in his own precept: " Be a disciple of Aaron, seek peace, love men, and devote thyself to the study of the law." Shammai was of a sterner and more uncompromising spirit than Hillel. He insisted upon the most rigid compliance with the precepts of the Law. The Mishna records that on the birth of a grandchild during the Feast of Tabernacles he had the ceiling removed and the room roofed in with boughs, that the infant too might keep the festival.

The distinctive tendencies of the two masters are reflected in their respective schools. The school of Hillel dealt with legal questions in a somewhat broader spirit than that of Shammai, but in reality there was no radical difference between these two schools of scribes. Their disagreements were about things which we should regard as trifles, as, for example, whether it was lawful to eat an egg laid on a feast day, or whether on a holy day one durst carry a ladder from one pigeon-house to another. In spite of some lofty ethical utterances standing to their credit, both Hillelites and Shammaïtes were casuists hampered by tradition. Narrow, however, as were the differences which separated them, great heat and bitterness were generated by their disputes. Now that the Pharisees were for the most part to be found in the schools, while the Sadducees were practically confined to the Temple, and these old traditional foes came less and less into contact, the Pharisees turned their weapons against one another. They felt what they reckoned the

errors of fellow-believers to be a much more serious
thing than the scepticism of the godless Sadducees; and
so strongly was the partisan spirit developed that they
sometimes resorted to violence. " This was a dark day,"
says the Jerusalem Talmud, " like that on which the
golden calf was made. The Shammaïtes killed some of
the Hillelites." [1]

In the Herodian age the Law became more and
more the authoritative basis of all regulations as to
worship and conduct. Owing to the tendency towards
a stricter limitation of the canon of Scripture, the naïve
method of obtaining guidance with reference to problems
of the present by the issue of pseudonymous writings
purporting to be revelations given to the pious in ancient
times no longer found favour. A solution was sought
in another direction—that of technical exegesis; and
here Hillel seems to have been the pioneer. He is said
to have laid a broad foundation for the industry of the
scribes by introducing certain new methods of interpretation, the underlying principle of which is the necessity
of this technical derivation from Scripture in the case of
every proposition advanced, in order to its recognition
as valid. And this principle he succeeded in establishing
so firmly that in the New Testament the method of
scriptural proof is used and accepted throughout. The
Sheba Middoth, or *seven rules*, of exegesis which found
recognition with the later rabbis are ascribed to Hillel.
These were the argument from the less to the greater;
the argument from analogy; the establishment of a
principle from a single text; comparison of a plurality
of texts in order to establish a main proposition;

[1] *Shabbath*, fol. iii. 3.

illustration of the general by the particular and of the
particular by the general; the use of one passage to
explain another; and attention to the light derivable from
the context. Through the expansion of the fifth into
eight, and the combination of the sixth with the second,
these rules were afterwards brought to thirteen, and embodied in every Jewish prayer-book. Although still of
value for hermeneutics, they were often so applied by the
rabbis as to support the most absurd conclusions. And
while, through the necessity for all legal maxims being
deduced from the Torah itself, Holy Scripture was
recognised as the sole authority, its authority was really
of little worth so long as by means of artificial exegesis
the entire Halacha could be placed under its ægis.
The inevitable result was the subordination of Scripture
to tradition. What availed it that the law of custom
had to find scriptural sanction, so long as the exposition
of Scripture itself was in the hands of the schools? If
the derivation of tradition from Scripture was a fiction,
the subordination of Scripture to tradition was a reality.
Although the scribes were not yet called rabbis in the
time of Herod the Great, what is known of them and
their rival schools entirely accords with the portraiture
drawn of the scribes and Pharisees in the Gospels. Not
content with claiming that the oral as well as the written
Law was revealed by God to Moses, they even exalted
the former above the latter, rejecting the commandments
of God that they might keep their own tradition.[1]

---

[1] Mark vii. 9. Rabbi Hillel is credited with having arranged the oral law
into six *sedarim* or orders, and it was committed to writing by R. Jehudah,
surnamed the holy, in A.D. 191, that the memory of it might not perish, whatever should become of the schools of the rabbis. This written collection is
called the Mishna, or "repetition" of the Law, and claims to be the oral

The type of piety created by this whole method of dealing with Scripture was as strained and artificial as the method itself. It was largely a matter of memory, of devotion to the letter as contrasted with the spirit of the sacred books, and of aptitude in applying texts or passages from them, regardless of the context, to the varied circumstances of life. That even such an attitude towards Scripture was not wholly fatal to godliness we may well believe, since earnest application to the oracles of God, however vitiated by such mechanical conceptions, must always be productive of some good. Yet the methods of the scribes were obviously detrimental to real piety, which is not a feat of memory but a fact of

Law delivered to Moses *plus* the accumulated traditions of the intervening centuries. The text of the Mishna furnished the basis of a fresh commentary named the *Gemara* or "complement," added as years went on, and composed of notes and discussions by famous teachers, together with a great deal of legendary matter. The combined texts of the Mishna and Gemara form the *Talmud*, which exists in two recensions, the Palestinian or Jerusalem, and the Babylonian. In both the Mishna is the same, but the Gemaras are different, the one having been arranged in the school of Tiberias, the other in that of Sura. The Babylonian is more voluminous, but less valuable, than the Palestinian. The Mishna, and not a little of the Gemara as well, is really the product of the period between the Exile and the Advent, although the Talmud was not closed in either of its versions till the fifth or sixth century of our era. That it is not absolutely devoid of system and rule, the internal division into Halacha and Haggada itself shews. Both were founded on *Midrash*, *i.e.* the searching into, or investigation of, the biblical text. The Halachic Midrash was "the exegetic development of passages of the Law"; the Haggadic Midrash was the working up of the historic and didactic parts of Scripture, an elaboration of them by the free use of the legendary element, suitable to the views and requirements of the age. As the Aramaic dialect had come to be the vernacular of Palestine, it was considered necessary to accompany the reading of the Scriptures in the synagogue by a running translation or paraphrase known as the *Targum* (interpretation). These Targumim were subsequently written down, the most famous being that of Onkelos (to the Pentateuch), and that of Jonathan (to the Prophets). Although not published until, perhaps, the third or fourth century of our era, they are undoubtedly based upon earlier works, and contain fragments as old as the time of John Hyrcanus.

experience, and which is concerned not with theoretical hair-splitting but with the most momentous issues of life.

We have already remarked that the character of the Pharisees is revealed not only in their opposition to the Sadducæan aristocracy, but also in their opposition to the plebeian and uneducated section of the community.[1] This latter antagonism probably dates from the Herodian age, although it was not till the latter part of the first century A.D. that it reached its full height. Practically from the beginning of the Christian era the Pharisee shared the Horatian sentiment,

Odi profanum vulgus et arceo.

There was at this time a transference of the exclusiveness long shewn by the Jews towards Gentiles, to men of their own nation. Members of opposing parties treated each other like heathen. With the arrogance of conscious power the Pharisees began to view with contempt whatever was unconnected with their own party. Hence the ever sharper distinction drawn between the Ḥăbērim and the Am-hăārez.

In the Old Testament the latter term is used in no depreciatory sense to designate the mass of the people as distinguished from the nobility. Now, however, it came to denote the people from whom the Pharisees separated themselves, and it obtained currency even as a term of reproach for individuals. "He is an Am-hăārez," was about the most contemptuous thing that could be said of a man. In the dogmatic deliverance

---

[1] See Note 19, p. 387, on Friedländer's view with regard to the Am-hăārez.

13

reported in the Fourth Gospel—"this multitude which
knoweth not the law are accursed"—we have a significant reflexion of the attitude of the Pharisees towards the
Am-hăārez, both individually and collectively. They
were outcasts from the fellowship of the learned. Their
sin lay in their want of culture. Those who identified
piety with learning despised them as an uneducated
mob, ignorant alike of written law and oral tradition.
If they did not perhaps quite correspond to the "babes"
and "little ones" so tenderly spoken of by Jesus in the
Gospels, they were certainly the "sinners" as distinguished from the pious Pharisees of the age. While
the category of Am-hăārez embraced all the ignorant
and unlearned, it was specially associated in the minds
of the pious with notorious sinners, and with hated
publicans who stooped to be catspaws of the foreign
lords. Hence the deep offence taken by the Pharisees
because Jesus did not hold Himself aloof from the dregs
of society: "this man receiveth sinners and eateth with
them."

The cleavage became specially acute after the
destruction of Jerusalem. What intercourse there was
between Hăbēr and Am-hăārez was strictly regulated, so
that the two classes were almost as effectually separated
as both were from the heathen. Intermarriage was
regarded as a calamity. While during the earlier part
of the first century the haughty scorn of the Pharisees
did not extinguish the feeling of respectful awe with
which the common people looked upon them as the
preservers of the Law, by its close—if we may trust the
testimony of a later time—the situation had become
embittered to the last degree. The Pharisees were

repaid in their own coin, and exposed to the hatred and contempt of what John Knox might have termed "the rascal multitude." While R. Akiba was still himself a plebeian, he is reported to have said, "O that a lettered man would cross my path, I would bite him like an ass."

Although the respectful attitude of the people towards the Pharisaic party was scarcely affected by the rise of the rival schools of Hillel and Shammai, the leadership of the Pharisees was gradually but surely superseded through the formation of the new party of the Zealots. This was a fanatical war party which aimed at the recovery of Jewish independence. During the Idumæan supremacy there had been a steady denationalisation of Israelitish piety; Herod made it his constant care to suppress the national spirit. But it revived with his death, and the Zealots were its leading representatives. They constituted no "fourth philosophical sect," as Josephus asserts, but were simply fanatical extremists who departed from the recognised non-political standpoint of the Pharisees. They were, in fact, dissatisfied Pharisees who formed a party of their own on the basis of combining politics with religion. While the Pharisees were pious churchmen, the Zealots were pious patriots. They were prepared to fight for their country as well as for the Law. For them patriotism was inseparable from religion. Their distinctive mark was this, that they held the recognition of foreign supremacy to be derogatory to the majesty of God; they refused to call any man lord. Tired of waiting for the realisation of the Messianic hope, they were eager to hasten it by an appeal to the sword. They took Phinehas for their patron saint, did their utmost to stir up discontent with Roman rule, and advocated a resort to war in order to wipe out the stain of foreign domination in Israel. Their zeal, however, was not according to knowledge. Although the Messianic hope was, so to speak, their life-element, the attitude taken up by them was thoroughly antagonistic to that hope, which is founded upon the conception of an ideal and invisible kingdom opposed to, and ultimately destined to supplant, the earthly kingdom. The pure form of this expectation is reflected not in the frenzied efforts of the Zealots, but in the beautiful picture of political passivity and religious faith drawn in the *Book of Daniel*, which represents men as content to count the days till the Almighty shall suddenly hurl from power the last of the heathen dynasties, and transfer the dominion to the saints.

Herod's surviving sons were Archelaus, Antipas, and Philip. Augustus divided his kingdom among them in terms of his last will, Archelaus being named, however, not king but ethnarch of Judæa; Antipas, tetrarch of Galilee and Peræa; and Philip, tetrarch of the north-eastern districts. During the time of our Lord's ministry Galilee was still under the sway of Herod Antipas, who was the slayer of John the Baptist. But Judæa was then no longer subject to Archelaus, who in the year A.D. 6 was deposed and banished by Augustus on a joint petition from Jews and Samaritans. As a part of the Roman province of Syria, its affairs were administered by procurators whose headquarters were in Cæsarea. Of these procurators or governors, Pontius Pilate was the sixth in order, and continued in office for about ten years. He was on a visit to Jerusalem

in connexion with the feast of the Passover when Jesus
was arraigned before him.   Philip was the most peace-
loving and popular of the Herodian princes, and ruled
as tetrarch for thirty-seven years.   It was to his
dominions—" the coasts of Cæsarea Philippi "—that
our Lord retired in order to make clear to His disciples
the fact of His approaching death.

The abolition of the vassal kingship and the establishment of direct Roman rule proved distinctly beneficial
to the Sadducees, who found themselves again at the
helm of the national government, and the official
representatives of the Jews in all transactions with the
sovereign power.   High priest and Sanhedrin were
invested with something of their old importance, and
had therefore every reason to be content under the
Romans.   That they developed the haughty spirit so
frequently begotten of place and power, is evident from
the narratives in the Acts and in Josephus, as well as
from the Talmud.   Their relations with the Pharisees,
however, were no longer actively, but only theoretically,
hostile ; they recognised the futility of disputing the
ecclesiastical rule of their opponents.   At the same
time, Church affairs were relegated to a position of much
less prominence than they had occupied hitherto.   True
to their traditions, the Sadducees embraced the
opportunity of advancing their own personal ends, and
of consolidating their own power as an aristocracy.
Nor were they at all scrupulous as to the means which
they employed.   In particular, their unprincipled
exploitation of the Zealots, whom they made their hired
assassins, was highly discreditable to them.   And it
was to recoil upon their own heads, for it was through

the revolt organised by the Zealots that they finally
lost their power. It is, however, to their credit that,
although drawn into the movement against their will,
the Sadducæan leaders performed their part like men,
and "went under with honour." Ananos, son of the
Ananos or Annas of the New Testament, was the last
representative of the ancient Jewish priesthood.
Speaking of the downfall of these aristocrats, Renan
strikingly says, " It was a world that disappeared."

That the new arrangement was probably as galling
to the Pharisees as it was gratifying to their opponents,
may be inferred from the praises bestowed by Josephus
and the Talmud upon Herod Agrippa I., whose brief
reign was to them like an oasis in the desert. This
king shewed all the adroitness of his grandfather in
humouring the religious susceptibilities of the Jews. It
was his policy, while resident in Palestine, to leave no
Pharisaic tradition unobserved. He even persuaded the
Emperor Caligula not to press his extraordinary demand
to have his statue erected in the Temple of Jerusalem.
Every day he offered the appointed sacrifice. His
persecution of the Christian Church [1] was of a piece with
the rest of his policy, for he judged that nothing would
be more acceptable to the Jews than the extirpation of
the Christians. But Herod's reign was of short duration,
and after his death the Pharisees found themselves again
in adversity. No doubt the Roman rule was less
irksome than the Idumæan, but after all this was in
their eyes a trifling matter compared with the fact that
the heathen paid no regard to the Law. At first they
transgressed it unwittingly, and then of set purpose.

[1] Acts xii.

With the Pharisees no civil benefits could atone for ecclesiastical insult, and they repaid the latter in bitter hatred of the Romans. Yet, in contrast to the Zealots, they were no advocates of war; and consequently, when at length the Sadducees had succumbed to the Zealots, and the Zealots to the Romans, there were none left to dispute with them the inheritance.

In spite of the mistaken attitude of the Zealots, their cause made headway owing to the worthlessness of the high priests and the misgovernment of the Romans. The discontent which had already found repeated expression under Cumanus (A.D. 48–52) developed into chronic rebellion under Felix (52–60). Not only the masses, but some even of the aristocracy, rallied to the support of the Zealots. The country was seething with revolution. Marauding bands seized the property of such as were loyal to the Roman rule; and although Felix had many of them crucified, the disorders continued. In place of the "robbers," as Josephus rather inaccurately terms them, there arose the Sicarii or Assassins,[1] whose deliberate policy it was to eliminate their antagonists by the use of the dagger. They represented the extreme section of the Zealots, and resolutely carried out their murderous designs. The *sica*, or short curved weapon from which they derived their name, was carried under their cloaks. So many friends of the Romans were secretly stabbed, especially at the festal seasons, that even the streets of Jerusalem became highly unsafe. It was a time of the wildest religious and political excitement. The trouble under

---

[1] So R.V. of Acts xxi. 38. The literal translation would be "dagger-men." A.V. renders "murderers."

Festus (60–62) equalled that under Felix. A reign of
terror had been created by the deeds of the revolutionists,
and hostility to Rome grew more and more intense.
After the appearance of a false Messiah who led the
people into the wilderness, and the death of Festus, who
failed to suppress him, Jerusalem was in a state of
anarchy. Under the procurators Albinus (62–64) and
Florus (64–66) the atmosphere became so charged with
electricity as to render a storm inevitable. Albinus was
an unprincipled money-grabber, who contrived to obtain
gifts both from the high priest Ananias and from the
Sicarii, while not interfering with the freedom of either;
Florus was an unscrupulous tyrant, compared with whom
even Albinus was a pattern of virtue. Roused to fury
by the action of Florus in robbing the Temple, and in
spite of the dissuasion of King Agrippa and leading
citizens both among the priests and the Pharisees, the
people rose in rebellion. It was resolved to discontinue
the daily sacrifice for the emperor. Cestius Gallus, the
governor of Syria, having made an ineffectual attempt
to storm the Temple mount, the principal men among
the Jews now identified themselves with the rebels.
Inspired by the memory of former victories over imperial
troops, the nation as a whole set itself to withstand the
might of Rome. But this was a vain dream; the
conflict was too unequal. After the Romans, aided by
the half-hearted measures of Josephus, who acted as
Jewish commander in Galilee, had subdued that bulwark
of Judæa, they laid siege to the capital. Dissatisfied
with the conduct of the war hitherto, the Zealots, who
were " the Jacobins of the Jewish revolution," forcibly
took the reins into their own hands, and, led by John of

Gischala, turned their weapons against all Jews who declined to adopt their revolutionary programme. Other parties were formed by one Simon ben Giora (= "son of the proselyte"), and by his son Eleazar. The internecine strife of these warring factions had largely consumed the strength of the Jews when, in A.D. 70, Titus appeared before the gates of Jerusalem. Only the ominous thud of the Roman battering-rams availed to stop the civil war. During five months the Jews offered a brave and desperate resistance. Then the city fell into the hands of the conquerors, and national recovery became hopeless.

As the influence of the Zealots increased, that of the Pharisees decreased. The latter, as the champions of ecclesiastical piety, could take no share in wild schemes of conquest; and after one of their leaders, Simon the son of that Gamaliel at whose feet sat St. Paul, had vainly made a joint effort with the priestly aristocracy to detach the people from the fanatical leadership of John of Gischala, they simply stood aside, and either retired into private life or fled from Jerusalem. But if for a brief period the victory lay with the votaries of aggressive political patriotism, the Pharisees not only regained their ascendancy, but became more powerful than ever, after the destruction of Jerusalem. This event directly led to the fall of the Sanhedrin and the exaltation of the rabbis. Now that Israel was once more a purely religious community, the doctors of the Law exercised undisputed sway. Rabbinical studies were carried on at various centres. The chief school, which was at Jabne (Jamnia), was founded by Johanan ben Sakkai, and had lustre. shed upon it by the great

name of Gamaliel II. (A.D. 90–110). Other famous
scribes of the period were the gentle R. Joshua, the
inflexible R. Elieser, and the popular R. Akiba, in whose
time, and probably at whose instigation, the oral Law
was first codified.   Although Pharisaic Judaism thus at
length triumphed over Jewish Hellenism, the national
spirit was not yet by any means extinguished.   In the
time of Hadrian the great revolt under bar-Cochba once
more plunged the country into a sanguinary strife which
lasted for more than three years.   On this occasion,
encouraged by the war between the Romans and the
Parthians, the Jews of the Dispersion also—in Egypt
and Cyrene, in Cyprus and Mesopotamia—caught the
infection, and were not easily suppressed.

For centuries, then, as Bousset remarks, "Palestinian
Judaism had been tossed to and fro between the two
poles, between a piety that stood aloof from everything
worldly, and therewith also from the national life, and
a wild political fanaticism.   In the Diaspora the situation was not materially different." [1]   Henceforth Judaism
was to bear an exclusively religious stamp.   At the same
time, with all its potentialities, it never grew into a
universal religion.   It failed to emancipate itself from
the national spirit, and to cut itself adrift from the
national life.   It gloried in its exclusiveness.   A Jew
regarded it as nothing less than a religious duty to keep
himself apart from other men.   Thus in spite of the
dissolution of the bond of State connexion, Judaism was
doomed to remain a sectional religion.   It was held fast
in the fetters of legalism, and circumscribed by the conditions of life peculiar to a single people.

[1] *Die Rel. des Jud.* p. 188.

The snapping of the political tie led only to a more rigid withdrawal from the world on the part of a nation "which could not live and could not die." In nothing, moreover, are the limitations of the later Judaism more manifest than in the central place given by it to the hope of the future. Notwithstanding the actual wreck of the national life, the pious Jew conjured up to himself a glorious future in which Israel should once more see palmy days, and should occupy a position of lordship on the earth. This became the dream of his life and the core of his faith.

No sketch of the influences at work in the Jewish life of this epoch would be adequate without a reference to the somewhat shadowy figures known as the Essenes. Although represented by Josephus as a third Jewish party, strictly speaking they were no such thing. They aimed at being, and were, simply a religious force. The Essenes are nowhere expressly mentioned either in Scripture or in the Talmud, and both in its origin and meaning the name remains obscure.[1] Seeing, however, that Josephus refers to Essenes as existing in the time of the Maccabæan prince Jonathan, and alludes to an Essene named Judas as living in the reign of Aristobulus I., the sect cannot have originated later than the middle of the second century B.C. According to Friedländer, its beginnings go back to the golden age of the Wisdom literature, and Essenism is to be regarded as the development of one of the prevailing religious tendencies

---

[1] The most likely derivation is from the Aramaic חֲסֵי, *pious*, plural חֲסֵין, equivalent to the form Ἐσσηνοί, and in the emphatic state חֲסֵיָא, equivalent to the form Ἐσσαῖοι. Lightfoot would derive from חֲשָׁאִים, "silent ones," *i.e.* with reference to their secrets.

in pre-Maccabæan Judaism, in short, as the ripe fruit of Jewish Hellenism.[1]

For the facts we are dependent upon Philo, Josephus, and the Roman historian Pliny. The two first agree in reckoning the number of the Essenes at about four thousand. Although found in every town in Palestine, they shewed a preference for villages. According to Pliny, they dwelt mainly in the neighbourhood of the Dead Sea. In the sources they are portrayed as a compact, well-organised body. They were really an esoteric brotherhood or monastic order, and as such were bound by the most rigid rules. Admission to the order was solemnised by the threefold gift of an apron, a white robe, and a mattock (symbols, presumably, of abstinence and purity), followed only upon a lengthened and double novitiate, and necessitated the taking of tremendous oaths of absolute obedience to the presidents, openness towards the members, and secrecy towards outsiders respecting the doctrines of the brotherhood. When Josephus speaks of four classes of Essenes, he includes, besides the regular members of the order, the junior and senior novices. The composition of the fourth class is not so clear; some think of the boys received with a view to their being trained in the principles of Essenism, others, of the guild of presidents. Discipline was rigorously enforced, and in cases of heinous transgression took the form of expulsion. Judgments were pronounced by a court of at least a hundred members, and were irreversible. The Essenes lived a communistic life in special quarters of their own. All

---

[1] *Die Religiösen Bewegungen innerhalb des Judentums im Zeitalter Jesu*, p. 114.

their belongings were common property, administered by chosen stewards for behoof of the entire order. This applied to food, housing, and even clothing; while in every town provision was made for shewing hospitality to journeying brethren. The latter circumstance raises an interesting question, namely, For what purpose did they travel? From the fact that open houses everywhere awaited them, it may be inferred that they travelled much. That their object was not merchandise or gain is certain, and Friedländer very pertinently asks, " What can they have had in view but propagandism? " This, of course, fits in well with his view that, like the " Wise " before them, and the Apocalyptists after them, they were the teachers of the people,[1] although they hedged themselves about with mysterious forms, and influenced the masses for the most part only indirectly through their pupils and adherents.

In respect of manners and customs, the Essenes had many peculiarities.[2] They wore a distinctive dress. While sending gifts to the Temple, they offered no animal sacrifices, deeming their own lustrations superior in point of purity. Theirs was a fellowship based not upon sacrifice, but apparently upon sacrament. Their midday common meal was at the same time a solemn diet of worship, a holy sacrament to which they came clad in white after having by a cold bath cleansed themselves on their return from the fields. A purifying bath had also to be taken in the event of contact with a foreigner, or even with an Essene of a lower grade. In

[1] This is denied by Lipsius. See Note 20, p. 388.
[2] Cf. the somewhat analogous case of the curious modern Russian sect of the Doukhobors. See Note 21, p. 389.

bathing and in performing natural functions they behaved with extreme modesty. Whether they abstained
from flesh and wine is uncertain, the generally accepted
view that they did so being based only on the analogy
of the practice of kindred sects such as the Therapeutæ
and Ebionites. But they forbade marriage, swearing of
oaths, and anointing with oil. Slavery and war they
abhorred. Renouncing trade as tending to covetousness,
they earned their livelihood by manual labour; the
majority of them were engaged in agriculture. They
were content with the same simple fare day by day; nor
were their clothes and shoes replaced until utterly worn
out. Their ideal, in short, was that of the simple, ascetic,
gentle life. They strove to live in conformity to nature.
Equally distinguished for their philanthropy and for their
piety, they were usually regarded as paragons of virtue.

It is perhaps a not unnatural result of their ardent
pursuit of the ethical, that less is known about the
doctrines of the Essenes than about their religious and
ascetic practices. That they occupied a peculiar position
both philosophically and theologically there can, however,
be no doubt. The statement of Josephus that they
diligently studied " the writings of the ancients " leaves
it uncertain whether the allusion is to the Scriptures,
or to their own esoteric books, or to such works as
those of Pythagoras. In any case, as philosophic
mystics who laid great stress upon morals and theology,
and cared little about logic and physics, they zealously
cultivated sacred science. If they investigated the curative
powers of roots and the medicinal properties of stones,[1]

---

[1] Josephus, *B. J.* ii. 8. 6. In this passage, which Friedländer considers
the key to the investigation of the kernel of Essenism, it must be admitted,

it was probably not so much the welfare of the body that they had in view as the development of their apocalyptic gnosis. In view of the sentiments expressed by the Chronicler and by the son of Sirach,[1] it is at least questionable whether their acting as "medicine men"[2] would have been regarded as consistent with a claim to superior piety. The religious ideas of the Essenes appear to have been essentially Jewish, but with certain decided exceptions or modifications. In respect of their belief in Providence, which was more absolute than that of the Pharisees; in respect of their veneration for Moses and the Law; and in respect of their sabbath observance, which was of the strictest possible type, they were Hebrews of the Hebrews. Apparently also, as a guarantee of ceremonial purity, their food was prepared and blessed by priests of Aaron's house,[3] while the allegorical interpretation of Scripture had a place in their worship. Intimately acquainted with the discourses of the prophets, many of them, moreover, were held in high esteem as foretellers of future events; indeed almost all whose names are known to us figure as seers or as interpreters of dreams.[4] At the same time the standpoint of the Essenes was marked by some curious deviations from Judaism. They adopted a dualistic anthropology not indigenous to Jewish thought. They did not hold the Pharisaic doctrine of the resurrection of the body, but spoke simply of the immortality

bodily well-being is specified as being, equally with spiritual, the object aimed at.

[1] Ecclus. xxxviii. 15; 2 Chron. xvi. 12. But see Chapter I. p. 53.

[2] Morrison, *The Jews under Roman Rule*, p. 336.

[3] Josephus, *Ant.* xviii. 1. 5; *B. J.* ii. 8. 5.

[4] *Ibid., Ant.* xii. 11. 2, xv. 10. 5, xvii. 13. 3.

of the soul. The material part of man they viewed as perishable; the spiritual, as destined to live for ever. Having come out of the purest ether in order to be imprisoned in the body as the consequence of a fall into sin, souls, when freed at death from terrestrial bonds, soar again to the heights, happy to have escaped from their long servitude. According to Josephus, it was this doctrine about the soul which captivated all who had once tasted the wisdom of the Essenes. The present world they viewed as evil, apart altogether from the human soul, which did not belong to it. But although they regarded as ungodly the world of sense as such, they yet held sin to be a transgression of the law of nature. Possessing their own secret books, they inquired into celestial things, and in particular prided themselves on knowing and concealing the names of the angels. Finally, if they did not worship the sun, in their numerous ceremonial lustrations they certainly came very near to the worship of water.

Although in the græcising phraseology of Josephus the three Jewish schools appear as clear-cut "philosophical sects," his statement of the facts may nevertheless be taken as at least broadly accurate.[1] It is the form rather than the substance of his description that is inexact. Assuming, then, that Essenism was substantially what he and the other authorities represent it to have been, how are we to explain it? It grew up exclusively on Jewish soil; was it also a purely Jewish product, or was it moulded by foreign influences?

Many scholars view Essenism as only an exaggerated Pharisaism. Its extreme veneration for Moses and

---

[1] See Note 22, p. 391.

the Law, its rigid sabbatarianism, and its straining after
ceremonial purity, are certainly thoroughly Pharisaic.
It was perhaps their desire to realise perfect Levitical
holiness that led the Essenes to live apart from others,
and to associate only with those whose common meals
were prepared by priestly hands.　From this standpoint
it is also easy to account for their communism with
regard to property, for their white attire, for the severe
tests applied to candidates for admission to the order,
for their scrupulous modesty, and even for their attitude
towards marriage, which involved ceremonial defilement.
Their belief that the emancipated spirits of the righteous
would gladly " mount upwards," may also perhaps be
regarded as a refinement upon the Pharisaic doctrine of
a bodily resurrection.　In an age affected by foreign
culture and by enervating luxury, the Essenes stood for
natural simplicity and frugality, and resisted all ostenta-
tion and extravagance; hence their antagonism to the
taking of oaths, to slavery, and to the use of ointment.[1]
Although their attitude with reference to these things
was not that of the Jews generally, it is sufficiently
explained by their asceticism.　In nothing to go beyond
natural requirements—that was the principle on which
they uniformly acted.　It was loyalty to this principle,
too, that crushed the commercial instinct; for their ideal
was that of a brotherhood no member of which should
work in his own interest, and every member of which
should labour for the collective benefit of all.

[1] This was not, of course, inconsistent with the one great oath taken by
them on admission to the order.　Bousset thinks their abstinence from
anointing oil was not the expression of an ascetic mode of life, but was
probably connected with the rejection of animal sacrifice—a protest against
the Old Testament priesthood, whose authority rests upon unction.

There remain, however, in Essenism certain non-Jewish elements incapable of explanation from the Pharisaic standpoint.[1] To this category belong its repudiation of animal sacrifices, its dualistic psychology, and the traditional prayers addressed to the sun at dawn. It has indeed been contended that in repudiating bloody sacrifices the Essenes were only carrying to an extreme the Pharisaic tendency to subordinate sacrificial rites to the study of the Law; that Josephus is responsible for the Platonic colouring given to the doctrine of man; and that by the prayers directed to the sun nothing further is meant than the recitation of the Shĕma' at daybreak. These contentions, however, are not convincing. A more spiritual conception of sacrifice had doubtless been reached by the prophets, and pervaded the Wisdom literature, while Philo defended the rejection of sacrifice on the ground that man must make himself the sanctuary of God. Nevertheless the attitude of the Essenes on this question constituted a distinct breach with Judaism as such. Even more

---

[1] According to Wendt, *The Teaching of Jesus*, i. p. 51 f., "the Essenes represent the tendency of Pharisaic legalism, so far as the latter was influenced by the idea of the transcendental character of God. But they exhibit that tendency in a more intense degree. Their rejection of animal sacrifices . . . which seems out of harmony with the rest of their legal obedience, is most simply explained as the consequence of their idea that to bring to God a bloody animal offering was derogatory to His transcendental character. Therefore they deemed it incumbent upon them to interpret the Old Testament command in reference to these offerings in an allegorising way. . . . Finally, the high regard paid to angels by the Essenes must be looked upon as a consequence of the same idea of the transcendental character of God, from which their tendency to legalism proceeded; and it might be a question worth considering, whether, in their peculiar sun-worship, we have not simply an expression of their reverence for the angels as the great "powers" through whose mediation, also according to the common Jewish idea, God works on nature, specially in the celestial phenomena of nature."

clearly does the alien element find expression in connexion with the Essene doctrines of the soul and immortality. The notions of the soul's pre-existence and of its temporary imprisonment in the body are absolutely un-Jewish. Also with reference to the custom of turning in prayer towards the sun,—a custom which came perilously near to an infringement of monotheism itself, involving as it did an invocation of the heavenly luminary as at least a living and exalted being,—it seems futile to question the presence of a tangible influence from the ethnic polytheistic side.[1] We are forced, then, to the conclusion that in the development of the singular religious society of the Essenes foreign influences were decidedly at work.

What these were, however, is not easy to determine. Whether in view of the many and composite waves of culture which swept over Palestine in the post-exilic period anything like certainty is attainable here may well be doubted. That we are to look to Buddhism or to Syrian paganism in this connexion is scarcely probable.[2] It is much more likely that the outside influences which helped to form Essenism were just those influences which affected Judaism itself, namely, the Greek and the Persian. The question, therefore, comes to be, was the foreign element in Essenism derived from Hellenistic or Zoroastrian ideas, or from a combination of both? It is interesting to find how many features of Essenism are common to Parsism and to Pythagoreanism. The white robes and the lustrations, the invocation of the sun and the repudiation

[1] So Bousset ; but see Note 23, p. 392.
[2] See, however, Note 24, p. 393.

of animal sacrifices, are equally characteristic of both. On the other hand, some peculiarities of the Essenes, such as their angelology and magic, favour the theory of Persian influence; others, such as their celibacy and their dualistic doctrine of man, point rather to a Greek origin. Probabilities are thus so evenly balanced as to render any definite pronouncement precarious. Lightfoot, Hilgenfeld, and Cheyne lean towards the hypothesis of Zoroastrian influences; Schürer, again, but for the important consideration that neo-Pythagoreanism itself contains elements that are of foreign and probably of Oriental origin, would follow Zeller in holding that it is to the Pythagorean school of Greek philosophy that we must trace what is non-Jewish in Essenism. Friedländer strongly advocates the theory of Greek influence, and maintains that Essenism was not only not of Pharisaic origin, but distinctly anti-Pharisaic in spirit and tendency.[1] He insists that it was not for the sake of Levitical holiness that the Essenes gradually withdrew from civic and social life. They did so in order to escape from the distracting bustle of the world.[2] It was their aim to rise to true holiness and communion with God, and they were convinced that this was possible only in a healthier atmosphere than that of cities, and through the practice of asceticism. According to this scholar, then, the fundamental idea of Essenism is the crucifixion of sense (*Sinnlichkeit*) through the observance of the greatest possible abstinence with a view to the ennoblement of the soul. Perfection is the end aimed at, and strict abstinence the means of attaining it. This whole ideal of life, however, is inspired not by

[1] See Note 25, p. 396.   [2] See Note 26, p. 396.

Pharisaism, but by Hellenism. The position taken up
by this writer is thus diametrically opposed to that of
Derenbourg, Ewald, and others, who look upon Essenism
as nothing but ultra-Pharisaism. We shall probably do
well to distrust both of these extreme views, neither
denying an admixture of foreign elements, nor, on the
theory of such an admixture, asserting it to be
exclusively Hellenistic. It seems safest on the whole
to conclude that both Zoroastrian and Pythagorean
influences were at work in the evolution of a system
which, while distinctly based upon Judaism, found in
these other schools of thought certain points of contact
which helped it towards the realisation of its own ideals.
But where joint influence of this sort may be reasonably
assumed, it is much too delicate an operation to attempt
an analysis so as to allocate the proportions on either
side. If, for example, the language used by Josephus
be correct, the Essene doctrine of the soul, while strongly
neo-Pythagorean, may also be viewed as a hebraised
combination of elements drawn from Oriental sources;
but who shall trace the precise process by which it came
at length to be formulated as an article in the creed of
a sect for which it appears to have won so many
adherents?

Another important question arises: Was there any
real kinship or original connexion between Essenism
and the religion of Jesus? Can the latter be in any
sense regarded as a product of the former? To this
we may unhesitatingly give a negative reply. If on
some subsidiary points the two systems are in substantial
agreement, they are nevertheless radically at variance.
The communism of the Essenes, their renunciation of

oaths, and the estimate put by them upon servants and the civil power, and upon riches and poverty, are reflected in the life of the early Church and in the teaching of our Lord. But far more marked are the points of difference. The Essenes were ascetics; the Son of Man came eating and drinking. The Essenes turned their back upon the world; Jesus moved about freely in it. Christianity knows nothing of the element of secrecy so characteristic of Essenism; Jesus taught openly, and not with closed doors. For the Essenes ceremonial purity was everything; for Jesus it was nothing. The Essenes acted on the principle that man was made for the sabbath; Jesus taught that the sabbath was made for man. The Essenes, moreover, rejected the doctrine of the resurrection, which formed the corner-stone of Christianity. In short, the agreement between Essenism and Christianity extends only to minor details, whereas the difference is vital.

Essenism is interesting not only as an illustration of the variety of religious experiences, but as shewing a certain elasticity even within the pale of Judaism. It proves that Pharisaic control of religious life and thought cannot have been absolute. High as was the esteem in which its votaries were held, however, Essenism in its organised form did not survive the destruction of Jerusalem. Subsequent to that event Judaism was represented only by Pharisaism. At the same time the influence of the Essenes lived on, and told especially upon the Gnostic sects which flourished on the east of the Jordan. It was probably through this medium that certain foreign elements grafted themselves upon Christianity. The Essenes must also be regarded as the precursors of Christian monasticism, although this appears to have originated not in Judæa, but in the deserts of Egypt. Their esoteric books were almost certainly devoted in large measure to angelology and eschatology; and that not a little of this secret literature has been transmitted to us through the Book of Enoch and other pseudepigrapha[1] is perhaps a warrantable conjecture, although no single extant Jewish apocalypse can confidently be pronounced to be of Essene origin. Indeed, as we shall have occasion to point out later on, there is reason to believe that it was from other circles that this species of literature emanated.

[1] So Wellhausen and J. E. H. Thomson. See Chapter **VI**.

CHAPTER VI

THE APOCALYPTIC MOVEMENT
AND LITERATURE

CHAPTER VI.

THE APOCALYPTIC MOVEMENT AND LITERATURE.

PART I.

IT has become usual to designate by the distinctive name of *apocalyptic* that period of Jewish religion and literature which covers the two centuries before Christ and the first century after Christ. Although it must now be regarded as permanently fixed, the name is not altogether a happy one. It takes no account of such constructive factors in the development of later Judaism as the scribal expansion of the Law, the synagogue service, or the cosmopolitan tendencies at work in the Dispersion. Even as applied to the apocalyptic literature, it scarcely does justice to the contents of these books; and although expressing quite appropriately the literary form into which for the most part they have been cast, may even convey a misleading impression as to their character. At the same time it is well fitted to indicate at least one main feature of the later Judaism, and in view of the influence of apocalyptic upon the New Testament, the determination of the nature and origin of this whole movement has an obvious importance for the student of Christianity.

The apocalypses [1] are the fruit of the new impulse

[1] The Greek word means " disclosures," " revelations."

given to Judaism by the Maccabæan struggle. They
are the most important literary expression of the revived
national sentiment which built up the Hasmonæan State,
and finally led to the disastrous conflict with Rome.
Although they were both popular and influential, very
few of them found a place in the canon of Scripture.
In these writings we have, however, a very valuable
reflexion of the political events and party relations
belonging to that interesting epoch of Jewish history,
when a discredited priestly aristocracy was superseded
by the democracy of the pious champions of the
Law.

We shall treat the subject under the following heads :
(1) the apocalyptic books themselves; (2) their special
characteristics; (3) the question of their origin; (4) their
main theological conceptions; (5) their influence upon
the New Testament; (6) the estimate to be formed of
their permanent value.

1. Of the pre-Christian books belonging to this
once popular species of literature none is so inherently
charming as the *Book of Daniel*, none achieved such
immediate success, and none has become invested with
such enduring sanctity. The course of events so
evidently stamped it with the Divine approval as to
secure for it at once a place in the sacred canon, and
it became the model upon which other apocalyptic
writings were framed.

The first part of the book consists of a series of
hortatory narratives, intended to encourage the oppressed
Jews to steadfastness by pointing them to the example
of faithful Israelites confronted with troubles similar to
their own. Of these narratives the last four are meant

to have a special bearing upon the Syrian persecution ; and in each case " the King," whether Nebuchadrezzar, Belshazzar, or Darius, is practically Antiochus IV. Epiphanes. He is the tyrant whose pride, sacrilege, and arbitrary intolerance are so graphically mirrored forth and so amply punished, while the Jews who are the victims of his cruelty are miraculously delivered. All this by way of consolation for the oppressed.

With the revelations of the second half of the book a star of hope appears above the horizon. The standpoint is that of the Babylonian exile. In a series of four visions there is unfolded to Daniel the subsequent course of events down to the establishment of the Messianic kingdom. These visions, which fill in the historical picture outlined in Nebuchadrezzar's dream,[1] represent the Greek dominion as the last of the great world-powers, special emphasis being laid on the Syrian monarchy and the impious reign of Antiochus Epiphanes. It is noticeable that at this point the predictions become more minute, and that they stop short just at the beginning of the Maccabæan revolt. The last vision [2] contains a very elaborate forecast of the relations and conflicts of the kings of Syria (" the north ") and the kings ot Egypt (" the south "). With still greater particularity the author goes on to describe the career of Epiphanes.[3] After referring to his debased nature and treacherous instincts, he outlines his wars with Egypt, foretells his malignant persecution of the Jews, and declares that he shall be called away from a victorious Egyptian campaign by tidings of trouble elsewhere, and shall " come to his end with none to

[1] ii.   [2] x.–xii.   [3] xi. 21–45.

help him." Although the tyrant's name is never
mentioned, his individuality is beyond dispute. With
his downfall Israel is to enter on happier times. The
brightest hopes for the future are expressed at the close
of the prophecy. Michael the guardian angel of the
Jewish people will appear, and those found written in
the book of life shall be delivered out of the appalling
tribulation of those times. Nor will the pious dead be
lost to the kingdom of God, for they shall rise again.[1]
Nowhere else in the Old Testament is the doctrine of
the resurrection so clearly expressed; and from this
time it began to influence devout Jews as it had never
done before. In the prophetic perspective of the *Book
of Daniel* the advent of the Messianic age follows close
upon the death of Antiochus, and the sequel of the
glorious struggle for spiritual independence in the time
of the Maccabees is represented as being nothing less
than the beginning of the realisation of God's kingdom
on the earth. Those who are meanwhile enduring the
bitter persecution of Antiochus are living in "the time of
the end," the close of which is distant by only three or
four years from the time of the suspension of the daily
sacrifice in B.C. 168.[2] Daniel is told to seal up his book
and quietly go his way. It is not intended for his contemporaries, but must be laid aside until the time of
the end, "so that many may (then) read it line by line,
and the knowledge (of God's purposes) be increased."[3]

Next in importance, and in its earliest sections the

[1] xii. 2.

[2] In xii. 11 the period is stated as being 1290 days from this date, while
in ver. 12 a special blessing is pronounced on him who shall wait and come
to the 1335 days.

[3] xii. 4.

nearest in date to the *Book of Daniel*, is the *Book of Enoch*. It is essentially a Palestinian production, preserved in an Ethiopic version made from a Greek translation of a Hebrew original, and is the longest extant work of its kind. Other Jewish apocalyptic books have been largely influenced by this "Jewish prototype of the Catholic Dante." [1] Until toward the close of the third century A.D., it was highly valued by the Greek and the Latin Fathers, some of them, Tertullian for example, even accepting it as inspired.[2] And it has undoubtedly exercised an important influence on the New Testament itself, in respect both of thought and language. According to Professor Charles, its influence in this direction has been "greater than that of all the other apocryphal and pseudepigraphal books taken together." [3]

The statement of Gen. v. 24, that Enoch walked with God, was held in later times to mean not only that he led a godly life, but that he was endowed with supernatural knowledge. In the *Book of Enoch* we have a literary embodiment of the knowledge which he was supposed thus to have gained. Although termed a book, it is really a composite collection of apocryphal writings issued under his name in the second and first centuries B.C.[4] The facts as to its origin sufficiently account for the heterogeneous nature of its contents.

---

[1] Baldensperger, *Das Selbstbewusstsein Jesu,* p. 9.

[2] Origen (*c. Cels*. v. 52, 54) hesitates in his attitude towards it ; Jerome (*De vir. illustr.*) calls it apocryphal ; Augustine (*De Civ. Dei*, xv. 23. 4) virtually rejects it.

[3] *The Book of Enoch, translated from Professor Dillmann's Ethiopic Text, Introduction,* p. 41.

[4] See Note 27, p. 399.

Whilst difference of opinion exists upon many points, critics are agreed that the book has been largely interpolated, and that the part of it known as *The Similitudes* [1] is of independent authorship.   The most important point chronologically is the interpretation of the "great horn" of ch. xc. 9.   If it be understood of Judas Maccabæus, then chs. lxxxiii.–xc. must have been written before his death in B.C. 161, for he is "still warring at the close of the rule of the twelve shepherds."   On the other hand, if, with Dillmann, Schürer, and others, we interpret it of John Hyrcanus, this section would be placed half a century later.   In any case, as it makes use of chs. i.–xxxvi., the latter must be of earlier origin. From the fact that no reference is made in these chapters to the persecution under Epiphanes, Charles infers that they must have been composed before B.C. 170, that is, earlier than the Book of Daniel.

In chs. i.–xxxvi. Enoch speaks of a vision which he saw of future judgment.   God would appear with His hosts on Mount Sinai to destroy the watchers (fallen angels) and ungodly men, and to confer light and joy and peace on the righteous.[2]   Then follows a detailed account of the fall of the angels, and of the punishment reserved for them.[3]   Enoch is commissioned to announce to them the coming judgment, and at their request intercedes for them ; but in vain.[4]   After this he relates how he was transported in vision over mountains and rivers, and under the guidance of the angel Uriel or Raphael saw the deep abyss into which would be plunged the angels who had seduced mankind.   There were also shewn to him the abode of departed spirits,

<hr>

[1] xxxvii.–lxxi.   [2] i.–v.   [3] vi.–xi.   [4] xii.–xvi.

and the divisions that separate them, and the garden of
Eden with the tree of knowledge of which Adam and
Eve had eaten.[1] In the next section of the book [2]
Enoch communicates to his son Methuselah two visions
which he had seen. The first vision deals with the
destruction of the world by the Flood ; the second gives
a history of the world down to the establishment
of the Messianic kingdom. As in Daniel, men are
symbolised by animals—bulls and sheep, wild beasts
and birds of prey. Apostate Israel is placed under the
charge of seventy shepherds (= *angels*), who are afterwards convicted of faithlessness to their trust. The
third division of the book [3] is also addressed to
Methuselah. Here the world-history is divided into
seven weeks, the events of which are recounted " from
the books." Enoch's own life is placed in the first week,
Noah's in the second, and Abraham's in the third. The
fourth witnesses the law-giving on Sinai. At the close
of the fifth the Temple is built. The sixth closes with
the Babylonian Exile. The seventh is a period of
apostasy reaching to the time of the author himself,
who boldly claims to instruct the righteous " concerning
God's whole creation." The eighth, that of the sword
and of righteousness, will see the establishment of the
Messianic kingdom ; in the ninth it will be revealed to
the whole earth. The tenth ends with the final judgment on the fallen angels. After that " sin will be no
more mentioned for ever." In none of these portions ot
the book is there any allusion to a Messiah in the sense
of the prophets. One passage [4] indeed speaks of " a
white bull " to whom all the beasts of the field paid

[1] xvii.–xxxvi.   [2] lxxxiii.–xc.   [3] xci.–civ.   [4] xc. 37.

homage; but although superior to the "sheep" who compose the rest of the religious community, he is at most a glorified man who only appears at the close of the world's history. Chs. xxxvii.–lxxi. record "the second vision of wisdom which Enoch the son of Jared saw." This part of the book consists of three "similitudes" or allegories. It is distinguished from the other portions by the prominence given to the Messiah-hope, and by its conception of the Messiah as the supernatural Son of Man. In the first similitude Enoch sees the mansions of the holy, and the Elect One (= the Messiah), the angelic host standing before the Lord of spirits, and the four archangels, Michael, Raphael, Gabriel, and Phanuel. "The secrets of the heavens" (of the lightning and the winds, of the clouds and the dew), and the chambers of the sun and the moon, are also revealed to him. In the second similitude Enoch sees the Elect One, or the Son of Man, seated on the "throne of His glory," which is also the throne of the "Head of Days," (= the Almighty), in order to judge the world. The judgment is followed by a resurrection of Israelites, and the righteous "all become angels in heaven." The third similitude contrasts the final blessedness of the righteous with the fate which shall overwhelm the wicked when the Messiah shall sit in judgment upon angels and men. The mighty ones of the earth shall quake with fear, but the righteous shall dwell with the Son of Man for ever and ever. Chs. lxxii.–lxxxii. form what is usually termed the *astronomical* book, and contain curious theories about sun, moon, stars, winds, etc., purporting to have been disclosed to Enoch by the angel Uriel, and intended to supersede the pagan conception of the sun's

course through the signs of the zodiac. Chs. cvi.–cvii.
are a fragment from a Noah apocalypse setting forth
his wonderful character from his birth, and predicting
the Deluge. In ch. cviii. Enoch finally exhorts the
righteous to wait confidently for the day of triumph,
when they will be set "each on the throne of his
honour."

The Enoch literature is a veritable mine of Jewish
folk-lore. The ideas of the fall of the angels and the
origin of demons, of the heavenly tables and the
imprisonment of evil spirits and disobedient stars, of
Gehenna and Paradise, etc., illustrate the trend of Jewish
popular beliefs already reflected in canonical and
rabbinical literature. Although the book has its
fantastic and even repellent side, and suggests the
magical atmosphere of the Arabian Nights rather than
the moral elevation of the Hebrew Scriptures, it contains
much that is valuable, and in particular exhibits a close
affinity with the eschatology of later Jewish and early
Christian literature. Even its grotesque nature-symbol-
ism and nonsensical physical and astronomical speculations, derived for the most part from Babylonian sources,
became, through the medium of Persian or Greek culture,
the possession of academic Judaism, and were made to
take on the hue of Biblical monotheism. Popular
Pharisaism itself began to assume a certain speculative
mystical tendency. In the time of our Lord both
Pharisees and Sadducees busied themselves about
weather forecasts,[1] and all sorts of silly occult arts.
And so from the spring of Babylonian and Persian
mythology there flowed down, through the *Book of*

[1] Matt. xvi. 2 f.

Enoch, a stream which influenced both the Talmud and the Gospels.   The book is also of great importance as affording much material for the study of doctrinal development in the inter-Testamental period.

In the *Testaments of the XII. Patriarchs* we have an example of a pseudepigraphic prophecy in which the ethical element predominates.   Discovered at Athens, and printed in a Latin version by Robert Grosseteste, Bishop of Lincoln, in the thirteenth century, these Testaments were issued in a Greek text (from a Cambridge manuscript) by Grabe in 1698.   They are also preserved in three other Greek manuscripts, as well as in an Armenian and an Old Slavonic translation. The work is modelled upon the Testament of Jacob in Gen. xlix.   As Jacob gave his dying charge to his sons, so the latter in their turn are depicted as conveying their last instructions to their descendants.   These exhortations are in each case based upon detailed haggadic references to the patriarch's own sins or virtues. Wherein they erred, they hold themselves up as a warning; wherein they excelled, they commend their own example.   Each patriarch also predicts the future of his tribe, and in nearly every case advises loyal adherence and submission to the tribes of Levi and Judah as those to whom God had given the supremacy ($\dot{\alpha}\rho\chi\dot{\eta}$).   Although in its present form the book un-doubtedly betrays the hand of the Christian interpolator,[1] it is not, therefore, necessarily of Christian authorship. The best authorities, indeed, now regard it as an origin-

---

[1] This is manifest from its repeated references to the Incarnation.   Cf. *Test.*, Sim. vi., vii. ; Levi ii., iv., xvi. ; Napht. viii. ; Asher vii. ; Benj. xi. ; Zeb. viii., ix. ; etc.

ally Jewish composition.[1]   Schnapp thinks that even this
was not a unity, and that at least two hands are traceable.   In support of this view he points, among other
things, to the double narrative regarding the fortunes of
the patriarch Joseph.[2]   This much at all events is
tolerably clear, that the book is mainly of Jewish origin,
and has been subjected to frequent revision.

For long it has been held that the original language
of the Testaments was Greek ; but Grabe's opinion, that
it was Hebrew, has recently been advocated by the
Jewish scholars Kohler and Gaster, followed by Resch [3]
and Charles.   In the last-named writer's recently
published critical edition of the book, and in his
" Hibbert " article, he adduces linguistic evidence to shew
that our Greek text is based upon a Hebrew original.
His chief argument is that many obscurities of the
Greek text are cleared away by re-translation into
Hebrew ; and the examples given are certainly interesting
and striking.   Perhaps, however, even in view of the
existence of a Testament of Naphtali in Hebrew, it
cannot be said that a Hebrew original has been
decisively proved ; at the same time it can no longer be
regarded as improbable.

The first or second century A.D., though necessary
to the theory of Christian authorship, seems too late a
date for the Jewish groundwork.   On the other hand,
from its frequent references to the Enoch literature, and
its affinities to the *Book of Jubilees,* it cannot be placed
earlier than the Maccabæan age.   According to Charles,

---

[1] Schürer, Schnapp (in Kautzsch), Charles (art. in *Hibbert Journal* for
April 1905).   See Note 28, p. 400.

[2] i.–x.[a] and x.[b]–xviii.   [3] *Stud. u. Krit.*, 1899, p. 206 ff.

the internal evidence clearly points to the time of " the Maccabæan priest-kings in the latter half of the second century," and even definitely to that of John Hyrcanus (B.C. 135–105). If this is the true date, then the Testaments must be held to have influenced the New Testament writings, instead of *vice versâ*, and in this way they become invested with an importance hitherto unrealised.[1]

According to Charles, the *Book of Jubilees* was written in Hebrew, and partly in verse, during the reign of John Hyrcanus (B.C. 135–105). Bousset, however, ascribes it to the reign of Alexandra—that epoch of Pharisaic reaction. It is a haggadic commentary to the canonical Genesis, and reflects the legalistic Pharisaism of the period. Its relation to Genesis is analogous to that of Chronicles to the Books of Samuel and Kings. We have in its pages a judaïsed version of primeval history. The author's object was to combat Hellenism, and to maintain the eternal validity of the Law, which he represents as having been observed in heaven before it was revealed on Sinai. The book is aptly named in view of its system of chronology, which divides the history of the world from the creation to the legislation on Sinai into jubilee periods of forty-nine years each. It assumes an impossible solar year of 364 days (*i.e.* twelve months of thirty days each, and four intercalary days), to which the ecclesiastical year of thirteen months of twenty-eight days each exactly corresponds. The whole chronology, for which the author claims heavenly authority,[2] is based upon the number 7. " Thus the week had 7 days; the month $4 \times 7 = 28$; the year

$52 \times 7 = 364$; the year-week 7 years; and the jubilee 7×7 years."

The *Book of Jubilees* has also been entitled the *Apocalypse of Moses*. And not inappropriately; for not only is the great Israelitish leader represented as the medium of all the revelations it contains, but the distinctively apocalyptic element is also present. Its author seems to anticipate the immediate advent of a Messiah sprung from Judah, and the gradual realisation of his kingdom through the simultaneous transformation of nature and man. In this age of Messianic blessedness, wickedness will be rooted out, and men will live to be a thousand years old. After death there will be no resurrection of the body, but the spirits of the righteous shall enjoy a blessed immortality.[1] It is further note-worthy that in this book we meet with a somewhat highly developed angelology. Four classes of angels are mentioned—angels of the presence, angels of sancti-fication, guardian angels over individuals, and angels presiding over the phenomena of nature. As regards demonology, the writer's position is largely reflected in the New Testament.

A very vivid reflexion of the opposition between Pharisees and Sadducees is contained in the interesting collection of psalms known as the *Psalter of Solomon*. From internal evidence the date may with practical certainty be fixed at the end of the Maccabæan age. Judæa is suddenly plunged into war[2] by the invasion of a foreigner[3] from the ends of the earth.[4] Although the authorities open the gates of the capital to him,[5] he

<hr/>

[1] xxiii. 27–30.　　　[2] i. 2.　　　[3] xvii. 7.
[4] viii. 5.　　　[5] viii. 16.

encounters resistance from a stronghold within the walls.[1] Being a powerful striker,[2] he beats down the battlements with the battering-ram.[3] Jerusalem is trodden under foot by the heathen,[4] and the sanctuary is desecrated.[5] Multitudes are slain,[6] and many persons deported to the West.[7] But the destructive dragon soon meets his doom on the mountains of Egypt by the seashore; his body is thrown to the waves, and there is none to bury him.[8] The historical situation here revealed is undoubtedly that of Pompey's conquest of Jerusalem (B.C. 63). The actual occurrences which marked that crisis in Jewish affairs could scarcely be more realistically or accurately mirrored. Some of the psalms were written a little later, for example the second, which relates the death of Pompey. As this took place in B.C. 48, we may safely place the entire collection between B.C. 70 and 45. Prior to the siege of Jerusalem by Pompey the Pharisees had attained to a position of supremacy under Alexandra, and our psalms are a protest against the secularisation of Israel during the Maccabæan rule. The Hasmonæans are represented as a race of usurpers who arrogantly seized on David's throne,[9] and whom God has justly recompensed. Even from the early days of the Maccabees the Ḥasīdîm, the forerunners of the Pharisaic party, were dissatisfied with the policy pursued, and clung to the ideal of the theocracy exemplified in those post-exilic times when as yet there was no thought of an earthly princedom. A worldly, warring priesthood like that of the Hasmonæans,

---

[1] viii. 19.   [2] viii. 15.   [3] ii. 1.
[4] ii. 19.   [5] i. 8, viii. 12 f.   [6] viii. 20.
[7] xvii. 11 f.   [8] ii. 26 f.   [9] xvii. 6.

combined as it was with the exercise of kingly power, was necessarily a thorn in their side. The later representatives of this dynasty, Alexander Jannæus and Aristobulus II., as adherents of the Sadducæan party, they viewed as sinful and lawless men. In the psalms accordingly the downfall of the Hasmonæans is hailed with satisfaction, and Pompey is denounced merely for his barbarity and impious profanation of the Temple.

That this is the only date to which these psalms can properly be referred, is further obvious from their whole tone and spirit. They reflect, and in fact constitute one of the most valuable witnesses for, the Pharisaic legalism of those days. Precisely herein lies their theological significance. Running through the whole eighteen songs is the sharp distinction between saints and sinners, between pious and godless. They are written in a strain of ardent piety, but the conception of righteousness is throughout of the most external character. The righteous are those who scrupulously observe the ceremonial Law, and fulfil all the Pharisaic prescriptions;[1] the sinners are their opponents, the Sadducees. Piety has no existence outside the ranks of the orthodox party; it is the monopoly of the poet's friends. The picture here drawn of Pharisaism enables us to understand the description and estimate of it given in the Gospels. " The righteousness of the scribes and Pharisees " could not pass muster with Jesus.[2] His ideal of righteousness was far as the poles asunder from the haughty self-righteousness of the Pharisee who " despised others." [3]

In their strongly developed Messianic expectation

---

[1] xiv. 2.   [2] Matt. v. 20.   [3] Luke xviii. 9.

these psalms reflect a notable feature of the religious sentiment animating the Pharisaic circles in which they had their origin. The writer looks for a personal Messiah who, as the son of David and king of Israel, shall cleanse Jerusalem from the heathen, smite the ungodly, and bring back the "Dispersion."[1] The heathen shall be subject to him, and of their own accord shall come to see his glory.[2] He shall rule not in the might of earthly power, but with the help of the Lord alone, being (ceremonially) pure from sin, and made strong in the holy spirit. Wisdom and justice shall be the pillars of his throne.[3] Through the exploits of the Maccabees the desire for a monarchy had once more taken possession of the Jewish mind. Recognising this, the Pharisees, who had previously been content with urging the claims of the Law, now sought to rally patriotic enthusiasm to their side by holding out the tempting prospect of a glorious future for Israel under a Davidic king.[4] Thus at length there would be realised a kingdom of the holy. Our psalmist's doctrine of rewards and punishments is simple and clear-cut. Although subject to the Divine decree as regards his general lot in life, man is free to choose righteousness or unrighteousness; and upon his choice depends his future destiny. If his works are righteous, he shall be raised again to eternal life;[5] if unrighteous, eternal perdition awaits him.[6]

The Book of the Secrets of Enoch (II Enoch), although perhaps widely circulated in the early centuries,[7] was

---

[1] xvii. 21 ff., xi. 2 f.   [2] xvii. 30 f.   [3] xviii. 7.
[4] xvii., xviii.   [5] iii. 12.   [6] iii. 11, xv. 13.
[7] According to Charles, its influence is traceable in Irenæus (*c. Hær*

lost for some twelve hundred years prior to its recent discovery in certain Slavonic manuscripts.[1]   Hence it is usually designated the " Slavonic," as distinguished from the older " Ethiopic," Enoch.   In its present form it appears to have been the work of a Jewish Hellenist who lived in Egypt in the first century A.D.   That the Slavonic text is derived from the Greek is clear from ch. xxx. 13, which states that the name Adam is formed " from the four substances: the East, the West, the North, and the South," that is, from the initial letters of their Greek names,[2] no similar result being obtainable in Hebrew.

Enoch is introduced as " a very wise man " who was privileged to see " the heavenly abodes," and " the unapproachable throne of the Lord."   In ch. i. two angels announce to him that he is to ascend with them into heaven.   After exhorting his sons to steadfast piety, and bidding them not seek for him till he is restored to them,[3] he is borne aloft by the angels.   In chs. iii.–xxi. Enoch describes his journey through the seven heavens in succession, giving details of what he saw in each. Much of the material in this section is found in the Ethiopic Enoch, but an entirely new setting is given to it.   Chs. xxii.–xxxviii. form the second division of the

v. 28) and others of the Church Fathers ; but Schürer characterises as "sehr unsicher" the patristic quotations given by this writer from the Slavonic Enoch.

[1] In an article by Kozak in the *Jahrbb. für Prot. Theol.* (1892), reference was made to a Slavonic version of the *Book of Enoch* ; but subsequent investigation shewed that the work in question was an entirely different one from the Ethiopic Enoch.   It has been made accessible to English readers in the translation of Morfill and Charles (1896).

[2] ἀνατολή, δύσις, ἄρκτος, μεσημβρία.

[3] Ch. ii.

book. Michael the archangel is directed to take from
Enoch his earthly robe, anoint him with the holy oil,
and clothe him with the raiment of God's glory, that he
may become like one of the glorious ones.   Enoch is
then enlightened by God Himself as to the secrets of
the creation and the history of mankind down to his
own time.   What we have here is virtually a gnosticised
expansion of Gen. i.[1]   After receiving a further revelation that God will send the Flood as a punishment for
the wickedness of men, Enoch is brought back by the
angels to the earth.   The concluding section [2] contains
Enoch's instructions and admonitions to his children,
the 366 books [3] in which he had written down the
revelations vouchsafed to him being commended to their
special study.   Many of the ethical precepts embodied
in this part of the work are reminiscent of Ecclesiasticus.
The book closes with a brief account of Enoch's translation to the highest heaven, a résumé of the main events
in his life, and a description of the festival held by his
sons at Achuzan, whence he was taken up to heaven.

Although from the date of its composition the
Slavonic Enoch can hardly have directly influenced the
writers of the New Testament, numerous coincidences of
thought and language help to remove obscurity from
some passages in the latter.   For example, with
Heb. xi. 3, "The worlds have been framed by the
word of God, so that what is seen hath not been made
out of things which do appear," we may with advantage
compare Slavonic Enoch xxiv. 2, "I will tell thee . . .

---

[1] It is noticeable that Greek names are given to the planets (Kruno,
Aphrodite, Ares, the Sun, Zeus, Hermes, the Moon (xxx. 3)).

[2] xxxix.–lxvi.   [3] xxiii. 6, lxviii. 2.

what things I created from the non-existent, and what visible things from the invisible"; and xxv. 1, "I commanded . . . that visible things should come out of invisible." [1]

The book also throws light upon certain aspects of religious thought, notably on the Jewish conceptions of the millennium and the seven Heavens. In chs. xxxii. 2–xxxiii. 2, God shews Enoch that the whole duration of this world is seven thousand years, that is, six thousand from the creation to the final judgment, to be succeeded by a thousand years of blessedness. The starting-point of this computation is the account given in Genesis of the creation. This was viewed as at once a history and a prophecy. It was held that as the world was created in six days, so the course of its history would extend to six thousand years, for with God a thousand years are as one day,[2] and that corresponding to the Divine rest on the seventh day there would follow a millennial rest of a thousand years. Charles has shewn that the detailed account of the seven Heavens in Slavonic Enoch probably represents only the full development of notions already existing in the ancient world, for example among the Babylonians and the Persians, and to some extent perhaps reflected in the Old Testament, regarding the plurality of the heavens.[3] The idea of at least a threefold division of the heavens was accepted by St. Paul,[4] and from the fact that both in his epistle

---

[1] For further examples, cf. the Introduction to Charles's edition.

[2] Ps. xc. 4; Jubilees iv. 30; 2 Pet. iii. 8, etc.

[3] Cf. the expression "the heaven of heavens" (Deut. x. 14; 1 Kings viii. 27, etc.). The plural form of the Hebrew word for "heaven" (*shamáyim*) may also point in this direction.

[4] 2 Cor. xii. 2 f.

and in Slavonic Enoch Paradise is assigned to the third heaven, it seems not improbable that he believed in the sevenfold division propounded in that work. This theory would help to explain some rather obscure expressions in his other writings, such as " against the spiritual hosts of wickedness in the heavens." [1] The presence of evil in the heavens was not alien to pre-Christian religious thought, and it is perhaps from this standpoint that we are to interpret Paul's statement that there are " things in the heavens " as well as " things upon earth " requiring to be reconciled to God. The reference is most likely to the fallen angels imprisoned in the second heavens.[2] This apostle's view as to " all the heavens " [3] seems to have been shared by the writer of the Epistle to the Hebrews, who speaks of Christ as " a great high priest who hath passed through ($\delta\iota\epsilon\lambda\eta\lambda\upsilon\theta\acute{o}\tau a$) the heavens,[4] and as " made higher than the heavens." [5]

The Assumption of Moses is a work which has come down to us only in fragmentary form. It is alluded to by Origen as the source of the legend about the strife between Michael and Satan regarding the body of Moses, and references to it occur also in Clement of Alexandria and others of the Fathers. It seems to have consisted of two distinct parts, the titles of which are given in the lists of apocryphal books as the Testament and the $\text{'}A\nu\acute{a}\lambda\eta\psi\iota\varsigma$ of Moses. The former section was discovered by Ceriani at Milan in 1861 ; but the latter, from which the quotations of the Fathers are taken, has been lost.

Ceriani's Latin version, which purports to be an

---

[1] Eph. vi. 12. [2] Cf. I Pet. iii. 19. [3] Eph. iv. 10.
[4] iv. 14. [5] vii. 26.

address from Moses to Joshua as his successor, contains
an apocalypse of Israelitish history from the entrance
into Canaan to the reign of Herod.[1]   Ch. vii. recounts
the rule of wicked and ungodly men prior to the end of
the times.   There follows in chs. viii.–ix. the description
of a cruel persecution in terms which point so evidently
to the tyranny of Antiochus Epiphanes as to render it
probable that in the present text the passage has been
misplaced.   Ch. x. is a confident anticipation of the
coming judgment upon the Gentiles, which will take
place after 250 weeks of years.   In ch. xi. Joshua
expresses his misgivings in prospect of the burden
laid upon him, and in ch. xii. Moses bids him be
of good cheer.   The book is of Pharisaic origin, and
was probably written in Hebrew shortly before the
death of Herod ; but the old Latin version is derived
from the Greek.

The Apocalypse of Baruch appears to be a composite
work, written from a Pharisaic standpoint, probably
subsequent to A.D. 70,[2] and preserved in a sixth century
Syriac text—itself a translation from the Greek, as the
latter seems to have been from the Hebrew—which has
been rendered into Latin.   Baruch records his experiences
before and after the destruction of Jerusalem, and claims
to forecast the history of Israel.   When he wrote, the
Jewish mind was still at a loss to understand how God
could have permitted such a calamity as the ruin of the

[1] ii.–vi.
[2] xxxii. 2–4. Thomson, who thinks this passage need refer only to
the profanation of the Holy of Holies by Pompey, fixes the date of composition
approximately at B.C. 59.   Charles regards these verses as an interpolation,
but assigns the writings which compose this book to " various dates between
50 and 90 A.D."

holy city. It can scarcely be decided whether this
work precedes or follows 2 (4) Ezra, with which it has
a close affinity, although in the latter the theological
problem as to the fewness of the saved seems to overshadow that as to the destruction of Jerusalem. In the
opening sections of Baruch an attempt is made to explain this disaster. It was for Judah's sins; and while
apparently the work of a heathen power, was really that
of the angels of God. Judgment will overtake the
ungodly, and that speedily.[1] The period of tribulation
will consist of twelve parts, each having its own special
visitation.[2] At the end of the twelfth time the Messiah
will return in glory, and all who have fallen asleep in
hope of him shall rise again.[3] These revelations come to
Baruch after much prayer and fasting, and in the valley
of Kidron he announces to the elders the future fate of
the city and temple. As he sits weeping on the ruins of
the sanctuary, a new revelation is vouchsafed to him.
He sees in vision a forest with a vine growing over
against it. From under the vine there issues a fountain
whose waters submerge the forest, and sweep it all away
except a single cedar. At length it, too, is uprooted, and
ordered by the vine to share the fate of the rest of the
forest. The cedar is then burnt up, while the vine
grows amid unfading flowers. By the forest is meant
the four world empires to which the Jews were subject;
by the vine, the Messiah, who will crush the forces of
the last and worst empire (the Roman); and by the
cedar, the last Roman leader, possibly Pompey.[4]
After receiving certain assurances regarding the nature
of the resurrection, Baruch sees another vision. A cloud

[1] xiii. 5.   [2] xxvii.   [3] xxx.   [4] xxxv.-xl.

comes up from the sea, its summit crowned with lightning, and discharges upon the earth dark and clear waters alternately, twelve times in succession. This is followed by a shower of very dark waters, whereupon the lightning flashes forth and heals the earth, and twelve rivers ascend from the sea and become subject to this lightning. After Baruch has prayed to God, the angel Ramiel is sent to interpret to him the vision. The cloud symbolises the duration of the present world ($ai\acute{\omega}v$); and the twelve parts of black and bright waters, twelve evil and good periods (all duly specified) in the history of the world prior to the Messianic era. The last and darkest waters of all represent a period of general confusion and tribulation; the lightning and the twelve rivers, the Messiah and the reign of peace to be inaugurated by Him.[1] Baruch declares his gratitude for the vision, receives the announcement of his approaching departure (though not by death) from the earth, and is directed to devote the forty intervening days to the instruction of the people. At their request he writes two epistles, one of which is conveyed by an eagle to the nine and a half tribes, and the other by three men to the exiles in Babylon. The first of these letters forms chs. lxxviii.–lxxxvi. of the *Apocalypse of Baruch* as we have it; the second has been lost.*

2 (4) *Esdras* contains seven visions ostensibly vouchsafed to Ezra in Babylon. In the first he complains of the sufferings of Israel as contrasted with the prosperity of ungodly nations, and is rebuked by the angel Uriel for thinking to comprehend the ways of the Most High.[2] In the second and third[3] Ezra is further rebuked, and

---

[1] lv.–lxxiv.   [2] iii. 5–13.   [3] v. 21–vi. 34, vi. 36–ix. 25.
* See Special Note on page 261.

taught that history must run its course, even wickedness having its appointed time. A more detailed account is given of the signs of the end than in the first vision. These shall herald the appearance and death of God's Son. After an interval of seven days, during which no one shall be alive upon the earth, the dead shall rise, and the Most High shall be revealed upon the seat of judgment, and consign men to the rest or torment earned by their deeds. For the wicked there will be sevenfold punishment, and for the righteous sevenfold bliss. Comparatively few will be saved. In the fourth vision,[1] under the imagery of a weeping woman transformed into a strong city, Ezra sees the desolation of Jerusalem repaired by the reinstitution of the sacrificial worship. In the fifth [2] he sees an eagle coming up from the sea with twelve wings and three heads; and out of the wings there grow eight little wings. The twenty wings and the three heads rule over the earth in succession until a lion comes and loudly rebukes the eagle for its insolent cruelty, and announces its imminent destruction. The eagle represents the fourth of Daniel's kingdoms as understood by the writer; the wings and heads are so many Roman rulers; and the lion is the Messiah, who shall judge and destroy these rulers and make glad the people of God for four hundred years [3] until the coming of the end. In the sixth vision,[4] Ezra sees a man rising up from the sea, and a multitude gathered to war against him; but they are burnt up by the flaming breath of his lips. He then calls unto himself another multitude which is peaceable; but at this stage Ezra awakes through fear. The man who comes up from the sea is he by whom the

---

[1] ix. 26–x. 59.   [2] xi. 1–xii. 51.   [3] Cf. vii. 28.   [4] xiii. 1–58.

Most High shall deliver his creation. His only weapon is the Law. The peaceable multitude represents the ten tribes returning from captivity. In the last vision,[1] Ezra is directed to set his house in order with a view to his approaching death, and to dictate to five scribes the contents of the Law which had been burnt. No fewer than ninety-four books, including the twenty-four of the Old Testament, are thus reproduced in the course of forty days.

Although extending to sixteen chapters in the Vulgate, the book properly consists of chs. iii.–xiv., two chapters at the beginning and two at the end being additions of Christian authorship. Different views are held regarding the date of its composition. The determining factor here is the interpretation put upon the vision of the eagle. It is clear that the author wrote during the reign of the third head; and if, as seems most probable, the three heads refer to the Flavian emperors (Vespasian, Titus, and Domitian), the work must have been written during the reign of Domitian (A.D. 81–96). Its sadness of tone is in strong contrast to the Book of Enoch. It has some doctrinal affinity with the writings of St. Paul, while its imagery resembles that of the Revelation of St. John. The style is verbose.

Except in the case of the *Testaments of the Twelve Patriarchs*, which are virtually moral sermons, the main object of most of these books is the consolation of the oppressed. There is, however, yet another type of apocalyptic literaturere presented by *The Sibylline Oracles*, the aim of which is distinctly propagandist. In form they resemble the utterances of the ancient Sibyl (or

[1] xiv. 1–50.

Sibylls) who authoritatively announced the destinies of
nations, and thus under a heathen mask seek to spread
Judaism in the pagan world.   Altogether they extend
to over four thousand Greek hexameters, divided into
fourteen books, and form a heterogeneous compilation of
Jewish and Christian materials, the earliest portions of
which were written about five centuries before the latest.
The fascinating element of mystery is present throughout.   In the hands of the various authors the Sibyl is
made to prophesy the fate of the world down to their
own times, in order that they may link on to it threats
and promises for the future.   The oldest parts of the
collection, dating probably from the Maccabæan period,
and admittedly Jewish, are contained in the *third book*,[1]
which reviews Israelitish history from the time of
Solomon, and makes unmistakable reference to Antiochus
Epiphanes and his successors.[2]   Towards the close
of this book [3] the Sibyl predicts the coming of the
Messianic king, and gives a detailed and glowing
picture of the prosperity in store for the righteous, and
of the judgment which will overwhelm the impenitent.
For the godly war will cease, and the earth be fruitful,
and the sea full of treasure.   The sons of the great God
will all dwell peacefully around the Temple, which will
be gloriously adorned.   Sun and moon will work for
them; sweet speech and songs shall be on their lips.
" And then will all islands and cities say, How greatly
the immortal God loves those men." [4]   On the other
hand, fiery swords will fall from heaven upon the wicked.
The fish of the sea, all animals on earth, and all souls
of men, will shudder before the immortal countenance.

[1] ll. 162–807.   [2] 612 ff.   [3] 652–807.   [4] 710 f.

The rocks and water-courses will flow with blood, and the clefts of high mountains be filled with corpses. The strongest fortifications of hostile men will fall to the ground because they have not acknowledged the law of the great God. Hellas is strongly urged to abandon her presumptuous pagan attitude, and so escape impending ruin. " But thou, unhappy Hellas, cease from arrogance; entreat the great-hearted Immortal one, and beware of again sending insensate people against this (holy) city.[1] . . . For He alone is God, and there is none else; He Himself also will consume with fire the hostile might of men. Make haste to stir up your heart, and flee lawless idolatry. Serve the Living One." [2] The end of all things upon earth will be betokened by the following signs: the appearance of swords in the starry heavens during the night; the descent of dust clouds, the blotting out of the sun's rays at midday, and the appearance of the moonbeams; the flowing of blood from the rocks; the sight of a conflict between infantry and cavalry, and of a wild-animal chase, in the clouds. " With this shall God who dwells in heaven accomplish the end of all things. May all therefore sacrifice to the great King." [3]

2. What, then, are some of the more distinctive features common to the Jewish apocalyptic writings?

The first thing to be considered here is the relation of apocalypse to prophecy. For while the apocalyptic writings are prophecies, they are not prophecies in the ordinary sense. Rather they represent a transformation of the older Hebrew prophecy with a view to the reconciliation of the prophetic promises to Israel with

[1] 732 ff.   [2] 760 ff.   [3] 796-807.

the present calamitous position of the nation under Syrian and Roman oppression. Traces of this type of writing are already met with in the Old Testament,[1] so that the transition from prophecy to apocalyptic was a gradual one, and the new species of literature introduced by the *Book of Daniel* was not entirely new. It is, in fact, the latest phase of Jewish written prophecy, the special object of which is to shew that as the prediction of judgment had been fulfilled in the Exile, so the prediction of the future glory of Israel, which had not been realised by the Restoration, would be fulfilled on the advent of the Messianic era.

But while in post-exilic times Old Testament prophecy drifted steadily towards apocalypse, it was not until the Maccabæan age that apocalyptic prophecy took definite shape as a new order of literature, and became the recognised vehicle of a particular trend of thought and sentiment. Great prominence had been given, especially by the older prophets, to the subject of sin and repentance, but now the centre of gravity, so to speak, was shifted. How long was Israel to be trampled upon by the heathen? When would the prophetic picture of her prosperity and glory be realised? Could a righteous God be indifferent to the suffering state of His righteous servants? Persecution forced these questions to the front, and under pressure of the problem thus presented arose the practice of reasserting the old but hitherto unfulfilled promises, and of developing them into the most dazzling visions of the future. This was the only form in which prophecy now existed, or could exist. It was the inevitable result

[1] See Note 30, p. 402.

of the political situation. With every fresh crisis in Jewish history arose the necessity of reconciling present disasters with the national hopes held out by the prophets.

The apocalyptists, then, drew their materials largely from the prophetic books, especially as regards eschatology. What concerned them most was not the civic and personal reformation of the people, but their deliverance from heathen oppression. Their interest centred in the day of the Lord as the day of Israel's redemption. They eagerly investigated the mysterious phenomena of the celestial world, and sought in these a key to the ills of the present and to the determination of the time and mode of their final resolution through the dawn of the Messianic age. They also in nearly every instance modelled their writings upon the visionary form adopted by Ezekiel and Zechariah. Notwithstanding these resemblances to later prophecy, however, the apocalyptic books possess, as we shall see, differentiating features of their own sufficient to constitute them a distinct species of literature.

The literary method of the apocalyptists was artificial. While no one felt that he could come forward as a fresh prophet, and in the spirit of the ancient seers claim attention for his message as that of Heaven itself, there were yet many whose religious enthusiasm made them eager to influence the public mind; and in order that their efforts in this direction might be the more weighty and successful, they fell upon the plan of issuing their writings under such great names of the past as Enoch, Moses, Ezra, etc. There thus resulted the somewhat curious phenomenon of books conveying prophetic instruction and exhortation for the present from the assumed historical standpoint of the past. From this standpoint the writers forecast the history of Israel and of the world down to their own time, when naturally they cease to be definite. The actual fulfilment, however, in past history of the alleged predictions tends to create confidence in the prophetic delineation of what is still future from the point of view of the reader. This delineation is usually of a very transcendental and world-embracing character. The activities of the celestial powers, the approaching judgment of the world and deliverance of Israel, the resurrection and future destiny of the righteous and the wicked, are all set forth in graphic colours. Unlike the prophets, the apocalyptists are never concerned with the historical present; their whole interest is concentrated on the future.

Although to the modern mind the practice of issuing books under forged names seems strange and even reprehensible, there is no reason to doubt that in taking this course the authors were perfectly sincere in their conviction of the truth of their revelations, and had no intention to deceive. Nor is there anything to shew that pseudonymous authorship was repugnant to the public conscience of the period. That the pseudepigraphic *Book of Daniel* should have been included in the canon of Scripture indicates that in the Maccabæan age men were more concerned with the contents of a book than with its authorship. Later on, too, our Lord speaks of this same work without appearing to doubt that it was written by "the prophet Daniel," and the genuineness of Enoch is similarly accepted by Jude. Hebrew writers cared little for fame,—witness the fact that the authors of such great works as the Book of

Job and Isaiah xl.–lxvi. should have been content to labour for the common good of the nation, and to remain unknown. On the other hand, this indifference to personal fame was accompanied by the tendency to make a free use of materials furnished by predecessors, and in point of fact most of the apocalypses were edited and re-edited until they came really to be composite works. It may, however, be said that this does not justify their issue under fictitious names. Probably not, but it may serve to explain, if not to excuse, such a practice. There is another consideration which is apposite here, namely, that the apocalyptic writers may have drawn largely from ancient traditions which in the course of the centuries had connected themselves with the great names of the past. In this way it becomes possible to think of them as honestly ascribing the real authorship to the ancient worthies under whose names they issued their works. But if it be difficult to vindicate the literary device of pseudonymity, it is equally so to homologate the opinion, expressed by a revered former lecturer under this foundation, that the presence of the fictitious element in the *Book of Daniel* excludes it from the category of Divine revelation.[1] Surely the message of faith and hope which the writer had to convey was too weighty and precious to be invalidated by its mere literary form.

Apart from the ethics of pseudonymity, however, we may ask what prompted recourse to such a method. It has been suggested that it was adopted in self-defence, seeing that the writers, living as they did under a

---

[1] Professor James Candlish, *The Kingdom of God, biblically and historically considered* (1884).

foreign despotism, could not with safety express themselves freely with regard to the outlook of their nation. But in that case anonymity would have been as serviceable as pseudonymity. A more likely explanation is to be found in connexion with the belief that prophecy had ceased with Malachi,[1] and with the fact that the canon was being gradually closed. Under the circumstances no prophetic writing, unless attached to a prophetic name, could carry authority or win for itself popular regard. But even if we can thus reasonably account for the pseudonymous character of apocalyptic literature at its rise and at its best, it is clear that latterly pseudepigraphy degenerated into a mere literary mode in the hands of men ranking far below the great prophets who spoke as the direct and authoritative messengers of God, and whose personality was in each case the element of peculiar value.

We have next to note the visionary-ecstatic form assumed by Jewish apocalypse. In the use of visionary symbolism there is a remarkable development from the simplicity of Amos to the more elaborate and complicated imagery of Ezekiel, Zechariah, and Daniel. Sometimes the images they see are not intelligible to the prophets themselves, and they beg for an interpretation of them.[2] After Daniel—assuming for convenience sake that the term revelation is applicable to subsequent apocalyptic works—the vision becomes *the* form of revelation. And necessarily so. No other vehicle of Divine communications could be so germane to the purpose of the writers, which was the heavenly unveiling

---

[1] 1 Macc. iv. 46, ix. 27, xiv. 41 ; Ps. lxxiv. 9.
[2] Zech. iv. 4 ; Dan. viii. 15.

of the future in order to a projection of supernatural activity into the sphere of the earthly.   In each case the apocalyptist claims to have been caught up into heaven, to have seen what is hidden from ordinary mortal ken, and to describe his exceptional experience, the truth of his message being made to hinge upon the reality of his translation.   Only through this medium could men hope to penetrate the secrets of the heavens and of the future. The heavenly, however, can never be quite adequately expressed; hence the need for the illustrative, if also partly beclouding, imagery peculiar to the vision.

In its literary form, the vision is characterised by the use of symbolic language, the imagery being sometimes of a very mysterious and fantastic kind.   It is intended to be understood literally, however, and not poetically. In making use of this extraordinary literary framework, what, it may be asked, had the author to begin with? The constituent elements of apocalyptic visions appear to be two—tradition and allegory.   The former supplied the writer with material which he adapted to the circumstances of his own time.   For example, the Old and the New Testament apocalyptist[1] both find in the Babylonian chaos dragon a figure suitable for their respective purposes.   Whether they employ the traditional figure merely with a view to literary effect, or whether they regard it as containing the key to the mystery with which they are confronted, is a question not easily answered.   Frequently the apocalyptist alludes to historical personages and events under the veil of allegory.   Although in Daniel Antiochus Epiphanes, and in Revelation Nero, are never mentioned

[1] Dan. vii.; Rev. xii.

by name, the former being designated "the little horn" and the latter the "beast," the references were obvious enough to intelligent readers of those days. The apocalypses are thus a strange combination of revelation and concealment. No doubt the element of mystery is frequently introduced merely by way of literary brocade; but behind the entire presentation undoubtedly lies the idea that the heavenly character of the revelation is proved by its mysterious dress, nay, that the more mysterious the symbols, the better fitted they are to adumbrate celestial truths.

Another question arises here: Do the apocalyptic visions represent genuine experiences on the part of the writers? It is certain that the prophets had visions both when "in the ecstasy" of overmastering Divine influence and when under normal mental conditions, and that these visions were actual occurrences and not merely literary fancies. Does this hold good of the apocalyptists also? Or are their visions simply the products of poetic phantasy? To what extent was the apocalyptist an independent agent? These are psychological questions which cannot be adequately discussed here. Two remarks, however, may be ventured. In the first place we must allow that, although in most cases apocalyptic writings must be pronounced literary fictions, they may nevertheless in some cases record real visionary experiences. It is psychologically conceivable that writers whose ideal it was to attain to ecstatic vision should sometimes have realised it through prayer and fasting. Such visions as those of Daniel and 2 (4) Esdras iii.–ix. seem to bear the stamp of reality. In the second place, it is difficult to regard apocalyptic visions as "pure creations of poetic fancy," for the simple reason that to do so would imply that the apocalyptist had no belief in the truth of his own message. This would be inconsistent with the claim of the New Testament apocalypse: "These are the true sayings of God."[1] If anything is certain with regard to apocalypse, it is that it aims at giving revelation, and at the same time attests the truth of it. To say this is not, of course, to deprive the writer of all individuality, or to destroy his freedom in the interpretation, expansion, or arrangement of the traditional material which lay to his hand; it only means that we must not so conceive of his independence as to make it impossible for him to believe in the truth of his own words.

The real significance of an apocalypse lies, however, not in its visionary-ecstatic form, but in its religious content, in its moral and spiritual import, primarily for the generation to which it was first addressed, but also in some degree for all time. This means that it is from the historical standpoint that the true value of an apocalypse must be estimated. Thus, for example, in order rightly to appreciate the *Book of Daniel* we must familiarise ourselves with the facts, and enter into the spirit, of the Maccabæan crisis. The key to the *Book of Enoch* is likewise to be found in an intelligent acquaintance with the story of the grasping worldliness of the priestly aristocracy. And so with the rest of the apocalypses; each must be viewed in its historical setting.

The aim of these writings is at once didactic and hortatory, although sometimes the one element pre-

[1] Rev. xix. 9, etc.

ponderates, and sometimes the other. Where the main object of the author is to impart instruction, the Divine mysteries and the surpassing excellence of Judaism are the favourite themes. But while some of these books are propagandist, in the majority of instances the chief purpose seems to have been to comfort the godly and warn the sinner by fostering faith in the bright future predicted for Israel. From this point of view the apocalypses have been aptly termed "Tracts for Bad Times."[1] They are practical messages of consolation to an age in which faith in God's righteous government of the world was sorely tried through the inscrutably hard lot meted out to His faithful servants. The natural occasion for such writings is a time when faith is endangered through stress of persecution or temptation to apostasy, and their burden is that however grievous the woes previously endured, or yet to be endured, the day of deliverance is coming, and is even nigh at hand. The virtue inculcated is faithfulness unto death; the reward promised is a crown of life.[2] While the apocalyptic literature represents the protest of the weak and suffering righteous against the intolerable oppression of the prosperous wicked, it also urges that there is no justification either for scepticism or despair. What the circumstances call for is rather a firmer faith in God and in the ultimate victorious destiny awaiting His people. The immediate future, indeed, might be even more agonising than the calamitous present;[3] nevertheless a happy change is imminent.

---

[1] See Anderson Scott's *Revelation* (Century Bible), p. 27, and Muirhead's *Eschatology of Jesus*, p. 67.

[2] Rev. ii. 10.   [3] Cf. Dan. vii. 23-26.

3. To what source are we to ascribe the origin of these writings? Upon this point great diversity of opinion prevails. Wellhausen thinks it a likely conjecture that we have here preserved to us extensive fragments of the secret books of the Essenes. This view has also been strongly advocated by Dr. J. E. H. Thomson,[1] the gist of whose argument is as follows: On the one hand we have a school whose esoteric books are wanting, and on the other a series of works produced by a school that is wanting; what more natural than that the two fit into each other? The apocalyptic books, moreover, exhibit the very features we should expect in the sacred writings of the Essenes. Besides, as there are satisfactory reasons for believing that these books cannot have sprung from the Samaritans, the Sadducees, the Pharisees, or the Zealots, there was no other source from which they could have come except the Essenes. This is an interesting working hypothesis, especially in view of the question as to the relation in which the Essenes stood to our Lord; but it involves the doubtful assumption that among them the sects included the whole population of Palestine. Ginsburg is quoted as asserting that "every Jew was *obliged* to belong to one or other of the sects"; but are there grounds for this assertion? According to Friedländer, in the post-Maccabæan age the majority of the people were outside the pale of the sects altogether.[2]

---

[1] *Books which influenced our Lord and His Apostles* (1891).

[2] "Denn es ist—und das kann nicht oft genug wiederholt werden—ein schwerer Irrtum, zu glauben, dass das ganze nachmakkabäische Judentum entweder pharisäisch oder sadduzäisch war; im Gegenteil, die grossen Massen des Volkes, die Ochloi (Am-haarez), blieben nach wie vor im Banne des hellenistischen Geistes, und wie die herrschenden Parteien, hatten auch

Others suppose the apocalyptic books emanated from the Pharisees; and no doubt there is much in them quite in keeping with the moral and religious ideals of Pharisaism. Seeing, however, that the Pharisees were keen ecclesiastics, and that the apocalyptists nowhere adopt anything like a party standpoint, or advocate any special programme, it is difficult to believe in the Pharisaic origin of this literature. Porter, who adopts this view in a modified form, thinks these books represent the earlier type of Pharisaism, but express the hopes and beliefs of Jews of different sects who agreed in their condemnation of the priestly and Sadducæar. classes.

According to Hassé, they were the product of the democratic schools of the scribes, *i.e.* of scribes who were not Pharisees. In consideration of their politica! neutrality, their sustained continuity, and their probable non-stereotyped points of view, he contends that this theory suits the facts. When, however, he asserts that we cannot otherwise " account for an Egyptian section of these writings," there having been " no Pharisees in Alexandria," this seems wide of the mark, the reference being presumably to the *Book of Wisdom*, which can scarcely be styled apocalyptic. Moreover, there seems no reason to regard the authorship of these books as the monopoly of literary scribes.[1]

sie, auch in nachmakkabäischer Zeit noch, ihre Lehrer und ihre Frommen."
—*Die Religiösen Bewegungen innerhalb des Judentums im Zeitalter Jesu*, p. 22.

[1] In this connexion Baldensperger emphasises the expression " Enoch the scribe" (1 Enoch xii. 3 f., xv. 1, xcii. 1), and points to the scholastic manner in which the subject-matter is frequently handled. He also adds : " Dieser Schulcharakter, der sich auch in dem durchgehenden Bestreben verräth, ein möglichst auf biblischen Grunde fussendes weltsystem zu entwickeln, erklärt

Friedländer tries to prove that the main features of apocalyptic are neither Pharisaic nor Essene, but suggest rather a Jewish-Hellenistic origin. He urges that post-Maccabæan Judaism is by no means summarily comprehended under the party names of Pharisees and Sadducees, and that the great mass of the people remained spell-bound by the Hellenistic spirit. As the Pharisees were the bodily, so the apocalyptists were the spiritual, heirs of "the pious" of the Psalms; they preserved the faith-contents of Mosaism without caring about oral tradition. They aimed at combining the spirit of Mosaism with the spirit of the age, with a view to the enlightenment of the heathen. So far from making religion the close preserve of the Israelitish people, they sought to bring the wide world within its range. According to this writer, such leading features of apocalyptic as its missionary spirit, its asceticism, its transcendent view of the Messiah, and the redemption of the world through the elect righteous, are irreconcilable with Pharisaic particularism, and are derived from Jewish Hellenism. Even where the standpoint is purely national, it has its analogue, he argues, in such poetical pictures of the Messianic age as occur in Book III. of *The Sibyllines*, a product of the Diaspora. But however convincing Friedländer's arguments are against the Pharisaic origin of this literature, they are not convincing in behalf of its Jewish-Hellenistic origin.

The probabilities, indeed, seem to point to an Oriental

hinlänglich, warum die Henochschriften, woran verschiedene Hände thätig gewesen, in einem Rahmen zu stehen kamen, und mag auch dafür bürgen, dass, wie die einzelnen Theile aus derselben Werkstatt hervorgegangen, sie auch zeitlich nicht zu weit auseinander liegen." — *Selbstbewusstsein Jesu*, p. 8.

rather than a Hellenistic influence. This is the view taken by Bousset, who while agreeing that Jewish apocalyptic is not a pure product of Jewish soil, but a syncretistic growth containing a large admixture of foreign elements, maintains that these were not Greek, but Persian. Some confirmation is lent to this theory by the existence of an Iranian apocalyptic similar in many respects to the Jewish. In both, according to Bousset, the world-drama is conceived as a battle between God and the devil; in both this æon has a definite duration, and is divided into distinct periods; in both the thought of the resurrection of the dead is connected with that of the great judgment; the thought of the world's destruction and of the judgment through fire, which are essentially Persian, occur at least here and there in Jewish apocalyptic also; finally, in the one as in the other the world-drama ends with the conquest and annihilation of the evil spirits. The points of resemblance are sufficiently striking. Is it certain, however, that the borrowing was on the Jewish side? According to Darmesteter, the date of the Avesta would suggest rather the dependence of Persian on Jewish apocalyptic. But this is not the view of Iranologists in general; and if Bousset is right, the antiquity of the eschatological ideas of the religion of Iran is not really affected by Darmesteter's investigations. No doubt the Bundehesh, which contains them in their developed form, is as late as the time of the Sassanides, but it is almost certainly a correct reproduction of the corresponding section of the Avesta. And as its statements in all essential points are corroborated by Plutarch, who bases his representation on the authority of Theopompus, a

writer belonging to the third century B.C., we are carried
back to a date sufficiently early to admit of the priority
of the Persian apocalyptic.

But objections other than chronological have been
brought against this theory.   While Bousset lays stress
on the resemblances, others point to the differences
between the Persian apocalyptic and the Jewish.   The
one, it is said, is optimistic, the other pessimistic; in the
one it is a dogma that *all* the dead shall rise again,
whereas in the other this first takes the form of a partial
resurrection of good and bad; the one is pervaded by
the idea of the destruction of the world by fire, the other
seldom alludes to such an idea.   To the first of these
contentions Bousset replies that even if true it would
be no proof against a dependence of Jewish on Persian
apocalyptic, but that in point of fact the Persian religion
is not so optimistic as is represented, seeing that judgment is preached in the Gathas.   In reply to the second,
without denying that the idea of the resurrection has an
organic connexion with Old Testament religion, he points
out that in New Testament times the thought of a
universal resurrection was already the ruling one.   To the
third he can only answer that the specifically Iranian
thought of the final conflagration of the world is found in
Books II. and III. of *The Sibylline Oracles.*

Bousset does not, however, rest his case solely upon
such resemblances in detail as are common to Persian
and Jewish apocalyptic.   The dualistic vein running
through the latter he regards as a strong proof of the
truth of his contention, for dualism is at once un-
Israelitish and a central feature of Iranian belief.
Attempts have indeed been made to shew that there is a

difference between Jewish and Persian dualism, seeing that in the one case the devil is represented as ruler of this entire world, and in the other as lord of only a part of it.   But it is in the Fourth Gospel and among the Gnostics that the devil first appears as the prince of this world.   Within the range of the apocalyptic literature he appears only as a power *in this æon.*   Certainly it is not easy to resist the impression that Persian and Jewish dualism are externally connected, and that in this particular at least there is a direct dependence of Judaism upon Parsism.   When Bousset further finds the explanation of the new element in Jewish apocalyptic in the cosmological principle underlying the dualistic structure of the Persian religion, it must be conceded that the apocalyptic hopes are on the same plane as those of that cult.   This view is, of course, rendered historically possible by the contact of the two religions in Babylon.

Amid so many conflicting theories, one can speak only with diffidence.   I incline, however, towards the view of Bousset, that the apocalyptic writings are essentially lay literature, books emanating from the comparatively uneducated section of the people, and reflecting in some important respects the influence of Oriental, and especially Persian, religion.   Acting upon the dictum ascribed to Solomon, that " of making many books there is no end," the scribes busied themselves with their oral tradition.   But among the non-professional classes there apparently arose many purveyors of popular literature, the very style of which is suggestive of its origin.   Its fondness for tales, legends, and fantastic imagery, its extensive use of dreams, parables, and angelic communications, and its uncritical spirit, seem to proclaim it to be of the people and for the people. Perhaps some Israelitish Carlyle began it—some strong soul outside of the strictly academic circles of the age, but with a stirring message for his generation. If the *Book of Daniel* be the earliest actual, as well as the earliest extant, specimen of this type of literature, its striking novelty, its moral elevation, and its spiritual fervour fit in well with such a view of its origin.

SPECIAL NOTE. See page 241.

Theologically, the Apocalypse of Baruch presents several points of interest. On the great question whether salvation is by faith or by works, and on the question of original sin, it is thoroughly anti-Pauline. Not only are the righteous themselves saved by their works, but their works are represented also as a shield for their unrighteous neighbours and as possessing an abiding meritorious value, in virtue of which God extends forgiveness to His people. Although Adam's sin brought physical death into the world, "every man is the Adam of his own soul." On the other hand, the doctrine of a bodily resurrection is strongly asserted. The earth will restore the dead precisely in the form in which they were committed to it, so as to facilitate their being readily recognised. Afterwards, however, "they shall be made like unto angels, and changed into every form they desire" (xlix–li). "The Apocalypse of Baruch is of exceptional interest to us because it affords us a clear illustration of Jewish thought in the last half of the first century of the Christian era, and shows us the sort of literature which the Apostle Paul would probably have produced if he had not become a Christian. The measure of the difference between the Apocalypse of Baruch and the Epistles of Paul is the measure of the influence of the Christian religion. The book enables us to see, too, what exactly Pauline theology owes to Judaism, and how Paul has purified and Christianised the Jewish elements which he incorporated into his new philosophy of religion." *

---

* Prof. H. T. Andrews, *The Apocryphal Books*, p. 84.

CHAPTER VII

THE APOCALYPTIC MOVEMENT
AND LITERATURE

CHAPTER VII.

THE APOCALYPTIC MOVEMENT AND LITERATURE.

PART II.

4. WE now proceed to discuss the main theological conceptions reflected in the apocalyptic literature.

In this connexion we note first the dualistic view of the world presented in these books. For the prophets the kingdom of God is still future. On its consummation His people shall be no longer downtrodden and oppressed, but shall attain a position of supremacy under the beneficent sway of the Messiah, the anointed king of David's line. Israel's enemies shall then be overthrown. As personified in Gog and Magog, they shall be destroyed by the Divine judgment in the valley of Jehoshaphat (Hinnom). The dispersed of Israel shall then congregate at Jerusalem, which together with the Temple shall be rebuilt in splendour.[1] The holy city shall thus become the exclusive abode of the saints, and no unclean person shall inhabit the fertile land. Its pious inhabitants shall be blest with a numerous progeny, and God shall be with them, forgiving their sins, creating in them a clean heart, and freeing them from all sickness and sorrow. Such is the scope of the older Messianic

---

[1] Cf. Tob. xiii. 16–18.

hope; and that it lived well into our period is clear from the glowing expression given to it in the *Psalter of Solomon*. But now within the circle of Messianic expectations a great change was wrought through the introduction of a more transcendental type of thought specially associated with the name *apocalyptic*. In the books so designated there is an enlarged horizon, the merely national outlook being superseded by the universal; while future hopes even of a strictly earthly character take on a supernatural hue. Hence to the question, wherein consists the specific difference between the older Messianic ideas and the later hope of Judaism as embodied in the apocalyptic writings, the answer is: Clearly in the introduction of the supernatural element and in the conception of a new order of the world. The bright future for Israel depicted in ancient prophecy was still a future that lay within the natural order of things, whereas the apocalyptic hope postulates a future blissful consummation in which there is a marvellous transcendental, unearthly element. For this a theoretical basis is laid in the division of the history of mankind and of the universe into two great periods—this and the future age. In the sharp contrast thus drawn between "this world" and "the world to come," between the present æon and the future æon, we find the centre of apocalyptic thought relatively to the national hopes of Judaism.

This world is conceived as essentially and increasingly bad, as in fact a kingdom of evil, under the influence and partly under the dominion of evil spirits, and as such irrevocably doomed to destruction. A world so constituted must necessarily pass away, but as its appointed end approaches Satan's power is all the more strenuously exerted to fill the cup of the righteous with misery, and to send a sword upon the earth. Although an invisible spirit, he is humanly conceived as the Antichrist, and sometimes, as in Daniel's picture of Antiochus Epiphanes, invested with the qualities of a despot; sometimes, as in Book III. of *The Jewish Sibyllines*, with those of a false prophet. This conception is clearly reflected in the New Testament.[1] As the conflict thickens and the destined change of worlds draws near, distresses and calamities increase. This is a common idea with the apocalyptists, who depict the woes preceding the end as the birth-pangs of the Messianic era. The thought underlying this eschatological dogma is that there must be painful throes before a new era can be born. These catastrophic signs of the end include the physical degeneracy of man, the failure and aberration of the powers of nature, portents in the skies and tumults among the nations and their rulers, as well as amongst the nearest relatives. Children will be born with grey hair;[2] the sown field shall appear unsown, and the springs of the fountains shall stand still;[3] blood shall drop out of wood, and stones shall speak; the sun shall shine in the night, and the moon in the day;[4] swords shall appear in the starry heavens, and a battle between footmen and horsemen shall be seen in the clouds.[5] All friends shall destroy one another;[6] the small minority of wise men shall be silent, and fools shall speak.[7] Thus shall the afflictions of Zion be fulfilled, and the seal set upon the world that is to pass away.[8]

---

[1] 2 Thess. ii. 1–12; Rev. xiii.   [2] Jub. xxiii. 25.   [3] 2 Esd. vi. 24.
[4] 2 Esd. v. 4 f.   [5] Sib. iii. 798 ff.   [6] 2 Esd. v. 9.
[7] Syr. Baruch lxx. 5, xlviii. 33.   [8] 2 Esd. iv. 19 f.

The future age is of an entirely different character from the present, being essentially good and eternal. It is of heavenly origin, a purely supernatural kingdom prepared by God before the foundation of the world, and destined to rise upon the ruins of the earthly. This is clearly stated in 2 Esd. iv. 17 ff.: "This world is full of sadness and infirmities. For the evil whereof thou askest me is sown, but the gathering thereof is not yet come. If therefore that which is sown be not reaped, and if the place where the evil is sown pass not away, there cannot come the field where the good is sown." That is to say, not only evil itself, but the world also as the soil in which it has taken root, will be destroyed. And for it there shall be substituted a new and better field: "For unto you is paradise opened, the tree of life is planted, the time to come is prepared, plenteousness is made ready, a city is builded, and rest is allowed, goodness is perfected, wisdom being perfect aforehand."[1] The kingdom of God is no longer conceived as an earthly kingdom, but as a heavenly, prepared and preserved until the end of the world. Does, then, the older form of the national hope no longer find expression in the apocalypses? It does, especially in parts of Enoch, but the prevailing conception is that which has just been described. What the writers generally have in view is not a return to the traditions of the Davidic kingdom, but a new earth formed upon a celestial model, and the ultimate transformation of the righteous into angelic beings.

But what is meant by this new earth? Is the expression to be interpreted ethically or literally? Do

[1] viii. 52.

the apocalyptists mean only that the world must be morally transformed in order to become the seat of the Messianic kingdom? Is it "a fundamental mistake to suppose that an apocalyptist has necessarily any quarrel with the earth or the world as such"?[1] Or has he in view an absolute upsetting of the present order of things, and a new order in which, for example, there may be no more any law of gravitation, just as in St. John's vision, after the first earth had passed away, "there was no more sea"?[2] To this it is difficult to give a precise answer on account of the lack of definiteness in the apocalyptic vision. In this transition period, when the older Messianic hope was being gradually transformed into the newer apocalyptic belief, "the line of demarcation between the earthly and the heavenly ideal was not always clearly or consistently drawn, so that it is not always easy to be confident in particular passages which of the two ideals the writer means to express."[3] All that can be said is that, notwithstanding the emphatically heavenly character of the kingdom, the general implication is that the earth, after undergoing a renewal so complete as to amount to its virtual destruction in its present form, will be the sphere of its realisation.

Although the contrast between the present and the future æon cannot be proved to have become axiomatic until towards the close of the first century A.D.,[4] it was no doubt current at a considerably earlier date. It has its basis, indeed, in the older prophetic pictures of

[1] Muirhead, *The Eschatology of Jesus*, p. 87.   [2] Rev. xxi. 1.
[3] Driver, *Daniel*, p. lxxxviii.
[4] 2 Esd. vii. 50 ; Syr. Baruch xliv. 9.

Isa. xxiv.–xxvii. ; Zech. xii.–xiv., etc.   It finds expression in the Slavonic Enoch, written probably before the destruction of Jerusalem,[1] and apparently in the Gospels.[2] St. Paul's frequent allusions to " this world " indicate that it was familiar to him also.   We may therefore take it that the dawn of Christianity found this conception ready to hand.

The peculiar significance of these new views lies, however, not so much in the transmutation of the earthly hope into a spiritual and heavenly, as in this, that they supplied the means of setting religion free from the trammels of nationalism.   The outlook is no longer confined to the Israelitish people, it becomes world-wide.[3] In Daniel the course of the world's history falls into two periods.   The first is that of the world-kingdoms, which are symbolised by animals, and succeed one another in a divinely appointed order.   The second is that of the universal kingdom of the saints, to which the dominion ultimately passes.   The two kingdoms are diametrically opposed, and the ever growing wickedness of the world-powers is suddenly arrested by the judgment and the dawn of the new age.   An over-whelming sense of the universality of the Divine purpose in reference to the events of human history pervades the book.   In the animal vision of the *Book of Enoch*[4] and in Baruch's vision of the cloud that rose out of the sea,[5] the writers similarly carry their presentation back even to primeval times.   " From the days of the creation till heaven and earth and all creatures be renewed " is the succinct description of the entire

---

[1] lviii. 5, lxxi. 6.   [2] Mark x. 30 ; Luke xviii. 30, xx. 34 f.
[3] See Note 31, p. 404.   [4] lxxxv.–xc.   [5] liii.–lxxiv.

course of this world given in Jub. i. 29. History is
regarded as a unity with a definite goal. The apocalyptists are thus in a position to view the rise and
fall of dynasties from a teleological standpoint, the
present being conceived as the necessary outcome of
past developments.

This doctrine of two æons strongly influenced the
newer hope of Judaism. It introduced into it a dualistic
element which asserted itself with growing emphasis as
time went on,[1] until it crystallised into the doctrine
of a direct opposition between God and the prince of
this world. Already in Daniel the saints are actively
opposed by the rebel angels,[2] and in the later Jewish
writings their arch-enemy is portrayed not merely as a
heathen despot, but as the prince of evil spirits in conflict
with the Most High (or the Messiah). The first clear
mention of a personal devil (Beliar = Satan, Sammael,
Mastema, Azazel) occurs in *The Testaments of the
Twelve Patriarchs*, dating probably from the Maccabæan
age. Two worlds, then, confront each other in sharp
antagonism. This world is evil, and for an appointed
time in subjection to Satan. The transition from the
present to the future age will be signalised by a battle
between God and the angels on the one side, and
Satan and the demons on the other. Victory shall
rest with God, and Satan will be driven from the earth.
"At the end of the times Satan and evil will be
no more." [3]

Thus had the Jewish Messianic hope become bound

---

[1] The development of the dualistic idea is briefly but clearly traced by
Bousset, *Die Jüdische Apokalyptik*, p. 20 ff. (1903). See Note 32, p. 404.
[2] x. 13.   [3] Jub. xxiii. 29.

up in the popular mind with an apocalyptic dualistic conception of the world. It was regarded as the *dénouement* in a drama of worlds, beginning with the fall of angels and men, and ending with the judgment. This decided drift of Jewish religious thought into dualism is a fact of great significance in the history of religion. It is clearly reflected in the Gospels, which represent the destruction of the kingdom of Satan as necessary in order to the establishment of the kingdom of God. Jesus cites the casting out of devils as a proof that the kingdom of God was on the point of realisation.[1] In the Fourth Gospel the dualistic vein is very marked; here the judgment of the world means the expulsion of its prince, the devil.[2] The same thing is true of the Apocalypse of St. John, which shews that foreign supremacy, and particularly that of the Roman Empire, was widely viewed as the work of the devil. God's final victory over Satan and his hosts will, however, usher in a brighter era. " Then will His dominion over all creatures appear, then will the devil have an end."[3]

This happy consummation will be preceded by the judgment, which is primarily conceived as a judgment upon Israel's foes. The idea, however, is gradually extended so as to embrace all the nations, and in common with the newly formulated doctrine of the change of æons there grew up the thought of a universal judgment of all creatures. In the apocalyptic literature "the great day," "the great judgment," are constantly recurring expressions, and the idea of judgment becomes purely forensic. The Lord is conceived no longer as "a man of war," but as the Judge, and nowhere more

---

[1] Matt. xii. 28 ; Luke xi. 20.   [2] xii. 31.   [3] *Ass. Mosis*, x. 1.

strikingly than in Dan. vii. 9 f., "I beheld till thrones were placed, and one that was ancient of days did sit: his raiment was white as snow, and the hair of his head like pure wool; . . . thousand thousands ministered unto him, and ten thousand times ten thousand stood before him: the judgment was set, and the books were opened." Judgment proceeds according to what is written in the books. Sometimes these are thought of as records of good and evil deeds, sometimes as containing the names of those destined to life and to death. Another conception which gained currency was that which represents the judgment as a weighing of men's deeds in the balances.[1]

Upon this new way of regarding history some interesting doctrinal positions soon grafted themselves.

For one thing, the apocalyptic writers offer a new solution of the problem which had so long exercised the best minds in Israel. The sufferings of the righteous are no longer viewed as the consequence of their sins, but purely as a necessary link in the chain of events. They form an essential part of the present order of things. History is treated as a theodicy in which present and future have their necessary place. No attempt is made to reconcile the misfortunes of the pious with the righteousness of God; the Gordian knot is cut by the simple assertion that this world is essentially bad, and that for the solution of all enigmas we must look to the world to come. The present supremacy of evil is occasioned by sin and strife in the world of spirits, but will cease on the arrival of the day of the Lord which is at hand.

[1] Dan. v. 27; Enoch xli. 1.

18

To the same cause is to be traced the practice of reckoning the time of the end of the present æon. This was based upon certain conceptions of what had already been divinely planned. " For he hath weighed the world in the balance; and by measure hath he measured the times; and by number hath he measured the seasons; and he shall not move nor stir them, until the said measure be fulfilled " [1] The world, then, had a regular course to run, and a distinct goal to reach. Moreover, its end was near: " The Most High also hath looked upon his times, and, behold, they are ended, and his ages are fulfilled." [2] These two ideas combined to stimulate inquisitiveness concerning the exact date of the world's end. If God had arranged the course of history according to a set plan, it should be possible for men enlightened by His spirit to trace it out in detail.[3] Hence the tendency to map out human history in sections, and to calculate the length of the different stages. To succeed in this attempt would be to measure the duration of the present world, and consequently to discover the time of Israel's deliverance from oppression. Daniel's delineation of the four world-kingdoms, and his interpretation of the seventy years of desolation foretold by Jeremiah as seventy " weeks " of years, formed the prelude to a long series of similar delineations and calculations. In many of the apocalyptic books, as an aid towards reckoning the time of the end, the world's history is divided into separate epochs, such as the ten weeks of the *Book of Enoch*, the ten generations of *The Sibyllines*, the twelve clouds of the *Syriac Baruch*, the twelve periods of 2 (4) *Esdras*, the seven weeks of

[1] 2 Esd. iv. 36 f.   [2] xi. 44.   [3] xiv. 5.

The Testaments of the Twelve Patriarchs, and the seven
seals of the Book of Revelation. *The Assumption of Moses*
reckons the entire duration of the world at 5000 years,
and Ethiopic Enoch at 10,000. But the most generally
accepted estimate was that put forward, for example, in
Slavonic Enoch, namely 7000 years, *i.e.* 6000 years +
1000 years of the Messiah's reign. Although Jewish
apocalyptic owed its religious influence to its insistence
upon the approaching end of this world, yet through the
extraordinary importance attached to these numerical
calculations piety soon assumed an unhealthy aspect.
For at bottom this was an irreligious tendency. Instead
of the calm patience that is content to bide God's time,
there grew up a spirit of curiosity which amounted to
an invasion of the prerogatives of heaven. It is noteworthy that while Jesus possibly shared the apocalyptic
sense of the nearness of this world's end, He expressly
dissociated Himself from the apocalyptic inquisitiveness
which sought precisely to determine the time of the
end.[1] Yet misplaced human ingenuity still sets itself
the futile task of trying to find out how near the world
is to its end—an inquiry apparently as fascinating as
it is presumptuous.

The new view of the world suggested in the apocalyptic literature is also naturally accompanied by a
decided alteration in the place given to, and in the
conception formed of, the Messiah. Seeing the judgment is regarded as the work of God Himself, there is
little or no place left for the Messiah, at all events in
those books which lay stress upon the idea of a world-
judgment. Such themes as the future æon, and victory

[1] Matt. xxiv. 36 ; Mark xiii. 32.

over the devil, have no real affinity with the ancient
picture of the Davidic king.   Consequently, in the
apocalyptic books the Messiah is either altogether absent,
as in *Daniel*, certain sections of *Enoch*, and *The Assumption of Moses*; or is relegated to the background, as in
2 (4) *Esdras* [1] and 2 *Baruch*; or is transformed into a new
figure of a more transcendental type, as in *The Similitudes
of Enoch*.   While the Messiah here retains the central
place, and is still a man, He is at the same time represented as pre-existent in a heavenly state, and as a
companion of God and the angels—in short, as the
supernatural Son of Man.[2]   This strikingly spiritual
conception of the Messianic idea is strongly reflected
in the judicial character ascribed to the Messiah.   He
stands at God's side, and virtually takes His place as
Judge, pronouncing sentence on angels and men.   As
the Anointed, the Righteous and Elect One, He shall
receive universal homage when seated on the throne of
His glory.

What is specially remarkable about this new picture
of the Messiah is that we cannot trace the stages of its
development.   Perhaps it did grow, and was no sudden
creation, yet apparently it emerges all at once, like
Athene from the head of Zeus.   Association of the
Messianic idea with a pre-existent heavenly being akin
to that personified in the Hellenistic Logos or the

---

[1] On some special peculiarities of the representation in 2 Esdras, see
Hastings' *Dictionary*, Extra Vol., p. 300.

[2] The same spiritualising tendency is seen in the rise of the idea of the
heavenly Jerusalem, the old expectation of a rebuilt earthly Jerusalem being
transformed into "the Jerusalem which is above."   The conception was a
familiar one in Jewish apocalypses (Enoch xc. 28 f. ; 2 Esd. vii. 26, etc.),
and finds expression also in the New Testament (Gal. iv. 26 ; Heb. xii. 22 ;
Rev. iii. 12, etc.).

Hebrew Wisdom was something absolutely new to Palestinian Judaism in pre-Christian times. And the precise origin of the idea of the heavenly man is still obscure. Some think the use of the phrase "Son of Man" as a Messianic title is to be traced to a misunderstanding of Dan. vii. 13 f.: "I saw in the night visions, and, behold, there came with the clouds of heaven one like unto a son of man, and he came even to the ancient of days, and they brought him near before him. And there was given unto him dominion, and glory, and a kingdom, that all the peoples, nations, and languages should serve him: his dominion is an everlasting dominion, which shall not pass away, and his kingdom that which shall not be destroyed." But, as Bousset remarks, "it is plainly inconceivable that so influential an idea as that of a heavenly, pre-existent Messiah should have arisen simply out of a misunderstanding of a biblical passage"; and this writer's theory, that Daniel probably found a mysterious concrete picture of the Son of Man already to hand, and made symbolic use of it, deserves consideration.

Whatever its origin, in its further development the new conception of the Messiah was greatly influenced by this prophecy of Daniel. The prophet probably speaks here, however, not of the individual Messiah, but of the glorified Israelitish nation. In point of fact the allusion is not to the Son of Man, but to *one like unto a son of man*, *i.e.* a figure in human form who receives the kingdom as representing "the people of the saints of the Most High." The Messianic interpretation appears to me to be untenable. It dates, however, from a very early period. The Septuagint translators even seem to have understood the reference as being to the Messiah. So also did the early Jewish rabbis. The form " Son of Man " [1] passed through the Jewish apocalyptic into the New Testament, and so has assumed great importance for Christian theology.

The contrast drawn between this and the future age further led to Chiliasm or Millenarianism. The effort to etherealise the national hope was only partially successful, for, after all, the prophetic forecasts of Israel's destiny could not be realised apart from this earth. With the individual it was otherwise; either a transfigured earth, or heaven itself might be his dwelling-place. Both the narrower temporal Messianic hope and the supernatural apocalyptic hope found literary expression. The former is reflected in the *Psalms of Solomon*; the latter attains its purest expression in Slavonic Enoch. But in several instances the two forms of thought are mixed up in a confused way without really coalescing. As an amalgamation between the old and the new thus proved impracticable, it became necessary to find some way of doing justice to both. Hence the millenarian idea, according to which there would first be a literal fulfilment of the prophetic promises to Israel, a period most frequently fixed at a thousand years, during which the Messiah would reign gloriously at Jerusalem, and then would be ushered in the future and eternal æon with its purely spiritual blessings. This conception of an intermediate kingdom was really introduced as a compromise,

---

[1] אֱנָשׁ כַּר (בֶּן־אָדָם) = ὁ υἱος τοῦ ἀνθρώπου = ὁ ἄνθρωπος. On the New Testament use and significance of the name " Son of Man," see Driver's *Daniel* (in *Cambridge Bible*); Muirhead's *Eschatology of Jesus*, Lect. IV.; and Wellhausen *Isr. und Jüd. Geschichte*,[3] p. 381.

and by means of it a chaotic mass of heterogeneous views was reduced to something like order. Just as the prophets conceived the Messianic age as lying in the immediate future, so the apocalyptists regard the end of this æon and the beginning of the new æon as at hand. Owing, however, to the impossibility of displacing all at once the older earthly hope, the Messianic kingdom was assigned a definite place between the two æons; and it was not until the days of Jesus and the apostle Paul that men began to believe in the immediate immanence of the transition from the one world-period to the other, and of the final judgment. In apostolic times insistence upon this was one of the most potent elements in Christian preaching, and proved a great stimulus to piety.

We meet with the millenarian idea first apparently in Enoch's vision of weeks, and in Book III. of *The Sibyllines*. Jesus makes use of apocalyptic images, but says nothing of a limited duration of the Messianic kingdom. It is doubtful whether chiliasm is implied in 1 Cor. xv. 23–28, but it is definitely expressed in Rev. xx. 6: "Blessed and holy is he that hath part in the first resurrection: over these the second death hath no power; but they shall be priests of God and of Christ, and shall reign with him a thousand years." Many early Christian writers went further than this, however, and were led into extravagance through taking the Jewish apocalypses as practically Christian documents; they accepted chiliasm as a tradition of the Church.

Jewish apocalyptic literature is further characterised by a transcendental conception of God and His relation to the world. No necessity was felt by the early

Hebrews for metaphysical speculation as to the being and attributes of God and His relation to the material universe. For them all such problems were settled by the fact that "in the beginning God created the heaven and the earth," and that since the days of Abraham onward He had been their covenant God, and had led them through all the vicissitudes of their history. Was not Zion the city of God, the holy place of the tabernacles of the Most High, and was not God in the midst of her? In the post-exilic period, however, there was developed a tendency to conceive God as dwelling in the distant heaven, as "afar off," and remote from the life of men. Prayer was directed not to a present Jahweh, but "toward heaven" or "unto heaven." [1] God was thought of as occupying an inaccessible throne, and owing to a false reverence care was taken to avoid speaking of Him in terms of the life of humanity. While this absolute, transcendental conception of God is more or less characteristic of the later Judaism generally, it is most marked in apocalyptic writings. The striking description of God in Dan. vii. 9 f. speaks to the imagination rather than the heart. This is still truer of the description of the palace of God in Enoch xiv. 17 ff.: "Its floor was fire, and above it were lightnings and the path of the stars, and its ceiling also was flaming fire. And I looked and saw therein a lofty throne: its appearance was as hoar frost, its circuit was as a shining sun and the voices of cherubim. And from underneath the great throne came streams of flaming fire so that it was impossible to look thereon. And the Great Glory sat thereon, and his raiment

[1] 1 Macc. iii. 50, iv. 10.

shone more brightly than the sun, and was whiter than any snow. None of the angels could enter and could behold the face of the Honoured and Glorious One, and no flesh could behold him." The sight made Enoch quake and tremble; but so long as the effect of proximity to the Divine is terror, so long as the ethical element is absent or in the background, religion must degenerate into a vapid supernaturalism.

The result of this whole way of conceiving of God and His relation to the world was the development of an elaborate hierarchy of angels and spirits in order to bridge the gulf thus created between God and men, and so meet what was felt to be an intellectual necessity. During the age of the prophets and the Law, angels had practically no function to discharge; Israel had to do directly with God Himself. But in view of the altered conception of God prevalent in the post-exilic period, and under the stimulus of Persian influences, the Jews came to think of Him as governing the world through hosts of angelic intermediaries, divided into different ranks and classes, with special functions assigned to each. Every nation was believed to have its own guardian angel.[1] The idea of the seven *ameshaspentas* of the Persian religion was reproduced in the seven archangels who are represented as the chiefs of the angelic host. Other features of the new development were the designation of angels by proper names, and the conception of elemental angels. In the *Book of Jubilees*, besides the two chief orders, the angels of the presence and the angels of sanctification, mention is made of a numerous class of inferior angels who super-

[1] Dan. x. 13, 20.

intend the phenomena of nature, " the angels of the spirit of the winds, and the angels of the spirit of the clouds, and of darkness, and of snow, and of hail, and of hoar frost," etc.[1]

Still more remarkable is the development in demonology reflected in the apocalyptic books. Apparently by means of a legendary expansion of the fragmentary narrative in Gen. vi. 1–4,[2] the origin of evil is traced to the fall of the angels, whose alliance with women had corrupted the earth. In Ethiopic Enoch lxix. 2 ff. are given the names of twenty wicked angels, together with the names of their chiefs. Their leader is Azāzel.[3] They are symbolised by disobedient stars, and are meanwhile imprisoned under the earth,[4] their presence there being attested by volcanic eruptions, earthquakes, and all the woes and diseases that afflict humanity. At the final judgment they will be consigned to eternal torment.

The attempt to refer the origin of evil to the degenerate angels or " sons of God "[5] led to the evolution of a personal devil as prince of this world. Although the belief in evil spirits is certainly characteristic of Jewish religion in more ancient times, it attained a particularly strong development in the apocalyptic period. Then for the first time do we meet with the idea of a kingdom of evil under monarchical rule, that, namely, of Satan and his hosts. Whereas the Satan of the Old Testament is an angel who serves Jehovah in the capacity of accuser, he now

---

[1] ii. 2, 18.   [2] See Note 33, p. 406.

[3] Semjāza in Eth. Enoch vi. 3, which Charles regards as an interpolated passage.

[4] Eth. Enoch xviii. 15, xxi. 6 ; Jude 5, 13.   [5] Gen. vi.

becomes the antipodes of God, the lord of the kingdom of evil, in short, "the devil." It is noteworthy that our Lord nowhere condemns the current belief in Satan and demons, and indeed He seems to have been to some extent influenced by the apocalyptic writings. Certainly the Gospels represent His whole activity as directed against Satan and his kingdom.

The apocalyptists stand at the opposite pole from that vulgar familiarity with God which Matthew Arnold justly rebuked when he said that some people speak of God as if He were a man living in the next street. And yet, in spite of all their supernaturalism, it must be admitted that "they turned the idea of the Divine transcendence to practical account." [1] Their argument was that a God who ruled the armies of heaven could be counted on to effect the deliverance of His oppressed people on earth. And the narratives in Daniel are indeed a standing proof of this, for the hopes which they breathe found expression at the very darkest moment in Israel's history.

A third feature in the theological conceptions of the apocalyptic writings is the notable development of religious individualism which they exhibit. The problem of the nation is still uppermost perhaps, yet religious individualism comes to active, if not pure, expression. There were two directions in which the difficulties arising from the discrepancy between the actual situation in Israel and the prophetic forecast made themselves acutely felt. A question was thus raised alike for the righteous nation and for the righteous individual. It was mainly the national destiny that was in the eye

[1] Muirhead, *op. cit.* p. 77.

of the Old Testament prophets; they foretold not only Israel's "resurrection" as a nation, but Israel's supremacy in the world as Jehovah's righteous people. But these bright hopes remained unrealised. In the Maccabæan age it was in its bearing upon the position of the righteous individual that the problem pressed most keenly. Individualism took a firm hold in the thought of reward in a future life, so that in order to the vindication of the Divine righteousness, it became necessary to assert the resurrection of the righteous individual as well as that of the righteous nation; and this was the special task that fell to the apocalyptic writers. In their execution of it they painted, as we have seen, upon a large canvas, giving a delineation of the history of the world and of the human race, describing the origin and development of evil, and predicting the final triumph of the good through the ushering in of a new æon. Then not only would the righteous nation possess the earth, but the righteous individual also, whatever his temporal lot, would receive the reward of his righteousness.

We are here face to face with a new and profoundly significant conception of human life. The doctrine of personal immortality was unknown to the older Hebraism. "Shall the dead praise thee," asks the Psalmist, "or they that go down into the pit?" While the ideas of immortality and resurrection were applied to the nation as a whole, they were never associated with the individual. Certainly the thought of a future life is implied, and a shadowy existence in Sheōl is assumed in the case of all the dead. Moreover, in some of the Psalms, notably the forty-ninth and seventy-third, the conviction of personal immortality comes out strongly. But the hope of a bodily resurrection for the individual first arose in the apocalyptic period, and first found expression in apocalyptic writings. Isa. xxvi. 19 really forms no exception, since it belongs to a post-exilic section of manifestly apocalyptic character. Apart from this passage, we have in Dan. xii. 2—no doubt within strict limits—a clear-cut assertion of the doctrine of a bodily resurrection for individuals, and from this time—that of the Maccabæan crisis—it continued to form a prominent feature of nearly all apocalyptic writings. The seer's words are: "And many of them that sleep in the dust of the earth shall awake, some to everlasting life, and some to shame and everlasting contempt." This is the first mention of the idea of a resurrection for the wicked, and of a difference in the destiny of the righteous and the wicked after death. The writer has in view Israelites only, and again only those who have taken a leading part either in advancing or obstructing the Divine kingdom; that is to say, he alludes specially to the martyrs and the apostates. There is here no thought of a resurrection for all; indeed this is expressly excluded.

The idea of a resurrection for all Israelites is first met with in Enoch li. 1 f.: "And in those days will the earth also give back those who are treasured up within it, and Sheōl also will give back that which it has received, and hell will give back that which it owes. And he will choose the righteous and holy from among them : for the day of their redemption has drawn nigh." And the doctrine of a universal resurrection of the dead is first clearly formulated, possibly under Christian influences, in 2 (4) Esd. vii. 32 : "The earth shall restore those that are asleep in her, and so shall the dust those that dwell therein in silence, and the secret places shall deliver those souls that were committed unto them," in 2 Baruch l. 2, li. 1 ff., etc., and in Sib. iv. 181 f.

As to the scope, nature, and time of the resurrection, there was no uniformity of belief. For the most part it is represented as confined to Israel; and even within this limit there are varying points of view. According to Dan. xii., only some, both of the righteous and the wicked, will be raised up; in the oldest part of *Enoch* [1] a resurrection of all the righteous and of only some of the wicked is contemplated; in *The Similitudes* expression is given both to the wider view that good and bad alike will share in the resurrection,[2] and to the narrower view that it will be limited to the righteous only ;[3] but the prevailing conception seems to be that none but the faithful will rise again.[4]   *The Testaments of the Twelve Patriarchs* and 2 *Maccabees* speak of a resurrection of the just, and this point of view is still reflected in the New Testament. Josephus represents the Pharisees as teaching that "the souls of good men only are removed into other bodies." In Revelation we have a combination of both conceptions.[5] At first the resurrection was viewed as a resurrection of the body; but during the last century before Christ, in accordance with the greater transcendence given to the Jewish hope of a blessed future, it came to be regarded as purely spiritual.[6] This

---

[1] i.–xxxvi.   [2] li. 1.   [3] lxi. 5.
[4] Enoch xci.–civ. ; 2 Macc. ix. 14, etc. ; Ps.–Sol. iii. 16, etc.
[5] xx. 4, 20.   [6] Enoch xci.–civ. ; Ps.–Sol.

was the position taken up by the Alexandrian Jews as
well as the Essenes. In 2 Macc. vii. both ideas are
conjoined, while in *The Similitudes* the older is still
adhered to. According to Enoch li. 1, the resurrection
will take place at the commencement, according to
2 Baruch and 2 (4) Esdras, at the close, of the Messianic
reign.

In the course of the second century B.C. the acceptance of the doctrine of the resurrection naturally gave
rise to the idea of future rewards and punishments, and
the thought of the resurrection is usually more or less
closely bound up with that of a world judgment to ensue
at the change of æons. And the aspect of Divine
judgment which now came into prominence was that it
would be a judgment upon individuals. The question at
issue was no longer merely that of adjudication between
Israel and her enemies, but the final destiny of every
man. Alongside of the national idea there grew up the
ethical, until the contrast between good and bad stood
forth in such strong relief that when at length it was
presented by Jesus in all its purity it fell upon not
altogether irresponsive ears. His hearers were already
so far prepared for that searching word : " What shall it
profit a man, if he shall gain the whole world, and lose
his own soul ? "

In the later Jewish literature the cleavage between
the righteous and the wicked is so sharp that the testing
of the judgment is represented as spelling for the
individual either eternal life or eternal condemnation.
The decisive factor in the case is a man's own works—
what he has done and left undone. Here we have
an undoubted triumph of religious individualism over

national religion; and although in the apocalyptic literature this conception rarely comes to pure expression, being frequently mixed up with the materialistic hope of a long life upon the earth,[1] the future life of the pious is at the same time not seldom more spiritually delineated as an exalted and supernatural life of heavenly glory. The righteous shall shine as the stars, and be like the angels. On the other hand, the wicked are consigned to irrevocable doom, with no further opportunity for repentance and prayer.[2] Sometimes their fate is represented as final destruction, and sometimes as eternal punishment by fire or darkness or rejection. At other times the distinction between the destiny awaiting righteous and wicked is expressed by saying that while the former shall rise again the latter shall be left in Hades. The idea of spiritual pain— pain due to the forsaking of God—as the portion of the wicked scarcely occurs.

Formerly the goal of Jewish hope lay in the supremacy of Israel and the overthrow of the heathen, but now the idea began to gain ground that with the advent of the new æon sin would wholly disappear. "The roots of unrighteousness . . . will be destroyed from under heaven" . . . "and sin will no more be mentioned for ever."[3] The community of the righteous shall appear, and the wicked shall be driven forth from the houses of the faithful, and even from the face of the earth.[4] The resurrection of the dead and the judgment of the world mark the close of the old æon and the beginning of the new. Then shall the faithful inherit " a

---

[1] 1 Enoch v. 9, etc. ; Jub. xxiii. 27 ff.   [2] 2 Baruch lxxxv. 12 f.
[3] Enoch xci. 8, 17.   [4] Enoch xxxviii. 1, xlvi. 8.

new heaven and a new earth." If the words are but
poetry as used by Second Isaiah, in the apocalyptic
books they have a more definite connotation. They
signify a world transformed, a world which shall be in
sharp contrast to the present æon, and from which sin
and sickness, death and devils, shall be utterly expelled.
Later on there rose a tendency to speculate as to the
process by which this stupendous change would be
brought about. In *The Sibyllines*[1] it is indicated that
the world will be destroyed by fire; in 2 Peter[2] that it
will be twice destroyed, once by water and again by fire.

The new world which is to rise upon the ruins of the
old, and in which earth and heaven are practically
merged into one, is represented as the abode of the
righteous,[3] who become angels in heaven,[4] and live in
immediate fellowship with the Lord of spirits.[5] Usually
they are said to be in Paradise, or the garden of Eden
transferred to heaven—a pre-existent, supramundane
abode which comes to manifestation at the day of
judgment, for the reception of the pious. There they
lead a blessed existence, eating of the tree of life and
drinking of the water of life. In this new earth and
heaven the wicked have no place. Until the resurrection
they share in Sheōl the general fate of the dead. Afterwards, according to one conception, they are condemned
to outer darkness, left in Hades, and have no resurrection; according to another they are tormented in hell-
fire. Just as formerly Israel's enemies were represented
as destined to meet a painful doom in the valley of
Hinnom (= Greek, Gehenna), the place of idolatrous

---

[1] iii. 46 ff.   [2] iii. 5 ff.   [3] Enoch xlv. 4 ff., li. 5.
[4] li. 4.   [5] lxii. 14.

19

sacrifices to Moloch, so were the ungodly now conceived as suffering there in sight of the pious Israelites on Mount Zion.[1]   Latterly, however, Gehenna was spiritualised into a transcendent place of punishment not only for apostates from Judaism,[2] but for kings and the mighty,[3] and for the nations generally.[4]   As in the new world there was no place for Gehenna, it vanishes henceforth from the sight of the righteous.[5]   In 2 (4) Esdras the furnace of Gehenna is regarded as pre-existent; it will appear at the last judgment, as will also the Paradise of delight and the heavenly Jerusalem.[6]

The emergence of the idea of a resurrection for individuals powerfully affected the whole range of thought connected with the " future-hope " of Judaism. Not only was this thereby individualised; it was also at the same time propelled in the direction of universalism, the thought of judgment being developed until it took in all men without exception.   With the belief in the resurrection there was also introduced a very marked spiritualising tendency.   In the new æon to which the faithful look forward everything will be upon a marvellously transcendental scale.   There will be a heavenly Jerusalem, and the risen righteous will be as the angels of God.   A further result of the growing belief in the resurrection was the importation of the moral element into the thought of the judgment.   There was a new consciousness that at the great assize the question at issue would not be the supremacy of Israel over the heathen, but the moral worth or worthlessness

[1] Enoch xxvii. 2 f. ; cf. Isa. lxvi. 24.
[2] Dan. xii. 2.
[3] Enoch xlviii. 8 f.
[4] Judith xvi. 17.
[5] Enoch lxii. 13.
[6] vii. 36.

of individual men.   Finally, it was due to the inspiration
of the resurrection idea that thoughts regarding a future
state began to assume definite shape, and that with the
dawn of the new æon there was associated the conception of a complete separation of men into the two
categories of good and evil, and of a corresponding
twofold destiny of everlasting life and everlasting condemnation.

It goes without saying that the thought of a future
retribution for individuals, once introduced, immediately
assumed cardinal importance for the religion of Judaism.
It did not, however, overshadow the idea of a national
glory.   In 1 Enoch only a single chapter is devoted to
theorising about the different destinies reaped by the
spirits of the dead, and even in the eschatological
discussion of 2 (4) Esd. vii. 36–126 it is about Israel's
future that the author is chiefly concerned.   This
helps us to understand the opposition shewn to the doctrine of the resurrection, and the keen controversy which
raged around it.   According to 1 Enoch,[1] "all goodness
and joy and glory" are in store for the righteous,
whereas the wicked "will have no peace."   On the
other hand, the author of Ecclesiastes treats this new-
fangled doctrine with sceptical sarcasm, affirming that so
far as death is concerned man and beast are on a level.[2]
Koheleth is answered, however, perhaps designedly, in
the *Book of Wisdom*, which asserts that "God created
man for incorruption."[3]   In the same way the writer
of the *Second Book of Maccabees* is at pains to correct
what seemed to him the defective attitude of the First
Book upon this point.   By the time of Christ, however,

---

[1] ciii.   [2] iii. 18–22.   [3] ii. 24.

belief in the resurrection had become an almost universally accepted dogma of Palestinian Judaism, and a test of orthodoxy. Still objected to by the Sadducees, it was adopted and proclaimed by Jesus and St. Paul, but in a more spiritual sense than that of the popular conception.

Although the appearing of the new heaven and the new earth formed the dazzling zenith of apocalyptic hope, it was nevertheless usual to depict this hope in very sensuous colours. The earthly and the material are often strangely mixed with a heavenly transcendentalism. Hence the confusion of thought which in these books so often perplexes the reader. The effect of all new ideas was neutralised by the fact that it was never found possible to rid the Jewish hope of national and material elements. Israel's supremacy in the new æon as the certain result of the judgment was the cherished idea which checked the growth of individualism. So far from emancipating piety from the national fanaticism, the influx of transcendentalism served but to feed it.

5. Another important point for consideration is the influence of Jewish apocalypse upon the New Testament.

It is an interesting circumstance that Christianity took over these books as a legacy from Judaism, which began to discard them. In early patristic literature they are quoted with approval, and even placed alongside of the Old Testament as a constituent part of Divine revelation. The Christians did not, however, receive them without modification; they interpolated and adapted them to their own requirements, particularly with the view of removing all uncertainty about the coming of the glorified Messiah as Judge. It is a

question debated among scholars whether even the
Apocalypse of John is not merely a christianised version
of an apocalypse originally Jewish. In any case the
influence of Jewish Apocalyptic is here most manifest.
Was, then, this assumption of apocalyptic literature by
early Christianity due to any real spiritual kinship
between it and the gospel of the kingdom? To what
extent is the apocalyptic element present in the Gospels
themselves? Did it influence the eschatology of
Jesus?

In a broad sense we may say the apocalypse paved
the way for Christianity. Doctrinally it represents a
distinct advance on *Ecclesiasticus,* and in the direction of
the teaching of Jesus. It was during the two centuries
previous to the Christian era that belief in the resurrection
and in future retribution for the individual was arrived
at, and this made the preaching of the gospel possible as
we can hardly conceive it would have been possible in
an age when for individuals there was no outlook beyond
the grave.[1]

While Jewish apocalypse was to a certain extent a
preparation for the gospel, it was, however, only a
preparation. The new hopes to which it gave rise
needed and received completion through the Evangel.
In the preaching of Jesus the doctrine of the resurrection
is purified, expanded, and clearly enunciated, and the
meaning of the terms heaven and hell as summing up the
rewards and punishments awaiting individuals in the
future are freed from all ambiguity. Thus when He
spoke of the necessity of fearing God, the almighty Judge
who can destroy both body and soul in hell, He was

[1] Sir. xiv. 18 f.

able, while striking a note that would vibrate in the souls of the people, at the same time to give precision and final shape to a conception already latent in Judaism, and only needing to be brought to its full development. It is further noteworthy that Jesus uses but sparingly the new terms "this world" and "the world to come," and that, though retaining the expression "the kingdom of God," and basing His preaching upon it, He not only spiritualises the idea into something very different from the popular beliefs associated with it, but also strips it of that specifically national reference always given to it in Jewish apocalyptic speculation. Even the thought of the millennium is eliminated. The sharp contrast drawn in the Pauline epistles between the age then present and the age to come, and the description of the former as "seen and temporal," and of the latter as "unseen and eternal," not only reflects the signal rapidity with which the belief in the world beyond took victorious possession of men's minds, but seems also to indicate that before his conversion Paul's eschatological ideas were much akin to those expressed in 2 (4) *Esdras* and in the *Apocalypse of Baruch.*

But there are certain specific points in regard to which the influence of Jewish apocalypse on the New Testament is peculiarly marked.

We find it reflected in the conception of the Messiah embodied in the Gospels. There "Son of Man" is used as the distinctively Messianic designation of Jesus—whether it was at the time of Christ a. current Messianic title, as Baldensperger maintains, is another question. But, as we have already seen, this name is closely associated with Jewish apocalypse, which thus supplied at least the frame into which was set the picture of Christ, the heavenly man, and future Judge of the world. To change the figure, this title was made the corner-stone of the earliest Christology. As a form of thought it was appropriated by primitive Christianity. The idea of God as Judge of all fell into the background, while that of pre-existence as applied to Christ reached ever fuller development. In his Bruce Lecture on *The Eschatology of Jesus*, Dr. Muirhead has shewn that there are no substantial grounds for holding with Baldensperger and others that Jesus publicly used the designation " Son of Man " only towards the close of His life. But, however this may be, it seems unquestionable that it was taken over from the apocalyptic books and launched on a new career of the greatest doctrinal significance. Strikingly enough, however, it is entirely absent from the New Testament epistles.

To Jewish apocalypse we further owe it that a certain vein of dualism runs through the New Testament writings. Jesus appears as the antagonist of Satan and all his hosts. He came to establish the kingdom of God, and to destroy the works of the devil. Although the popular belief in demons did not lend itself to theological treatment, and has no prominent place in the Pauline epistles, the apostle speaks of the devil as "the god of this world," "the prince of the power of the air." And in the Fourth Gospel we have an approach to a regular dualistic system. Two kingdoms confront each other— those of light and darkness, truth and falsehood, freedom and bondage; those of Christ the Saviour of the world, and the devil the prince of this world. This point of view is distinctly reminiscent of Jewish apocalypse.

The New Testament expectation of the nearness of "the end" is also a heritage from the apocalyptic books. There can be no doubt that the strongly eschatological trend of primitive Christianity—so finely expressed by St. Paul in the words: "The night is far spent, the day is at hand"—derived its inspiration from this source. Although after the destruction of Jerusalem under Titus the belief that the last period of history had been reached grew faint in Jewish circles, it continued universal among Christians. It was certainly shared by the apostles. But what of our Lord Himself? Did He also entertain it? While we are here upon ground where we must tread reverently, there need be no nervous dread as to the possibility of an affirmative answer. His own distinct statement is that He did not know: "Of that day or that hour knoweth no one, not even the angels in heaven, neither the Son, but the Father."[1] This seems the best point from which to start in any discussion of this grave theme. Our Lord's words make it plain that it did not lie within the scope of His Messianic commission to disclose the course of future history, or to predict the time of "the end." From the fact of His nescience it follows that His impression as regards the time of the Parousia may not have been a constant quantity. It may have oscillated somewhat in view of new developments in the providential order, and the extreme limits of oscillation on either side may possibly be reflected in those passages respectively which speak of the Parousia as if it were to be long deferred, and those other passages which seem to imply that He considered it as nigh at hand. His express disavowal of knowledge

[1] Mark xiii. 32.

with reference to this matter even warrants the further
inference that it is not inherently impossible that He
should have entertained an *impression* regarding it which
events did not verify, and that "He by no means required to feel this want of knowledge to be a defect
which was peculiarly unbecoming for Him as the Son." [1]
To deny this is to contradict His own words, and to
maintain that He must have known what He Himself
says He did not know.   However offensive to Christian
sentiment the bare idea of Jesus being in ignorance or
under the slightest misapprehension with regard to
anything, it must be recognised that, seeing it was on
His own shewing no part of His office as Messiah to
forecast the course of the future development on earth
of the kingdom of God, the mere fact of His actual
return being either earlier or later in time than He may
have anticipated, can in no way detract from His perfect
fulfilment of all righteousness as the Son of God.   The
question is part of the larger problem as to the limitations of our Lord's human knowledge.   The references
of Jesus to this subject are contained in the following
passages of the Synoptic Gospels.   "Verily I say unto
you, there be some here of them that stand by which
shall in no wise taste of death till they see the kingdom
of God come with power," or as St. Matthew has it, "till
they see the Son of Man coming in his kingdom." [2]
"This generation shall not pass away until all these
things be accomplished." [3]   "When they persecute you
in this city, flee into the next: for verily I say unto you,

[1] Wendt, *The Teaching of Jesus*, ii. p. 344.   See Note 34, p. 406.
[2] Mark ix. 1 ; cf. Matt. xvi. 28.
[3] Mark xiii. 30 ; cf. Matt. xxiv. 34.

ye shall not have gone through the cities of Israel till the Son of Man be come." [1]   On the assumption that these sayings are substantially genuine,[2] a natural reading of the language does seem to convey the impression that our Lord Himself looked for the consummation of the kingdom in the not distant future.   Wendt speaks of this as " manifestly presupposed," Bousset says " it cannot be denied," Charles regards it as " proved beyond question," and Sabatier is of the same opinion.

Yet this view is beset with serious difficulty.   Not only does it imply defective insight on the part of our Lord with regard to the future development of the kingdom, but it conflicts with His own utterances. Several passages suggest that the Parousia will take place only after a protracted period of waiting.   Such are the parables of the Ten Virgins and the Unmerciful Servant.   In a further series of parables—those of the Mustard Seed, the Leaven, and the Blade, the Ear, and the Full Corn—He teaches the gradual and slow growth of the kingdom.   All these parables indicate that its final triumph will be attained only in the ordinary course of human development.   Then—not to build exclusively upon parables—Jesus speaks of the propagation of the gospel among the Gentiles as a necessary prelude to the final consummation of the kingdom,[3] and this was not practicable within a single generation.   At the same time, He so clearly foresees its victorious establishment that He can speak of it as on the eve of being accomplished ; and in this sense His words were understood by the first disciples, who were therefore also led to confound

---

[1] Matt. x. 23.   [2] See Note 35, p. 408.
[3] Matt. xxiv. 14, xxvi. 13 ; Mark xiii. 10; Luke xxi. 24.

the destruction of Jerusalem with the end of the world.

How then are we to reconcile the two sets of passages—those which speak of our Lord's second coming as quite near at hand, and those which suggest that it may be long delayed?

There is much to be said for the theory supported by A. B. Bruce and others, that the great eschatological discourse recorded in Matt. xxiv. and Mark xiii.[1] is not a unity, but a piecing together on the part of the evangelists of sayings uttered on separate occasions, with the result that future events are represented as closer at hand than the words of Jesus really warranted. This hypothesis would certainly explain the fact that in the discourse we seem to have an admixture of passages referring to the approaching end of the Israelitish state with passages which clearly point to another but more distant crisis.[2] With less probability Colani, followed by Wendt and Charles, maintains that an independent apocalypse, of Jewish-Christian authorship and written shortly before the fall of Jerusalem, has been worked into the Parousia discourse, to the consequent confusion of the text.[3]

According to Godet and others, the passages which seem to imply the imminent nearness of the end refer to the destruction of Jerusalem, and not to the end of the world, so that it is only the former that Jesus places

---

[1] Cf. Luke xxi.

[2] Matt. xxiv. 43-50; Mark xiii. 34-37.

[3] On this theory, harmony would be restored to Mark xiii. by the excision ot vers. 7-8, 14-20, 24-27, 30-31; while these passages read consecutively form "a very short though complete apocalypse, with its three essential acts," and a brief appendix. Charles, *Eschatology*, p. 325 f.

within the lifetime of the current generation. This would be a satisfactory solution were it well grounded, but to limit thus the significance of words some of which at least are deeply embedded in eschatological discourses seems arbitrary.

A recent writer, who says, " The cumulative evidence in my judgment goes to shew that He had no such idea of an immediate return as the Apostles ascribed to Him," [1] bases his conclusion on other grounds, holding that Jesus merely spiritualised current eschatological terms, and that while seeing with penetrating glance the true significance and final issues of moral facts and forces, " He saw them in no exact temporal perspective, or the relations of far and near." Interpreting the address to the high priest (" Henceforth ye shall see the Son of Man sitting at the right hand of power, and coming on the clouds of heaven " [2]) as meaning simply that in spite of apparent defeat " the invincible might of His gospel was about to be manifested," Dr. Forrest argues that in the passages already referred to our Lord's words are to be understood in the same sense. But is it certain that Matt. xxvi. 64 does not itself refer to the Parousia ? [3] The other contention, that Jesus may have prophetically viewed as near to each other things far separated in time, cannot be disputed, although it may be supplemented with the remark of Wendt, that " Jesus had no consciousness that this nearness was only apparent and in perspective, and did not correspond to the real circumstances."

---

[1] Forrest, *The Authority of Christ*, p. 323.
[2] Matt. xxvi. 64.
[3] " Cum sessione a dextris conjunctus est reditus ad judicium."—Bengel.

There are those who would carry the spiritualising tendency much further. Many are now disposed to interpret the Parousia itself in a purely spiritual sense, and to regard it merely as " the perpetual Spiritual Advent of our Saviour in the perpetual communication of His presence." [1]   According to this view there is no outward and visible coming of Christ to judgment to be looked for: " the Parousia is a process with an eternal import, and not a past epoch or future event."   It is a parable of salvation and judgment, and even more closely connected with salvation than with judgment. The key to the whole matter is found in the teaching of the Fourth Gospel: " It is expedient for you that I go away: for if I go not away, the Comforter will not come unto you, but if I go, I will send him unto you.   And he, when he is come, will convict the world in respect of sin, and of righteousness, and of judgment; of sin, because they believe not on me; of righteousness, because I go to the Father and ye behold me no more; of judgment, because the prince of this world hath been judged."   In support of this contention it is urged that an earthly apocalypse is " physically, geographically, and spiritually " inconceivable.   Christ's well-known practice of speaking in parables, the impossibility at that stage of presenting in its real significance the truth concerning the spiritual dispensation, and the appropriateness of a catastrophic delineation of the new era which, whether sudden or gradual in its advent, " could not but be subversionary," are also adduced as arguments against

---

[1] F. W. Orde Ward, B.A., in an article upon " The Parable of the Parousia," contributed to *The Interpreter* for Jan. 1907.   The further quotations in the text are also from this article.

putting a matter of fact interpretation upon the Saviour's eschatological teaching. Its advocates claim that this explanation is the easiest way out of "an embarrassing difficulty, not to say a desperate *impasse*," and that it is quite reconcilable with the language of apostolic writers even in passages like 1 Thess. iv. 16 f., which have usually been considered conclusive in favour of a material Parousia. It is held that in view of the comparative silence of Jesus regarding the unseen world they were obliged, "though assuredly inspired," to fall back upon the old imagery of angels and clouds and visions and trumpets which the Hebrew prophets had made familiar. Attractive in some ways as this theory is, it is questionable whether it does not create difficulties at least as great as those which it seeks to surmount. It may harmonise with the truth of the Christian's present communion with Christ, but what of those who have died during the progress of the development of the kingdom? Does the Parousia come for the individual at death? And what of the resurrection? Is it to be regarded as purely spiritual too? This theory leaves it uncertain what the eternal life involves. Are those spiritually prepared for the great triumph of the kingdom just to remain on in the world? What significance are we to attach to the Saviour's prayer: "Father, that which thou hast given me, I will that where I am, they also may be with me; that they may behold my glory," or to the declaration of St. Paul: "When Christ, who is our life, shall be manifested, then shall ye also with him be manifested in glory?" While worthy of consideration, this way of interpreting the Parousia leaves many problems unsolved.

6. There still remains the question regarding the permanent value of all this literature.

It is not surprising that many should have regarded these books as practically worthless for present-day theology. Even a scholar and theologian like A. B. Bruce somewhere says of them that while they have a certain interest and importance for the student, the general public has only one duty to discharge with regard to them, and that is to leave them severely alone.[1] Broadly speaking, we must allow that there is force in the remark, and that in view of their contents and style these writings can never again become popular literature. Their bizarre imagery, their labyrinthine complexity, their excessive supernaturalism, are fatal barriers to popularity with moderns. Besides, it is only indirectly that they can be said to have a message for our day. The semi-scientific views of the world and of history by which the apocalyptists account for the temporary ascendency of evil are of no real value to us. Their high-flown delineations of heaven and of heavenly beings are but an expression in terms of the imagination of faith in God and the unseen universe. Yet their writings are of value historically, not only as reflecting the inner life and external conditions of the period when they were composed, but also as representing a peculiar phase in the development of human thought. From a spiritual point of view, moreover, they are by no means to be accounted worthless. That element in them which

[1] "Scholars may revive a professional interest in apocalyptic, and it is not to be denied that the exegete of the New Testament may learn something from their labours ; but the great heart of humanity has only one duty to perform towards it, and that is to consign it to oblivion."—*Apologetics*, p. 293.

proved the stay of God's people under oppression and persecution was not ephemeral.   These books furnish an illustration on a grand scale of the eternal truth that " the just shall live by faith."   Their appeal is to the world unseen, to the eternal righteousness, in short to the fact of God.   Alongside of the great and funda- mental truth of the Divine authority is set that of human responsibility.   The apocalyptic writers also proclaim the approaching victory of good over evil, and claim that in spite of appearances the justice and beneficence of God will be made patent to all.   They are the champions of a lofty idealism, and their writings form a plea for God and immortality too strong to be ignored.   As a key to the future course of the world's history, or to the secrets that lie hid within the veil, they are indeed useless; but as a species of religious poetry they can still be read to edification.   In the aggregate, and apart from the specific programme outlined in any single book, they bear impressive testimony to the fact that human history is a unity through which the Divine purpose runs, its onward course being simply the evolution towards the one, but in their view *not*

> " far-off, divine event
> To which the whole creation moves."

The weak point in the apocalyptic conception is that the righteous have merely with folded hands to wait for the appointed time of the Divine interposition for the destruction of evil.   In spite of this, however, the apocalyptists rendered a service to religion by their advocacy of faith as opposed to materialism.   Their glowing enthusiasm, too, proved a healthy antidote to the crusted legalism of the age, while their interest in the coming of God's kingdom opened for Jewish saints a wider and nobler vista than could possibly be seen so long as religion was narrowly regarded as the mere working out of a man's own salvation.[1]

The question regarding the permanent value of this literature is, however, largely bound up with that of the significance of the apocalyptic element in the teaching of Jesus. Unhappily this remains a moot point. Two extreme views are held. On the one hand, Wellhausen and others seem to regard the apocalyptic element in the Gospels as a mere Jewish excrescence, out of harmony with the ethical precepts of the Master, and, like the accounts of miraculous healing, tending to obscure His real image. These critics are therefore inclined to explain it away as alien and worthless. On the other hand, according to Baldensperger and his school, it is precisely the apocalyptic element that constitutes the fundamental and distinctive feature in the personality of Jesus, and dominates His entire ethical standpoint. To His enthusiastic temperament the end of all things is at hand, and therefore in His eyes earthly relationships and institutions are of little account. While both of these views—based as they are upon opposite conceptions of the individuality of Jesus—no doubt contain a certain measure of truth, neither of them can command acceptance.

[1] As an American scholar has said, " Their message for us, their abiding truth, is their conquest of self and the world, their resolute choice of the part of God against the apparent interests of the hour, the spirit, at its highest, of martyrdom."—F. C. Porter, *The Messages of the Apocalyptical Writers*, p. 74.

20

To set aside as spurious, or as an importation by the Evangelists, the whole apocalyptic element in the Synoptic Gospels, is not so much historical criticism as reckless caprice. In these apocalyptic passages there may be some sayings which the tradition has not preserved in the precise form or context in which they were uttered; there may possibly even be some which cannot stand the application of the critical tests. But to eliminate them all, so as to deny to Jesus the prediction of His second Advent in glory and in power, is to deny the essential trustworthiness of the narratives.

But if the wholesale deletion of the apocalyptic passages as being of no significance for Christ's teaching be an unsatisfactory solution of the problem, that which, with Baldensperger and Johann Weiss, regards these as its very core and essence is no better. If Jesus lived under "the powers of the world to come," He lived not less intensely for the present. To represent Him as a visionary enthusiast intoxicated by Jewish apocalypse, is to draw not a faithful portrait, but a caricature. It is true that for Jesus the kingdom of God lies in the future: He teaches His disciples to pray for its coming. But it is also true that He regards it as already in His Person present among men. To lose sight of this double aspect of the kingdom is to land ourselves in confusion.[1] It is the merit of the Baldensperger school that it lays stress upon the Parousia as necessary to the consummation of the kingdom, and so brings into due prominence what is belittled by those who would excise the apocalyptic element from the Gospels. But it shares

[1] Charles, *Eschatology*, p. 320 f. ; Cairns, *Christianity in the Modern World*, p. 172.

the weakness of its opponents in putting forth a one-sided view of Christ's teaching and ignoring its other aspects.

Naturally we desiderate some way of combining the two apparently conflicting elements, the ethical and the apocalyptic, into a higher unity, in preference to that mode of conception according to which these are so antagonistic as to compel us to choose between them as expressions of Christ's teaching. An interesting attempt has recently been made to supply this lack by the author of *Christianity in the Modern World*, who finds a principle of synthesis in a proper understanding of the idea of the kingdom of God. This writer's contention is that in the eschatological discourses of Jesus we have a veiled presentation, such as the political situation rendered inevitable, of the social and national side of Christian ethics. " The social side of Christianity is, as it were, masked under the idea of the Parousia. It is masked, but it is also conserved ; for so long as the idea of the Parousia remained, there was no fear that acquiescence in the present evil order would react hurtfully upon Christian faith and morality. Had it not been for the Parousia hope, the early Church might have been prematurely hurled against the Empire as a Revolutionary force, or through enforced acquiescence in its evils have become a merely pietistic association, a new Essenism on a larger scale."[1] If this theory is right, then not only does the ancient criticism, revived by Mill and Mazzini, with reference to the undue individualism of Christian ethics, lose its point entirely, but the most pressing need of our time

[1] *Op. cit.* p. 214.

is supplied, and that from a highly unlikely quarter seeing that what has hitherto been one of the enigmas of the New Testament would be made to throw light upon the path of duty with reference to social questions so much canvassed to-day.

Probably this is too much to hope for. Even if we do view the apocalyptic passages in this light, how are we to apply them to the practical problems of our time? Admitting that they contain veiled guidance upon such matters, say, as the nationalisation of the land, capital and wages, or the provision of old age pensions, how are we to penetrate behind the veil so as to discern the will of the Saviour? This is the difficulty which Professor Cairns has to meet. He brings us up to a locked door, and says that what we want is inside, but he does not furnish us with the key by means of which we can effect an entrance. To say that one who earnestly contemplates the glorious Advent of Christ as the goal of history will order all his life with a view to "the winning of the world for his Lord," is doubtless to proclaim an edifying truth, but it certainly does nothing to convert the perplexing apocalyptic passages of our Lord's teaching into a *vade mecum* with regard to social questions.

And here it seems relevant to remark that, apart altogether from their apocalyptic sections, the Gospels, particularly in the Sermon on the Mount, clearly assert those principles of unselfishness, justice, and fairness by which Christian men must be guided in all their social and national relations. There is, of course, no detailed directory of conduct; but great principles, applicable to all the exigencies of life, are enunciated, illustrated, and

enforced.   Do we really require anything more explicit?
Do we need the help of this ingenious and fascinating,
but somewhat artificial and elusive, theory?   The
criticism of Mill and others can be met without it; and
it is not enough to say that the teaching of Jesus on
social problems is contained in disguised form in the
apocalyptic passages of the Synoptic Gospels unless it
can be shewn with some explicitness what that teaching
is, and in what respects it adds to the ethical instructions,
so amazingly tactful and wise, elsewhere recorded.   Our
Lord was continually dealing with the social problem,
but there is no special solution for any particular time
intended.   We are left to apply the great principle of
brotherhood in every relation of life.   Now either Professor Cairns means that in his view the apocalyptic
element in Christ's teaching contains something more
definite than this, or he does not.   If he does, we are
entitled to ask, wherein consists this advance upon the
general position taken up in the Gospels; if he does
not, then his theory leaves matters just where they were
before.

At the same time, it is not the case that in the
Sermon on the Mount we have a full presentation of
Christ's teaching.   This cannot reasonably be limited
to a statement of the root principles of religion and
morals.   It is impossible to ignore His demand for
faith in Himself, and that both as present Saviour and
as future Judge.   "Whom say ye that I am?"   "What
think ye of Christ?"   These questions He pressed upon
friend and foe alike.   He also clearly announced that
"the Son of Man is come to seek and to save that which
was lost," and expectantly anticipated "the day when

the Son of Man shall be revealed," and "shall send forth his angels, and they shall gather out of his kingdom all things that offend, and them which do iniquity." The testimony He thus bore to Himself is as much entitled to rank as an integral part of His teaching as is the ethical element to which some would give exclusive prominence. Nor is it easy to judge otherwise with respect to the apocalyptic factor,—which, indeed, is a part of this testimony, inasmuch as it asserts His glorious Advent as Judge,—or to see why it should necessarily clash with the ethical. As Christ was "a greater than Solomon," so also He was a greater than Elijah or any other prophet. Cairns has rendered excellent service in emphasising the wide range of the Personality of Jesus as more than either sage or prophet, as well as the twofold aspect of the kingdom as militant and triumphant. If he has failed to establish his main point, his is yet a particularly fresh and attractive treatment of a theme which is being studied with growing interest at the present day.

In any case the significance of the apocalyptic element is presumably greater than Wellhausen and his school would allow, and less than Weiss and Baldensperger would claim. Although Jesus makes use of a style of expression borrowed from Jewish apocalypse, yet, as Dr. Bruce has said, "He borrowed from the past in such a way as to transmute traditional data into a new conception." Apart from its Jewish garment, the teaching is essentially His own, and amounts to an assurance that He will come again in glory and in power, to bring the kingdom to complete and final victory, and to judge the world in righteousness. Still the very fact that the form of language in which He clothes these truths is that of Jewish apocalyptic, gives to the literature bearing that name a certain abiding value for the student of Christianity; and to say with Dr. Bruce that " a stray phrase may have found its way into His vocabulary from that quarter, but beyond this an influence emanating thence is not discernible in the Gospels," [1] is, in the opinion of the present writer, to appraise that value too slightly.

[1] *Apologetics*, p. 292.

CHAPTER VIII

HELLENISTIC JUDAISM

CHAPTER VIII.

HELLENISTIC JUDAISM.

UNDER the Diadochoi the Alexandrian Jews had their own special quarters assigned to them in the "Delta" (the north-eastern portion of the city), so that they might better retain the purity of their religious life; but although continuing for the most part to reside there, already in Philo's time they had spread themselves and their houses of prayer over the whole city.[1] According to this writer, there were no fewer than a million Jews in Egypt; and of these a large proportion lived in Alexandria, two of the five districts into which the city was divided being virtually appropriated by them. From the first they had equal rights with the Macedonians, and exercised their own municipal government. They had also a national chief of their own, a vassal prince or "ethnarch," whose prerogative it was, according to Strabo, to "preside over the people and decide processes

---

[1] "Zahlreiche Bethäuser in der Stadt bewiesen ihren Glaubenseifer. Vor allen prangte die grosse Basilika mit doppelter Säulenhalle, welche von solcher Grösse war, dass der Custos mit einem Tuche winken musste, um den hintenstehenden anzudeuten, wann sie auf die Stimme des Vorbeters mit Amen einzufallen hätten. Von ihr ward gesagt: 'wer sie nicht sah, hat die Ehre Israels zu jenen Zeiten nicht gesehen,' Succa, 51. 2."—Siegfried, *Philo von Alexandria*, p. 6.

and dispose of contracts as if he ruled an independent community." [1]

From the third century B.C. Alexandria became the centre of civilisation. Literally and metaphorically, it was the heart of the world. As a great international emporium of trade, it stood unrivalled, and afforded ample scope for the trading propensities of the Jew. As the home of science and philosophy, it also provided him with the opportunity of bringing the truths of revelation into fruitful contact with the imagination of the East and the culture of the West. The intellectual atmosphere of the place was unique, and characterised by extraordinary activity. Hebrew religion, Greek speculation, and Oriental mysticism acted and reacted upon each other. In their mutual relations there was at once the warlike clash of opposition, and the peaceful process of assimilation. It was a time of religious and philosophical eclecticism. Every one, whatever might be his particular creed, was affected by the general interchange of thought. New forces were thus called into play. Philosophy had transferred its headquarters from Athens to Alexandria, where it could feed on fresh pastures, and its scope and influence inevitably became enlarged. Through its union with Hellenism the Oriental imagination gave rise to that pantheistic mysticism which stamped itself indelibly not only upon Neoplatonism and the Kabbalistic lore of the Jews, but also upon Christian theology. By introducing the religious element, Judaism also helped powerfully to mould the moral and spiritual life of the period. Under the alchemy of a process marked at once by opposing tendencies and by syncretistic appropriation

---

[1] Quoted by Josephus, *Ant.* xiv. 7. 2.

of elements from antagonistic creeds, striking results were produced.   As in India at the present day,[1] the provincial was transmuted into the cosmopolitan; the sectional was taken up into the larger category of the universal; the limitations of nationalism were dissolved in the wider intercourse of humanity.   This applied not only to general manners and customs, but even to morality itself.   Another fruit of the syncretism of the age was the remarkable spirit of toleration which prevailed in the community; no one was pilloried because of his religious belief or practice.

Possessed in an exceptional degree of the linguistic faculty, the Jews were not long in acquiring the Greek language after their settlement in Egypt.   It was, of course, a peculiar dialect that they spoke,[2] but they made such constant use of it that they soon forgot their native Hebrew.   Their primary object in learning Greek was no doubt the furtherance of their material well-being, and not the desire to come into contact with Greek thought. Yet their knowledge of the Greek tongue, once acquired, brought within their mental horizon the whole field of Hellenistic culture.   And they were greatly attracted by it.   Everything conspired to bring about this result. Apart from the eclectic spirit of the age, and the readiness of the Greeks to allegorise their mythology by way of indicating that their numerous pantheon represented only so many different phases of the activity of the one

[1] "Charles Kingsley's *Hypatia* is a vivid picture of the fermentation of belief, thought, and life in ancient Alexandria, which marks Calcutta, Bombay, and Madras under parallel conditions at the present day."—Dr. George Smith, *Short History of Missions*, p. 54.

[2] This must not be understood as holding good with regard to *the syntax*.   See Notes 36 and 37, pp. 409, 411.

God, the special circumstances at Alexandria favoured the *rapprochement* between Jew and Greek. In the lectures delivered by the Greek professors in the Museum, students of Greek philosophy could find all needful stimulus and guidance, while the treasures laid up in the Library afforded every facility for sustained research. The friendly attitude of the three first Ptolemies was also an important factor in the situation, the century during which they occupied the throne constituting the golden age of the Jews in Egypt. Jews held high office in the State, and played a considerable part in the colonisation of certain towns like Cyrene. Under Ptolemy IV. Philopator (221–204) they appear to have fallen into disfavour, and even to have endured much cruel treatment, if we are to accept the legendary story of 3 Maccabees as founded to some extent upon historical fact. But by the time of Ptolemy VI. Philometor (180–146) they were once more in high favour at court, and two Jewish generals, Onias and Dositheus, practically controlled the kingdom. Their relations with the ruling powers were again less happy under Ptolemy VII. Physcon (146–117); but this monarch ceased to molest them when, in B.C. 138, the Romans took them under their protection.

Such was the environment—commercial, intellectual, social, and political—in which the Jewish-Alexandrian philosophy came into being. It took its rise in one of the wealthiest cities of the world, in a society more cosmopolitan than any other then existing, under the most favourable political conditions, and at an epoch of exceptional activity in literature and art. Amid such surroundings, Jews were necessarily more accessible to new ideas than were their brethren in Palestine.

Occasional visits to the Temple only served to give them
a more spiritual impression of the national worship than
that entertained by those who were constant witnesses of
the mechanical ceremonial of Pharisaic legalism. The
exclusiveness which was maintained in Jerusalem was
impossible in Alexandria, where the Jews had to practise
the same tolerance that was extended to themselves.
But with a more tolerant spirit came also broader views,
and a desire to emancipate themselves from the narrow
groove of their own national traditions; and so they
became philosophers.

The initial stage in the development thus brought
about was the acquisition by the Alexandrian Jews of
the Greek tongue.[1] From this it was an easy step to
the adoption of Greek names and customs, the pursuit of
Greek philosophy, and the appropriation of Greek wisdom.
Especially for the more active minds among the Jews,
Hellenism had a charm not to be resisted. Some declared themselves Stoics, others embraced the tenets of
the Peripatetics, while the majority adhered to the
Platonic school as most akin to the Old Testament.
With the aid of the Greek language and philosophy, the
scientific study of religion seemed a far larger thing than
it could ever be while prosecuted within the limits of
their own literature. Whatever the special school of
philosophy to which they attached themselves, all agreed
in entertaining a certain contempt for the simple religious
teaching of their fathers; yet their national pride, as
well as, presumably, some measure of faith, prevented
them from breaking with Judaism. In taking to abstract
speculation they still remained Jews outwardly, and

[1] See Note 37, p. 411.

freely employed the new philosophical methods as
weapons for apologetic and missionary purposes. The
forces of Hellenism and Judaism thus combined to create
a type of thought and life richer than that which either
of them could have produced singly, and the strength of
the copartnery lay in the fact that the one supplied what
the other lacked. The Jew gave to the Greek a religious
conception of the world ; the Greek presented the Jew with
the means of giving scientific shape to his religious ideas.

Serious problems were thus raised, however, for these
Jewish-Alexandrian philosophers. In particular, alongside of a revelation at once Divine and adequate, what
room was there for the conclusions of human philosophy?
The truth of the latter must in any case be tested by
their agreement or disagreement with Holy Scripture.
Accordingly, in order to fortify their own position, the
Jewish Hellenists were driven to harmonise the Platonic
philosophy with the Mosaic Law, and to assert that the
former was borrowed from the latter. As the traces of
Platonism found in the Septuagint were in themselves
insufficient to establish this, the theory was supplied
with a fictitious basis. This was done first through the
story of Aristeas, which affirmed the transference from
the Hebrew to the Greek text of the verbal inspiration
claimed for the former, and then through the unfounded
assertion of "the Peripatetic" Aristobulus that there
existed an earlier translation of the Law for use in the
synagogue, upon which the Alexandrian was based.
By the one fiction the whole difficulty was reduced to
a matter of interpretation, and so relegated to the
alchemy of the allegorical method, by which it was
possible to extract from the Scriptures almost any

meaning whatever. And under shelter of the other it was easy to represent Plato as merely " an Attic Moses." The Bible came thus to be used largely as a stalking-horse for human speculation. In the struggle that necessarily ensued, the religion of Jahweh, through having to accommodate itself to philosophy, lost its essential character, and, being diverted from its real mission, sustained inevitable and serious injury. At the same time it gained something from its association with the wisdom of the Greeks, and ultimately asserted itself as the predominant partner.

What, then, were the different stages by which the Jewish philosophy of Alexandria reached its full development? To trace these it is not necessary that we should deal exhaustively with every extant Hellenistic Jewish writing issued during the two centuries before Christ; the development will be made sufficiently clear by reference to certain of the leading documents in question.

1. *The Pseudo-Aristeas* (Aristæus).[1]—The alliance between Hellenism and Judaism was very adroitly prepared by the so-called letter of Aristeas. This Greek composition, which bears a name unknown to history, emanated from Alexandria, probably about B.C. 200,[2] and purports to narrate the origin of the Septuagint. Both the writer Aristeas, an honoured official at the court of Ptolemy II. Philadelphus, and his brother, the cultured Philocrates, to whom it is addressed, are

---

[1] Not to be confounded with the Jewish historian of the same name mentioned by Eusebius.

[2] So Schürer. Kautzsch, however, places the date of composition between B.C. 96 and 63, with a leaning towards the superior limit. So also Wendland, the most recent editor of the book. Bousset ascribes it to a still later date (B.C. 40–A.D. 30). But see G. A. Smith, *Jerusalem*, ii. p. 441, *n.* 2.

ostensibly pagans who entertain a deep respect for Judaism; but they only wear a heathen mask. Twice over the author fails to write in character, and unwittingly distinguishes his own times from the past age of Philadelphus (28, 182). In reality we have here a story with a purpose, the end in view being to glorify Judaism in the eyes of the Greeks, and to recommend the Jewish Law by adducing royal testimony to its worth. The treatise is not written in a controversial vein; the writer is content with trying to create a favourable impression among the heathen with regard to the Jewish people and their religion.

Briefly, the legend is to this effect: Ptolemy II. Philadelphus had a zealous librarian, Demetrius Phalereus, who advised his royal master to procure a Greek translation of the Jewish Law as containing the wisest legislation in the world. Acting on this suggestion, the king sent Aristeas and another courtier named Andreas to Jerusalem, with letters and gifts to Eleazar the high priest, asking for his co-operation in the work. To this request Eleazar responded courteously, and sent him seventy-two experienced scholars (six from each tribe), with a copy of the Law. At court, where the deputies were received with unusual honour, the king was astonished at the wisdom shewn by them in answer to his questions. After a week had passed, during which they were daily invited to the royal table, Demetrius conducted them to beautiful and retired quarters in the island of Pharos, where they completed the translation of the Pentateuch in seventy-two days. It was read first to the Jewish community of Alexandria, who officially certified its accuracy and decreed its finality, and then to King Ptolemy, who was "greatly amazed at the insight of the lawgiver," and ordered the careful retention of the books in his library. The translators, laden with presents for themselves and the high priest, were then sent back to Judæa.

The mere fact that the letter is spurious tends to throw doubt upon its historical trustworthiness; and there are other considerations which point strongly in the same direction.[1] While, therefore, there is every reason to ascribe the translation of the Law to the time of the second Ptolemy (284–247), it is improbable, to say the least, that we owe it to the literary taste of that monarch, according to the shewing of the letter of Aristeas. But indeed the writer's object is not primarily historical. For him the historical framework is valuable only in so far as it is fitted to exalt the Jewish religion in the estimation of the Greeks. The same motive underlies the glowing descriptions of Jerusalem and the Temple which are inserted in the narrative. His aim evidently is to strike the imagination of pagan readers, and to impress them with the worth of a religion emanating from so fine a country, having its head-quarters in such a beautiful city among the mountains, and so splendidly equipped as regards temple and

---

[1] According to Hermippus Callimachus (*ap.* Diog. Laert. v. 78, in Müller's *Frag. Hist. Græc.* iii. 47), a reputable writer under Ptolemy IV. Philopator (221–204), Demetrius Phalereus, who appears to have helped in founding the Library under Ptolemy I. Soter (321, King 306–285), was banished immediately on the accession of Philadelphus. If this is correct, the tradition is discredited at the core. Further, Aristeas is unaware that Arsinöe was childless; Ptolemy's naval defeat by Antigonus near Cos is alluded to as a victory; the philosopher Menedemus is wrongly represented as attached to the court of Philadelphus; the authors Theopompus and Theodectes are chronologically misplaced; even the historicity of the high priest Eleazar is uncertain.

priesthood. This conclusion is further supported by
the fact that in the artificial and monotonous politico-
religious conversations between Ptolemy and his guests,
questions and answers are so drawn up as practically
to form "a résumé of Jewish dogma, a catechism of the
Law of Moses."[1] It is also significant that at the close
the king is made to declare that he had derived great
advantage from their exposition of the principles of
government.

The letter of Aristeas is more, however, than a mere
recommendation of Judaism to the favourable notice of
the heathen. To some extent it represents a positive
attempt to bridge over the gulf that separated Jew and
Greek theologically. Passing by other and minor
indications of this, we may note the manner in which
the writer recognises the distinction, so characteristic of
Alexandrianism, between the Most High (θεὸς μέγιστος, ὁ
κυριεύων ἀπάντων θεός) and the particular gods (θεοὶ
μερικοί) who collectively stand in a subordinate
relation to Him. In pleading with Ptolemy for the
liberation of Jewish slaves within his dominions, Aristeas
uses the argument that they had received their Law,
and he his knowledge, from the same God, "the creator
and guardian of all, whom also all men worship, and we
ourselves under the name of Zeus."[2] Traces of the
Alexandrian religious philosophy appear even in the
utterances put into the lips of Eleazar the high priest.
Viewing all as one creation, Aristeas asks him to explain
why according to the Jewish Law some animals should

---

[1] Herriot, *Philon le Juif*, p. 65.

[2] Τὸν γὰρ πάντων ἐπόπτην καὶ κτίστην θεὸν οὗτοι σέβονται, ὃν καὶ πάντες,
ἡμεῖς δὲ μάλιστα προσονομάζοντες ἑτέρως Ζῆνα (16).

be reckoned unclean, and some kinds of food forbidden. In his reply Eleazar goes into considerable detail, pointing out that through the prohibitory precepts in question the Jews were defended as by walls of brass from prejudicial fellowship with men of other nationalities, and further, that there was " a deeper sense of the Law " in respect of which all its precepts were not only amply justified, but also of equal value. By way of making good the latter assertion, the writer already has recourse to the method of allegorical interpretation which the Jewish-Alexandrian philosophers were yet so fully to develop. He unfolds, for instance, the secret of the legal provisions with respect to clean and unclean animals. The language, he says, is figurative. Moses did not legislate with reference to mice and weasels,[1] but these holy commands were given with the view of awakening pious thoughts and building up character. Eleazar is also made to ascribe the great merit of the Jewish religion to its monotheistic doctrine. Polytheism and the animal worship of Egypt it counts as folly. Its fundamental teaching is that God is one, that His power permeates and governs all, that not the most secret of man's actions remains hid from Him, and that He sees the future as He sees the present. We have here a tolerably clear reflexion of the Alexandrian doctrine of the world-spirit through whom and in whom is all, and that to such an extent that He can Himself be called the All.[2]

2. *The Septuagint.*—Of prime importance for the study of Hellenistic Judaism is the Greek translation

[1] Lev. xi. 29.

[2] Dähne, *Geschichtliche Darstellung der Jüdisch-Alexandrinischen Religionsphilosophie*, ii. p. 209 f.

of the Scriptures known as the Septuagint. This is indeed the basis of the entire structure, and—to use the felicitous comparison of Schürer—as much bound up with it as is Luther's translation of the Bible with German Protestantism. Its antiquity, its exegetical value, its formative influence upon New Testament Greek, its independent witness to the text of the Old Testament—all combine to invest it with exceptional interest and value.

The middle wall of partition that had hitherto divided the Jews from other nations was effectually broken down by this epoch-making work. Although the legend of Aristeas, which assumed various forms in the writings of the Fathers,[1] is undoubtedly fictitious, the Septuagint may possibly have originated in the literary taste of Ptolemy Philadelphus, but the *raison d'être* of the work is more probably to be found in the growingly felt necessities of the Hellenistic Jews themselves. As Hebrew was now known only to the priests and the learned, a Greek Bible became indispensable for the great mass of the community. Some regard the Septuagint as the gradually evolved product of the translation into the vernacular of the synagogue lessons from the Law and the prophets, according to the custom introduced by Ezra. On this theory we should have to regard its origin as analogous to that of the Targums, which contain in written form the oral Aramaic translation or paraphrase by means of which the Jews of Asia were enabled to understand the sacred books.

---

[1] Philo adds a new detail. According to his account the translators were isolated, yet their renderings when compared were found exactly to coincide. This embellishment is already rightly denied by Jerome.

Others view the Septuagint as a result of the Jewish propaganda among the heathen.   In any case its linguistic character stamps it as the work of Jewish-Alexandrian scholars, and not that of deputies from Jerusalem.[1]

It is noteworthy that the story of Aristeas refers to the Pentateuch only.   This was certainly translated first, the other books having been added afterwards, at different times, and by at least five different hands. The exact dates at which the several books were rendered are not ascertainable, but the Prophets were dealt with before the Hagiographa, some parts of which were apparently not written till the age of the Maccabees. Not to mention certain other historical data pointing to the same conclusion, the prologue to *Ecclesiasticus* states that by B.C. 132 the entire Old Testament was extant in Greek.[2]   The best executed portion of the translation is undeniably the Pentateuch ; but it is no less true of this than of the whole collection to which the name of Septuagint has come to be applied, that the language is so harshly Hebraistic in character that no Greek could have perfectly understood it.   The very structure of the sentences is strongly Hebraic ; Greek words have new meanings thrust upon them by their being made to connote all that the corresponding Hebrew terms do ;[3] and new words are used which do not occur in classical Greek.[4]   How are we to account for these linguistic

---

[1] For illustrative examples see H. A. A. Kennedy, *Sources of N.T. Greek*, p. 24 f.

[2] But see Note 1, p. 363.

[3] *E.g.* δόξα, δικαιοσύνη, εἰρήνη, ὀφείλημα, etc.

[4] *E.g.* ἀλλοφυλισμός, 2 Macc. iv. 13, vi. 24.   See on this whole subject H. A. A. Kennedy, *op. cit.*   The learned author's examination of the Book of Deuteronomy shews that of 313 of the more uncommon words used, 36, or 11 per cent., are peculiar to the Septuagint.

features of the Septuagint Greek? Everything points to the likelihood that, while necessarily from the circumstances of its origin "deeply impregnated with Semitic characteristics," the Septuagint largely reflects the colloquial Greek of Alexandria as spoken in the third century B.C.[1]

In the very production of the Septuagint, which was completed gradually, and was probably, at least as regards the prophetical and poetical books, due to private enterprise, we have a standing memorial of the extent to which Greek influence now pervaded Jewish life.[2] It was no longer essential for Jews of the Dispersion to be acquainted with the Hebrew language in order to remain in possession of the truths of the Hebrew religion; they read the Scriptures, as they transacted their business, in the vernacular tongue. And although there may be difference of opinion as to the extent of it, there can be none as to the fact that the Hellenistic influence is already reflected in the Septuagint. No sooner did the Old Testament Scriptures wear a Greek dress than there began to be infused into them a Greek spirit. This is so far discernible in the very process of translation.[3] It is impossible to

---

[1] "On the one hand it has many elements in common with the writers of the κοινὴ διάλεκτος, on the other it is often a transcript of the vernacular. But the predominant features in its vocabulary are—(*a*) The creation of a theological terminology rendered necessary by the original of which it is a translation, and (*b*) The expression in Greek form of special Jewish conceptions and customs due to the same cause." Kennedy, *op. cit.* p. 164. On the syntax of the Septuagint see Note 37, p. 411.

[2] See Note 38, p. 412.

[3] "Toutefois il convient de se rappeler que, même dans la traduction la plus libre, on ne doit pas s'attendre à trouver autre chose et plus que des indices obscurs du *Credo* philosophique des traducteurs."—H. Bois, *Essai sur les Origines de la Philosophie Judéo-Alexandrine*, p. 130.

resist the conviction that the translators were in sympathy with the tendency of the times to reconcile Judaism with the culture of the West. There are traces of Jewish-Alexandrian philosophy in the Septuagint,[1] the germs, at any rate, of the doctrine afterwards developed by Philo. Yet it would be easy to exaggerate here. The translators were tied down to the Biblical text, and it was only in isolated instances, and even then very delicately, that they could put forward their philosophical views. It was, however, a necessary consequence of the contact of Judaism with Hellenism that the Alexandrian philosophy should stamp itself to some extent upon the Greek translation of the Hebrew Scriptures. The Egyptian Jews were equally concerned to maintain the authority of their sacred books and to conserve their philosophical standpoint as to the transcendence of God. Refraining as they did from applying even the worthiest titles to the Deity, it was distasteful to them to find passages of Holy Writ in which He was spoken of in terms of human being and working. The Septuagint translators therefore set themselves to tone down at least the grosser anthropomorphic expressions about God and His relation to the world.[2] In this connexion, by

---

[1] This is denied by Freudenthal, *Jewish Quarterly Review*, ii., 1890, p. 205 ff. Bois, on the other hand, writes: "Dans une version qui serait strictement exacte, il n'y aurait pas de place, à coup sûr, pour les vues particulières aux traducteurs. Mais la version des Septante est loin d'être stricte. . . . Dans plusieurs passages ou rencontre certains changements d'un caractère tel qu'on ne peut alléguer, pour en rendre compte, ni l'incurie ou l'ignorance des traducteurs, ni l'usage d'un texte différent du nôtre. On dirait qu'on est en présence d'adaptations intentionelles des Ecritures à des opinions modernes et hellénistiques."—*Op. cit.* p. 130 1.

[2] In a few isolated passages the use of the Divine name is avoided by the substitution of ἄγγελος (Job xx. 15; Ps. viii. 6; Isa. ix. 6; Hos. xii. 4, etc.), while in Ex. iv. 16, xviii. 19 we have the expression τὰ τοῦ θεοῦ.

means of slight but subtle alterations, the text of the
Greek translation has accordingly been adapted to the
Hellenistic standpoint. Although many of the examples
of such adaptation put forward by Dähne [1] are disallowed
by Siegfried, Herriot, Drummond, and other scholars,
there are at least enough of unmistakable instances to
prove that the path of Hellenism was appreciably
smoothed by the labours of the Seventy.[2]

In explanation of this aloofness from anthropomorphism which characterises the Septuagint we have two
conflicting theories. Some think the modifications of
the Hebrew text so slight as to make it quite un-
necessary to view them as the result of the latent
influence of a foreign philosophy, and prefer to regard
them as the natural evolution of dogma among a people
who were advancing in civilisation. Others, with more
reason, maintain that we can trace here at least the
rudiments of the system afterwards built up by Philo.
This view has certainly been carried too far by Gfrörer
and Dähne, who write sometimes almost as if the
Jewish-Alexandrian philosophy had already assumed its
final shape at the time of the translation of the old
Testament into Greek. All that can be said with
safety is that among cultured Jews of the period, and
apparently owing to Hellenistic influences, there was
a growing tendency to dissociate the idea of God from
everything that savoured of human imperfection or
limitation, or seemed to bring Him into close contact
with men. The argument that the theory of Greek
influence is vitiated by the fact that changes are not

[1] *Op. cit.* ii. pp. 11–72.
[2] See Note 39, p. 414.

made throughout systematically, the theophanies for
example being retained in the Septuagint as in the
Hebrew Bible,[1] is lacking in historic sense. The
translators were not writing another Bible; they were
not exponents of a developed philosophy; they did
not set themselves rigidly to remove every anthropomorphic expression from the Old Testament. What
they did was to introduce in various directions such
modifications, whether slight or marked or subtle, as
to leave us in no doubt regarding the general bent of
their minds, and even sometimes the special colour of
their thought.

3. *Aristobulus.*—The first known representative of
pure Jewish-Alexandrian religious philosophy was Aristobulus. He is usually spoken of by the Fathers as a
Peripatetic; but as his writings certainly contain Pythagorean tendencies also, it is safest to style him an
Eclectic. Eusebius and Clement identify him with the
philosopher mentioned in 2 Macc. i. 10 as "King
Ptolemy's teacher." Although there has been a good
deal of discussion concerning the period when he wrote,
it is practically certain that he lived at Alexandria under
Ptolemy Philometor (B.C. 180–146). Clement[2] says he
wrote βιβλία ἱκανά, which seems to mean not that he
wrote a variety of treatises, but that his work was one of
considerable size. With the exception of two passages
quoted by Eusebius,[3] it has entirely perished. There is

---

[1] Herriot, *op. cit.* p. 96.

[2] *Strom.* v. 14.

[3] *Præp. Ev.* viii. 10, xiii. 12. The quotations in Clement (*Strom.* i. 22,
vi. 3) supply no additional material. Cyril of Alexandria (*contra Julian.*
p. 134, ed. Spanh.) erroneously ascribes to Aristobulus a passage from the
third book of the Ἰνδικά of Megasthenes. Cf. Clement, *Strom.* i. 15.

no doubt, however, about its character. This is clear both from the descriptions of those who knew it, and from the fragments which have been preserved. Eusebius calls it "an interpretation of the sacred laws," Jerome "an explanatory commentary," and Anatolius "an exegetical treatise," upon the Mosaic Law. The general tendency of the work is evident from the passages quoted by Clement and Eusebius. It does not appear to have been a consecutive exposition of the sacred text, but rather a sort of philosophical digest of the contents of the Mosaic legislation, drawn up with the view of proving that Judaism, rightly understood, had anticipated the principal tenets of the various schools of Greece. These, he contended, had been taken from the Pentateuch, of which some portions had long been translated. This fact had been obscured by the literal interpretation of Scripture, but was revealed by the application of the allegorical method. Aristobulus therefore set before himself a twofold aim—the allegorical interpretation of Scripture, and the winning over of Greek philosophers and poets to Judaism.

According to this Jewish-Alexandrian philosopher, the Bible contains a truly spiritual conception of God; but this is arrived at only by discovering the hidden meaning which underlies its statements. These must be expounded in a "God-worthy" way, and this service he endeavours to render. With the view of removing the unpopularity attaching to the Law on account of its anthropomorphisms, he gives elaborate comments upon such passages as attribute to the Deity hands, arms, etc. He asks his royal patron not to interpret them according to the letter, but in what he calls a natural manner, and in accordance with a conception of God from which the physical, mythical, and anthropomorphic has been entirely eliminated. "For often," he says, "our legislator Moses, when desiring to express an idea, purposely makes use of *sensible* expressions in order to do so." Not to recognise this is to be without the key to the Mosaic writings.[1]

It may be said on behalf of this writer that in adopting the peculiar method of Biblical interpretation which he did, his intention was simply to present the essential truth of Scripture apart from its particular historical setting. But whatever service he may have rendered in the way of bringing out the moral and spiritual teaching of the sacred writings is more than counterbalanced by the crop of extravagances which followed in his wake, and for which he was mainly responsible. To any passage which had either come to be literally inapplicable, or which according to its plain reading was unintelligible, the allegorical method was applied with wonderful effect. But the use of it was not limited to such cases; it was virtually extended to the whole of Scripture. And Scripture suffered much in the process. Such was the vitality of this method of interpretation that a century and a half elapsed before it came to full maturity in the writings of Philo. We find it still in vogue after the commencement of the Christian era. St. Paul occasionally resorts to it. It has a place in the Epistle to the Hebrews. It was in general favour among the Gnostics. It was much affected by Origen, who expressly replies to the attack made by Celsus not

---

[1] For examples of this writer's method of interpretation, see Note 40, p. 418.

only upon the Mosaic history, but upon those who understood it allegorically.[1]

The effort to unify philosophy and Judaism is also reflected in the extant fragments from the pen of Aristobulus.[2] He finds a note of similarity between Moses and the Greek philosophers in their interpretation of the expression "the voice of God." By this he says we are not to understand audible words, but the preparation of an act. This is what Moses means when he says, "God spake, and it was done." Pythagoras, Socrates, and Plato speak of having heard the voice of God in precisely the same sense. In both cases the meaning intended to be expressed is that they have understood the inner laws of the world. Again, Aristobulus expresses the view that we cannot directly apprehend Godhead; we can only recognise the Divine power as dwelling in the world. From eternity God and matter have been distinct. All His relations with the world are mediated by His wisdom, which is the source of all light, and the parent of idealism. Aristobulus points out that in holding that all light comes from wisdom the Peripatetics and Solomon are at one;

[1] *c. Cels.* i. 17.

[2] We have already seen that this writer maintained the derivation of Greek philosophy from the Jewish Law. Clement (*Strom.* i. 22) professes to quote from him verbally as follows: "Aristobulus, in his first book addressed to Philometor, writes in these words: 'Plato followed the laws given to us, and had manifestly studied all that is said in them. And before Demetrius there had been translated by another, previous to the dominion of Alexander and of the Persians, the account of the departure of our countrymen the Hebrews from Egypt, and the fame of all that happened to them, and their taking possession of the land, and the account of the whole code of laws; so that it is perfectly clear that the above-mentioned philosopher derived a great deal from this source, for he was very learned, as also Pythagoras, who transferred many things from our books to his own system of doctrines.'"

and from the excellence of God he infers the excellence
of His Law, which requires piety, justice, and modera-
tion—the very virtues, be it noted, to which Philo
afterwards gave special prominence in certain of his
writings.   The rest of the seventh day is another thing
which Aristobulus deems it necessary to explain.   He
cannot suppose that God ever really rested or ceased to
act upon the world.   If Scripture represents Him as
resting on the seventh day, this is in order to signalise
the worth of the number seven, which is the symbol of
reason, the seventh and highest faculty in man." [1]   In
proof of the virtue of this number, Aristobulus quotes
some verses from Hesiod, Homer, and Linus.   Another
illustration of the spirit and method of this writer is
found in his treatment of a poem ascribed to Orpheus,
and still preserved in its original form.   This Aristobulus
largely supplements from the Pentateuch.   A meeting
between Orpheus and Moses is falsely invented and
gravely chronicled.   The poem asserts the immortality
of God; but Aristobulus improves upon this, and
represents Him as absolutely beyond the grasp of the
human soul, and visible only to pure intelligence.   This
whole theory of the dependence of Greek philosophy on
Judaism may strike us as somewhat puerile; but even
three or four centuries later it was firmly believed in by
Clement of Alexandria, who speaks of the Greeks as
"pilferers of all manner of writing." [2]   The idea had
been mooted even before the time of Aristobulus.
About the beginning of the Seleucid era (B.C. 312) the
historian Megasthenes wrote: "All that was said about

[1] Here we have a point of contact with the Pythagorean philosophy.
[2] *Strom.* vi. 4.

nature by the ancients is said also by those who philosophise beyond Greece: some things by the Brahmins of India, and others by those called Jews in Syria."[1] Megasthenes, however, only noted the coincidence; Aristobulus sought to account for it on the supposition of plagiarism from Jewish sources. That this view afterwards found many adherents even among the Greeks themselves is clear from its acceptance by Hermippus[2] and others, who were perhaps led to adopt it from the desire to trace their beliefs to an Oriental source. It found expression among the Jews of the Middle Ages, who represented Aristotle as recognising on his deathbed the God of Israel.[3] In the fifteenth century Reuchlin, and in the seventeenth Huetius, still tried to shew that all true philosophy comes from the Hebrews.

In view of the subsequent development given to his two leading ideas, the importance of Aristobulus is certainly not to be measured by the brief fragments of his writings which have been preserved. He was the first full-fledged Jewish-Alexandrian philosopher, and laid the foundation of the structure which others were to rear. Some recent critics regard the entire work of Aristobulus as spurious. The truth seems to be that in his simplicity he sometimes quotes as genuine verses of

[1] Clement, *Strom.* i. 15.
[2] Didot, *Frag. hist. gr.* iii. 41.
[3] According to the testimony of the Fathers, Aristobulus was an Aristotelian. Ravaisson (*Metaph. d'Aristote*, ii. 356) makes the interesting suggestion that possibly the spurious work *De Mundo*, which has been ascribed to Aristotle, may have been the work of Aristobulus, whose idea of a Divine power pervading nature it exactly reflects. "Ne peut-on pas reconnaître dans le faux Aristote, comme dans le faux Orphée (que d'ailleurs il ne manque pas de citer), le Juif Alexandrin, imbu de la physique stoïcienne?"

Homer, Hesiod, etc., what are clearly Jewish forgeries.[1] But this is no sufficient reason for doubting the authenticity of his work generally.

4. *The Book of Wisdom*, etc.—Jewish-Alexandrianism appears in a more fully developed form in the *Book of Wisdom*. This indeed is its finest literary product. It represents the high-water mark of Jewish religious thought in the period between the Old and New Testaments, and in some of its ideas has a remarkable affinity with the Johannine books and the Epistle to the Hebrews.[2] Some of its beautiful expressions have become the permanent possession of the Christian Church. From the circumstance that Solomon is several times introduced as the speaker, although he is not actually named,[3] it has been called the *Wisdom of Solomon*. The book, however, is plainly the work of an (unknown) Alexandrian Jew, and its ascription to Solomon is quite in accordance with a well-known literary method of the times. Chronologically, it comes after *Ecclesiasticus*, and before Philo; but the date of composition cannot be more precisely determined. From the clear-cut philosophical conceptions of the writer it seems reasonable, however, to suppose that he lived as late as the middle of the first century B.C.[4] Regarding the unity of the book widely different opinions are entertained. Some consider it "the well-

---

[1] See Note 41, p. 418.

[2] Of the writer Ewald says: "In the nervous energy of his proverbial style, and in the depth of his representation, we have a premonition of John, and in the conception of heathenism a preparation for Paul, like a warm rustle of the spring ere its time is fully come."—*Hist. of Israel*, v. p. 434.

[3] See especially ix. 7 f.

[4] Bousset assigns it to be the period between B.C. 30 and A.D. 40.

arranged product of a single author,"[1] while others regard it as of composite origin.[2] For our present purpose the question is of little consequence. The main burden of the book is the folly of idolatry and the excellence of true wisdom as embodied in the Jewish Law. Although rhetorically addressed to the kings and judges of the earth,[3] its teaching is quite as much designed to rebuke the faithless among the Jews themselves as to convert heathen readers into proselytes to Judaism. While the writer thus appeals to all " heathen-minded readers," whether of Jewish or Gentile extraction, he also seeks to console the faithful under persecution by dwelling upon the temporal happiness which attends the pursuit of wisdom, and by pointing to the bliss of immortality.[4]

The Hellenistic trend of the book is very pronounced. It was originally written in Greek by one whose mastery of that language is in evidence on every page. If Hebraisms occur, there is also a coinage of new words which implies an intimate acquaintance with the Greek tongue. The book distinctly reflects the influence of Hellenic culture generally. Greek phrases, figures, and allusions abound. The skilfully constructed sentences[5] and flowing rhetoric[6] betray a Greek education. The author is familiar with Greek poetry, and with the respective tenets of the various schools of Greek philosophy. An instance of the Greek logical argument known as the *Sorites* occurs in vi. 17–20.

---

[1] Siegfried in Kautzsch, *Die Apokryphen*, etc.
[2] Stevenson, Introduction to *Wisdom* in the *Temple Bible*.
[3] i. 1, vi. 1 ff.   [4] iii. 1, 4.
[5] xii. 27, xvii. 2, etc.   [6] xvii.–xix.

One is struck with the absence of the objectivity so
characteristic of the Hebrew Scriptures. The writer
frequently makes reflexions of his own, reasoning in
dialectic fashion, and basing his conclusions on
experience,[1] and sometimes states, like a pulpiteer or
rhetorician, how he is going to treat his subject.[2]

A few concrete examples will shew to what an
extent, alike in thought and in expression, the book
bears the stamp of Hellenism. In support of the
position that God is not the author of death, the writer
says, " Nor hath Hades royal dominion upon earth." [3]
This personification of Hades (= the Hebrew Sheōl) is
apparently borrowed from the Greek mythology, and
is certainly not after the manner of the older Hebraism.
Equally foreign to the latter is the description of
reason as " a spark kindled by the beating of our
heart," [4] and of God as " the first author of beauty." [5]
In at least two passages [6] the doctrine of the Divine
providence finds quite abstract and theological expression. It is a palpably Grecian and didactic
condemnation of idolatry to say that " men . . .
invested stones and stocks with the incommunicable
Name." [7] Wisdom is said to be " initiated into the
knowledge of God," [8] and manna is described as " ice-like
grains of ambrosial food." [9] Whether or not there is an
allusion to the Greek idea of the river of Lethe in the
expression " falling into deep forgetfulness," [10] the Stoic
enumeration of the four cardinal virtues (" soberness
and understanding, righteousness and courage ") is

---

[1] xiii. 3 f., etc.   [2] vi. 22 f.   [3] i. 14.   [4] ii. 2, R.V. marg.
[5] xiii. 3.   [6] xiv. 3, xvii. 2.   [7] xiv. 21.   [8] viii. 4.
[9] xix. 21.   [10] xvi. 11.

undoubtedly reflected in viii. 7, and the Pythagorean
doctrine of the pre-existence of the soul in viii. 20.[1]
In xix. 4 Jahweh's hardening of Pharaoh's heart
to pursue the Israelites after having allowed them to
depart is represented in terms of a philosophical
determinism which recalls the Greek Nemesis; the
Egyptians were lured to their doom by "necessity."[2]
The abstract mode of thought characteristic of
Hellenism appears, however, not only in single expressions and phrases, but also in the treatment of
scriptural incidents. An example of this is the
allegorising reference in xvi. 5 ff. to the lifting up
of the brazen serpent in the wilderness.[3] In the Old
Testament narrative we have a simple objective statement of facts; there is no explanation of the facts.
In the *Book of Wisdom* it is otherwise; the spiritual
significance of the incident is expounded at length,
and the outward details only alluded to in a general
way. The serpents were sent upon the people "for
admonition," and the brazen serpent was "a token of
salvation to put them in remembrance of the commandment of thy law." Not only so; the writer in a
speculative vein not natural to a Jew uninfluenced by
Hellenism, distinctly guards his readers against a false
interpretation of the narrative, and adds, "For he that
turned toward it was not saved because of that which
was beheld, but because of thee, the Saviour of all."
Here, then, we see the allegorising tendency of the
Alexandrian Jews in full play.

The Greek influence is also clearly traceable in the
psychology of the book. As already stated, the writer

---

[1] Denied by F. C. Porter.   See Additional Note, p. 423.
[2] Cf. R.V. marg.   [3] Num. xxi. 4 ff.

holds the Pythagorean doctrine of the pre-existence of
the human soul. " Being good," he says, " I came into
a body undefiled." [1]   It is impossible to find the source
of this teaching in the Old Testament, the attempt to read
it into such passages as Deut. xxix. 15, Job xxxviii.
19 ff., and Ps. cxxxix. 15, being forced and unnatural.
Another tenet of Greek philosophy is adopted by our
author, namely, the Platonico-dualistic doctrine that
the body is only an " earthly tabernacle " for the mind.[2]
It must return to dust when " required to render back
the soul which was lent." [3]   If he scarcely goes so far as
to maintain with Philo that the body is the principle
of all evil, he certainly regards it as a perpetual drag
upon the progress of the soul.

The pseudo-Solomon seeks to prove the existence
of God from the visible works of creation: " From the
greatness of the beauty even of created things cor-
respondently (ἀναλόγως) does man form the image
of their first maker." [4]   In this fact we have a further
Hellenistic trait.   To the unsophisticated Jew the being
of God is not a matter for demonstration; it is an
axiom, the postulate underlying all his thought.   But
in Jewish-Hellenistic circles there was a growing
tendency to represent human knowledge of the Deity
as limited to the bare fact of His existence.   It was
reserved for Philo formally to assert the impossibility
of defining God in His essence; but the *Book of
Wisdom* already approaches to this position when it
says: " Hardly do we divine the things that are on
earth . . . and who ever gained knowledge of thy
counsel, except thou gavest wisdom, and sentest thy

---

[1] viii. 20.   [2] ix. 15.   [3] xv. 8.   [4] xiii. 5.

holy spirit from on high?"[1]   The work, however, is not altogether free from anthropomorphisms,[2] and God is not always spoken of as a passionless Being.

But the presence of the Greek influence is in nothing more manifest than in the conception of Wisdom itself as the intermediary between God and the world, and in the epithets applied to it as such.   The Hebrew doctrine is hellenised; the writer describes Wisdom after the manner of a Greek philosopher discoursing of the *Nous*.   She is " a breath of the power of God," " a clear effluence of the glory of the Almighty," " an effulgence from everlasting light," " an unspotted mirror of the working of God," and " an image of his goodness."[3]   Wisdom is apparently elevated into a substance and invested with a spirit.   " There is in her a spirit quick of understanding, holy, alone in kind, manifold, subtil, freely moving, clear in utterance, unpolluted, distinct, unharmed, loving what is good, keen, unhindered, beneficent, loving toward man, stedfast, sure, free from care, all-powerful, all-surveying, and penetrating through all spirits that are quick of understanding, pure, most subtil."[4]   The difficult question as to whether in the writer's mind Wisdom is merely a Divine attribute, or at most a poetical personification, or whether it is a Divine personality separate from, though always subordinate to, God, belongs more properly to the development of doctrine within the period.   Here the broad fact to be grasped is that the *Book of Wisdom* is really transitional, and that, therefore, its doctrine of Wisdom is naturally something intermediate

[1] ix. 16 f.   [2] Cf. i. 10, iv. 18, v. 16, vii. 16, x. 20.
[3] vii. 25 f.   [4] vii. 22 f.

between that of the Old Testament and the Logos
theory of Philo.   A great step is already taken towards
the formulation of the latter in the unification of the
Divine intermediaries under a single name.   The writer
seems to use wisdom as the equivalent of several other
terms.   The parallelism in ix. 17 makes it virtually
certain that Wisdom and God's "holy spirit" are
identical.   This conclusion is confirmed by the fact that,
like Wisdom, the spirit of God is an all-pervading
principle.[1]   The same thing holds good with regard to
the Word.   Like Wisdom, the Word is the medium of
creation,[2] all-powerful [3] and all-healing,[4] and bearing the
sword of God.[5]   As sharing God's throne,[6] Wisdom
also stands for the supreme Power,[7] Justice,[8] Providence,[9]
and Mercy.[10]   It was essentially as the image of God's
goodness [11] that Wisdom presided at the creation of the
world out of formless matter, and became the artificer
of all things.[12]   This idea was afterwards to find very
exalted expression in the writings of Philo, but already
in the *Book of Wisdom* it is elaborated with much
clearness and force.   " Thou hast mercy on all men,
because thou hast power to do all things, and thou
overlookest the sins of men to the end they may repent.
For thou lovest all things that are, and abhorrest none
of the things which thou didst make ; for never wouldest
thou have formed anything if thou didst hate it.   And
how would anything have endured, except thou hadst
willed it ? or that which was not called by thee, how
would it have been preserved ?   But thou sparest all

---

[1] i. 12, xii. 1, compared with vii. 23.   [2] ix. 2.   [3] vii. 23, xviii. 15.
[4] xvi. 2.   [5] xviii. 15 f.   [6] ix. 4.   [7] i. 3.   [8] i. 8, xi. 20.
[9] xiv. 2 f.   [10] x. 4.   [11] vii. 26.   [12] vii. 21, viii. 6.

things because they are thine, O Sovereign Lord, thou lover of men's lives (= souls); for thine incorruptible spirit is in all things." [1]

In this book the subject of retribution also is handled in an obviously philosophical spirit. The writer lays down the principle that punishment is exactly proportionate to transgression: " by what things a man sinneth, by these he is punished." [2] In illustration he points to the case of the Egyptians, whose destruction of the male children of the Hebrews in the Nile was punished by the experience of " clotted blood instead of a river's ever-flowing fountain," and whose worship of " reptiles and wretched vermin " was followed by avenging plagues of the same " irrational creatures." Alongside of the righteous retribution thus meted out in this life the writer sets down his brilliant conception of the future lot of the righteous. In a passage of great beauty he remarks upon the blindness of the wicked to the fact that the prize of immortality awaits the blameless soul. God made man for incorruption. It was only by the envy of the devil that death entered into the world. The souls of the righteous are in the hand of God. " They are in peace. For even if in the sight of men they be punished, their hope is full of immortality." [3] A graphic picture is also drawn in ch. v. of the revulsion of feeling produced in the wicked when at last they are confronted with the victims of their abuse. Afraid, and " amazed at the marvel of God's salvation," they shall penitently acknowledge their folly

---

[1] xi. 23–xii. 1.
[2] xi. 16. This view occurs, however, in 2 Macc. xiii. 7—a Pharisaic work.
[3] iii. 4.

in reckoning as madmen the sons and saints of God, and in setting so much store by pleasure and riches and arrogance—things which "all passed away as a shadow." In all this the way was to a large extent prepared for Philo's doctrine, that after death the souls of the righteous dwell in the supersensible world among the angelic powers.

The *Book of Wisdom*, then, is a genuine creation of the Jewish-Alexandrian philosophy. Here at all events there can be no question of detecting isolated traces of Greek influence; it is so pronounced as to amount to an actual transformation of Judaism. We see Hebrew religion so intermingled with Greek beliefs that the resultant product is a philosophy which deliberately seeks to remove God to a distance from the world and to create a host of intermediaries. It is a philosophy not to be identified with Platonism, Stoicism, or any other particular school. As its leading idea was the fusion of Judaism and Hellenism, it naturally assimilated everything conducive to this object, from whatever source derived. The significance of the *Book of Wisdom* lies precisely in the fact that it reflects the Judaism of a period when the utmost efforts were made to secure this fusion.

To suppose, however, that everything in the *Book of Wisdom* is inspired by the thought and culture of Greece, would be as absurd as the contention of those Jews who held that all Greek philosophy had been taken from the Bible. Although the work is impregnated with Hellenism, the theological standpoint of the writer remains essentially Jewish. This is clear both from the form and from the contents of the book. The use of Hebraic turns of expression, of the simplest connecting particles, and of the parallelism distinctive of the proverbial philosophy of the Hebrews, already convey the stamp of Judaism. In its whole spirit and purport, moreover, the work is that of a loyal and earnest-minded Jew, whose Judaism, so far from being irksome to him, as was the case a little later on with Josephus and Philo, is openly proclaimed and contrasted with the false philosophy which would make pleasure rather than righteousness the guide of life. The spectacle of so many being led by the Greek materialism to abandon the faith of their fathers draws forth his strong protest.[1] Living amongst Hellenists whose principles and practice differed so widely from his own, he seeks to furnish professors of the Jewish religion with a solid and philosophically reasoned basis of belief. Did they " seek after wisdom ? " In its truest form it lay enshrined in Judaism. The choice of the term σοφία was peculiarly happy, inasmuch as it covered at once the whole circle of truth embraced in Greek philosophy and all that the Old Testament had taught about Ḥokhma. Thus it comes to pass that if the writer is influenced by the different schools of pagan philosophy on the one hand, on the other his conception of Divine Wisdom is exclusively based on Proverbs.[2] His point of view is therefore neither exclusively Greek nor exclusively Jewish, but Græco-Jewish, in short, Jewish-Alexandrian.

Two other literary remains of Hellenistic Judaism claim at least passing mention—*The Jewish Sibyllines* and the *Fourth Book of Maccabees*. The former constitute a confused mass of miscellaneous material which

---

[1] i. 16–ii. 24. [2] viii. and ix.

is the despair of critics.   Even the Jewish and the Christian elements can only here and there be with certainty
distinguished.   But the oldest portions of the collection,
contained in the third book, and dating from about
B.C. 140, are undoubtedly of Jewish-Alexandrian origin.
A heathen guise is assumed with the aim of propagating
Judaism.   In Greek hexameter the Sibyl prophetically
addresses the heathen, proclaiming the one true God, and
denouncing the sin and folly of idolatry.   Eternal
blessedness is promised to the penitent, while the
severest judgment is threatened in case of impenitence.
The distinctive features of Hellenistic thought are unmistakably present.   Greek and Jewish legends are
intermingled.   There is throughout a studious effort to
avoid speaking of the Deity in terms of the life of
humanity, as well as a frequent reiteration of the
conviction that Judaism is destined to triumph over
heathenism and to become the religion of the whole
world.   The conception of the heathen gods as demons,[1]
the frequent connexion of God with light, and the description of man as roaming in darkness (out of which,
however, it is his duty to emerge, striving after the
light),[2] suggest the influence of Alexandrianism.   It is
also significant that no allusion is made in the poem to
Christian faith or practice, and that the language used
with reference to the absolute exaltation of the Divine
Being [3] is such as to exclude the worship of the
Redeemer.   This exactly coincides with the fact that
the notion of a concrete personal Messiah was alien to
the purely ideal outlook of the Jewish-Alexandrian
school.

[1] Ver. 22.   [2] Ver. 25 ff.   [3] Vv. 7, 16.

The so-called *Fourth Book of Maccabees* is a philosophical discourse upon " the supremacy of pious reason (= religious principle) over the passions," and affords a good example of Judaism and Hellenism in combination. In xv. 31 the steadfastness of " the mother of the Maccabees " in face of a flood of passionate impulses is compared to the manner in which at the time of the Deluge the ark withstood the force of the waters. Some would find in this an echo of the allegorical interpretation of the Flood current among the Hellenistic Jews.[1] Although written in fluent and correct Greek, and clearly reflecting the Stoic philosophy, 4 Maccabees is the work of an earnest-minded and devout Jew, who is anxious that his co-religionists should loyally adhere to the Mosaic Law in spite of the seductions of Hellenism on the one hand and the pains of persecution on the other. It is not to human reason as such, but to *pious* reason, or reason based upon the observance of the Divine Law, that he ascribes the mastery of the passions. As the result of a philosophical discussion, he concludes that this lordship extends to all the affections except forgetfulness and ignorance, which are defects inherent in reason itself. This conclusion is supported by examples from Jewish history, special stress being laid upon the heroism of the priest Eleazar, and of the seven brethren and their mother, who in the persecution under Antiochus Epiphanes endured the most barbarous cruelty rather than deny the faith. From the troubled present the writer contemplates the future with calmness, being assured that the sufferings of the righteous will be

[1] Dähne, *op. cit.* ii. p. 196. For Philo the flood means the uprising of the passions against the rational will, while Noah is the reason which seeks to protect men against this flood.

followed by a blessed immortality. The book dates probably from the Herodian age.

Finally, it may be noted here that if the writings of the period unmistakably bear the stamp of the Greek learning, there was also a corresponding attempt to inoculate Greek literature with Hebrew theology. Surprising results were sometimes obtained by means of slight textual alterations. In this way it became possible to represent Sophocles as a teacher of monotheism, and Homer as an authority on sabbath observance.[1] Those who wrote on sacred themes took the Greek classical poets as their models of style. Thus a certain Theodotus composed an epic poem upon the history of ancient Shechem, and an otherwise unknown Philo dealt similarly with Jerusalem, while an Ezekiel wrote a tragedy upon the Exodus.

5. *Philo.* — The Jewish - Alexandrian philosophy reached its fullest development in the writings of the illustrious Philo (*c.* B.C. 20–A.D. 50), who not only outstripped all others in the effort to wed Jewish belief with Hellenic culture, but also influenced very strongly the development of Christian theology. Although no names of its representatives have come down to us, it would be a mistake to suppose that it had none in the interval between the appearance of the *Book of Wisdom* and the works of Philo. But Philo so far eclipsed all his precursors that it is little wonder if nearly all of them have fallen into oblivion. Aristeas, Aristobulus, and even the pseudo-Solomon, were forgotten on the advent

---

[1] For suspected quotations from these and other Greek poets see Clement, *Strom.* v. This writer evidently took them from the work of the pseudo-Hecatæus on *Abraham.*

of him who put the copestone upon the structure which they had helped to rear.

Philo was a native and citizen of Alexandria. He does not appear to have lived in affluence,[1] like his brother Alexander, who held the post of *alabarch* or chief collector of customs on the Arabian side of the Nile, but he at all events belonged to an influential Jewish family. It is clear from his writings that he disliked the Egyptians, and could never forgive their cruel treatment of the Hebrews. The Alexandrians in particular were obnoxious to him on account of their shameless spoliation of the Jews, and he stigmatises them as " adepts in flattery, jugglery, and lying."[2] A lover of Greece and of the Greek learning, he was yet a Jew to the core, " attached to all the traditions of his religion and of his race "; and we know from the *De Providentia* that he made at least one pilgrimage to Jerusalem. " There is," he says, " on the Syrian shore a town named Ascalon. I passed it when I was sent to the temple of my fathers in order to pray and offer sacrifices there."[3] Even apart from this express statement, the fact might have been inferred from the circumstantial account of the Temple and the priesthood in the second book of the *De Monarchia*. In A.D. 40, when an old man, Philo headed a Jewish embassy to Rome which sought to dissuade the Emperor Caius from requiring Divine honour of the Jews. It would appear that in the later period of his life, although much against his will, he was a good deal immersed in politics.[4] The appeal

[1] In *De spec. leg.* ii. 5 he eulogises the rich who were willing to live " like the rest of us who are poor."
[2] *Leg. ad Caium*, 25.　　　[3] *Sermo* ii. § 107.　　　[4] *De spec. leg.* iii. 1.

to Rome was unsuccessful.   More attention was paid to
Apion, chief advocate for the non-Jewish population of
Alexandria, who, perceiving the dilemma of the Jews,
behaved themselves towards them with greater truculence
than ever.   Beyond these facts nothing is known of
Philo's personal history.

We are left in no dubiety, however, either as to the
aims he set before himself or as to the general principles
by which his life was regulated.   These are sufficiently
manifest from his works.[1]   Like Aristobulus, he was
chiefly concerned to establish the Jewish origin of the
doctrines derived from Greek philosophers.   Assuming
the absolute authority of the Mosaic Law not only as in
itself true, but as the source and sum of all truth, he
proceeded to deduce from it the most approved conclusions of Greek philosophy, with the view of convincing
his Jewish brethren that these had already been taught
by Moses.   On the other hand, he sought to point the
Greeks to the Pentateuch as the source of all that was
profoundest in philosophy and best in legislation.   This
twofold aim he kept before him in all his literary work.
He was the interpreter of the Greek to the Jew and of
the Jew to the Greek.   As a Greek he was an eclectic
philosopher with a marked preference for the doctrines
of Plato, the Stoics, and the later Pythagoreans.   As a
Jew he clung loyally to the religion of his fathers, and

[1] Philo was a voluminous writer, but many of his works are no longer
extant.   The bulk of those which, in whole or in part, have come down to
us, deal with the Pentateuch.   They include (1) an explanation of it in the
form of a catechism ; (2) a great allegorical, *i.e.* esoteric and scientific,
commentary on Genesis ; (3) a more popular digest of the Mosaic legislation for non-Jewish readers.   Philo's style is modelled upon the Greek
classical authors, particularly Plato.

had some knowledge of Hebrew, and even of the Halacha or traditional law, while in the Haggadic inter-pretation of Scripture he excelled. Himself both Jew and Greek, he tried to bring others into the same category by hellenising the Jews and judaising the Greeks. He sought on the one hand to indoctrinate his fellow-countrymen with his own pale conception of Judaism as modified by elements imported from Greek philosophy, and on the other hand to persuade the Greeks that in virtue of the Mosaic revelation the highest religious knowledge belonged to the Jewish people.

Philo laboured arduously at this double task, and relied upon the already established method of allegorical interpretation as the scientific instrument of its accom-plishment. This method had been applied to the Homeric poems even before the time of Plato. It was also in extensive use among the Stoics, and soon developed into a regular system with definite rules and methods. In the hands of Philo as an interpreter of the Old Testament, allegorism becomes a fine art. His con-tention is that, while Scripture is the depository of truth, it requires to be interpreted with the aid of allegory. In other words, he starts from the principle that a hidden meaning underlies the sacred narrative. He grants that the legal enactments of Scripture must be strictly and literally observed, but thinks it absurd to suppose that it should occupy itself with simple genealogies, accounts of battles, etc. More especially the literal sense is inadmissible where it is obscure or unintelligible, or less elevated than the allegorical sense, or where it ascribes to God anything unworthy of His

Divinity.[1]   In general, however, the written record is susceptible of only one spiritual interpretation.

A few examples will best convey some idea of Philo's method as an expositor of the Old Testament.   Stories like those of the creation, the forming of woman out of man's rib, and the descent of God to inspect the tower of Babel, he regards as so palpably unreasonable that they must have been intended to carry a deeper meaning than that which appears on the surface.   By the creation of woman out of the rib of man, for instance, is meant that sense (that is, the soul's affections) has been formed by one of the powers of the understanding.   The sabbath rest means simply inward peace.   The garden of Eden represents the virtue which God has planted in the human heart; its situation in the East indicates that virtue, dawning in the soul, dispels its darkness; the four rivers by which it is watered are the four (Platonic) cardinal virtues; all four flow out of the great river of Goodness; this, again, proceeds from Wisdom, which " disports itself in the Majesty of God the Creator." For Philo the figures of the patriarchal age are idealised types of character and conditions of soul.   Abel is the personification of saintliness, Cain of egoism, Noah of righteousness.   Abraham, who migrated from Chaldæa, denotes the advance from heathen ignorance to the desire for Divine instruction.   Ishmael symbolises unregulated passion, and Isaac (= " the laughter ") joy in Divine truth.   Jacob, " the man who saw God," denotes the perfect ascetic who has emancipated himself from the

---

[1] The student will find the Rules of Allegory detailed and illustrated with extraordinary thoroughness and patience in Siegfried's *Philo von Alexandria*, p. 168 ff.

23

world of sense, and found his true home in the sacred word; Esau, on the other hand, denotes sensual appetite. When it is said that " man was created " in the image of God,[1] the preposition κατὰ indicates that he was created not the image of God Himself, but after the image of God the Logos. With reference to the animals which Abraham was instructed to offer in sacrifice, it is said that " he took unto him all these and divided them in the midst."[2] In the apparently redundant expression μέσος, Philo finds the dogma of the equal parts into which God divides all things through the λόγος τομεύς.[3] According to him, it was not Abraham who took and divided, but the Logos Himself.

To quote examples would be endless, but it may be pointed out that as practised by Philo, allegorism yields very wonderful and very mixed results. By this process, which was in many respects virtually a Hellenistic application of the method of the rabbinical Midrash, he contrives to extract the leading psychological and ethical theories of Greek philosophy from three chapters in Genesis.[4] Often, it must be acknowledged, it serves to open up rich veins of spiritual truth; at other times it leads to what is utterly ridiculous. Lacking the wholesome safeguard of the critical spirit, it affords ample scope for imaginative caprice. Precisely herein lay its attractiveness for Philo, to whose genius as a Jew it belongs to think in pictures. But the interpreter often allows his method to run away with him. Owing to the constant necessity of allegorising, and of pursuing in each case the allegory to its utmost limits, he is

---

[1] Gen. i. 27.
[3] *Quis rer. div. hæres*, 28 ff.
[2] Gen. xv. 10.
[4] ii.-iv.

sometimes led not only into the most extraordinary digressions and obscurities of thought, but also into contradictory statements on such important points as the eternity of matter, the relation of God to the Logos, and the personality of the Divine Powers. The extravagances of allegorism were still more strikingly exhibited two or three centuries afterwards in the writings of Origen, the great Christian teacher of Alexandria.[1] Needless to say, the use of allegory does not, in Philo's estimation, detract in any way from the authority of Scripture. On the contrary, it only leads him to assert it the more. He affirms the inspiration not only of the content, but also of the form of revelation. Every word and letter is God-given. What may seem to be a free way of handling the sacred text is in reality the philosophic insight that guards it from misunderstanding. This certainly gives point to the remark of Lipsius that "allegorical exposition of Scripture and a mechanical theory of inspiration always go hand in hand."[2]

Philo was a philosopher as well as an exegete. That he has given us his philosophical ideas in the form of Biblical commentaries makes the study of them more difficult than if they had been conveyed directly and in a compact system. Yet owing to the ample material there is to hand, and by a comparison of passages, it is easy to follow the main trend of his thought. Of philosophy as such he had the loftiest conception. For him it meant in the first place the study of God, His Divine Logos, and the sensible world, and then of virtue

---

[1] See Note 42, p. 420.
[2] In Schenkel's *Bibel-Lexicon*, i. p. 91.

and vice in every creature.[1]   His ethics is the consequence of his metaphysical theory of God and the world.
According to Philo, there is a true and a false philosophy.
The latter is represented in Scripture by Balaam, and in
Egypt by those whom he calls the Sophists, and whom
he compares to unclean swine who " divide the hoof, but
chew not the cud." [2]   True philosophy, on the other
hand, is identical with universal science. It supplies
the principles which lie at the foundation of each
separate art, and the definitions by means of which
progress in the various departments is made possible.

Only in a few points does Philo's philosophy remain
distinctively Jewish.   He dissociates himself from
popular paganism by maintaining that there is but
one God, who is exalted absolutely above the world,
and is to be worshipped without images.   But even here
his position is not opposed to Greek *philosophy*, which
indeed has strongly influenced his doctrine of God.
The specifically national and particularistic standpoint
of Judaism is abandoned in favour of the cosmopolitan
standpoint of Greek philosophy.   Wisely to observe the
Mosaic Law is to be a citizen not of this country or of
that, but of the world.

Philo conceives God as pure Being, of whom no
quality can be predicated without degrading Him to
the level of the finite and imperfect.   He is eternal,
unchangeable, and immaterial—not liable to human
passions, and raised above human virtues.   As uncreated,
He is unknowable and inexpressible, self-sufficient, and
having neither relations nor attributes.   We know that
He is, but not *what* He is.   By these negations Philo

---

[1] *De spec. leg.* iii. 34 ; *De confus. ling.* § 20.   [2] Lev. xi. 7.

seeks only to establish the perfection of God and His absolute elevation above the world, and therefore does not hesitate to make the contradictory assertion that God contains and is the source of all perfection, and pervades all things.

As the perfect Being, God cannot enter into relations with the world of corruptible matter. But although contact with the universe is impossible for God in His own proper being, He nevertheless acts upon it through the medium of His Ideas or Forces or Logoi, *i.e.* partial powers of the universal reason. These intermediaries Philo identifies not only with the Platonic Ideas and Stoic Forces, but also with the Dæmons of the Greeks and the Angels of the Jews. Among the infinite variety of the powers two are supreme—goodness and might. It must be said, however, that Philo has no clear-cut conception of these mediating forces. At times he speaks as if they were mere abstractions, at other times as if they were persons. But this is the necessary result of the premises from which he starts. As the media through which He works in the world, His ideas must be inseparable from God; while at the same time, on the assumption of God's aloofness from the world, they must rank as independent entities.

In Philo's philosophy we meet with a still higher generalisation than that which ranges the powers under the two personifications of goodness and might. This is the Logos, a term which he found ready to hand, and whose elasticity of meaning rendered it peculiarly suitable for his purpose. Out of materials gathered from Jewish and Gentile sources alike, Philo constructed a philosophy of religion in which the Logos was represented as a mediatorial hypostasis standing between God and the world.   The Jewish elements in this conception are those of the Wisdom, the Spirit, and the Word of God. Platonism contributed to it through its doctrine of ideas and of the soul of the world, and Stoicism through its identification of God with the reason which operates in the world.   The Logos is related to God as Wisdom, and is the full expression of the Divine mind.   He is the sheckinah or glory of God, the firstborn Son of God, the second God.   As regards His relation to the other Divine powers or ideas, He comprehends them all, reconciles them, and directs them.   To the world He stands related as the organ of creation, and as the pilot of its destinies.   The Logos is further represented as mediating between God and man, and as sharing both natures.   He is at once God's ambassador, and the High Priest who atones and intercedes for men.   The weakness of Philo's position is that he makes the idea of the Logos "oscillate obscurely between personal and impersonal being."[1]   Clearly the Logos cannot be regarded as at once a person distinct from God and at the same time as only a certain property of God actively operating in the world.

The root-principle of Philo's philosophy is that of the dualism of God and the world.   He assumes the pre-existence of shapeless matter, and places it as a second principle alongside of God.   Hence creation in the strict sense cannot be ascribed to the Deity; the world was merely formed or arranged into a cosmos by the Logos and the powers, by whose means also it is preserved. Philo's dualism is further apparent in his doctrine of

[1] Zeller, *The Philosophy of the Greeks*, iii. 2, p. 278.

man, which is essentially Platonic. He conceives the air to be peopled with souls. Those who dwell in the upper parts are the intermediaries between God and the world, but those who are nearest the earth are attracted by sense, and descend into sensible bodies. Man, therefore, has a higher and a lower origin. On one side he is, like the angelic powers, an emanation of Deity; on the other he is a creature of sense, tainted with sin, and dwelling in a mortal body. As the source of evil, the body is the prison of the soul, which would fain rise again to God.

The view of man thus propounded formed the basis of Philo's ethic, of which the leading principle is the rejection of the sensuous, the rooting out of the passions. He adopts the teaching of the Stoics with respect to the four cardinal virtues and the four passions, and with them considers morality the only good. But his morality differs from that of the Stoics in having a religious basis. Man is not thrown back upon himself, but taught to look to God for deliverance from the bonds of sense and the power to become wise and virtuous. In this way alone can man fulfil the true end of his being and attain to the vision of God. This can be reached even in this life. "Often when I have come to write out the doctrines of philosophy," says Philo, "though I well knew what I ought to say, I have found my mind dry and barren, and renounced the task in despair. At other times, though I came empty, I was suddenly filled with thoughts showered upon me from above, like snowflakes or seed, so that in the heat of Divine possession I knew not the place or the company, or myself, what I said, or what I wrote."[1] To pass beyond this ecstasy the soul

---

[1] *De Migr. Abr.* 7.

must be altogether freed from the body and return to its original state. This takes place at death, provided the soul has not become attached to the things of sense, in which case it must enter into another body. A sharp distinction is drawn between the seeing and the blind. " The former lift up their eyes to heaven, contemplating the manna, the Divine Logos, the celestial and imperishable nutriment of the soul which loves beautiful sights ; the latter broods over the roots of the ground." Unswervingly to abide in God alone—that is the height of happiness. As Herriot has said, " This is the last word of Philo, the extreme consequence of a method which has allegory for its starting-point, ecstasy for its favourite process, and mysticism for its result." [1]

Although Philo's influence, both in Jewish and in pagan circles, was not small, it was nevertheless considerably neutralised by the perfecting of legalistic Judaism on the one hand and the rise of Christianity on the other.[2] His labours had, moreover, important and unforeseen results in connexion with the development of Christian doctrine. In the opinion of many, clear traces of Philonism occur in the New Testament itself, notably the conception of the Logos in the prologue to St. John's Gospel. Be this as it may, Philo's influence upon the post-apostolic age was undoubtedly potent.[3] It was neither an unmixed good nor an unmixed evil. The task of the Christian theologian was vastly facilitated by

---

[1] *Philon le Juif*, p. 199.   [2] See Note 43, p. 422.

[3] " Almost all the Greek Fathers of the first century, as well as the Alexandrians, the Gnostics as well as their adversaries, and even the great Greek theologians of subsequent centuries, have, some more, some less, either directly or indirectly, consciously or unconsciously, drawn from Philo."—Schürer, *Geschichte*,[3] p. 562, Eng. tr. II. iii. p. 381.

Philo's conclusion regarding "the possibility and the mode of an eternal distinction in the Divine unity"; but, on the other hand, his position as a Platonic philosopher militated against a true understanding of the Atonement. For him the Incarnation is impossible, vicarious suffering meaningless, and faith of less importance than knowledge; and although the Logos is spoken of as Mediator and High Priest, these terms do not connote to him what they connote to the Christian. Whatever else the Logos may be, he is not the Messiah, nor is he Jesus. If, moreover, in opposition to the ascetic spirit which would make a glorious hereafter contingent upon self-torture in this life, Philo did excellent service by representing the soul as the centre of its own blessedness, and the vision of God as the highest reward, he also did much harm by the extent to which he allowed his allegorism to run riot in the interpretation of the Hebrew Scriptures.

APPENDIX I.

———◆———

NOTES.

NOTE 1. See p. 3.

*The Chronological Statement in the Prologue to
Ecclesiasticus.*

THIS runs thus : Ἐν γὰρ τῷ ὀγδόῳ καὶ τριακοστῷ ἔτει ἐπὶ τοῦ
Εὐεργέτου βασιλέως παραγενηθεὶς εἰς Αἴγυπτον καὶ συγχρονίσας,
εὖρον οὐ μικρᾶς παιδείας ἀφόμοιον. If the reference is to the
thirty-eighth year of King Euergetes, we must understand it of
Ptolemy VII. Physcon Euergetes II., the only Egyptian king
bearing the surname Euergetes whose reign extended to more
than thirty-eight years, and regard the date specified as = B.C. 132.
On this interpretation, however, the ἐπί which stands between
the number and the name of the king appears to be pleonastic.
Some accordingly view the number as applicable to the year
of the prologue-writer's own age. This would still make it
possible to think of the older Euergetes who reigned only twenty-
five years (B.C. 247–221), in which case the translator would
have lived about a hundred years earlier. But it is difficult to
see for what reason he should have mentioned the year of his
own life in which he came to Egypt, and most expositors are
agreed that only the year of the reign of Euergetes can
be meant. Deissmann cites several nearly contemporary
authorities to shew that the ἐπί is not really pleonastic, but

represents a Greek idiom peculiar to the locality. "In an Inscription from the Acropolis, as old as the third century B.C., we find in line 24 f. the words ἱερεὺς γενόμενος ἐν τῷ ἐπὶ Λυσιάδου ἄρχοντος ἐνιαυτῷ. Still more significant for the passage in Sirach are the following parallels of Egyptian origin. The Inscription of the Rosetta Stone (27th March, 196 B.C.), line 16, runs thus : προσέταξεν [Ptolemy v. Epiphanes] δὲ καὶ περὶ τῶν ἱερέων, ὅπως μηθὲν πλεῖον διδῶσιν εἰς τὸ τελεστικὸν οὗ ἐτάσσοντο ἕως τοῦ πρώτου ἔτους ἐπὶ τοῦ πατρὸς αὐτοῦ [Ptolemy iv. Philopator]. Though Letronne, in view of the alleged want of precedent for this usage of ἐπί, tries a different interpretation, he is yet forced to acknowledge that, if we translate the concluding words by *until the first year* [*of the reign*] *of his father,* the whole sentence is made to fit most appropriately into the context ; the priests, who are hardly inclined to speak of the merits of Epiphanes for nothing, would be again but manifesting their ability to do obeisance to him, and, at the same time, to extol the memory of his father. Had Letronne known the example from the Prologue to Sirach, perhaps he would have decided for this way of taking ἐπί, which so admirably suits the context. The two passages mutually support one another. But the usage of ἐπί is further confirmed by other passages of Egyptian origin. In *Pap. Par.* 15 (B.C. 120) two αἰγύπτιαι συγγραφαί are mentioned, which are dated as follows : μιᾶς μὲν γεγονυίας [τοῦ ΙΗ′ ἔτους παχ]ὼν ἐπὶ τοῦ Φιλομήτορος, *the one of Pachou* (Egyptian month) *of the eighteenth year* (*of the reign*) *of Philometor* ; ἐτέρας δὲ γεγονυίας τοῦ ΛΕ′ μεσορὴ ἐπὶ τοῦ αὐτοῦ βασιλέως, *the other of Mesore* (Egyptian month) *of the year thirty-five* (*of the reign*) *of the same king.* Finally, *Pap. Par.* 5 begins thus : βασιλευόντων Κλεοπάτρας καὶ Πτολεμαίου θεῶν Φιλομητόρων Σωτήρων ἔτους Δ′ ἐφ′ ἱερέως βασιλέως Πτολεμαίου θεοῦ Φιλομήτορος Σωτῆρος Ἀλεξάνδρου καὶ θεῶν Σωτήρων, κ.τ.λ. If the interpretation advocated by Brunet against Brugsch [Brugsch translates thus : *under the priest of* '*the*' *King Ptolemy*], viz., *under King Ptolemy . . . the priest of Alexander* [the Great] *and of the gods,* be correct, then this passage also must be taken into consideration."—*Bible Studies,* p. 340 f.

NOTE 2. See p. 5.

The Relative Value of the Inscriptions and the Papyri.

"The gains from the Papyri are of much wider extent than those from the Inscriptions. The reason is obvious. We might almost say that this difference is determined by the disparity of the respective materials on which the writing was made. Papyrus is accommodating, and is available for private purposes; stone is unyielding, and stands open to every eye in the market-place, in the temple, or beside the tomb. The Inscriptions, particularly the more lengthy and the official ones, often approximate in style to the literary language, and are thus readily liable to affectation and mannerism; what the papyrus leaves contain is much less affected, proceeding, as it does, from the thousand requirements and circumstances of the daily life of unimportant people. If the legal documents among the Papyri shew a certain fixed mode of speech, marked by the formalism of the office, yet the many letter-writers, male and female, express themselves all the more unconstrainedly."
—Deissmann, *Bible Studies*, p. 179 f. See also this writer's more recently published *Light from the Ancient East.*

CHAPTER I.

NOTE 3. See p. 16.

The Diaspora.

The Dispersion included "the twelve tribes" (Jas. i. 1). In 2 Macc. i. 27 the term is used of those in bondage, but it soon came to be applied to all those residing out of Palestine, and even to the place of their sojourn (Judith v. 19; cf. John vii. 35; 1 Pet. i. 1). Partly through the colonising policy of the Diadochoi (successors of Alexander), who offered tempting inducements to emigrants, and partly through the voluntary migration of Jews, who found Palestine no paradise for peaceable citizens, to most of the trading centres of the ancient world, the Dispersion began to assume the proportions of a considerable movement. According to Willrich, indeed, there was no such thing as a Jewish Diaspora prior to the Maccabæan revolt. But this view is untenable. Not only is it totally subversive of the credibility of Josephus as a historian, but it is also incompatible with the fact that Antiochus Epiphanes already found a strong hellenising party in Judæa prepared to co-operate with him in his ill-advised attempt to force paganism upon that country. We have the testimony of Hecatæus of Abdera, a historian who lived at the court of Ptolemy Lagos, that many Jews were led to abandon their own customs through contact with Persians and Macedonians. At the same time it is no doubt the case that subsequent to the Maccabæan revolt the dispersion increased to an extent never witnessed before. A century before the Christian era, Jews had settled in all parts of the known world. The historical evidence on this point is abundant. About B.C. 140, we have the lament of *The Sibylline Oracles* (iii. 271) that "every land and every sea was filled with them." Cf. also 1 Macc. xv. 16–24, where it is stated that the Romans, in renewing their old league with the Jews, sent intimation thereof "to King Ptolemy," likewise "to Demetrius the king, and to Attalus, and to Arathes, and to Arsaces, and unto all the countries, and to Sampsames, and to the Spartans, and unto Delos, and unto Myndos, and unto Sicyon, and unto Caria, and unto Samos, and unto Pamphylia, and unto Lycia, and unto Halicarnassus, and unto Rhodes, and unto Phaselis, and unto Cos, and unto Side, and unto Aradus, and Gortyna, and Cnidus, and Cyprus, and Cyrene. But the copy hereof they wrote to Simon the high priest." All this implies a wide dispersion of the Jews. Josephus (*B. J.* ii. 16. 4) says there was "no nation in the world which had not among them part of the Jewish people." The same author (*Ant.* xiv. 7. 2) quotes Strabo as saying: "It is not easy to find a place in the world that has not admitted this race, and is not mastered by them."

Weizsäcker (in Schenkel's *Bibel-Lexicon*, art. "Zerstreuung") rightly calls attention to the fact that the Dispersion is not wholly explained by the historical circumstances. Their religion enabled the Jews to remain a nation among the nations. Wherever they went they were "the people of God," and a standing witness to monotheism. It was through the Jewish Dispersion that Christianity obtained a foothold in every quarter of the civilised world.

NOTE 4. See p. 18.

The Lack of spiritual Proportion in legalistic Judaism.

"Denn das ist überhaupt das Wesen des Judenthums: die höchsten und die abstossendsten Gedanken, das Grossartige und das Gemeine liegen unmittelbar neben einander, untrennbar verbunden, das eine immer die kehrseite des anderen. . . . Das Judenthum ist wie die consequenteste und folgenschwerste, so vielleicht auch die bizarrste Bildung, welche die religiöse-politische Entwickelung Asiens geschaffen hat. Die alte Frage, ob die Juden ein Volk sind oder eine Religionsgenossenschaft, ist schief gestellt: vielmehr ist gerade das das Wesen dieser Bildungen, dass sie das Volksthum in Religion umsetzen und dadurch im Stande sind, weit über die Grenzen des ehemaligen Volks hinauszugreifen. Das ist, ausser etwa im späteren Parsismus, nirgends in so umfassendem Maasse geschehen wie in Judenthum. Das Erbtheil des Volksthums bleibt der Gemeinde: die Hoffnungen welche das Volk aufrecht erhielten, sind zu Verheissungen für die Gläubigen geworden, diese leben in den Formen der ehemaligen Nation. Dadurch werden Züstande und Anschauungen einer längst vergangenen Zeit für alle Zukunft conservirt, Bitten und Bräuche, die ehemals naturwüchsig waren, aber längst widersinig geworden sind, die Nachkommen bis in die fernsten Geschlechter aufgezwängt. Die Juden scheppen sich an ihnen bis auf den heutigen Tag. Der göttliche Segen, den sie vor der Uebernahme des Gesetzes erwarteten, ist ihr Verhängniss, ist der schwerste Fluch geworden."—Ed. Meyer, *Geschichte des Alterthums*, iii. p. 218 ff.

NOTE 5. See p. 20.

Jewish Propagandism.

It was quite in keeping with the character of Judaism that it should endeavour to propagate itself. Under the Greek and Roman supremacy, especially after the time of the Maccabees, Jewish propagandism was vigorously, and, in many instances, successfully, carried on both in Palestine and throughout the Dispersion. "Among the mass of the people," says Josephus, "there has for a long time now been a great amount of zeal for our worship; nor is there a single town among the Greeks or barbarians, or anywhere else; not a single nation to which the observance of the sabbath as it exists among ourselves has not penetrated; while fasting, and the burning of lights, and many of our laws with regard to meats are also observed" (*c. Apion*, ii. 39). The 'proselytes' receive distinct mention in the comprehensive list of Acts ii. 9–11, and apostolic preaching was everywhere addressed to the 'God-fearing' Gentile as well as to the Jew. The women of Damascus (Josephus, *B. J.* ii. 20. 2) and of other places adhered in great numbers to the observances of Judaism, and among them were many of exalted rank (Acts xiii. 50). The case of the Ethiopian treasurer (Acts viii. 26) shews also that the converts included men occupying positions of trust and influence. The most brilliant example of the success of Jewish proselytism, however, w.s the conversion of Izates, King of Adiabene, together with his entire household (Jos. *Ant.* xx. 2. 4). That in Rome also Judaism made considerable headway is manifest from the attention bestowed upon it by the satirists (Horace, *Sat.* i. 4, 142 f.; Juvenal, *Sat.* xiv. 96 ff.). The methods used to win converts were not always justifiable. In some instances, whole tribes, *e.g.* the Idumæans under Hyrcanus, and the Itureans under Aristobulus, were forced to profess Judaism (Jos. *Ant.* xiii. 9. 3; 11. 3). Those who did so spontaneously were actuated by various motives; some to effect a marriage (*Ant.* xx. 7. 3), others to escape military service (*Ant.* xiv. 10. 13), others from a sense of religious need (Acts vi. 5, xvii. 4).

When we take into account the hostile feeling of paganism which, besides circulating many gratuitous slanders against the Jews, ridiculed their abstinence from swine's flesh, their sabbath observance, and their refusal to adopt any form of image-worship, and detested their proud exclusiveness, it may seem strange that the principles of Judaism should have made any progress at all in heathen centres. Schürer ascribes the triumph won by the Mosaic cultus against great odds to three circumstances, namely, the shrewd way in which the votaries of Judaism kept its attractive side to the front; the fact that the Jewish religion aimed at realising a moral and happy life, and could in spite of its repulsive externals give a greater deliverance from sin than heathenism in any of its forms could offer; and the tendency of the age to patronise Oriental religions in general and monotheistic systems in particular.

NOTE 6. See p. 32.

The Tendency towards Universalism and Individualism in Religion.

"So werden Universalismus und Individualismus die charakteristischen Züge aller Religionen und aller Culte. Jeder Cultus beansprucht der höchste, womöglich der einzig berechtigte, jede Gottheit eine grosse kosmische Macht zu sein, und sie alle wenden sich nicht mehr oder nicht mehr ausschliesslich an eine Volksgemeinschaft, sondern in erster Linie an jeden Einzelnen, ihm versprechen sie jeglichen Gewinn auf Erden wie im Jenseits, sicherer als irgend ein anderer Gott. Nicht mit einem Schlage ist die Umwandlung fertig geworden: aber sie beginnt in der Perserzeit. Die grosse Concurrenz der Religionen bereitet sich vor, welche die spätere Jahrhunderte des Alterthums erfüllt. Jetzt ist es auch möglich geworden, eine Gottheit fern von ihrem Wohnsitz zu verehren, losgelöst von dem Heimathsboden und dem eigenen Volke: das Band, welches Gott und Verehrer verbindet, ist nicht mehr national und politisch, sondern persönlich und daher unzereissbar. Sklaven, Kaufleute, Handwerker, die ihrer Heimath dauernd entfremdet werden, nehmen ihre

Gottheit mit sich, gründen ihr Heiligthümer, gewinnen ihr in der Fremde Anhänger, so gut wie der Fremde, der an eine Cultusstätte kommt, der Gottheit seine verehrung zollt und dauernd für ihren Dienst gewonnen werden kann. Daher beginnen alle Culte eifrig Propaganda zu machen, sei es, dass sie sich bemühen, den Kreis der Verehrer des Heiligthums zu erweitern, sein Ansehen und seinen Einfluss zu steigern weit über die Nachbargebiete hinaus, sei es, dass sie die Ideen und Riten ihrer Religion zu massgebender Bedeutung zu erheben suchen." —Ed. Meyer, *Geschichte des Alterthums*, iii. p. 169 f.

NOTE 7. See p. 48.

The syncretistic Character of later Judaism apparent from its Treatment of primitive Legends.

" Der synkretistische Charakter der spätjüdischen Literatur wird auch sichtbar, wenn wir die Legenden, welche dieselbe selbständig und unabhängig von der alttestamentlichen Erzählung gebildet oder überliefert hat, ins Auge fassen. Ich will hier nur die wichtigsten in Betracht kommenden Stücke nennen, die Esther-, Tobit- und Judith- Legende und die erzählenden Stücke des Buches Daniel. Dass im ESTHERBUCHE keine ursprünglich jüdische Erzählung vorliegt, sondern eine wahrscheinlich babylonische Sage, die mit einem leichten jüdischen Firnis bedeckt ist, ist so gut wie gesichert. Mögen auch die meisten Einzeldeutungen der, wie es scheint, sehr komplizierten Estherlegende, noch nicht feststehen, so weisen doch die Namen Esther (Isthar), Mardochai (Marduk) nach Babylon. Auch das Fest der Loose (Purimfest), wird irgendwie fremder Religion und Sitte entlehut sein, wenn hier sicheres auch noch nicht herausgestallt ist. Die Erzählung des TOBITBUCHES scheint ebenfalls eine überraschende Beleuchtung von religionsgeschichtlicher Seite zu bekommen. Die Tobitlegende ist nämlich vielleicht eine jüdische Umarbeitung der im Folklore weitverbreiteten Legende von dankbaren Toten Nach der Legende schützt der Held derselben den Leichnam des Toten vor Misshandlung. Der dankbare Tote gesellt sich dann dem Helden als Reisebegleiter, er hilft ihm, die reiche Braut erringen, und schützt ihn vor dem Schlangendämon, der allen früheren Verlobten der Braut in der Brautnacht ein rasches Ende bereitet hat. Ein Zusammenhang des Tobitbuches zu dieser Legende erscheint zum mindesten wahrscheinlich. Jedenfalls liegt dann im Tobitbuch eine ausserordentlich feine und verständige Bearbeitung der Legende vor. Das charakteristische an dieser Beobachtung ist eben immer wieder dies, dass ein Jude es wagt, eine so specifisch heidnische, auf niederster Stufe stehende Legende zu bearbeiten.—Von hier aus löst sich noch ein Rätsel. Seit der Entdeckung der interessanten ACHIKARLEGENDE ist man auf die interessanten, gar nicht wegzuleugnenden Beziehungen der Tobit- zur Achikarlegende aufmerksam geworden. Die Achikarlegende ist eine Illustration—vielleicht die älteste— zu dem Spruche: wer andern eine Grube gräbt, fällt selbst hinein. Achikar, der weise Minister des Assyrerkönig's Senacherib, wird von seinem missratenem Neffen schändlich verraten, vom Könige zum Tode verurteilt, von einem Beamten des König's, dem er früher eine Gnade erwiesen, insgeheim gerrettet. Als dann der König in seinem Rätselwettstreit mit dem ägyptischen König seiner bedarf, wird er wieder aus Tageslicht gezogen ; er führt siegreich die Sache seines Königs und überantwortet den schändlichen Neffen seiner wohlverdienten Strafe. Es kann kaum ein Zweifel sein, dass die Legende ihrem Ursprung nach heidnisch (vgl. namentlich die Armenische Recension). An einer Reihe von einzelnen Angaben und den hineingearbeiteten mythologischen Zügen wird das vollkommen evident. Wenn nun die jüdische Tobitlegende direkt auf jene Erzählung anspielt, den Tobit zu einem Verwandten des Achikar macht und sich auch sonst in ihrer Spruchweisheit mit den Sprüchen der Achikarlegende berührt, so lässt diese Beobachtung zweierlei Deutung zu. Entweder hat die jüdische Litteratur der späteren Zeit sich danach auch der Achikarlegende bemächtigt, und den Achikar zum jüdischen Helden umgestaltet, so dass dann die umgewandelte Achikarlegende die Tobitlegende beeinflusst hätte,—oder es hat dem jüdischen Bearbeiter der Tobitlegende diese Legende bereits in einer Gestalt vorgelegen, in welcher

diese in Beziehung zur (heidnischen) Achikarlegende gesetzt war
In beiden Fällen wird der enge Zusammenhang der jüdischen
Legende mit heidnischem Folklore deutlich. In ähnlicher Weise
wird übrigens auch die Judithlegende, vielleicht auch die Jonas-
legende zu beurteilen sein. Auch die Geschichtserzählung des
Danielbuches muss einer ähnlichen Beurteilung unterliegen.
Jene Geschichten sind sicher nicht frei erfunden, vielmehr werden
wir fast in ihnen allen eine Umarbeitung babylonischer Erzäh-
lungen vermuten dürfen. An einem punkt können wir das auch
noch nachweisen. Die merkwürdige Erzählung von Nebukadnezars Wahnsinn, die noch jetzt in der vorliegenden Form ihre
heidnische Herkunft deutlich verrät, hat ihre Grundlage in einer
babylonischen Legende von einem Traum Nebukadnezars und
dem Ende dieses Herrschers, welche uns der orientalische
Chronist Abydenus aufbewahrt hat." — Bousset, *Religion des
Judentums*, p. 467 ff.

NOTE 8. See p. 52.

Greek Words in Daniel.

"Nous sommes assez mal renseignés sur le nombre des
termes ou des tournures que la conquête d'Alexandre imposa
au vocabulaire et à la grammaire hébraïques. Si nos renseigne-
ments étaient plus complets, nous verrions sans doubte les
emprunts faits au grec, à peu près nuls dans la vielle langue
hébraïque, devenir de plus en plus nombreux dans les documents
de plus en plus jeunes. La conquête avait importé des idées
nouvelles; pour les exprimer, il fallait des mots nouveaux. Ce
sont ces mots nouveaux que H. Derenbourg, dans une mono-
graphia très intéressante (*Mots grecs dans Daniel* p. 235 f.), a
voulu dégager du *Livre de Daniel*, écrit palestinien, de 168 ou
169 avant l'ère chrétienne. Ces mots sont peu nombreux.
Toutefois H. Derenbourg signale l'influence des mots grecs
κῆρυξ, κέρας, σῦριγξ, κίθαρις (doublet poétique de κιθάρα),
συμφωνία (en hébreu *soumpōneyāh*), φθέγμα (en hébreu *pitgâm*),
πέτασος (? en hébreu *petîsch*), μανιάκης (en hébreu *hamînekã'*),

et quelques autres influences qui semblent plus douteuses (examples : νόμισμα et nebizbâh ; πρότιμοι et partemīm ; λαμπάδες πυρός, lappîdî êsch)."—Herriot, *Philon le Juif*, p. 24.

The use of Greek words in Daniel has of course an important bearing on the question as to the date of the book. "Whatever might conceivably be the case with κίθαρις, it is incredible that ψαλτήριον and συμφωνία can have reached Babylon *c.* 550 B.C. Any one who has studied Greek history knows what the condition of the Greek world was in the sixth century B.C., and is aware that the arts and inventions of civilised life streamed then into Greece from the East, not from Greece eastwards. Still, if the instruments named were of a primitive kind, such as the κίθαρις (in Homer), it is *just* possible—though, in view of the fact that the Semitic languages have their own name for the 'lyre,' by no means probable—that it might be an exception to the rule, and that the Babylonians might have been indebted for their knowledge of it to the Greeks; so that had קיתרס stood alone, it could not, perhaps, have been pressed. But no such exception can be made in the case of ψαλτήριον and συμφωνία, both *derived* forms, the former found first in Aristotle, the latter first in Plato, and in the sense of concerted music (or, perhaps, of a specific musical instrument) first in Polybius. These words, it may be confidently affirmed, could not have been used in the Book of Daniel unless it had been written *after the dissemination of Greek influences in Asia through the conquests of Alexander the Great.*"—Driver's *Daniel*, p. lviii f.

CHAPTER II.

NOTE 9. See p. 60.

Israel's Connexion with Palestine.

This idea of Canaan as the land of Jahweh implied no doubt a somewhat primitive and parochial conception of deity.

To the average Hebrew, Canaan was Jahweh's land, just as Moab was the land of Chemosh. In Semitic religion generally each nation had not only its own land but its own god, and the god was as closely associated with the land as with the nation. A god had a vested right, so to speak, in his land, irrespective of his relation to the inhabitants. Thus even in the event of the removal of his worshippers, the land was still theoretically *his* land. The new settlers, drafted into Samaria by the king of Assyria after the deportation of the ten tribes, imported their own gods; but the havoc wrought among them by lions led them to acknowledge "the god of the land" (2 Kings xvii. 24 ff.). On the other hand, it was an accepted principle that a god could not be fitly worshipped outside of his own land (Josh. xxii. 19; 2 Sam. xxvi. 19; Hos. ix. 3 ff.). This idea finds expression even in connexion with the worship of Jahweh. Naaman asks for two mules' burden of Palestinian soil in order to render possible the worship of the God of Israel at Damascus; and the exiles in Babylon were at a loss how to sing the Lord's song in a strange land (Ps. cxxxvii.). Cf. W. Robertson Smith, *Religion of the Semites*, p. 91 f.

It would be absurd to think of Israel's connexion with Palestine as merely accidental. There was a special function assigned in Providence to both land and people. God, who has determined for all nations the bounds of their habitation, placed Israel in the Holy Land as in a sheltered nook where they might be preserved amid all the upheavals of the ancient world, and might receive the religious training which should fit them to become the bearers of revelation to all mankind. "There is no land which is so much a sanctuary and an observatory as Palestine: no land which, till its office was fulfilled, was so swept by the great forces of history, and was yet so capable of preserving one tribe in national continuity and growth: one tribe learning and suffering and rising superior to the successive problems these forces presented to her, till upon the opportunity afforded by the last of them she launched with her results upon the world. . . . If a man can believe that there is no directing hand behind our universe and the history of our race, he will, of course, say that all this is the result of chance. But, for most of us, only another conclusion is possible. It may best be expressed in the words of one who was no theologian but a geographer—perhaps the most scientific observer Palestine has ever had. Karl Ritter says of Palestine: 'Nature and the course of history shews that here, from the beginning onwards, there cannot be talk of any chance.'"— G. A. Smith, *Historical Geography of the Holy Land*, p. 112 f.

NOTE 10. See p. 70.

The Wranglings of the Schools.

"The discussions of the school often degenerated into disputes, and the contending scribes did not hesitate to insult one another, for there was no law to interfere and punish the offender. Jews indeed have never known how to argue calmly. Jesus raised His protest against this use of violent language so common in His time. Such opprobrious terms as fool, imbecile, idiot, were in frequent use, and the word Raca was constantly to be heard. We can scarcely form an idea of the rancour of these quarrels, and of the bitter mutual hatred in which these scribes indulged. This hatred was fostered by the spirit of the times, and by the constant agitation of the people rising gradually into a perfect paroxysm of exasperation against the foreigners. The followers of Hillel and Shammai were even more bitter against each other than the Pharisees and Sadducees . . . 'This was a dark day,' says one of the Talmuds, 'like that on which the golden calf was made. The Shammaïtes killed some of the Hillelites.'"—Stapfer, *Palestine in the Time of Christ*, p. 302 f.

CHAPTER III.

NOTE 11. See p. 112.

The Ḥasīdîm essentially a religious Party.

"Wenn die Asidäer schon im Jahre 162 ihre Wege von denen der Makkabäer trennten, so haben sie für die Richtung, wohin jene steuerten, ein feines Gefühl gehabt.

"Aus dieser Erörterung erhellt erstens, dass die Asidäer nicht eine vorzugsweise patriotische Partei waren, nicht die Seele des Aufstandes und verschieden von den 'Treuen des Judas,' zweitens, dass sie vielmehr eine streng kirkliche Partei waren, dass sie nur für's Gesetz kämpften und Friede schlossen, so bald es von wegen des Gesetzes erlaubt oder geboten war. Diese Züge passen zu dem Namen der 'Frommen,' zu der Thatsache, dass die Schriftgelehrten ihre Führer, endlich zu der Wahrscheinlichkeit, dass die Essäer ihre fortsetzung waren—um der Pharisäer hier noch zu geschweigen. Darnach nimmt es auch kein wunder, dass sie nur so selten und nebenbei von der Ueberlieferung erwähnt werden, in sonderbarem Contrast zu der Hartnäckigkeit, mit der sie in den neueren Geschichtswerken fortdauernd als Subjekt alles Handelns erscheinen."—Wellhausen, *Die Pharisäer und die Sadducäer*, p. 85 f.

NOTE 12. See p. 113.

Did Judas Maccabæus conclude a Treaty with the Romans?

"The details of the narrative in 1 Macc. viii. have been called in question by many critics, although the fact of a treaty having been concluded between the Jews and the Romans has been generally admitted. Wellhausen, *e.g.*, while asserting that the journey to Rome, the negotiations with the senate, and the return to Jerusalem, could not have been accomplished in a single month, goes on to say: 'This would be decisive, only I am not convinced that the usual assumption is correct. For the festival of Nicanor's day is unintelligible, if the sensation of victory had been forthwith effaced through a reverse of the worst description. It is not maintained that the statement of 1 Macc. viii. 17 (2 Macc. iv. 11) is drawn purely from the imagination' (*Isr. und Jüd. Gesch.*² p. 250, note 3). That the narrative does contain inaccuracies (vv. 8, 15, 16), is not to be denied. These, however, may be accounted for by the defective means of international communication in those days, and still more by the fact that the interests of the Jews were practically confined to agriculture and their ancestral religion. The writer's graphic picture is upon the whole 'not unfaithful' (Rawlinson), and has 'quite the character of that *naïveté* and candour with which intelligence of that sort is propagated in the mouth of the common people' (Grimm). In spite of what is said in ver. 13, he is apparently blind as to the dangers attending negotiations with the Romans."—The author's comment *ad loc.* in *Cambridge Bible for Schools*, p. 157.

After pointing out that the ostensible treaty records contained in 1 Maccabees are really the products of the writer's own pen, Niese proceeds: "Davon abgesehen ist jedoch die Thatsache, dass Judas mit den Römern Freundschaft schloss, so gut wie nur möglich bezeugt. Auch Josephus im *Bellum Judaicum* spricht davon in unverdächtiger Weise, Justinus erwähnt es und schliesslich wird wenigstens die jüdische Gesandtschaft nach Rom vom 2 Makkabäerbuche in einer beiläufigen und ganz unbefangenen Notiz so erwähnt, dass an ihrer Wirklichkeit kein grund zu zweifeln vorliegt, zumal da auch die Zeitumstände sehr dafür sprechen. Denn Judas suchte in Rom gegen Demetrios einen Rückhalt und hatte auch Grund, auf Erfolg zu hoffen; denn die Römer waren jenem Fürsten durchaus feindlich gesinnt; wenn sie ihn auch anerkannten, so haben sie ihm doch nie verziehen, das er gegen ihren Willen auf den Thron gelangt war, und daran ist er dann schliesslich zu Grunde gegangen.

" Man hat nun gesagt, mit einem Rebellen wie Judas würden die Römer kein Bündniss geschlossen haben. Dagegen verweise ich auf ihr verhalten gegen Timarchos, der sich als babylonischer Satrap gegen Demetrios erhob ; er erhielt vom Senat eine sehr ermuthigende Antwort, und es ist wahrscheinlich genug, dass man sich den Juden gegenüber nicht anders verhielt. Ob nun damals schon ein förmliches Bündniss mit dem Römischen Volke geschlossen ward, oder ob die Gesandten der Juden nur einen freundlichen senatsbeschluss und eine Verwendung bei Demetrios erreichten, darüber kann man zweifeln ; denn da die Bündnissurkunde in der überlieferten Form unecht ist, so ist es wohl denkbar, dass der Schriftsteller ein Senatusconsult zu einem Bündniss umgearbeitet habe."—*Kritik der Beiden Makkabäerbücher*, p. 88 f.

NOTE 13. See p. 118.

The High-Priesthood in post-exilic Times.

"For nearly four centuries the high-priesthood, although held subject to the dictation of foreign secular authority, had been hereditary in the house of Joshua, the coadjutor of Zerubbabel. But on the accession of Antiochus Epiphanes, and in the person of Jason, who bribed the Syrian king to take it from his brother Onias III. and confer it upon himself, it had suffered the deepest degradation. A further step was taken when Epiphanes sold the office to Menelaus, a Hellenistic Benjamite, and therefore not even of priestly family. Alcimus, who had been appointed by Eupator, and acknowledged by Demetrius, possessed this qualification, and on that account was welcomed at first by many pious Israelites. Since the death of Alcimus the office had remained vacant for seven years, until now, in a moment of happy inspiration, Alexander Balas bethought himself of nominating Jonathan to fill it, in order thereby to secure his goodwill and support in the contest against Demetrius. As a member of a priestly family, and in view of the fact that the legitimate successor to the dignity had fled to Egypt after the murder of his father Onias III. (Jos. *Ant.* xiii. 3. 1), Jonathan was, of course, quite as eligible as any other, even from the standpoint of the law."—The author's note on 1 Macc. x. 20 in *Cambridge Bible for Schools*.

NOTE 14. See p. 124.

The Issue of Jewish Coins under Simon.

"The right of coinage was, in fact, an attribute of the independence which had been granted to Judæa, or at all events had been interpreted as such, and was enjoyed at this period by several free cities of the Syrian kingdom. The coins issued in virtue of the assumption of this privilege are to be regarded not so much as coins of Simon as of the civic commune of Jerusalem in his day. The year numbers on the coins may also be those of a civil era of Jerusalem, 'as also other cities of Phœnicia, such as Tyre, Sidon, Ascalon, had begun toward the end of the second century B.C., in token of the freedom which they had obtained, to adopt a cycle of their own' (Schürer, 1. i. p. 258). If, on the other hand, they denote the year of Simon, it is strange that among extant specimens (which are numerous) there should be only one with the stamp of the year 5, and none with that of the years 6 and 7, seeing that Simon reigned for eight years. It is, of course, possible that the practice of stamping on the coins the year of issue was after a time discontinued. The silver coins struck were of the value of a shekel, a half-shekel, and a quarter-shekel. On one side they bear the inscription, 'Jerusalem the holy,' and on the other 'Israel's shekel,' or 'half-shekel,' etc. These belong to the years 1, 2, and 3. Copper coins were also issued, all as yet discovered bearing the inscription, 'Year 4 of the emancipation of Israel.' Both classes of coins were inscribed in the old Hebrew (Phœnician) characters, but under the later Hasmonæan princes these were displaced by the Greek. These Jewish coins were formed after the Greek models, but give no name or portrait profile of any high priest or prince. They are adorned with simple symbols, *e.g.* a cup, a lily branch, a grape cluster, a palm, etc. For engravings of them see Madden, *Coins of the Jews*, p. 67 ff."—The author's note on 1 Macc. xv. 6 in *Cambridge Bible for Schools*.

NOTE 15. See p. 128.

Possible Reference of the Eulogy of Ecclus. l. 1–21 to Simon, son of Mattathias.

"The unquestionable importance of this high priest, the unprecedented honours conferred upon him, and the esteem shewn him in a most demonstrative manner by his people, render such a eulogy as this natural, while the author's taste would dictate the features to be mentioned. That he should close with a prayer for the preservation of the high-priesthood in Simon's family and a reference to the promise to Phinehas is significant. The priests and the people had made Simon's pontificate hereditary (1 Macc. xiv. 41). But a high priest marching sword in hand against the enemy was a new type, and demanded a justification in the Law. This was found in the example of Phinehas (Num. xxv. 6). The assurance there given of an everlasting priesthood as a reward for such zeal helped to legitimatise the new pontifical family, and the emphasis shifted for a time from Aaron and Zadok to Phinehas (1 Macc. ii. 26; Ps. cvi. 30; Ecclus. xlv. 23). Simon was the son of Mattathias, son of Johanan. In ch. l. 1 the text is uncertain. While the Greek manuscripts give his father's name as Onias, the Syriac has Nethaniah and the Hebrew Johanan, and in the Ethiopic it has fallen out entirely. It is possible that the original read only 'Simon, the high priest.' 'Son of Mattathias, son of Johanan,' may be a later addition, of which the former name, in the form of Nethaniah, was preserved by some texts, the latter only by others. Such additions, omissions, and changes are not seldom found."—N. Schmidt, Introduction to Ecclesiasticus in the *Temple Bible*.

CHAPTER IV.

NOTE 16. See p. 144.

Recent Controversy on the Sanhedrin.

"The scholarship of our time has been sharply divided over the question of the character and organisation of the Great Sanhedrin of Jerusalem. Our information on the subject is derived, as has been said, from three sources: the Gospels, Josephus, and the Talmudic literature. The evidence of the last differs in many respects from that of the two former: the question is, which of them are we to trust? To cite only recent disputants, Jewish scholars like Zunz and Grätz accept the tradition of the Talmud that the Sanhedrin was presided over not by the High Priest, but by successive 'pairs' of leaders, whose names it gives; and with them some Christian scholars like De Wette are in agreement. On the other side, Winer, Keil, and Geiger have, in contradiction to the Talmud, asserted either the constant, or the usual, presidency of the High Priest; while Jost has defended an intermediate view, that the Sanhedrin enjoyed its political rights only in theory, but was prevented from putting them into practice through the usurpation of them by the High Priests and others. Another question is, when was the Sanhedrin definitely constituted? . . . The whole subject has been admirably expounded and discussed by Kuenen in his essay on 'The Composition of the Sanhedrin.' His results are hostile to the Talmudic account of the Sanhedrin, for he believes he has proved that a Sanhedrin of the type described or implied in the New Testament and Josephus not only coincides with the Jewish form of government since Alexander the Great, but actually existed since the third century B.C., and that the modifications which it underwent before its collapse in 70 A.D. may be stated, if not with certainty, at least with great probability. Kuenen's conclusions were generally accepted till recently Dr. Adolf Büchler, in *The Synedrion in Jerusalem*, etc., offered an argument for the

existence of two great tribunals in the Holy City, with separate
authorities, religious and civil; and this view has been adopted
by the *Jewish Encyclopædia* in its article 'Sanhedrin.'

"The view, of which Kuenen was the chief exponent, and
which has been generally accepted, is that the Great Sanhedrin
in Jerusalem was a single court, the supreme tribunal of the
Jewish nation, which met usually in a hall in the southern part of
the Temple enclosure known as the *Lishkath hag-Gāzîth* or
Chamber of Hewn-stone, but which under stress of circumstances
might also meet elsewhere. There they interpreted the Law,
and in criminal cases gave sentence. Their power over Jews
was, subject to the Procurator's approval of their sentences of
death, unlimited; and in certain cases they did not wait for
references from the lower courts, but acted directly. According
to the *Mishna*, they alone could try a false prophet or an
accused High Priest, or decide whether the king might make
an offensive war; and Josephus adds that the king was to do
nothing without the High Priest and the opinion of the Senators,
and if he affected too much luxury, was to be restrained. Also,
they judged directly accused priests and other persons. The
Mishna adds that Jerusalem or the Temple Courts could not
be extended without the consent of the Sanhedrin. The
number of the latter was seventy-one.

"This view of the Sanhedrin rests upon the evidence of the
New Testament and Josephus, with illustrations from Talmudic
literature when this agrees with it; and with the rejection of
the rest of the Talmudic evidence as late and unhistorical. Dr.
Büchler, however, has made a fresh examination of the Talmudic
evidence, and has come to the conclusion that there were two
great Jewish tribunals at Jerusalem, possessing different powers:
one with civil authority, the Sanhedrin of Josephus and the
Gospels, one a Sanhedrin with purely religious functions. The
former, he thinks Josephus indicates, sat in the town, or on
the west edge of the Temple mount. The latter was entitled
'the great Beth-Din, which is in the Lishkath hag-Gāzîth,' or
'the great Sanhedrin which sits in the Lishkath hag-Gāzîth.'
This second tribunal had to decide on the purity of priests and

other exclusively religious matters. Neither Josephus nor the Gospels report of their Sanhedrin that it judged cases concerning priests, the temple service, or any religious questions, but ascribe to it exclusively judicial processes, penal sentences, and perhaps cases of a political nature. With these the Talmud does not associate the 'Great Beth-Din in the *Lishkath hag-Gāzîth.*' Dr. Büchler bases his theory on no mean foundation of evidence; his argument is generally reasonable, and his conclusion that there were two supreme courts meets some difficulties which are not removed by the view that there was only one. Still, the following considerations appear to me to be hostile to it. Neither in the Gospels nor in Josephus is there any proof of this duality in the supreme national authority. Had it existed, the descriptions of the Jewish constitution by Josephus would certainly have contained some explicit notice of it; nor do the citations by Dr. Büchler from Josephus necessarily imply it. Nor have we found any evidence of a second supreme court in our survey of the constitutional history previous to New Testament times. Nor does the Talmud itself afford an unambiguous statement that there were two courts—a curious phenomenon, which would certainly have articulated itself somewhere in that vast literature, as it would in Josephus, had it actually existed. There is, too, the fundamental idea of the Jewish system that the civil and religious sides of life were not separate but everywhere interpenetrating, if not identical; and the impossibility, as we have seen, of deciding what matters were religious and what not. To these considerations may be added the fact, as Dr. Büchler admits, that the *Lishkath hag-Gāzîth* was so situated, on the southern edge of the inner court of the Temple but with a door into the outer court, that a body, partly consisting of laymen, might have gathered in it. The solution of the problem may be in some such arrangement as we found the Chronicler to record or suggest, whereby cases purely of the ceremonial law were decided by the priestly members of the Sanhedrin only. But in that case the High Priest would surely have presided; while in the Beth-Din, which Dr. Büchler takes as the supreme religious court, the Talmud says he did not preside!"—G. A. Smith, *Jerusalem*, i. p. 418 ff.

———

NOTE 17. See p. 150.

What do we learn from rabbinical Literature as to the real Nature of the Cleavage between Pharisees and Sadducees?

After criticising Grätz, who finds in the *Megillath Ta'anîth* a number of memorial feasts of an anti-Sadducæan character, Wellhausen proceeds: " Weitere differenzen zwischen Pharisäern und Sadducäern finden sich in der Mischna verzeichnet, namentlich Jadaim 4, 6 f. Authentisch sind diese Angaben wohl jedenfalls, sehr lehrreich aber sind sie an sich nicht, sondern werden es erst durch die Behandlung, die man ihnen angedeihen lässt.

" m. Jadaim 4, 6 : 'Wir haben euch vorzuwerfen, ihr Pharisäer, dass ihr behauptet, die heilige Schrift verunreinige die Hände, nicht aber die Schriften Homers.' Geiger versteht die Pointe. Er sagt Urschrift S. 146: 'Die Sadducäer in der Hochhaltung der eigenen priesterlichen Heiligkeit behaupteten nemlich, dass wer sie berühre, dadurch auch geheiligt werde, desgleichen auch, wer die heiligen Gegenstände berühre, die Pharisäer dagegen behaupteten, man ziehe sich dadurch grade eine Unreinheit zu. Um dies an einem schlagenden Beispiele als widersinnig zu bezeichnen, heben nun die Sadducäer die erwähnte Consequenz hervor.' Die Voraussetzungen dieses Verständnisses sind, um einen bis zur Ungerechtigkeit milden Ausdruck zu wählen, völlig unsicher, und wären sie sicher, so nützten sie dem Verständnisse nichts. Die angeführte Stelle der Mischna nemlich lässt sich durchaus aus sich selbst verstehen, und um so unnöthiger ist es, hier nach einer tiefsinnigen Pointe zu suchen, als die weitere Discussion den Grund des auffallenden pharisäischen Verfahrens sehr einfach und ohne jeden tendenziösen Witz zu Tage bringt. Jochanan b. Zakai verweist die Gegner darauf, dass ja auch die Gebeine eines Esels nicht verunreinigen, wohl aber die eines Menschen, sei es auch des edelsten. Die Antwort, welche die

Sadducäer darauf haben, ist Wasser auf seine Mühle. Sie sagen nemlich: 'weil man Sie hochschätzt, behandelt man sie als unrein, damit nicht etwa Jemand aus seines Vaters und seiner Mutter Knochen Löffel macht.' Das selbe Princip, erwiedert Jochanan, liegt auch dem analogen Verfahren der Pharisäer in Bezug auf die verschiedene Behandlung der Bibel und Homers zu Grunde: die unreinheit schützt das Heilige vor Profanierung. Was kann man Graderes verlangen? Dies ist übrigens keineswegs der einzige, aber ein sehr interessanter Fall, dass Heilig und Unrein sich in dem Begriffe des Unnahbaren berühren.

"m. Jadaim, 4, 7: Ausgegossenes Wasser wird nach den Sadducäern durch das Ausströmen selbst unrein, die Pharisäer aber leugnen, dass dies als Grund der Verunreinigung genüge, und werden darob hier angegriffen. Eine solche Lappalie, dass es für Geiger nothwendig ist, die tiefere Bedeutung aufzudecken. 'Ihr rechnet es, wollen die Sadducäer sagen, dem Unreinen zu Gute, wenn es nur von einem Reinen herkommt; ebenso haltet ihr an den späten Schwächlingen des hasmonäischen Hauses fest, weil sie von grossen Ahnen abstammen.' Die Voraussetzung, dass die Pharisäer mehr als die Sadducäer an dem hasmonäischen Hause festhielten, wäre erst noch zu beweisen; an sich ist das Gegentheil glaublicher, denn so lange die Hasmonäer regierten, waren bekanntlich die Sadducäer die hasmonäische Partei und die Pharisäer ihre wüthendsten Gegner. Ebenso stammt die weitere historische Aufhellung der Controverse aus einem Irrlichte. Auf den Vorwurf der Sadducäer erwidern nemlich die Pharisäer: ihr selbst haltet doch auch das Wasser eines Aquäducts für rein, sogar wenn es aus einem Kirchhof herkommt. Geiger legt dieser treffenden und sachgemässen Antwort folgenden tendenziösen Sinn unter: 'Ist Herodes, wollen die Pharisäer sagen, nicht dadurch zum Throne gelangt, dass er überall um sich her Leichen gehäuft, kann der als berechtigt gelten?' Diese Deutung erklärt gar nicht die charakteristische Fassung der Antwort, abgesehen davon, dass es noch sehr zweifelhaft ist, ob die Sadducäer dem Herodes sehr gewogen waren. Ueberhaupt aber ist gar kein Anlass da zu vermuthen, dass die Pharisäer etwas anderes sagen wollten, als was sie sagten."

25

After dealing exhaustively with the other references to the Pharisees and Sadducees contained in the ra~~~nical literature, Wellhausen says : " Wer daraus einen durchgreifenden Gegensatz inhaltlicher Principien herauslesen will, der darf nicht blöde sein. Die Sadducäer sollen sich als selbstsüchtiger Klerus zeigen, der seine Prärogative als auszubeutendes Monopol behandelt, die Pharisäer dagegen als Vertreter des Gemeindeprincips, des polemisch gefassten Grundsatzes vom allgemeinen Priesterthum." —*Die Pharisäer und die Sadducäer*, p. 63 ff.

CHAPTER V.

NOTE 18. See p. 186.

The Herodians.

The Herodians are thrice mentioned in the Gospels (Matt. xxii. 26 ; Mark iii. 6, xii. 13), but are not referred to by Josephus or any contemporary author. From the data available it is not possible to define their position with exactness. Since Origen's time it has been usual to regard them as Jews who were content to pay tribute to the Romans ; but they were more probably Jewish nationalists who preferred the native monarchy with all its faults to the direct dominion of Rome. They differed from the Pharisees in being not a religious, but a political, or, at all events, a diplomatic party. Why then did they join with the Pharisees in their opposition to Jesus? Perhaps, as those who were "satisfied with the leaven of Herod," they considered the Messianic predictions sufficiently fulfilled in his person and power, or perhaps they dreaded the result of any movement which might lead to complications between the Herodian dynasty and the Roman authorities. In any case they favoured the Herodian kingdom " as representing that union of Hellenism and Judaism which seemed to enable Jews to make the best of both worlds. Such a re-establishment, however, was hindered by the preachers of Messianism, and the friends of Herodianism recognised Jesus as one of these. So these 'spies,' as they are called

(Luke xx. 20), put the insidious question to him, 'Is it lawful to give tribute unto Cæsar, or not,' simply 'that they might catch him in talk,' and accuse him to the governor."—Art. "Herodians" in *Encyc. Bib.*

NOTE 19. See p. 193.

Friedländer's View with regard to the Am-hāārez.

Friedländer denies that they were so ignorant, and holds that they had for their teachers the pious apocalyptists. "Freilich, wenn man in hergebrachter Weise annimt, dass das palästinensische Judentum samt und sonders entweder pharisäisch oder sadduzäisch war, wenn man sogar das Judentum in der Diaspora von dem pharisäischen Geiste beherrscht sein lässt, dann allerdings bleibt es unverständlich, wie aus diesem Milieu das Christentum hervorgehen konnte.

"Nun gab es aber neben dem offiziellen auch ein nichtoffizielles Judentum in Palästina, welch letzeres sich aus den Massen des sogenannten 'Landvolkes,' den Am-haarez, rekrutierte und weder zu den Pharisäern noch zu den Sadduzäern zählte, vielmehr sich gegen beide feindlich abschloss, von ihnen verachtet und gehasst, das aber seine eigenen Lehrer hatte: die frommen Apokalyptiker. . . .

"Nach dem bewährten Beispiel der pharisäischen Schriftgelehrten, die ihren ganzen Hass und ihre unsagbare Verachtung über dieses ihrer Führerschaft unerreichbare, 'Landvolk' ausgossen, ist auch die moderne Religionsforschung geringschätzig über dasselbe hinweggegangen und hat sich dadurch des einzigen Schlüssels beraubt, mit dessen Hilfe das geheimnisvolle Dunkel, das die Geburt des Christentums umschliesst, wenigstens einigermassen gelüftet werden kann. Dieses Landvolk, Am-haarez, gilt heute noch als der 'idiotische Pöbel,' als ein loser unwissender Haufe, der sich frech über Gesetz und Recht hinwegsetzte, Lehre und Zucht hasste und einen schweren Makel am jüdischen Volkskörper bildete.—Das war es aber durchaus nicht, am allerwenigsten in vorchristlicher Zeit, wo es noch von gottbegeisterten jüdischen—allerdings nicht pharisäischen—Männern geleitet wurde. Erst als diese zu schwinden und ihre erhebenden Lehren seltener zu werden anfingen, um die Zeit also, als die tobenden Kriegstürme über Judäa hereinbrachen, denen Tempel und Reich zum Opfer fielen, da verviel auch das Landvolk, 'es war verschmachtet und verstreut, wie Schafe, die keinen Hirten haben.'"— *Die Religiösen Bewegungen innerhalb des Judentums im Zeitalter Jesu*, pp. 15 f., and 78 f.

NOTE 20. See p. 205.

Were the Essenes Teachers of the People?

This is denied by Lipsius. "Die Essäer kommen als Aerzte, Wahrsager, Traumdeuter, Exorcisten, aber nicht als Lehrer und Prediger mit dem Volk in Berührung; ihre frommen Uebungen behalten sie ebenso wie ihre tugendhaften Gesinnungen für sich, ohne auch nur den Versuch zu wagen, ihre reinen religiösen Anschauungen zum Gemeingut der Nation zu erheben. Hierin liegt auch der principielle Unterschied zwischen ihnen und dem gewaltigen Busprediger Johannes, dessen Askese und Taufpraxis sonst so viele Berührungen mit essäischen Wesen bietet. Noch schärfer prägt sich aber der Gegensatz aus, wenn wir von Johannes dem Täufer zu Jesus fortgehen. Fast alles, was Jesus im Gegensatz zu pharisäischem Wesen redet und thut, trifft immer zugleich auch das Essäerthum mit, ja zum Theil in gesteigertem Mass. Die ganze Lebenssitte Jesu, sein ungezwungener Verkehr mit allerlei Volk, ja gerade vorzugsweise mit den für unrein geachteten, seine hohe Freiheit von jeder rituellen Engherzigkeit, seine Opposition gegen alles Gewichtlegen auf äussere Reinheit, auf Sabbatfeier und Fasten, seine sorglose Theilnahme au geselligen Freuden, au Gastmählern und Festlichkeiten, ja selbst eine ganze Reihe specieller Vorschriften und Anweisungen an die Seinen beweist, dass von essäischen Wesen auch nicht eine Ader in ihm war. Der Essäismus war von Haus aus unfähig, etwas neues zu schaffen; von vornherein als Sekte angelegt, ist er Sekte geblieben und hat überall, wo er späterhin auf das

Christenthum einwirkte nur sektenbildend gewirkt."—Art. "Essäer" in Schenkel's *Bibel-Lexicon.*

NOTE 21. See p. 205.

The Russian Doukhobor a Sort of modern Essene.

"What I saw of the Doukhobors and heard from those who have intimate association with them belied the unfavourable stories which I was told in England, and which were given by what I heard in the Eastern provinces. They are of the poorest type of Russian peasantry. Their uncouth appearance, their shaggy skin coats, their lowering countenances, together with the idea that the men put the women folk to the plough and worked them like horses, produced a feeling of resentment among those of whiter skin who regarded themselves as more civilised.

"The Doukhobors are deeply religious, but with a blind, mystic, superstitious religion which is impervious to reason. They live in daily expectation of the second advent of the Messiah. A frenzied faith that the advent is near will send them on a pilgrimage in the depth of winter seeking the Messiah. They cause much anxiety to the officials. Last year they set off on a pilgrimage, making practically no provision for feeding themselves, and turning their stock out upon the snow-swathed wilderness. Government officials, however, got the stock, sold the animals, and held the money in trust for the owners. In time the pilgrims were persuaded to return to their homes. At intervals they have renewed inclinations to search the world for the Messiah. I was at Saskatoon immediately following Lord Minto, the then Governor-General, who had arrived after a ten-days' horse ride from Edmonton, by way of Battleford. I was told how the poor Doukhobors, hearing of the coming of a great man, were with difficulty restrained from greeting Lord Minto as divine.

"But though their fanaticism may bring a smile to the lips of those who are more worldly, their lives are full of self-sacrifice. Most of them left Russia some five years ago [*i.e.* in 1900] for the wilds of Canada. As a religious sect they had planned the exodus from their native country for a long time. They knew hardships would be awaiting them. They regarded it as criminal to take very small children with them. So full were they of pious restraint, that no children were born into the community for several years. Indeed, when four or five thousand of them first reached Winnipeg, there was only one baby amongst them all.

"Hundreds of homesteads have now been taken up. But the Doukhobors mostly live for their community. They share in common. They own their own steam threshing outfits, and have purchased saw mills to provide lumber for their own people. I do not think, however, that the 'commune' will last. Already many of the Doukhobors are beginning to lose their Russian prejudices, and are adapting themselves to Canadian ways. They have the best agricultural machinery to be obtained, and I recall meeting a banker who told me it was amazing the amount of money they were saving. The more energetic and intelligent Doukhobors are giving some signs of wavering in loyalty to the 'commune.' They don't see why the best workers should share and share alike with the worst. Still the strong religious feeling which pervades the sect keeps up a sympathetic Socialism between all sections. The more adventurous borrow from the banks, and there have been no bad debts. I met a man who lent money to a Doukhobor. It was to be repaid by a certain date. At that time the weather was terrible. Yet the Doukhobor rode 150 miles to pay his debt. That is typical.

"A few years back the coming of the Doukhobors to the Dominion was by no means welcomed. Now they have proved themselves good farmers, frugal, virtuous, honourable in all their dealings; and I never heard anything but praise about them from anyone entitled to express an opinion."—*Canada As It Is* (p. 158 ff.), by John Foster Fraser.

"There has been a tendency for the new lands of Canada to become dotted with nationalities with marked distinctions from each other. This is prejudicial to the scheme of making Canada a homogeneous nation.

"Take the case of the Doukhobors, the South Russian sect

advocating Universal Brotherhood. Sterling and worthy though they be, universal brotherhood is what, as a sect, they are stoutly resisting. A little over two years ago the leaders of the Douk-hobors in Assiniboia petitioned the British Columbian Govern-ment to grant them land where they might live without reference to any other Authority than that of God. The application was refused. The fanaticism of the sect has caused bodies of them to make pilgrimages in the bitter winter to hail the second coming of Christ. Because they could not do as they liked, they declared Canada was not a land of religious freedom.

"Foolishness ran through their piety. They petitioned the Sultan of Turkey. Here are one or two extracts from the document: 'We cannot submit ourselves to the laws and re-gulations of any State, or be the subjects of any other ruler except God. . . . They refuse to give us any land unless we promise to obey all the laws of Canada. We declare before God that that is impossible, and that we would sooner bear any oppression than be false to Him. Now we turn to your Majesty and beg you to shew grace to us and our families, not only as a monarch, but as a fellow-being. As pilgrims of God we beg you to give us hospitality and shelter in your wide dominions. . . .' Fancy such a petition to the Commander of the Faithful! Pity comes in thinking of the poor people."—*Ibid.* p. 290 f.

NOTE 22. See p. 208.

Credibility of the Account of the Essenes in Josephus.

Only three authorities—Pliny, Philo, and Josephus—mention the Essenes. Pliny naturally draws his material mostly from the other two, who were Jews, and virtually contemporaries. With the possible exception of the *Apologia pro Judæis* (*ap.* Euseb. *Præp. Evang.* viii. 11), the so-called writings of Philo in which reference is made to the Essenes, namely, *De Vita Contemplativa*, and *Quod Omnis Probus Liber*, chs. xii. xiii., are now generally admitted to be spurious. Much, therefore, turns upon the credibility of Josephus. On this point, unfortunately, opinion is greatly divided. (1) De Quincey regards the whole narrative as the invention of a mendacious rascal, and maintains that no such sect ever existed. It is the newborn brotherhood of *Christians* that is described under the name Essenes. The essay in which this writer expounds his theory, if not convincing, is certainly ingenious, and, needless to say, eminently readable.

(2) A directly opposite view is taken by Friedländer, who not only maintains the trustworthiness of the narrative of Josephus, but also draws considerably upon the Philonic sources. He argues that Josephus as a Pharisee may surely be credited when speaking of a Jewish sect which completely outshone the Pharisees, and asks what the Essenes were to him that he should exalt them so? So far from being an inventor, Josephus as the apologist of his people simply makes use of an important and world-renowned sect to illustrate "what incomparable ethical perfection sprang up on the soil of Mosaism."

(3) Between these two extremes many prefer to steer a middle course, and while recognising that Josephus frequently gives a certain colour to his narrative, are nevertheless prepared to regard it as in the main substantially true. Cheyne, for example, says, "We must not follow Josephus blindly. He either suppresses, or but lightly touches upon, one of the most important Pharisæan doctrines, that which relates to the judgment, the resurrection, and the 'kingdom of God.' Can we hesitate to believe that he deals similarly with the Essenes?" And again, "Still I hesitate to accept such a radical criticism as Ohle's (Ohle undertakes to shew that the accounts of Essenism in Josephus are spurious). There is much in Josephus's account of the Essenes which altogether tallies with our previous expectations, and can be explained either from native Jewish or from Zoroastrian beliefs."—*Origin of the Psalter*, pp. 419, 446.

NOTE 23. See p. 211.

Were the Essenes Sun-worshippers?

The question practically turns upon the interpretation of the words of Josephus, *Bell. Jud.* ii. 8. 5 : Πρὶν γὰρ ἀνασχεῖν τὸν ἥλιον οὐδὲν φθέγγονται τῶν βεβήλων, πατρίους δέ τινας εἰς αὐτὸν εὐχὰς, ὥσπερ ἱκετεύοντες ἀνατεῖλαι. Lightfoot, taking them in their literal sense, regards the Essenes as sun-worshippers, and finds in this a strong proof of Persian influence. Friedländer, on the other hand, protests against putting a literal interpretation upon the words of Josephus here. To do so is, in his opinion, to judge of the Essenes as hostile Roman writers did of the Jews in general, when they called them cloud-worshippers (cf. Juvenal, *Sat.* xiv. 96, " Nil præter nubes et cœli numen adorant"). He thinks nothing more is intended than the Jewish habit of praying at sunrise with hands and eyes directed towards the east (Wisd. xvi. 29; Sib. iii. 591 f.), and that the Essenes were no more sun-worshippers than the early Christians who, according to Tertullian, were similarly looked upon as such by the heathen. "Others . . . believe that the sun is our god. We shall be counted Persians, perhaps, though we do not worship the orb of day painted on a piece of linen cloth, having himself everywhere in his own disk. The idea no doubt has originated from our being known to turn to the east in prayer."—*Apol.* c. xvi.

NOTE 24. See p. 211.

The foreign Element in Essenism.

While fully conscious of the difficulty of the problem, Lipsius looks to Syrian heathenism as affording the most probable solution. "Es ist unmöglich, diese Zeitmeinungen, die uns in den verschiedensten Umgebungen begegnen, auf ihre ursprünglichen Mischungsverhältnisse zurückzuführen. Mit demselben Recht, mit welchem die einen auf griech. philosopheme zurückgingen, haben andere an Einflüsse des Parsismus gedacht; noch näher legt sich, zumal beim Vergleich mit älteren gnostischen Sektenmeinungen, mit den sogenannten Ssabiern, den Mandäern u. a., der Gedanke an vorderasiatisches, insbesondere syr. Heidenthum, wie es bei dem aramäisch redenden Mischvolk Galiläas, Samariens und des Transjordanlandes in der nachexilischen Zeit von neuem sich ausbreitete, und mit der religiösen Weltanschauung des A.T. aufs wunderlichste sich kreuzte. Neben dem, gegenüber dem Parsismus minder scharf ausgeprägten Dualismus, der doch auch sonst zu einer Weltflüchtigen Askese führte, zeigen sich spuren einheimischer oder wenigstens einbürgerter Naturreligion; so vielleicht schon in dem an die aufgehende sonne gerichteten Morgengebet (Josephus, 'Jüdischer Krieg,' ii. 8. 5), welches freilich keine eigentliche Aubetung der sonne als eines Gottes, aber auch schwerlich das gewöhnliche jüd. Schemagebet (5 Mos. 6. 4–9) gewesen sein wird, sondern wol eine Anrufung des himmlischen Lichts oder auch der Sonne als eines, wenn auch nicht göttlichen, doch lebendigen und erhabenen Wesens. Eine weitere Spur liegt wol ferner in der magischen Vorstellung, welche die Essäer ähulich wie die Mandaer und Elkesaiten von der reinigenden und entsühnenden Kraft des Wassers gehegt zu haben scheinen, desgleichen in den von ihnen berichteten magischen Curen und Dämonenbeschwörungen. Unter den alten Schriften, deren sie sich 'zur Heilung der Seele und des Leibes' bedient haben sollen (Josephus, 'Judischer Krieg,' ii. 8. 6), sind vermutlich Zauberbücher nach Art der dem Salomo zugeschriebenen zu verstehen, von welchen Josephus anderwärts redet ('Alterthümer,' viii. 2. 5). Dieselben enthielten also Beschwörungsformeln zur Austreibung böser Geister; ausserdem gingen auch Curen mittels heilskräftiger Pflanzen und Steine bei ihnen im Schwange ('Jüd. Krieg,' ii. 8. 6). Die werke der Barmherzigkeit, in denen den Essäern ausdrücklich auch Fremden gegenüber freie Hand gelassen war, sind wahrscheinlich ebensolche magische Curen. Hiermit hängt endlich auch die von ihnen berichtete Wahrsagekunst und Traumdeuterei zusammen, in welcher sie Bewunderung der Zeitgenossen erregten ('Jüd. Krieg,' ii. 8. 2; 'Alt.' ii. 8. 12; cf. xiii. 11. 2, xv. 15. 5, xvii. 13. 3). Alles dies weist wol auf starke Einflüsse einer, namentlich bei der Heidnischen Bewölkerung Palästinas und Syriens weitverbreiteten Superstition, die keineswegs ausschliesslich oder auch nur vorzugsweise hellenischen Ursprungs ist. Auch die ebenfalls auf einheimischer Naturreligion beruhende

Anrufung der elementaren Mächte bei verschiedenen Weihen, Gelübden, Beschwörungen u.s.w., die uns später bei Ebioniten und Elkesaiten begegnet, war wol schon bei den Essäern im Gebrauch. Die jüd. Dogmatik ward durch diese und ähnliche, ursprünglich auf einem fremden Boden gewachsenen Vorstellungen und Braüche nicht unmittelbar berührt; es schien möglich, ihnen sich hinzugeben und doch dabei ein gesetzesfrommer Jude zu bleiben. Einiges, wie die Dämonenbeschwörungen und magischen Curen, hatte auch bei den Pharisäern Eingang gefunden; sie entsprechen nur einem allgemeinen Zug der Zeit, dem die Essäer in ihrer Abgeschiedenheit vom nationalen Gemeinwesen vielleicht nur widerstandsloser nachgaben. Auf jüd. Boden verpflanzte Pythagoräer sind sie darum noch nicht, trotz der zahlreichen Berührungen mit neupythagoräischem Wesen, welche Zeller beibringt; nicht einmal ein Absenker des jüd. Alexandrinismus sind sie zu nennen, vielmehr scheint die Entwickelung deren Resultate die Darstellungen des Philo und Josephus zusammenfassen, sich durchaus auf palästin. Boden vollzogen zu haben. Bestimmteres über die allmähliche innere Umgestaltung des Essäismus lässt sich bei der Lückenhaftigkeit unserer Nachrichten nicht mehr ausmitteln. Die fortschreitende Zuspitzung der echt chaldäischen Reinheitsangst zu einer wirklich dualistischen Weltanschauung, also die Ausdehnung der ursprünglich aus echt jüd. Motiven entsprungenen Grundgedanken über die jüdisch noch mögliche Grenzlinie hinaus, ist ohne Zweifel, ähnlich wie die Entwickelung des jüd. Alexandrinismus, allmählich und unbewusst vor sich gegangen, unter der Einwirkung von mancherlei dem palästin. Juden nicht blos räumlich nahe tretenden, sondern auch geistig durch wirkliche oder scheinbare Verwandtschaft mit innerjüd. Tendenzen sich empfehlenden Zeitmeinungen. Immerhin ist die wenigstens mittelbare Berührung mit griech. Ideen, wie schwer sie auch sich nachweisen lässt, doch immer noch glaubhafter als die neuerdings alles Ernstes befürwortete Uebertragung des buddhistischen Mönchthums auf jüd. Gebiet."—Art. "Essaer" in Schenkel's *Bibel-Lexicon.*

NOTE 25.   See p. 212.

Is Essenism of Pharisaic Origin?

The following passage shews how vigorously Friedländer
ranges himself on the negative side of this question. "Aber
nicht nur nicht pharisäisch ist der Essenismus, er ist sogar streng
antipharisäisch! Der Pharisäismus spricht jenen, die die Aufer-
stehung des Leibes leugnen, oder auch nur behaupten, dieselbe
werde in der Thora nicht gelehrt, den Anteil an dem künftigen
Leben ab und lässt sie für ewige Zeiten in der Gehenna gerichtet
werden; der Essenismus hingegen verwirft stracks die Aufer-
stehungslehre, ganz im Geiste des jüdischen Alexandrinismus
den Leib für sundhaft erklärend, den der Fromme schon bei
Lebzeiten abtöten müsse; dagegen huldigt er einer, wie Josephus
berichtet, ungemein erhebenden Lehre von der Unsterblichkeit
der Seele, die ebenfalls ganz zweifellos der Jüdisch-Alexandrinischen Schule entlehut ist. Der Pharisäismus verpönt die
Ehelosigkeit als eine krasse Verletzung des göttlichen Gebotes;
der Essenismus preist sie und huldigt ihr. Der erstere hält den
Opferdienst im Tempel für eine untastbare göttliche Institution;
der letztere verwirft ihn, und führt andere Heiligungen an seine
Stella ein, bricht mit dem officiellen Judentum und wird deshalb
aus dem Tempel ausgeschlossen.—Solche und andere, in der
Folge noch zu berührende fundamentale religiöse Differenzen
bildeten eine unüberbrückbare kluft zwischen beiden Sekten, so
dass es ganz unerfindlich ist, wie ernste Forscher über sie
hinweg, auf unbedeutende äusserliche Ähnlichkeiten hin, zu
der Überzeugung gelangen konnten, der Essenismus sei lediglich
eine Steigerung des Pharisäismus!"—*Die Religiösen Bewegungen*,
etc., p. 130.

NOTE 26.   See p. 212.

What led the Essenes to seek Seclusion?

"Der Hang zur Einsamkeit ist jederzeit ein gewichtiges
Symptom, und als solches figuriert es vor allem im Judentum.

Denn Einsamkeit ist dem jüdischen Wesen an sich fremd. Es sind nirgends innerhalb des mosaischen Volkstums Ansätze, keime für eine Existenzform gegeben, die sich über das soziale Medium emporhebt. Das Judentum trägt einen entschieden demokratischen Charakter, das Wort in seiner weitesten Bedeutung genomen, also nicht als politischer und ökonomischer Wert. Wohl mochte es alexandrinischer Interpretationskunst gelingen, auch diesem neuen Ideal einen würdigen Adelsbrief zu schaffen. Wohl hingen Abraham, Moses und andere gefeierte Männer des alten Bundes in der Einsamkeit ihren frommen Betrachtungen nach, im ahnungsvollen Schauen des Ewigen und seiner Herrlichkeit versunken. Ihnen aber war die Einsamkeit und die Fülle von Gesichten, die sich in ihr bot, niemals Selbstzweck sondern Vorbereitung. Sie waren einsam, um sich innerlich zu stärken und für ihre grosse Mission reif zu werden. Ganz anders die essenische und jüdisch-hellenistische Einsamkeit. Sie ist die Krone und nicht die Wurzel des Lebensbaums. Hier ist das Verhältniss ein umgekehrtes. Zuerst aufgehen in den grossen Zwecken der Gesamtheit, dann sinnvolle Kontemplation. Den Preis der Einsamkeit erwirbt sich der, der vorerst unverdrossen in Reih und Glied gestanden hatte. Man zahlt seine Schuld an die Mitwelt, indem man für sie arbeitet. Man heimst den Lohn der Arbeit ein, indem man sich mit jener Bemühung das Recht auf Einsamkeit erwirbt.—Das Buch des alten Bundes ist durchtränkt von sozialer Gesinnung. Vor ganz Israel verkündet Gott seine zehn Gebote. Aus diesem boden entspross kein Wert, der sich von der Gesellschaft emanzipiert, der die gedankenvolle Isolation zum moralischen Imperativ verklärt. Fremde Einflüsse beginnen sich da zu zeigen. Wenn man sie auch vor der Hand nicht zu lokalisieren vermag, es genügt anfangs, sie als solche gekennzeichnet zu haben. Das Märchen von der pharisäischen Herkunft der Essener muss angesichts eines solchen Phänomens schweigen. Den Pharisäer zog kein inneres Bedürfuiss von der 'freundlichen Gewohnheit des Wirkens,' von den trauten Kreisen der Gemeinschaft ab. Ihn lockte nicht der Wunsch 'Gott zu schauen,' ins Gefilde der

Einsamkeit. Es kann also nicht gelengnet werden, dass man hier auf fremden Boden sich versetzt findet. Aus dem sozialen Charakter des Mosaismus ist der Sprung in weltflüchtiges Anachoretentum keineswegs zu erklären. Lassen wir also die unfruchtbare Spekulation, die mit sophistischen Mitteln bloss verjährte Irrtümer decken soll, und rechnen wir mit Realitäten. Der Essenismus mit seinem hochragenden Eigenban an Ideen und Idealen ist aber eine solche Realität und lässt sich nicht zum Schattenspiel des Pharisäismus verflüchtigen. Wenn sein grundbegriff Einsamkeit also nicht aus dem Mosaismus geflossen ist, dann restiert bloss die andere Möglichkeit einer Herkunft aus dem Geist des Hellenismus. Auch hier wird man wohl einer Reihe von Einwänden begegnen. In das Wesen des Griechentums ist nicht weniger sozialer Geist geprägt, als in das des Judentums. Die drei grossen Denker, die ja vielleicht als die Einzigen sichtbare Spüren in die jüdisch-hellenistische Religionsphilosophie eingezeichnet haben konnten: Sokrates, Plato und Aristoteles waren keine Säulenheilige oder Wüstenmänner. . . .

"Vor allem muss man den zweifachen Gedankenkern in dem an sich fliessenden und relativen Begriff der Einsamkeit festhalten. Einsamkeit ist nicht notwendig die absolute Abkehr des Individuums von seinesgleichen, das Anachoretentum, das zu seinem Wohnort die Wüste kürt. Es gibt auch eine Einsamkeit zu vielen, eine sozial organisierte Einsamkeit. Eine solche war eigentlich der Essenismus. Er war einsam der Masse, dem grossen Haufen gegenüber, vor dem er sich vornehm abschloss. Aber diese Einsamkeit sublimierte nicht zum Extrem der Wüstenheiligen, sondern trug einen im höheren Sinn socialen Charakter. Hier aber erweist sich das Griechentum zweifelos vorbildlich. . . .

"Was nämlich sich als der eigentliche Nerv des Einsamkeitsideals immer klarer aus dogmatischen Umhüllungen und liturgischem Apparat herausschält, das ist die eminente Potenzierung des theoretischen, des rein philosophischen Elementes, das hierin seinen Ausdruck und seine höhere Weihe empfängt. Es ist das Verlangen, Gott zu schauen, durch inbrünstige Hingabe an den Erkenntnistrieb der Welt tiefstes Geheimnis in sich aufzunehmen. Der antisoziale, besser gesagt, der antiplebejische Charakter ist nicht der Sinn, der Kern des Essenismus, sondern bloss eine folgerichtige Konsequenz aus jenem Hang."—Friedländer, *op. cit.* p. 125 ff.

CHAPTER VI.

NOTE 27. See p. 223.

Contents of the Book of Enoch.

According to Charles, the whole is divisible into six parts as follows :—

(1) Chs. i.–xxxvi., written at latest before B.C. 170.

(2) Chs. lxxxiii.–xc., written between B.C. 166–161.

(3) Chs. xci.–civ., written between B.C. 134–94, or possibly between B.C. 104–94.

(4) Chs. xxxvii.–lxx., written between B.C. 94–79, or B.C. 70–64.

(5) Chs. lxxii.–lxxviii., lxxix., lxxxvii., of uncertain date.

(6) Fragments from a lost Apocalypse of Noah, and other interpolations, scattered throughout the book, written some time before the Christian era.

Beer in Kautzsch groups the contents thus :—

A. Kap. i.–v. : Eine Einleitungsrede zum ganzen Buche.

B. Kap. vi.–cv. : Die Hauptmasse, bestehend aus :

    I. Kap. vi.–xxxvi., dem angelologischen Buch.

    II. Kap. xxxvii.–lxxi., dem messiologischen Buch.

    III. Kap. lxxii.–lxxxii., dem astronomischen Buch.

    IV. Kap. lxxxiii.–xc., dem Geschichtsbuch.

    V. Kap. xci.–cv., dem paränetischen Buch.

C. Kap. cvi.–cviii. : Der Schluss des ganzen Buchs.

NOTE 28. See p. 229.

Original Language of the Testaments of the Twelve Patriarchs.

The case for a Hebrew original has been presented by Charles in the *Hibbert Journal* (April 1905). His contention is that in addition to frequent Hebraisms in style, and " paronomasiæ or plays upon words and proper names, which are lost in the Greek (but) can frequently be restored by retranslation into Hebrew," there are " obscure or unintelligible passages " which on being rendered into Hebrew lose their obscurity and become quite clear. "Before dealing with illustrations, I would first observe that there are two recensions of the Greek text. Sometimes these agree word for word through whole sentences and paragraphs. At times they disagree in a single word or phrase or entire paragraph. Now in the case of such disagreements we find that sometimes one text is obviously right and the other corrupt, and that by retranslation of the two into Hebrew we understand at once how the mistranslation in the one case arose : or, again, both may be corrupt, and retranslation enables us to discover the original text underlying the corruptions. I will now give some examples. First, in the Test. Reub. iv. i. Reuben says to his children, according to our recension : 'Expend your energies on good works and on learning' ($\mu o \chi \theta o \hat{v} \nu \tau \epsilon \varsigma$ $\dot{\epsilon} \nu$ $\ddot{\epsilon} \rho \gamma o \iota \varsigma$ $\kappa a \lambda o \hat{\iota} \varsigma$ $\kappa a \grave{\iota}$ $\dot{\epsilon} \nu$ $\gamma \rho \acute{a} \mu \mu a \sigma \iota \nu$); the second recension is here unintelligible : 'Expend your energies on works and departing in learning' ($\mu o \chi \theta o \acute{v} \nu \tau \epsilon \varsigma$ $\dot{\epsilon} \nu$ $\ddot{\epsilon} \rho \gamma o \iota \varsigma$ $\kappa a \grave{\iota}$ $\dot{a} \pi o \pi \lambda a \nu \acute{\omega} \mu \epsilon \nu o \iota$ $\dot{\epsilon} \nu$ $\gamma \rho \acute{a} \mu \mu a \sigma \iota \nu$). If we translate both into Hebrew we see that the difference between them arose from reading יְשָׁרִים ($= \kappa a \lambda o \hat{\iota} \varsigma$) wrongly as וְסָרִים ($= \kappa a \grave{\iota}$ $\dot{a} \pi o \pi \lambda a \nu \acute{\omega} \mu \epsilon \nu o \iota$), *i.e.* וְסָרִים. Again, in Test. Levi vi. 10 all the versions agree in describing the Shechemites as 'forcibly carrying off the wives of strangers and banishing them.' Now, the Hebrew word for 'banish,' יְדִיחוּ, means also 'to seduce to idolatry.' This suits the context. Again, in xiii. 5 we have the following couplet, according to the first recension :

> ' Do righteousness, my sons, on earth,
> That you may be made sound in heaven.'

For 'may be made sound' the second recension has simply 'may find.' But neither yields any right sense. When retranslated, their Hebrew equivalents shew that the true text, from which they each differ by a slight corruption, was probably:

> 'Do righteousness, my sons, on earth,
> That you may have treasure in heaven.'

In the Test. Jud. ii. 2 one recension reads: 'I prepared it for my father and he ate'; the other: 'I prepared food for my father.' The difference arose in Hebrew by the transposition of two letters. Again, in iii. 3 of the same Test. Judah says: 'I hurled a stone of sixty pounds and gave it to his horse and killed him.' Here 'gave' (נתתי) is unintelligible, but its equivalent in Hebrew differs but slightly from a word כתותי, which means 'crushed,' or from הכיתי, which means 'smote.' Thus, 'I hurled a stone of sixty pounds and smote his horse and killed it.'

"Sometimes the translation of the true text and likewise that of its corruption are embodied in the Greek, as occurs occasionally in the LXX. A single instance will suffice. In Test. Naph. vi. 2 we have the following peculiar statement: 'A ship came sailing along full of salt food without sailors.' Here 'full of salt food' = מָלֵא מֶלַח or מְלֵא מֶלַח, which is simply a corruption of בְּלֹא מַלָּח = 'without sailors.'

"I shall content myself with two more examples. In Test. Jud. xix. 2, Judah says, after his sin with Tamar: 'Had not the prayers of my father run, I should have died childless.' Here had run = רצו, corrupt for נרצו = 'had been accepted.' In Test. Dan. i. 4, Dan declares: 'I confess that in my heart I rejoiced at the death of Joseph, and I was glad that he was sold.' This, of course, is nonsense. The nonsense is due to the intrusion of a single letter in the Hebrew. When removed, the text runs: 'I confess that I had resolved on the death of Joseph, and that I was glad that he was sold.'" See, further, this writer's recently issued edition of the book.

NOTE 29.   See p. 230.

Date of the Testaments of the Twelve Patriarchs.

Charles tries to shew that in nine instances quotations (direct or implied) from Slavonic Enoch occur in *The Testaments of the Twelve Patriarchs*. In this he has been followed by Bonwetsch, the German translator of the first-named book. Schürer, on the other hand (*GJV*,[3] iii. p. 213), is decidedly of opinion that in no single case can the contention be made good. He also asserts that the discrepancies between the descriptions of the Heaven of Heavens in Slavonic Enoch and the briefer description in the Test. of Levi (chs. ii.–iii.) preclude the supposition that the author of the latter work was acquainted with the former.   When Charles published his edition of Slavonic Enoch he held that the Testaments belonged to the second century A.D.   Now he is convinced that this work dates from the reign of John Hyrcanus (B.C 135–105); see *Hibbert Journal* for April 1905.   But as he places Slavonic Enoch between B.C. 30 and A.D. 70, either *its* date must be put back more than a century (which cannot well be done, since according to Charles himself "Ecclesiasticus is frequently drawn upon"), or it must be admitted that Schürer is right, and that the supposed quotations from it in the Testaments are purely imaginary.

NOTE 30.   See p. 246.

Development towards Apocalypse within the Old Testament itself.

There was a prior development, even within the Old Testament itself, which prepared the way for the apocalyptic writers. This appears from the tangible distinction between pre-exilic and post-exilic prophecy.   The first representative of the latter is Ezekiel, whose transcendental conception of God, employment of complicated imagery and symbolical visions interpreted by angels, and comparative lack of subjectivity, are in considerable contrast to the older type of prophecy. Instead of the summons to repent, we have the proclamation of a change to be super-naturally wrought in the human heart; and the ushering in of the Messianic age is viewed as a thing apart from either the co-operation or obstruction of man. These features are largely reflected in all post-exilic prophecy, which gravitates more and more towards apocalypse. But they are most pronounced in Zechariah, Joel, and certain sections of the Book of Isaiah. Zechariah's forecast of the last judgment, his highly developed angelology, his use of the vision as a form of revelation, his contribution to the vocabulary of hope, and his recourse to imagery derived from foreign sources (*e.g.* the seven eyes of Jahweh, iii. 10), represent a distinct step in the direction of apocalypse. For the apocalyptists valuable materials were also supplied in Zech. ix.–xiv., which depicts the miseries antecedent to the Messianic age, Jahweh's defence of Jerusalem against the final siege on the part of the heathen, and His acknowledgment by the survivors as "the King, the Lord of hosts." In his treatment of the Day of the Lord, Joel also drifts into apocalypse. The prediction of a spiritually revived Israel and the delineation of the signs in heaven heralding the day of judgment became classical among the Christian apocalyptists of the two first centuries. In the apocalyptic section of Isaiah formed by chs. xxiv.–xxvii. we are for the first time face to face with two conceptions which afterwards attained great popularity among apocalyptic authors, namely, the punishment along with the kings of the earth of the wicked angels or tutelary genii of the nations (possibly, however, the reference is to the stars as objects of false worship) and the resurrection. The way was further paved for the apocalypse by the idea of the reappearance of Elijah (Mal. iv. 5) and by various oracles against foreign nations (Isa. xiii., xiv.; Jer. l., li.; Ezek. xxv.–xxxii.). In the apocalyptic literature the former conception was extended so as to include the return of Moses, Isaiah, and Jeremiah, and the denunciations of the latter were used against the galling yoke of the Syrians and Romans.

CHAPTER VII.

NOTE 31. See p. 270.

The apocalyptic Conception of the Kingdom as a World-Empire.

"The kingdom is one. In other words, it is a world-Empire. No other view of it is possible. The whole apocalyptic literature belongs to a period when, practically speaking, small kingdoms are no more. It is a day of empires, and the world is one. Now, I venture to think that this aspect of things reveals one of the points at which the apocalyptic mode of presentation, as seen particularly in Daniel, must have possessed a certain attraction for our Lord. The Gospels inform us clearly enough that the imperial idea had for Him the attraction of a temptation; but it is not difficult to see that, while He rejected the showy forms of empire that had come and gone in this world, He believed in an empire of men, founded not upon the self-assertion of superior races or individuals, but upon their self-sacrifice, and maintained, not by force of arms, but by the eternal strength of righteousness and the overflowing omnipotence of humility and love. The world was far enough away from such a kingdom. But such a kingdom would come to the world in the good time of God. The power was already there in Himself and in all who believed with Him in a Father in heaven, to whom all things were possible."—Muirhead, *The Eschatology of Jesus*, p. 87 f.

NOTE 32. See p. 271.

The Development of the dualistic Idea.

"Die Idee entsteht und wächst sehr langsam. Bereits der Verfasser der späten, in den ersten Teil des Jesaia eingesprengten Apokalypse (c. 24–27) redet in seiner geheimnisvollen Weise von dem Heer der Höhe, das beim Gericht Gottes in Gefangenschaft gesetzt werden solle. Zu diesen dunklen Andeutungen bietet das äthiopische Henochbuch gleichsam den Kommentar Hier (c. 89 f.) wird die Idee entwickelt, dass

Gott seit der Vernichtung und dem Exil des Volkes Israel sein
Weltregiment an die 70 Völkerhirten abgetreten habe, und dass
diese das ihnen zugesprochene Strafmandat Gottes übertreten
und als böse Mächte in der Welt gehaust haben. Dem
entspricht es, wenn beim grossen Gericht Gottes jene Hirten-
engel vor allem gestraft werden, und wenn nach der Wochen-
vision in der letzten Woche das ‘grosse Gericht über die Engel’
stattfinden soll. Eine andere aber verwandte Anschauung ist es,
wenn in den Henochbüchern das Unglück, die Sünde, vor allem
der Götzendienst auf die Engel, die in den Tagen Henoch's sich
mit den Menschentöchtern vermischten und deren Nachkommen,
zurückgeführt wird. Wieder eine andere Wendung des Ge-
dankens liegt im Buch Daniel vor. Der Zeichnung des
furchtbaren vierten Weltreich's und der Gestalt des Verfolgers
des Juden Antiochus IV. (c. 7–8) liegt deutlich die Idee eines
am Ende der Tage erfolgenden Kampfes Gottes mit dem
Drachen ungeheuer zu Grunde, ein Mythus, der dann rein und
nicht mit historischen Zügen übermalt in der Offenbarung
Johannes c. 12 (vgl. auch Ps. Salom. 2), hervortritt.—Die
eigentliche Idee eines persönlichen Widersachers Gottes, der an
der Spitze eines bösen Geisterreiches steht, findet sich zum
ersten Mal in deutlicher Ausprägung in den Testamenten der
Patriarchen, eines ihrer Grundlage nach wahrscheinlich aus der
Makkabäerzeit stammenden Schrift. Hier steht Beliar, der
Fürst der bösen Geister, der Herrscher der wilden Tiere, der
Urheber der Not und der Sünde, der Fürst der Finsternis und
Luge in schroffem Gegensatz Gott gegenüber. Hier gewinnt
der Gedanke eines endgültigen Sieges Gottes über Beliar und
seine Schaaren entscheidende Bedeutung. Spuren des Dogmas
vom Teufel finden sich auch in dem den Testamenten zeitlich
nahestehenden Buch der Jubiläen in den Bilderreden des
Henochbuches. Im neutestamentlichen Zeitalter ist das Dogma
von Teufel fertig. Diejenige Apokalypse, die wir als einzige
mit Bestimmtheit gerade in das Zeitalter Jesu setzen können,
die Assumptio des Moses, beginnt die Schilderung des Endes
mit den Worten: ‘Und dann wird sein (Gottes) Regiment über
alle seine Kreatur erscheinen, dann wird der Teufel ein Ende

haben.' Jesus setzt in seiner Predigt das Dogma vom Teufel als gegeben voraus. Wir brauchen nur an das eine Wort zu errinern: 'Wenn ich im geiste Gottes Dämonen vertreibe, dann ist die Herrschaft Gottes (d. h. der Sieg Gottes über Teufel und Dämonen) gekommen' (Mtth. xii. 28). Paulus, in dessen Weltanschauung wie es scheint der mehr populäre Teufelsglaube einigermassen zurücktritt, nennt doch den Teufel den Gott dieser Welt (2 Kor. iv. 4). Im Johannesevangelium wird wieder der dualistische Gegensatz zwischen Gott und dem Fürsten dieser Welt, dem Vater der Lüge und der Finsternis, central, genau wie in den Testamenten der Patriarchen."—Bousset, *Die jüdische Apokalyptik*, p. 20 ff.

NOTE 33. See p. 282.
Legendary Expansion of Gen. vi. 1–4.

"Bestimmte dualistische Gedanken und Vorstellungen werden für uns erst seit der zweiten Hälfte des zweiten vorchristlichen Jahrhunderts (nach Daniel) sichtbar. Zunächst hat hier die Gen. 6. 1 als Rudiment aufgenommene Sage von der Vermischung der Göttersöhnen mit den Menschentöchtern oder vielmehr eine ausführlichere Erzählung dieser Sage, die sicher unabhängig neben Gen. 6 stand, weitergewirkt. Schon in der Grundschrift des 1. Henoch bekommt diese Sage eine principielle Bedeutung. Es entwickelt sich an ihr die Idee einer gefallenen Engelwelt. Mit ihr tritt für den Verfasser der älteren Henochbücher das Böse in die Welt hinein. Die gefallenen Engel sind die Urheber alle böser Zauberei auch der heidnischen Astrologie und Wissenschaft."—Bousset, *Die Religion des Judentums*, p. 326.

NOTE 34. See p. 297.
Did our Lord expect the Parousia in His own Time?

Charles arrives at the conclusion that "according to the teaching of Christ the parousia was to be within the current generation.

"We must, accordingly, admit that this expectation of Christ was falsified. But the error is not material. It is in reality inseparable from all true prophecy. For the latter, so far as it relates to fulfilment, is always conditioned by the course of human development. Herein lies the radical difference between Apocalyptic and Prophecy. The former determines mechanically the date of consummation of a certain process, irrespective of human conduct; the latter determines only the ultimate certainty of that consummation. Moreover, Old Testament prophecy, and likewise Jewish Apocalyptic, represent the consummation of the kingdom as following immediately on its establishment. Thus all the past gave its suffrage to Christ's expectation. Furthermore, as Christ was convinced that all the prophecies of the Old Testament were fulfilled in Him, and that the age introduced by Him was *final* and *ultimate* as regards things religious and spiritual, the expectation was in the highest degree natural that this age would be *final* and *ultimate* in a temporal sense also. But whereas the fact that the kingdom should be consummated was a matter of transcendental importance, the time of that consummation had no immediate significance, religious or spiritual. Provided with all knowledge that was needful for His vocation, Christ yet confessed that the knowledge of this date had been expressly withheld (Mark xiii. 32). By his unique and perfect communion with God He possessed an independent and authoritative judgment in things essentially spiritual and religious, but not in other spheres. In the latter He was dependent on the thought and development of His time."—*Eschatology*, p. 331 f.

"Titius (*Jesu Lehre vom Reiche Gottes*, Mohr, 1895) is confident that Jesus expected the end of the world in His own time, but he holds that the expectation did not so possess His mind as not to pass readily, through His surrender to His Father's will, into the larger reality."—Muirhead, *op. cit.* p. 87, *note.*

CHAPTER VIII.

NOTE 35. See p. 298.

The eschatological Sayings of Jesus.

On this subject Harnack (*Dogmengeschichte*,[3] i. 65, 97 ; Eng. trans. i. 101 f.) remarks : " The Jewish apocalyptic literature, especially as it flourished since the time of Antiochus Epiphanes, and was impregnated with new elements borrowed from an ethico-religious philosophy, as well as with Babylonian and Persian myths (Greek myths can only be detected in very small number), was not banished from the circles of the first professors of the gospel, but was rather held fast, eagerly read, and even extended with the view of elucidating the promises of Jesus. . . . It was an evil inheritance which the Christians took over from the Jews, an inheritance which makes it impossible to reproduce with certainty the eschatological sayings of Jesus. Things directly foreign were mixed up with them, and, what was most serious, delineations of the hopes of the future could easily lead to the undervaluing of the most important gifts and duties of the gospel. An accurate examination of the eschatological sayings of Jesus in the Synoptists shews that much foreign matter is mixed with them (see Weiffenbach, *Der Wiederkunftsgedanke Jesu*, 1875). That the tradition here was very uncertain, because influenced by the Jewish Apocalyptic, is shewn by the one fact that Papias (in Iren. v. 33) quotes as words of the Lord which had been handed down by the disciples, a group of sayings which we find in the Apocalypse of Baruch about the amazing fruitfulness of the earth during the time of the Messianic kingdom." M. Réville (quoted by Gardner, *Exploratio Evangelica*, 1908, p. 279) also maintains that the prophetic utterances regarding the last things are not after the manner of Jesus. " N'est-il pas surprenant que les enseignements de Jésus, même quand il énonce des idées qui ne sont pas précisément nouvelles, ont toujours un cachet original, indi- viduel, frappé nettement à sa marque personnel, et qu'ici, au

contraire, c'est ce qu'il y a de plus banal dans les apocalypses
qui nous est présenté comme sa révélation suprême?" If
these sayings are not properly ascribed to Jesus, but are to be
viewed as importations by the evangelists from foreign sources,
then the problem indeed becomes insoluble. No doubt, even on
the supposition that they are genuine utterances of our Lord, they
are to be read as poetry, not as prose. This does not, however,
mean the elimination of their essential content as predictions
of the second Advent, and of a future judgment.

NOTE 36. See p. 317.
The Hellenistic Dialect.

(1) "Il était impossible que ces relations de plus en plus
fréquentes et intimes avec un monde nouveau et si avancé dans
tout ce qui tient à la civilisation, n'exerçassent une influence
profonde sur la fraction de la nation juive qui y participa plus
directement. Nous n'avons pas à nous occuper de cette
influence, en tant qu'elle dut se montrer dans les habitudes de
la vie sociale; nous nous hâtons de signaler un phénomène
plus curieux et plus immédiatement en rapport avec la sphère
des idées dont nous étudions l'histoire. C'est le fait de l'adoption de la langue grecque par les familles juives établies hors
de la Palestine et même dans les villes maritimes de la mère-
patrie. Après la religion, la langue est bien la chose la plus
étroitement liée avec la vie intime d'un peuple, son héritage le
plus sacré et le plus inaliénable. Eh bien, le peuple juif, dans
la dispersion, en fit le sacrifice avec une facilité qui resterait une
énigme, si nous n'avions pas déjà constaté que l'intérêt materiel,
et non pas même celui qui est justifié par le besoin, a été le seul
mobile de cette migration d'un genre nouveau. Cet intérêt seul
pouvait amener les juifs à remplacer la langue de leurs pères par
un idiome étranger. Ils s'appropriérent ce dernier pour l'usage
de la vie commune d'abord, et arrivèrent bientôt à ne plus
pouvoir s'en passer dans les autres sphères de la pensée. Mais
rien n'est plus singulier que l'idiome qui naquit ainsi presque au

hasard du contact des deux nationalités. Les juifs s'emparèrent de ce que nous appellerions le trésor de la langue grecque, c'est-à-dire de tous les mots qui la composent, ainsi que des formes grammaticales qui en sont inséparables. Comme ils durent prendre les uns et les autres dans la bouche d'une population très-mélangée elle-même et en partie peu cultivée, le fond même de la langue qu'ils apprirent était déjà très-différent de celui de l'ancienne langue littéraire des Hellènes. Mais c'était bien pis encore pour ce qui en constituait l'esprit. Ils ne parvinrent pas à le saisir ; la syntaxe qui, partout, fait le caractère propre d'une langue à son état de perfection et qui est la chose capitale pour le grec surtout, ils ne la comprirent point, on pour dire plus vrai, ils ne s'en soucièrent pas, ils l'ignorèrent. Ils continuèrent à penser selon le génie de leur idiome sémitique, si différemment façonné sous ce rapport, et traduisant ainsi leur pensée mot à mot de l'hébreu en grec, ils produisirent un langage tout particulier, hébreu d'esprit et grec de corps, jargon bâtard dans l'origine, mais acquérant peu à peu droit de cité dans le monde par son usage étendu, se légitimant par une littérature aussi remarquable qu'exceptionelle, et destiné à laisser des traces profondes jusque dans les langues modernes les plus cultivées et les plus répandues. Car c'est surtout par son application aux idées religieuses que ce langage particulier est devenue célèbre et influent. Il servit bientôt à traduire la loi pour les juifs d'Égypte qui commençaient à oublier la langue sacrée, et peu à peu tous les autres livres de l'ancienne Alliance furent transcrits en grec à leur tour. Enfin, les apôtres qui vinrent prêcher ou écrire en grec, n'eurent guère que le dialecte helléniste à leur disposition ; ils durent lutter, sans toujours triompher, contre la pauvreté désespérante d'une langue dont les moyens tout matériels n'étaient pas en rapport avec la tâche élevée qu'on lui imposait.

"Ce changement de langue, phénomène très-intéressant par lui-même déjà, n'était encore qu'un fait extérieur si l'on veut. Mais il ne faut pas juger l'esprit qui dirige les destinées de l'humanité d'après le mouvement plus on moins bruyant qui se fait à la surface des événements. L'avenir du monde se prépare à une profondeur où l'œil de l'observateur ne pénètre guère.

Le courant nouveau qui se forme au fond ne peut se manifester que tardivement et par des symptomes d'abord peu appréciables à travers les flots de la surface. Le fait de la métamorphose des juifs hébreux en juifs héllénistes ne présente pas seulement cet intérêt statistique ou philologique que nous avons dû signaler d'abord : il cachait dans son sein des conséquences qui se révélèrent plus tard et dont la portée va droit au cœur de l'histoire de la théologie chrétienne."—Reuss, *Histoire de la Théologie Chrétienne au siècle Apostolique*, i. p. 95 ff.

(2) "We can see from the Septuagint what sort of Greek was spoken in Hellenistic capitals—very coarse and rude as compared with Attic refinement, interlarded with local words, which would differ according to the province and its older tongue, but a practical and handy common language, such as Latin was in the Europe of the Middle Ages."—Mahaffy, *Alexander's Empire*, p. 154.

NOTE 37. See pp. 317, 319, 328.

The Syntax of the Septuagint.

"The syntactic 'influence' of the Alexandrian translation was less powerful by far than the lexical. The spirit of the Greek language was, in the imperial period, sufficiently accommodating where the enlarging of its stock of terms was concerned ; the good old words were becoming worn out, and gropings were being made towards new ones and towards the stores of the popular language—as if internal deterioration could again be made good by means of external enlargement. But notwithstanding all this, it had a sense of reserve quite sufficient to ward off the claims of a logic which was repugnant to its nature. The alleged 'Jewish-Greek,' of which the Alexandrian translation of the Old Testament is supposed to be the most prominent memorial, never existed as a living dialect at all. Surely no one would seriously affirm that the clumsy barbarisms of the Aramæan who tried to make himself understood in the Greek tongue were prescribed by the rules of a 'Jewish-Greek' grammar. It may be, indeed, that certain peculiarities, particularly with regard to the order of words, are frequently repeated, but one has no right to search after the rules of syntax of a 'Semitic Greek' on the basis of these peculiarities, any more than one should have in trying to put together a system of 'English High-German' from the similar idioms of a German-speaking Englishman. We need not be led astray by the observed fact that Greek translations of Semitic originals manifest a more or less definite persistence of Semitisms; for this persistence is not the product of a dialect which arose and developed in the Ghettos of Alexandria and Rome, but the disguised conformity to rule of the Semitic original, which was often plastered over rather than translated. How comes it that the Jew Philo and the Benjamite Paul stand so distinctly apart from that of such Greek translations? Just because, though they had grown up in the Law, and meditated upon it day and night, they were yet Alex· andrian and Tarsian respectively, and as such fitted their words naturally together, just as people spoke in Egypt and Asia Minor, and not in the manner of the clumsy pedantry of the study, submitting line after line to the power of an alien spirit. The translators of the Old Testament were Hellenists as well as were Philo and Paul, but they clothed themselves in a strait-jacket —in the idea perhaps that such holy labour demanded the putting on of a priestly garment. Their work gained a success such as has fallen to the lot of but few books : it became one of the 'great powers' of history. But although Greek Judaism and Christianity entered into, and lived in, the sphere of its ideas, yet their faith and their language remained so uninjured that no one thought of the disguised Hebrew as being sacred, least of all as worthy of imitation,—though, of course, there was but little reflexion on the matter."—Deissmann, *Bible Studies*, p. 296 f.

NOTE 38.   See p. 328.

Influence of the Septuagint on popular religious Thought.

Deissmann (*Bible Studies*, pp. 271–300) gives an interesting account of " an epigraphic memorial of the Septuagint " discovered

at Adrumetum, south-east of Carthage, in 1890, and dating from
the time of Origen. The tablet is "a love-spell dressed in the
form of an energetic adjuration of a demon, by means of which
a certain Domitiana desires to make sure of the possession of
her Urbanus. The technical details of the spell have no direct
significance for our subject; we are interested only in the
formulæ by which the demon is adjured. . . . We may at once
take for granted that these formulæ were not composed by Domitiana herself. She copied them, or had them copied, from one
of the many current books of Magic ; and in doing so had her
own name and that of the person loved inserted at the respective
places. . . . On this assumption the historical value of the formulæ
is increased, for the formulæ thus employed in the third century
must have been extracted by the writer of the book in question
at a certainly much earlier date from the Alexandrian Old Testament. In the Magic books now in Paris, Leiden, and London,
which were in the main composed before the third century, we find
quite a multitude of similar adjurations compiled from biblical
materials, and the task of subjecting these to a critical survey is
well worth while." That that author was a Greek Jew is indicated both by its almost complete freedom from Hebraisms and
by the way in which it heaps up attributes of God after the style
of 2 Maccabees (ii. 1, 24 ff., etc.) and other Jewish Greek writings
of the period. "Thus the tablet of Adrumetum is a memorial
of the Alexandrian Old Testament. Not only does it reveal
what a potent formal influence the Greek Bible, especially the
praise-book thereof, exercised upon the classes who lived outside
of the official protection of the synagogue and the Church, and
who thus elude the gaze of history, but it lets us also surmise that
the eternal thoughts of the Old Testament had not wholly lost
their germinative power even where, long after and in an obscure
place, they had seemingly fallen among thorns."

NOTE 39. See p. 330.

Are there Traces of Greek Philosophy in the Septuagint?

We may note first the systematic use of κύριος and θεός for Jahweh wherever He is regarded in the Hebrew text as actively working. Dähne's attempt, however, to ascribe to these terms the meaning they ultimately acquired in the religious philosophy of Philo, and to shew that as used in the Septuagint they denote not only the supreme God, but also intermediary beings or higher powers, is not convincing. The same thing has to be said of his discovery of the Alexandrian tenet that no human name can be applied to God in the translation of Lev. xxiv. 16, "he that blasphemeth (נקב) the name of Jahweh" by the Greek verb ὀνομάζω. This may not be strictly accurate, but not to mention that Aquila (a later authority no doubt) translates similarly, it is a very slight deviation on which to build so much. Again, in the Septuagint rendering of Ex. iii. 14, "I am" is expressed by the participle ὁ ὤν. In this Dähne detects the Philonic doctrine that we know merely that God is, but not what He is. But the rendering need not denote anything more than the eternal or self-existent Being, and Philo himself accepts it as the nearest equivalent of the Hebrew text. On the other hand, the tendency to avoid anthropomorphism (ascription of members of the human body) and anthropopathy (ascription of affections of the human mind) to set forth the moral and spiritual activity of God is undoubtedly traceable in a number of passages which have been altered in accordance with Alexandrian views. Thus in Josh. iv. 24 for "the hand of Jahweh" is substituted the abstract expression, "the power of the Lord," and in Isa. vi. 1 for "the skirts of his robe" we have simply "his glory." In Ex. xxiv. 10, where the Hebrew text reads, "they saw the God of Israel," the Septuagint has, "they saw the place where stood the God of Israel." [Herriot, however, points out with force that even with this alteration little was gained from the philosophic point of view, for "supposer Dieu se tenant en un certain lieu, c'est aussi peu conforme aux idées judéo-Alexandrines que prétendre qu'on le

puisse voir en personne."] Similarly, in Isa. xxxviii. 11, Hezekiah's lament, "I shall not see the Lord in the land of the
living," becomes "I shall not see the salvation of God." In
2 Chron. vi. 2 the Heb. text speaks of the Temple as the
dwelling-place of God Himself, but in the Septuagint Solomon
is made to say, "I have built a house to thy name." Of the
slave who voluntarily renounces freedom it is said in Ex. xxi. 6
that "his master shall bring him unto God," but the Greek translation phrases it, "unto the judgment of God." In Ps. xvii. 15,
"thy likeness" is rendered by "thy glory." The hellenising
hand is particularly traceable in passages which speak of God
as "a man." Thus in Isa. xlii. 13, where the Heb. text has
"Jahweh shall go forth as a mighty man," the Septuagint reads,
"The Lord God of powers (τῶν δυνάμεων, according to
Drummond = 'armies,' according to Dähne = essentially Divine
powers, yet not individually one with God) shall go forth";
while in the same passage, as also in Ex. xv. 3, in place of the
concrete designation "a man of war" we have the abstract notion
of "stirring up war."

Interesting also is the treatment of passages dealing with
God's relation to the world. The insertion of the word ἔτι in
the Septuagint rendering of Gen. ii. 19 is by Dähne adduced as
evidence that the translators desired to give expression to Philo's
view that while the *ideas* of the animals were previously formed
in the spiritual world, the actual material existences represent
a further creation. Curious as the use of the adverb is, this is
perhaps to read too much of Philo into the cosmology of
the Pentateuch. The same thing is true with regard to
several of the passages from the opening chapters of Genesis
(i. 11, ii. 5, etc.) which are founded upon by Dähne. But this
writer also finds the Alexandrian cosmology reflected in the
Septuagint rendering of Isa. xlv. 13. The Heb. text gives:
"Thus saith Jahweh that created the heavens; he is God; that
formed the earth and made it; he established it." The Greek
translation is : οὗτος ὁ θεὸς ὁ καταδείξας τὴν γῆν, καὶ ποίησας αὐτὴν,
αὐτὸς διώριζεν αὐτὴν, κ.τ.λ. Since καταδείκνυμι means to bring
to visibility, to shew clearly, and διορίζω means to divide by

limits, to set bounds to, Dähne would find here the Platonic doctrine that the visible world is the projection or image of an invisible world (κόσμος νοητός), and that the creation represents a process cf division. In this instance Bois (*Essai sur les Origines de la Philosophie Judéo-Alexandrine*) is disposed to agree with Dähne: "Il est bien vraisemblable qu'on doit admettre ici que la traduction de ce passage est décidément inspirée par une conception philosophique grecque." But it is questionable whether we have here really anything more than the Hebraic representation of God as dividing the light from the darkness, and by the fiat of His will calling the world into existence and giving to it sensible forms. On the other hand it seems clear that in Gen. i. 2, ἡ δὲ γῆ ἦν ἀόρατος καὶ ἀκατασ-κεύαστος, there is a reference to the κόσμος νοητός, for there is no other conceivable explanation of such a rendering of the תהו ובהו of the original. This is allowed even by Siegfried, who pronounces the whole question as to the influence of Greek philosophy upon the Septuagint "streitig," and speaks of the "ausserordentliche Flüchtigkeit" of the alleged parallels. Strangely enough, it is questioned by Bois, who regards the Hellenistic influence as indubitable.

The later doctrine of guardian angels seems also to be read into the Pentateuch. In Deut. xxxii. 8, where the Heb. text speaks of the Most High having assigned to the nations their inheritance "according to the number of the children of Israel," the Septuagint reads "according to the number of the angels of God." This deviation appears to reflect a distinctly Platonic influence, and at all events it became the basis of a belief which found widespread acceptance among the Jews (Dan. x. 20; Acts xii. 15).

Dähne finds a reflexion of the Platonic psychology in the words of Gen. iii. 14: ἐπὶ τῷ στήθει σου καὶ τῇ κοιλίᾳ. But it is more reasonable to view this as an instance of double translation or as a combination of two textual variants than as an allusion to the division of the human faculties into the λογιστικόν, the θυμικόν, and the ἐπιθυμητικόν (assigned to the head, the heart, and the belly). In Job vii. for "my soul chooseth strangling and death rather than my life" (lit. than *these* my bones), the Septuagint reads: Ἀπαλλάξεις ἀπὸ πνεύματός μου τὴν ψυχήν μου, "Thou wilt separate my soul from my spirit." This decided variation may well have been due to the recognition of the distinction between soul and spirit. It is difficult also to regard the use of the philosophical term ἡγεμονικός as purely accidental; but when Dähne explains the addition "in thy hand," Deut. xxx. 14, as due to the later Jewish-Hellenistic theory relative to the distribution of the active powers of man, one feels that he is needlessly ingenious.

Bois concludes a discussion of the question at issue in the following terms: "Il est certain qu'il y a déjà du judéo-alexandrinisme dans les Septante: y en a-t-il beaucoup? Il est certain que les auteurs de cette traduction ont été influencés par la philosophie grecque: dans quelle mesure? C'est ce qu'il est délicat de décider.

"Mais il semble qu'à côté de doctrines et de termes empruntés à la philosophie grecque (théorie des idées, doctrine de la matière préexistante, termes anthropologiques, notions anthropologiques), la version des LXX contient, dans sa notion de Dieu, l'essence du judéo-alexandrinisme, savoir la véritable raison d'être et le germe du Logos philonien.

"Ce résultat est de la plus haute importance. Car cette version des Septante, c'est précisément la seule forme sous laquelle la plupart des Juifs Alexandrins connurent les livres de l'Ancien Testament. Cet amas de traductions, d'origine et de mérite différents, devint lui-même inspiré à leurs yeux, aussi inspiré que les originaux. Et c'est ainsi que la "haie" sacrée, qui devait entourer et abriter les documents de l'ancienne alliance, se trouva, en Egypte, singulièrement élargie, enserrer et légitimer le berceau de la philosophie des judéo- alexandrins. La fameuse haie laissera bientôt tout passer. Car, un peu en fait déjà, et complètement en puissance, la philosophie grecque, le philonisme sont introduits et acceptés dans la place sainte."

NOTE 40. See p. 333.

Examples of the allegorical Method of Interpretation adopted by Aristobulus.

By way of applying his method Aristobulus points out that by God's hand we are to understand simply His power. Just as, when Ptolemy himself performs a great action, his subjects say, "The king's hand is strong," meaning the king is powerful; so when Moses says, "The Lord hath brought you up from Egypt with a mighty hand" (Deut. vii. 8), he alludes to the power of God which gave effect to His will. Again, the expression στάσις θεία is not, he says, to be taken in the literal sense of God's stability, but in the figurative sense of the organisation of the world (ἡ τοῦ κόσμου κατασκευή), with its clear divisions of sun from moon, land from water, man from beast, etc. "For God is over all, and all is subject to Him, and has received from Him its stability, so that man can discover that it is immovable. . . . Thus we can speak of God's stability." Aristobulus also explains allegorically the descent (κατάβασις) of God on Mt. Sinai in fire (Ex. xix. 18). We are not to think of a local descent, such as the language used might seem to imply, but of the advent of Divine power. Cf. Clement, *Strom.* vi. 3.

NOTE 41. See p. 337.

Ascription of spurious Verses to Greek Poets.

One of the weapons by which a Jewish propaganda was carried on under a heathen mask was the ascription of spurious verses to Greek poets, in numerous passages of whose writings apologists for Judaism found the fundamental doctrines of their creed—the unity, spirituality, and transcendence of God, and retributive judgment for men. Clement of Alexandria, indeed, quotes from Greek poets many verses that are genuine; but in his writings, as well as in those of Aristobulus, and in the pseudo-

Justinian works *Cohortatio ad Græcos* and *De Monarchia*, there are also many which are pure forgeries. We have already referred to the appeal to Hesiod, Homer, and Linus (not Callimachus as Clement wrongly states) with regard to the sabbath, and to the poem ascribed to Orpheus, which Schürer characterises as "one of the boldest forgeries ever attempted. It is a supposed legacy to his son Musæus, in which, having arrived at the close of his life, he expressly recalls all his other poems, which are dedicated to polytheistic doctrines, and proclaims the alone true God" (Eng. trans. II. iii. p. 300). Spurious verses are also attributed to the comic poets Philemon, Menander, and Diphilus, and to the great writers of tragedies, Aeschylus, Sophocles, and Euripides.

Who was responsible for these forgeries? Both Clement of Alexandria (*Strom.* v. 14) and the *De Monarchia* (chs. 2–4) contain nearly all the spurious verses in question (for complete list see Schürer, II. iii. p. 298 ff.), and appear to have derived them from a common source. Now what this was is distinctly indicated by Clement (*Strom.* v. 14, 113); it was the work of the pseudo-Hecatæus on Abraham. Not content with giving many authentic extracts from the Greek poets, this writer seems to have deliberately set himself to supplement them in order to make them satisfactory exponents of monotheistic beliefs. His work *On Abraham*, or as it is also more generally entitled *On the Jews*, was issued under the name of the historian and philosopher Hecatæus of Abdera, who flourished at the court of Ptolemy Lagos in the fourth century B.C. This forged treatise may, however, have been based upon actual portions of the real Hecatæus. That the latter in his history of Egypt entered into particulars concerning the Jews is clear from the long extract in Diodorus Siculus, who, however, wrongly calls him Hecatæus of Miletus. According to Schürer, the pseudo-Hecatæus wrote in the third century B.C.; according to Willrich (*Judaica*, p. 97), after the time of John Hyrcanus, that is, at the earliest, about 100 B.C.

NOTE 42. See p. 355.

Allegorism in the hands of Origen.

I transcribe the following from my volume on Origen in the
" World's Epoch-Makers " series (p. 78 ff.) :—

" As a Jew, even Philo had to pay some regard to the literal
and historical sense of the Old Testament; but the reins of
Origen's imagination knew no such restraining influence. For
him allegorical exegesis meant license to father his own speculations upon a sacred text which was venerated as the depository
of all truth.

" In opposition to the Jews and judaising Christians, who
denied that their legal sacrifices and ritual were denuded of
their value and importance by the coming of Christ, Origen
maintained that to observe the law outwardly in the letter
now that its spiritual sense has been revealed, is no longer
religion but superstition, and a hindrance rather than a help to
piety. 'Compared with the gospel, the law is like those earthen
vessels which the artist forms before casting the statue in bronze ;
they are necessary until the work itself is finished, but their
utility ceases with the completion of the statue' (*In Levit.*
Hom. x. 1).

" With Origen the aggressiveness of the Gnostics weighed even
more powerfully than the conservatism of the Jews. Learned,
versatile, speculative, this class of opponents devoted their
oratorical and literary powers to wrecking the faith of the simple.
Undoubtedly the strong point of Christian preaching was an
unbroken tradition reaching from the creation to the times of
Christ. The Gnostics sought to undermine this position by
violently separating the New Testament stem from the Old
Testament root. They ridiculed the story of Noah's ark, and
the God who had to send His angels to ascertain what was
happening in Sodom. They criticised mercilessly whatever
in the Old Testament offended their moral sense, *e.g.* the
atrocities of the Jewish wars, with the view of representing
them as sanctioned by a cruel God utterly unlike the good God

of the gospel. Cultured Greeks, although otherwise drawn to the sacred writings, were shocked at such tokens of barbarity, and hesitated to declare themselves Christians. Under these circumstances Origen does not, like Clement, content himself with pleading that in God justice and goodness are harmoniously combined. He boldly cuts the knot by maintaining that the narratives and commands to which his opponents took exception are not literally true; that the kings slain by the Israelites are only figurative names for vices that have dominion over men; and that the nations which they are said to have exterminated are not to be regarded as composed of men, but of the enemies that assail men's souls. What the Spirit has in view in such passages is not the narration of historical events, but the communication of mysteries, under the veil of facts, for the soul's edification. They thus serve a pædagogic purpose, and are vehicles of the highest truth. The forbidding aspect of the upper garment cannot alter the fact that ' the king's daughter is all glorious within,' and while it may repel the ignorant, it only acts as a spur to redoubled effort on the part of the spiritually enlightened. In the hands of Origen, therefore, allegorism in its negative aspect becomes an apologetic weapon, by means of which he defends Christianity against the hide-bound externalism of the Jews and the blasphemous criticism of the Gnostics; but as the result of his fantastic interpretations, the history itself, of course, disappears. Lest, however, his view should be regarded as invalidating entirely both the historical and legislative portions of Scripture, Origen is careful to state that the passages having a purely spiritual meaning are few in comparison to those that are true historically, and that in regard to the Decalogue and such New Testament precepts as 'Swear not at all,' etc., there is no doubt that they are to be observed according to the letter, although in such cases a deeper meaning also may disclose itself to the advanced Christian.

"It has been suggested that, even irrespective of any controversy with Jews or heretics, Origen would still have been driven to these extremities by the mere conditions of preaching in his

time. The preacher's custom was one day to read and expound
a page of scripture, the next day to read and expound the page
following. In the case of historical books, which were not
written exactly for edification, one can understand what
embarrassment he would experience. Only by effacing their
historical character could he draw edifying lessons from texts
but little edifying in themselves. Origen's *Homilies* certainly
shew how ready he was to sacrifice the literal sense and at all
hazards to discover a meaning suitable to the moral and
spiritual needs of his hearers. Any other course would in his
opinion have been wrong. 'Those do injustice to Moses, who,
when the Book of Leviticus or some portion of *Numbers* is read
in the church, do not set forth spiritually what is written in the
law. For necessarily those present on hearing recited in the
church either the rites of sacrifice or the observances of the
sabbath and other similar things, are displeased, and say, How
is it necessary to read that here? Of what use to us are Jewish
precepts and the observances of a despised people? That
concerns the Jews; let them attend to it if they please' (*In
Num.* Hom. vii. 2)."

NOTE 43. See p. 360.

*The living Word of God the real Bridge between God
and Men.*

"Philo von Alexandria und die palästinensische schriftgelehrsamkeit bilden die äussersten Spitzen, in welche die
gesetzliche Religionsauffassung auslief. Das *lebendige Wort
Gottes*, welches von dem Gesetz auf endgiltige feste Form
gebracht werden sollte, damit die gottesfürchtigen Juden in
allen Stücken den Willen Gottes erfüllen könnten, wurde auf
der einen Seite in eine philosophische Lehre aufgelöst, die
unfähig war, den Verkehr Gottes mit den Menschen von dem
allgemeinen Wirken des einen Logos in der Welt zu unter-
scheiden und so ihn sicher zu stellen, und auf der andern Seite
in eine Unmasse atomistischer Regeln und Satzungen zerlegt und

verdichtet, die wie ein undurchdringlicher Zaun den Ausblick auf Gott unmöglich machten. Von einer Unmittelbarkeit der Religion, wie sie die Propheten als die wahre innige Verbindung der einzelnen Menschenseele mit Gott erlebten und für alle von der Zukunft erhofften, und wie sie noch der Dichter Hiobs in heissem Ringen gegenüber der nomistischen Fassung siegreich behauptet hatte, war keine Rede mehr. Das lebendige Wort Gottes war erstarrt, ein Prophet stand nicht mehr auf; seine Stimme wäre auch nur wirkungslos an dem gelehrten System und dem starren Gesetz abgeprallt. Da hat Gott die Rettung gebracht, nicht mit einer anderen Lehre oder einem anderen Gesetz, sondern durch die Sendung seines Wortes in lebendiger Kraft, das zu den Herzen der Menschen hindurchdringt und ihnen eine selbständige und unmittelbare Erkentnis des Willens Gottes verleiht. Weder in den cultischen Riten oder den Satzungen der Schriftgelehrten, noch in der philosophischen Weisheit ist für jeden die Brücke zwischen Gott und den Menschen zu finden; sondern, wie die Propheten erhofften, nur das lebendige Wort Gottes bildet die wahre Verbindung. *In Jesus ist dieses Wort in lebendigen Kraft erschienen:* ὁ λόγος σὰρξ ἐγένετο καὶ ἐσκήνωσεν ἐν ἡμῖν (Ev. Joh. i 14)."—Marti, *Geschichte der Israelitischen Religion*, p. 335 f.

ADDITIONAL NOTE. See p. 340.

The Pre-existence of the Soul in the Book of Wisdom.

In a paper on this subject, contributed to vol. i. of *Old Testament and Semitic Studies in Memory of William Rainey Harper* (Chicago University Press), Prof. F. C. Porter, of Yale, says: "The Platonic doctrine of the pre-existence of the soul is not found in the Book of Wisdom. It is not the natural meaning of the one verse which is thought to assert it (viii. 20); it is not sustained by the two Platonic phrases (ix. 15, xi. 17) which are adduced in its support; it has not its inevitable accompaniments, its roots and fruit, in the writer's views as to the world in general, which, so far as they are not Jewish, are Stoic in character, nor in his conception of the origin and nature of sin, nor in his view of death and his doctrine of immortality. It is not asserted that the book contains no idea of the pre-existence of the soul. A certain sort of pre-existence is implied in viii. 19, 20, xv. 8, 11, 16, xvi. 14; but it is not the pre-existence of the person, the conscious moral self; it is not of the Greek, but of the Jewish, type. A doctrine of the pre-existence of the soul of which no use is made to refute a current material-istic notion (ii. 2, 3); with which the belief in immortality, though earnestly urged, stands in no relation; from which no theoretical or practical inferences are drawn in the direction of an ascetic suppression of the body; which has nothing to do with the theory of ideas,—can surely not be called Platonic."

APPENDIX II.

—◆—

BIBLIOGRAPHY.

THE following works are set down, without any attempt at classification, in their (approximate) chronological order. The list includes only the more modern literature. Although comparatively few of these books deal comprehensively with our period, all treat of some portion or aspect of it. Many changes in prices have taken place since this list was compiled. The prices specified are the pre-war prices and should now be disregarded.

PRIDEAUX : The Old and New Testament connected in the history of the Jews and neighbouring nations from the declension of the kingdom of Israel and Judah to the time of Christ. Originally published in 2 vols. (1716–1718). There have been many subsequent editions. Diffuse and out of date, but still worth consulting. Cheap second-hand copies are numerous.

HARTMANN : Die enge Verbindung des Alten Testaments mit dem Neuen (1831). Discusses fully the Sanhedrin and the Synagogue.

COTTON, H. : The Five Books of Maccabees translated into English (Oxford University Press, 1832. - 10s. 6d.).

DÄHNE : Geschichtliche Darstellung der jüdisch-Alexandrinischen Religionsphilosophie (1834). The first systematic treatise on the subject, and still well worth reading. Procurable second-hand for 3s. or 4s.

GFRÖRER : Geschichte des Urchristentums (2 vols., 1838). The first valuable attempt at a systematic presentation of Judaism.

VITRINGA : The Synagogue and the Church (1842). An abridgment of *De Synagoga Vetere*, issued in 1726.

BRUCH : Weisheitslehre der Hebräer (1851).

FRITZSCHE UND GRIMM : Kurzgefasstes Exegetisches Handbuch zu den Apokryphen des AT's (1851–9). This still remains the best commentary.

LÜTTERBECK : Die Neutestamentliche Lehrbegriffe oder Untersuchungen über das Zeitalter der Religionswende, die Vorstufen des Christenthums und die erste Gestaltung desselben (2 vols., 1852). Vol. i. is mainly a discussion of the religious condition of Judaism in the time of Christ.

RAPHALL : Post-Biblical History of the Jews from the close of the Old Testament, about the year 420, till the destruction of the Second Temple in the year 70 (2 vols., 1856).

HERZFELD : Geschichte des Volkes Israel (3 vols., 1847–1857. 10s. 6d. second-hand). Vol. ii. deals with the political history, and vol. iii. with the inner development, of our period.

HILGENFELD : Die Jüdische Apokalyptik (1857). A standard work.

GEIGER : Urschrift und Uebersetzungen der Bibel (1857). Treats of the bearing of the inner development of Judaism upon the text of the Old Testament.

JOST : Geschichte des Judentums und seiner Secten (3 vols., 1857–59). Vol. i. deals with the development of Judaism down to A.D. 70.

MILMAN : The History of the Jews (3 vols., 1829–30 ; new ed. 1892). Vol. i. and the first part of vol. ii. deal with the inter-Testamental period.

NICOLAS : Des doctrines religieuses des Juifs pendant les deux siècles antérieures à l'ère chrétienne (1860. 2s. second-hand). Characterised by Bousset as "recht unbrauchbar," yet readable, and not devoid of merit.

BOST : L'Époque des Maccabées, histoire du peuple juif depuis le retour de l'exil jusqu' à la destruction de Jérusalem (1862. Fr.3.50).

BAUMGARTEN : Der National - Jüdische Hintergrund der NT Geschichte (im Jahrbücher für Deutsche Theologie, 1864–65).

EWALD : Geschichte des Volkes Israel (7 vols., 3rd ed. 1864–68. Eng. tr. in 8 vols., 1867–86. About 30s. second-hand). Vol. v. is devoted to the history of Ezra and of the Hagiocracy in Israel to the time of Christ. An epoch-making work.

REUSS : Histoire de la theologie chrétienne au siècle apostolique (2 vols., 3rd ed. 1864. 5s. second-hand. Eng. tr. 1872. 12s. 6d. second-hand). Vol. i. contains succinct and able chapters on the Synagogue, Pharisaism, Sadduceeism, Jewish Theology, Hellenism, Alexandrine Philosophy, Essenism, and Messianic Hopes. (Scarce.)

LANGEN : Judentum in Palästina zur Zeit Christi (1866. 3s. second-hand). A very interesting book, written from the dogmatic standpoint of the Roman Church. Unlike Gfrörer, Langen does not use the rabbinical writings as sources.

WORDSWORTH, Bishop C. : The Church and the Maccabees (Rivingtons. 1s.). "Two inspiring sermons which still have a sale, and deserve it."

DERENBOURG : Essai sur l'histoire et la géographie de la Palestine, d'après les Thalmuds et les autres sources rabbiniques. Part I. Histoire de la Palestine depuis Cyrus jusqu' à Adrien (1867). Contains very valuable matter.

WEBER UND HOLTZMANN : Geschichte des Volkes Israel (2 vols., 1867). Relates the history from Alexander the Great to Hadrian. Similar in method to Ewald, but much briefer.

HITZIG : Geschichte des Volkes Israel von Anbeginn bis zur Eroberung Masada's im J. 72 nach Chr. (2 vols., 1869). Comparatively full treatment of the period subsequent to Alexander the Great.

GRAETZ : Geschichte der Juden. A voluminous work of Jewish authorship. Vols. ii. and iii. deal with our period. Vols. iii.-xi. appeared in 1853-70 ; vols. i. and ii. in 1874-76. 4th ed. in 1888. Price £3, 16s.

KEIM : Geschichte Jesu von Nazara (3 vols., 1867-72 ; Eng. tr. in 6 vols.). The earlier portion of this work treats of the Herodian age and of the inner condition of Judaism during that period. Cheap second-hand copies obtainable.

KUENEN : De godsdienst van Israel tot den ondergang van den joodschen staat (2 parts, 1869-70). Eng. tr., The Religion of Israel to the Fall of the Jewish State (vol. iii., 1881-82. 6s.).

VERNES : Histoire des idées messianiques depuis Alexandre jusqu' à l'empereur Hadrien (1874. 2s.).

WELLHAUSEN : Die Pharisäer und Sadducäer (1874. 5s.). An excellent little book, but unfortunately out of print. Schürer says, "This short monograph gives more information about the inner history of Judaism during our period than many an extensive work."

SCHÖNEFELD : Ueber die messianische Hoffnung von 200 vor Christo bis gegen 50 nach Christo (1874. 80 pf.).

SIEGFRIED : Philo von Alexandria als Ausleger des Alten Testaments an sich selbst und nach seinem geschichtlichen einfluss betrachtet (1875. 6s. second-hand). Very scholarly and thorough.

STANLEY : Lectures on the History of the Jewish Church (3 vols., 1875-76. 36s.). Now to be had in cheaper form. Vol. iii. : From the Captivity to the Christian Era. Largely indebted to

Ewald, finely descriptive, and strong in seizing on picturesque incidents.

HAUSRATH : Neutestamentliche Zeitgeschichte (3 vols., 1868–74 ; 2nd ed. in 4 vols., 1873–77. Eng. tr., 2 vols., 1878. 10s.). Graphic and interesting.

DRUMMOND : The Jewish Messiah. A critical history of the Messianic idea among the Jews from the rise of the Maccabees to the closing of the Talmud (1877. 15s.). A very good book, but scarce.

STAPFER : Les idées religieuses en Palestine à l'époche de Jésus-Christ (2nd ed., 1878. 6s.).

WÜNSCHE, A.: Beiträge zur Erläuterung der Evangelien aus Talmud und Midrasch (1878. 11s.). Good and interesting.

CONDER : Judas Maccabæus and the Jewish War of Independence (1879. 4s. 6d.). "Brings out, perhaps more forcibly than any other writer, the military genius of ' the Hammer.' "

WEBER, F. : System der altsynagogalen palästinischen Theologie aus Targum, Midrasch und Talmud dargestellt (1880). New and posthumous editions under somewhat different titles in 1886 and 1897. A standard work of importance.

BISSELL : The Apocrypha, in Lange-Schaff's Commentary (1880. 15s. net).

LUCIUS : Der Essenismus (1881. 3s.).

DE SAULCY : Histoire des Maccabées ou princes de la dynastie asmonéenne (1880. 8s. 6d.).

SEINECKE : Geschichte des Volkes Israel (2 vols., 1884. 15s.) Vol. ii. : From the Exile to the Destruction of Jerusalem by the Romans.

CHURTON : The Uncanonical and Apocryphal Scriptures (1884. 7s. 6d.).

BACHER : Die Aggada der Tannaïten (2 vols., 1884–90. 4s.). An indispensable supplement to Weber's work, which does not sufficiently distinguish between the older and more recent of the haggadistic sayings.

STANTON : The Jewish and Christian Messiah : A Study in the Earliest History of Christianity (1886. 10s. 6d.).

MACKINTOSH, R. : Christ and the Jewish Law (1886. 6s.). An acute and valuable treatment of this important subject.

STAPFER : La Palestine au temps de Jésus-Christ d'après le Nouveau Testament, l'historien Flavius Josèphe et les Talmuds (1855 ; 5th ed. 1892. 4s. Eng. tr. 1886). Largely archæological.

BALL, C. J. : The Variorum Apocrypha (Eyre & Spottiswoode. 6s. 6d.). Contains useful short notes on the various readings and renderings.

Bibliography 429

MAHAFFY, J. P. : Alexander's Empire (1887. 5s.). A volume of the "Story of the Nations" series.

STADE : Geschichte des Volkes Israel (2 vols., 1888. 32s.). Vol. ii. (latter half) : Das Ende des jüdischen Staatswesens und die Enstehung der Christentums (by O. Holtzmann). This work might be called "Ewald up to date."

REUSS : Die Geschichte der heiligen Schriften alten Testaments (1881 ; 2nd ed. 1890. 15s.). Combines history of the literature with that of the people.

CHEYNE : Job and Solomon, or the Wisdom of the Old Testament (1887. 12s. 6d.).

DRUMMOND : Philo Judæus (1888. 2 vols., 21s.).

MORRISON : The Jews under Roman Rule (1890. 5s.). A volume of the "Story of the Nations" series.

BOIS : Essai sur les origines de la philosophie judéo-alexandrine (1890. Fr.6). A valuable treatise.

HUNTER, P. HAY : After the Exile : A hundred years of Jewish History and Literature (1890. 2 vols., 5s. each).

TOY, C. H. : Judaism and Christianity (1890. 12s. 6d.). Traces the development of religious thought in the inter-Testamental period. A valuable study.

RYLE AND JAMES : The Psalms of the Pharisees = Psalter of Solomon (1891. 15s.). A reliable handbook.

LOOMAN : Geschiedenis der Israeliten van de babylonische ballingschap tot op de komst van den Heere Jezus Christus. Meteen aanhangsel, inhondende de geschiedenis der Israeliten van Herodes I. tot op de verwoesting van Jerusalem (1867 ; 3rd ed. 1891).

DEANE : Pseudepigrapha (1891. 7s. 6d.). A "popular" survey.

THOMSON : Books which influenced our Lord (1891. 10s. 6d.). Racily written.

STRACK UND ZÖCKLER : Apokryphen des Alten Testaments (1891. M.8).

CHWOLSON : Das letzte Passamahl Christi und der Tag seines Todes (1892. M.4.65). "Contains, among much that is important, an essay on the Pharisees."

HENDERSON, A. : Palestine : Its Historical Geography (1893. 2s. 6d.). Section 99 gives "a brief account of the places which became notable during the wars of the Maccabees."

BALDENSPERGER : Das Selbstbewusstsein Jesu im Licht der messianischen Hoffnungen seiner Zeit (1892. 4s.). Valuable. More recently by the same writer : Das spätere Judentum als Vorstube des Christentums (1900. 60 pf.).

REINACH : Jewish Coins. Eng. tr. by MARY HILL (1903. 3s. 6d.).

VOLZ : Jüdische Eschatologie von Daniel bis Akiba (1903. 7s.).

SMITH, G. A.: The Historical Geography of the Holy Land (1894. 15s.). A standard work.

RENAN : Histoire du peuple Israel (vol. 5. 1894). A graphic review of the history of our period. Eng. tr. in 3 vols.

CARPENTER, J. E.: Life in Palestine when Jesus lived (1894. 1s.).

PFLEIDERER : The Philosophy and Development of Religion (2 vols., 1894. 15s. net). Vol. ii. ch. 2 : "The Preparation of Christianity in Judaism." Characterised by this writer's usual grasp and clearness of insight.

HOLTZMANN, O.: Grundriss der Neutestamentlichen Zeitgeschichte (1895. 4s. 6d.). A short summary.

GUNKEL : Schöpfung und Chaos (1895. 10s.). Deals with some fundamental questions relating to the genesis of later Judaism.

KENNEDY : Sources of New Testament Greek, or the Influence of the Septuagint on the Vocabulary of the New Testament (1895. 5s.).

MAHAFFY, J. P.: The Empire of the Ptolemies (1895. 12s. 6d.). A standard history.

WILLRICH : Juden und Greichen vor der Makkabäischen Erhebung (1895. M.4). See Note 3, p. 365.

MEYER, E.: Die Enstehung des Judentums (1896. 6s.). Cf. the section on "Die Anfänge des Judentums" in his Geschichte des Altertums, III. i. 167–236 (1901).

BERTHOLET : Die Stellung der Israeliten und der Juden zu den Fremden (1896. 7s.). A monograph of special value, dealing not merely with a side issue, as its title might suggest, but with the most fundamental problems of Judaism.

BUHL : Geographie des alten Palästina (1896. M.6.60).

SCHULZ : Alttestamentliche Theologie (5th ed. 1896. 12s.) Contains a brief review of our period. Eng. tr. in Clark's series.

HÖLSCHER : Der Sadduzäismus (1906. M.2.80). "A striking monograph" (Rev. G. H. Box).

WEISS, H.: Judas Makkabaeus (1897. 2s. 6d.). Written from the Roman Catholic standpoint. The writer refers to 2 Maccabees as "this so long unjustly depreciated part of the Biblical canon."

STREANE : The Age of the Maccabees, with special reference to the religious literature of the period (1898. 6s.).

KENT : A History of the Jewish People. Part III. : The Greek Period of Jewish History (1899. 6s.).

BÜCHLER, A.: Die Tobiaden und die Oniaden im II. Makkabäerbuche und in der verwandten jüdisch-hellenistischen Literatur (1899. M.7).

WILLRICH, H.: Judaica. Forschungen zur hellenistisch-jüdischen Geschichte und Literatur (1900. M.5.60). In this work Willrich follows up his "Juden und Griechen," on the main contention of which see Note 3, p. 365.

WELLHAUSEN: Israelitische und Jüdische Geschichte (1894, 4th ed.; 1901, 5th ed. 10s.). A work of the greatest value. Contains within short compass an able and illuminating presentation of the development of Jewish piety in the post-exilic age.

CORNILL: Geschichte des Volkes Israel von den ältesten Zeiten bis zur Zerstörung Jerusalems durch die Römer (1898. 8s., bound). Those who are acquainted with this writer's "The Prophets of Israel" will turn with interest to his book on Israelitish history.

FAIRWEATHER AND BLACK: The First Book of Maccabees, with the Text of the Revised Version (Cambridge Bible for Schools) (1897. 2s. 6d. net).

HERRIOT: Philon Le Juif: essai sur l'école Juive d'Alexandrie (1898. Fr.7.50). Like most French works, clear and readable. Book I. discusses Jewish Alexandrianism before Philo. Book II. treats of the Life of Philo, and gives a classification of his writings. Book III. contains an exposition, and Book IV. an examination, of his philosophy.

DALMAN: Die Worte Jesu (1898. 8s. 6d. Eng. tr. 1902. 7s. 6d.). A treatise of exceptional worth. Specially rich in linguistic investigations, and dealing with quite a number of questions vitally affecting Jewish religion.

CHEYNE: Jewish Religious Life after the Exile (1898. 6s.). Third series of "American Lectures on the History of Religions." Informing, suggestive, and well worth reading.

SCHÜRER: Geschichte des Jüdischen Volkes im Zeitalter Jesu Christi (3rd ed. 1898–1901, 3 vols. 40s. 4th ed. 1908). Eng. tr. of the second ed. 1886–1890, Index 1891, in Clark's "Foreign Theological Library" (New Series), 5 vols. A monumental work, indispensable for every student of post-exilic Judaism.

LATIMER: Judea from Cyrus to Titus (1899).

SHAILER MATHEWS: A History of New Testament Times in Palestine, 175 B.C. to 70 A.D. (1899. 3s. 6d.).

HÜHN: Die Messianischen Weissagungen des israelitisch-jüdischen Volkes bis zu den Targumim (1899. 9s. 6d.). A careful study, based on historical sequence, of all Messianic passages, presumed or real, in the Old Testament, Apocrypha, and Pseudepigrapha, and the Targums.

GUTHE : Geschichte des Volkes Israel (1899. 6s.). Something of the nature of an epitome ; an enlarged form of the article "Israel" in the Encyclopædia Biblica.

MONTEFIORE, C. G. : Bible for Home Reading (Macmillan. 5s. 6d.). "Contains reflective comments on 1 and 2 Maccabees."

CHARLES : A Critical History of the Doctrine of a Future Life in Israel, in Judaism, and in Christianity ; or Hebrew, Jewish, and Christian Eschatology from Pre-Prophetic Times till the close of the New Testament Canon (The Jowett Lectures for 1898–99. 15s.). An acute and valuable treatment of the subject, although the writer is perhaps disposed to rely too much upon the results of critical emendations of the text of the sources. Charles has rendered a great service to students of the Jewish pseudepigraphic writings by his editions of the Book of Enoch, the Apocalypse of Baruch, the Assumption of Moses, the Ascension of Isaiah, the Book of Jubilees, the Book of the Secrets of Enoch, and the Testaments of the XII. Patriarchs.

SCHECHTER AND TAYLOR : The Wisdom of Ben Sira (1899. 10s. net).

GASTER, M. : The Chronicles of Jerahmeel (1899. 10s. net). Jerahmeel is "the oldest and best corpus of apocryphal and pseudepigraphal books of which any literature can boast."

WELLHAUSEN : Skizzen und Vorarbeiten VI. (1899. 8s.). The writer here enters into a controversy with Gunkel on the subject of the Apocalyptic literature. See p. 225 ff.).

SMEND : Lehrbuch der AT Religionsgeschichte² (1899. M.11.50).

NIESE : Kritik der Beiden Makkabäerbücher (1900. 2s. 6d.).

KAUTZSCH : Die Apokryphen und Pseudepigraphen des Alten Testaments (2 vols., 1900. 20s.). Contains, besides a general Introduction, brief but adequate introductions to the several books, a German text, and a critical commentary. Altogether a most serviceable work.

SCHLATTER, A. : Israel's Geschichte von Alexander dem Grossen bis Hadrian (1901. 3s.). Brief but suggestive.

RIGGS : History of the Jewish People during the Maccabæan and Roman Periods (1900. 5s.). A companion volume to Kent's "History of the Jewish People."

EDERSHEIM : The Life and Times of Jesus the Messiah (2 vols., 1884, 1886², 1900³. 24s.). Embraces a great mass of (critically unsifted) material from late Jewish tradition.

DEISSMANN : Bible Studies : Contributions chiefly from Papyri and Inscriptions in the history of the Language, the Literature, and the Religion of Hellenistic Judaism and Primitive Christianity (Eng. tr. 1903². 9s.). Full of interesting and valuable material.

HOLTZMANN: Die Jüdische Schriftgelehrsamkeit zur Zeit Jesu (1901. 50 pf.).

SALMOND: The Christian Doctrine of Immortality (1895; 5th ed. 1901. 14s.). Perhaps the best book on the subject.

WENDT: Lehre Jesu (2nd ed. 1901. 12s.). Eng. tr. of Part II. (from the first ed.), in 2 vols., 1892. 21s. First Section: The Historical Foundation of the Teaching of Jesus.

MOSS, R. W.: From Malachi to Matthew (1893. 2s. 6d.) Useful.

FAIRWEATHER: From the Exile to the Advent (1911³. 2s.).

MOULTON, R. G.: The Literature of the Bible (1901. $1). Contains an interesting chapter on "Old Testament Wisdom," in which the Books of Wisdom and Ecclesiasticus are discussed fully from their literary side.

BEVAN E.: The House of Seleucus (2 vols., 1902. 36s.). A very valuable work.

WERNLE: Die Anfänge unserer Religion (1901; 2nd ed. 1904. 7s.). In the Eng. tr. (2 vols., 1903. 21s.), pp. 12–36 of vol. i. deal with Judaism and the Fulness of the Time.

BOUSSET: Die Religion des Judentums im neutestamentlichen Zeitalter (1903, 1906². 10s.). Exceedingly valuable. See also the same writer's Die Jüdische Apokalyptik (1903).

SCHRADER: Die Keilinschriften und das Alte Testament. Dritte Auflage, mit Ausdehnung auf die Apokryphen, Pseudepigraphen und das Neue Testament, neu bearbeitet von Dr. H. Zimmern und Dr. H. Winckler (1903. 21s.). This important work comprises two sections, "History and Geography" by Winckler, and "Religion and Language" by Zimmern.

BALDENSPERGER: Die Messianisch-Apokalyptische Hoffnungen des Judenthums (1903. M.4).

FRIEDLÄNDER: Geschichte der Jüdische Apologetik als Vorgeschichte des Christenthums (1903. M.8).

FRIEDLÄNDER: Griechische Philosophie im AT (1904. M.5.40).

BEVAN, E.: Jerusalem under the High Priests: Five Lectures on the Period between Nehemiah and the New Testament (1904. 7s. 6d.). A well-written popular sketch.

MUIRHEAD: The Eschatology of Jesus, or the Kingdom Come and Coming (the Bruce Lectures for 1903) (1904. 6s.). Interesting, able, and scholarly.

PORTER: The Messages of the Apocalyptical Writers (1905. 3s. 6d.). The Introduction (pp. 3–75) is specially valuable.

MARSHALL, J. T.: Religious Beliefs in the Time of Christ. HASSÉ, LEONARD: The Apocalyptic Schools of Judaism in Biblical Times. (Manchester University Press, 1905.)

28

FRIEDLÄNDER : Die Religiösen Bewegungen innerhalb des Judentums im Zeitalter Jesu (1905. 7s.). An important and well-
written book, if sometimes rather violently polemical. The
author, himself a Jew nurtured on Pharisaic traditions, maintains that Pharisaism, favoured by the change of political relations consequent upon the Maccabæan victories, broke through
the natural development of Judaism as hitherto dominated by
the spirit of the prophets and the Wisdom literature, and
alienated it from its original and peculiar mission. It was
the Hellenistic Jews who followed the original and true traditions of Israel, and cherished the universalism preached by
the great prophets, whereas the Pharisees forced the religious development into the narrow and artificial groove of
legalism.

HOLLMANN-HALLE : Welche Religion hatten die Juden als Jesus
auftrat? (1905. 40 pf.). In the "Religionsgeschichtliche Volks-
bücher" series.

HENDERSON : The Age of the Maccabees (Temple Series. 9d. net).

DAVIDSON, A. B.: The Exile and the Restoration (Clark's "Primers").

SKINNER, J.: Historical Connection between the Old and New
Testaments (Clark's "Primers." 6d.).

GRANT, C. M.: Between the Testaments ("Guild Text-Books." 6d.
net). Gives a short account of the Literature as well as the
History of the Period.

SEDGWICK, S. N.: The Story of the Apocrypha (S.P.C.K. 1s. 6d.).

SNELL, B. J.: The Value of the Apocrypha (1905. 1s. 6d.) A
series of Sunday evening "Lectures."

KENT : The Student's Old Testament. Vol. ii. treats of Israel's
Historical and Biographical Narratives (1905. 12s. net).

MAHAFFY : The Progress of Hellenism in Alexander's Empire
(1905. 5s. net).

MILNE RAE, G.: The Historical Connection between the Old and
New Testaments (Temple Series. 9d. net).

ABRAHAMS, ISRAEL : Festival Studies (1906. 2s. 6d.). Gives an
account of Hanucah, when the heroic exploits of the Maccabees
are commemorated.

ABRAHAMS, ISRAEL : Judaism (1907. 1s. net). An illuminating
little book by a modern Jew.

OESTERLEY AND BOX : The Religion and Worship of the Synagogue (1907. 10s. 6d. net). Interesting to the student of the
Apocrypha. Uses the term "Jewish" loosely (Schürer).

THE TEMPLE APOCRYPHA (J. M. Dent. 6 vols. at 1s. each) : Contains Introductions to the several books.

Bibliography 435

ANDREWS, H. T. : Apocryphal Books of the Old and NT.

MARTI : Geschichte der Israelitischen Religion (5th ed. 1907).

GENUNG : Hebrew Literature of Wisdom (1907).

HELBING : Grammatik der Septuaginta (1907).

SMITH, G. A. : Jerusalem : The Topography, Economics, and History from the Earliest Times to A.D. 70 (2 vols. 1908).

PENTIN, H. : Judith (1908).

MOULTON, J. H. : Grammar of NT Greek³ (1908). See also Moulton's inaugural lecture in the University of Manchester, "The Science of Language and the Study of the NT" (1906), and his article "From Egyptian Rubbish-Heaps" (*London Quarterly Review*, April 1908).

HART, J. H. A. : Ecclesiasticus (1909). Interesting, scholarly, and indispensable: Mr. Hart challenges the generally accepted view of the date of Ecclesiasticus, and would place it fully a century earlier.

OESTERLEY, W. O. E. : The Doctrine of the Last Things : Jewish and Christian (1909). "A fascinating book."

HUGHES, H. M. : The Ethics of Jewish Apocryphal Literature (1909).

GREGG, J. A. F. : The Wisdom of Solomon (1909).

THACKERAY, H. ST. JOHN : A Grammar of the OT in Greek, according to the Septuagint.

HARRIS, J. RENDEL : The Odes of Solomon, now first published from the Syriac version (1909).

SHARMAN, HENRY BARTON : The Teaching of Jesus about the Future, according to the Synoptic Gospels (Eng. ed. 1909).

MILLIGAN, G. : Selections from the Greek Papyri (1910).

DOBSCHÜTZ, ERNST VON : The Eschatology of the Gospels (1910). An "admirably careful and balanced study of the subject."

SCHWEITZER : The Quest of the Historical Jesus : A Critical Study of its Progress and Results from Reimarus to Wrede (1910).

PROKSCH, D. OTTO : Studien zur Geschichte der Septuaginta.

KENT : The Sermons, Epistles, and Apocalypses of Israel's Prophets from the Beginning of the Assyrian Period to the End of the Maccabæan Struggle (1910).

ABBOT, EDWIN A. : The Son of Man, or Contributions to the Study of the Thoughts of Jesus (1910).

PFLEIDERER, O. : Primitive Christianity : Its Writings and Teachings in their Historical Connections (Eng. tr. 1910). Contains a valuable chapter on the religion of Mithra.

SCHNEIDER, HERMANN : Entwickelungsgeschichte der Menschheit. Band ii. Kultur und Denken der Babylonier und Juden (1910).

STRACK : Sanhedrin-Makkoth, die Misnatraktate über Strafrecht und Gerichtsfahren (1910).

EMMET, C. W. : The Eschatological Question in the Gospels (1911). A reply to Schweitzer.

SCOTT, E. F. : The Kingdom and the Messiah (1911).

DEISSMANN : Light from the Ancient East : The NT illustrated by recently discovered Texts of the Græco-Roman World (1911²). In this interesting work it is conclusively proved that many so-called specifically " Biblical " Greek words were current in ordinary Greek.

OTTLEY, R. L. : The Religion of Israel.

BENSLY AND JAMES : The Fourth Book of Ezra. Contains the text of the Latin version. A fine piece of scholarship.

DAUBNEY, W. H. : The Three Additions to Daniel.

SANDERS AND FOWLER : Outlines for the Study of Biblical History and Literature. Ch. ix. deals with the Maccabæan Age.

BUTCHER, S. H. : Harvard Lectures on Greek Subjects. Contains a chapter which contrasts Hebraism and Hellenism.

SCHECHTER : Studies in Judaism, including "A Glimpse of the Social Life of the Jews in the Age of Jesus the Son of Sirach."

BRUCE, TAYLOR, R. : Ancient Hebrew Literature.

HAUPT : The Book of Nahum. The writer regards this book as a liturgical collection of four poems—the first two, Maccabæan.

SHARPE, S. : The History of the Hebrew Nation and its Literature. Some of the author's conclusions are questionable.

STRACHEY, J. ST. LOE : The Practical Wisdom of the Bible. Books of the Apocrypha are utilised.

HAUPT, P. : Purim. Interesting to students of the Books of Esther and Judith.

NAU, F. : Histoire et Sagesse d'Ahikar l'Assyrien. Of especial interest to students of the Apocrypha.

LANSDELL, H. : The Tithe in Scripture. Ch. vii. deals with the teaching of five books of the Apocrypha on the subject.

TISSERANT, E. : Ascension d'Isaie. Based on the Ethiopic version, and containing scholarly Introduction and Notes.

OESTERLEY, W. O. E. : The Jewish Doctrine of Mediation. Includes the teaching of the Apocrypha and Pseudepigrapha.

MONTEFIORE, C. G. : The Synoptic Gospels. Contains various references to the Jewish Apocryphal literature.

VITEAU AND MARTIN, FR. : Les Psaumes de Salomon (1910).

BRÉHIER, E. : Les Idées Philosophiques et Religieuses de Philon d'Alexandrie (1908). Comprehensive and valuable.

SANDAY, Prof. W. : The Apocalyptic Element in the Gospels. Article in *Hibbert Journal* (Oct. 1911).

STONE AND SIMPSON : Communion with God : The Preparation before Christ and the Realisation in Him (1911).

WELLS : The Choice of the Jews : A Tragedy and a Lesson (1911). The author handles his historical facts with skill.

STADE, B. : Biblische Theologie des Alten Testamentes. Die Jüdische Religion von der Zeit Ezra's bis zum Zeitalter Christi von Dr. A. Bertholet (1911).

BOX, G. H. : The Ezra-Apocalypse, translated from a critically revised text, with critical introduction, notes, and explanations.

KENT, C. F. : The Makers and Teachers of Judaism (vol. iv. of the Historical Bible). Covers the period from the fall of Jerusalem to the death of Herod the Great.

WORSLEY, F. W. : The Apocalypse of Jesus (1912). Written from the point of view that the life of Jesus was a new Apocalypse itself.

OESTERLEY, W. O. E. : Ecclesiasticus in the Revised Version (1912)

BERNARD, J. H. : The Odes of Solomon (1912).

CHARLES, R. H. : Between the Old and New Testaments (1912).

ABBOT, E. : Light on the Gospel from an Ancient Poet (1912). A painstaking study of the Syriac " Odes of Solomon " recently discovered by Dr. Rendel Harris, and supposed to have been written by a Christian Jew.

MEYER, ED. : Der Papyrusfund von Elephantine. Dokumente einer jüdischen Gemeinde aus der Perserzeit (1912).

UNGNAD, A. : Aramäische Papyrus aus Elephantine (1912).

TOWNSHEND, R. B. : Antiochus Epiphanes (*Hibbert Journal*, 1913).

WICKS, H. J. : The Doctrine of God in the Jewish Apocryphal and Apocalyptic Literature (1914).

MERCER, A. B. : Extra-Biblical Sources for Hebrew and Jewish History (1914).

FOWLER, WARDE, W. : Roman Ideas of Deity in the Last Century before the Christian Era (1914).

ANGUS, S. : The Environment of Early Christianity (1914).

LEGGE, F. : Forerunners and Rivals of Christianity : Studies in Religious History from 330 B.C. to 330 A.D. (in 2 vols.).

OESTERLEY, W. O. E. : The Books of the Apocrypha.

HILL, H. ERSKINE : Apocalyptic Problems (1916).

STREATFIELD, F. : Preparing the Way : Influence of Judaism of the Greek Period on the Earliest Development of Christianity (1918).

INGE, W. R. : The Philosophy of Plotinus (1919).

KENNEDY : Philo's Contribution to Religion (1919).

APPENDIX III.

GENERAL INDEX.

APPENDIX IV.

PASSAGES OF THE BIBLE, APOCRYPHA, AND PSEUDEPIGRAPHA.

1. OLD TESTAMENT.

29

2. APOCRYPHA AND PSEUDEPIGRAPHA.

3. NEW TESTAMENT.

APPENDIX V.

JOSEPHUS, PHILO, AND TALMUDIC LITERATURE.

1. JOSEPHUS.

2. PHILO.

3. TALMUDIC LITERATURE.

Printed by MORRISON & GIBB LIMITED, *Edinburgh.*